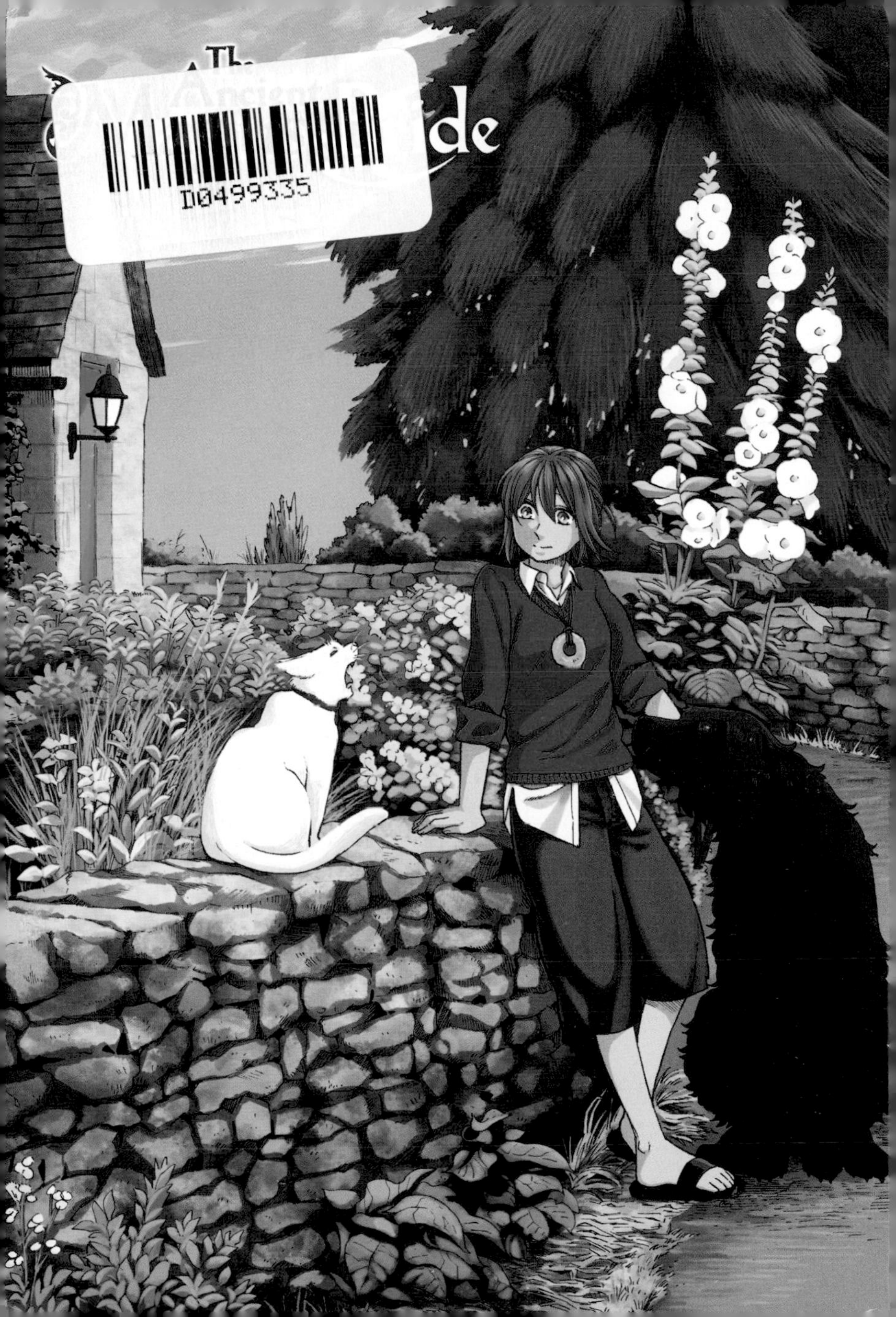

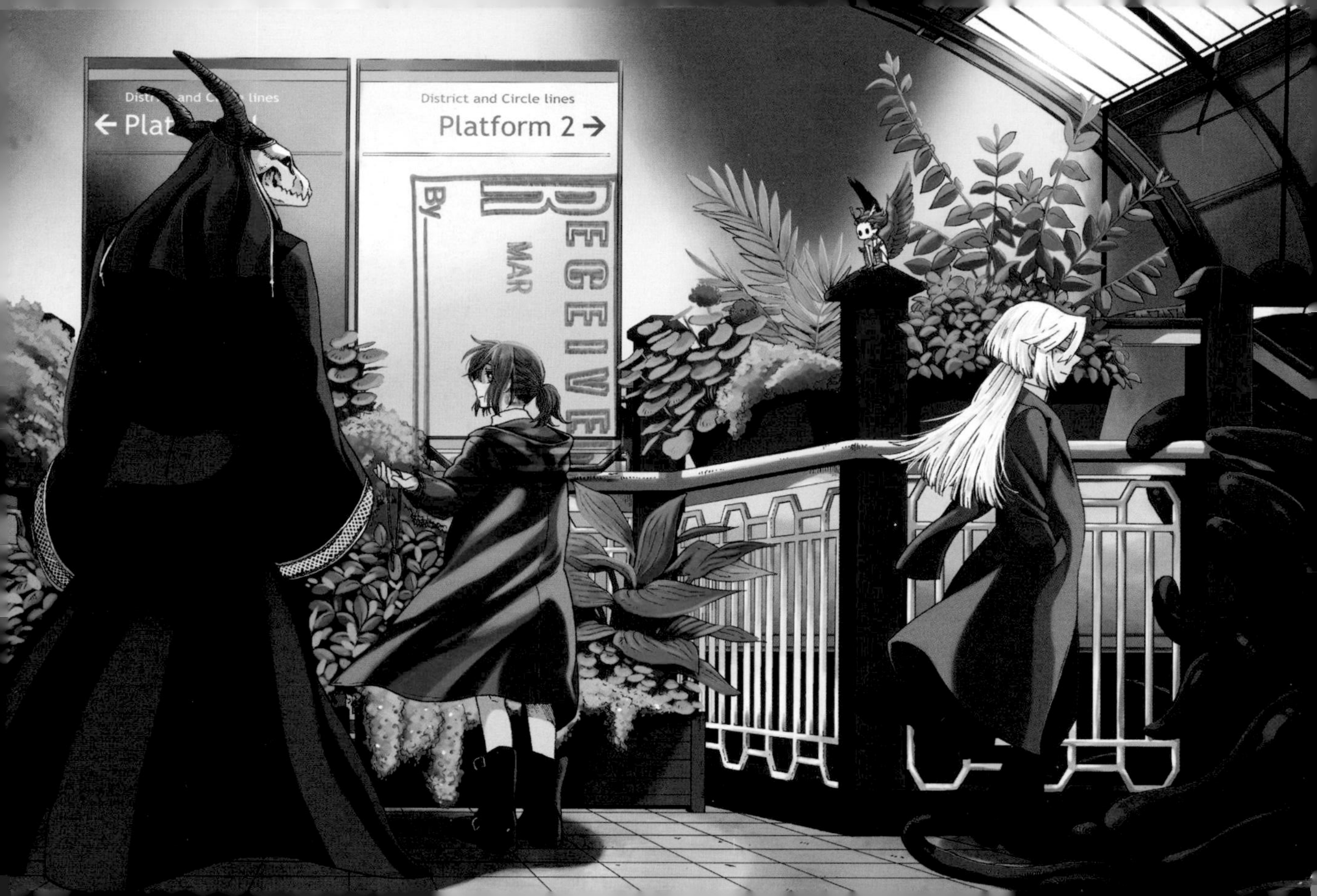
District and Circle lines
Platform 2 →
RECEIVE
MAR
By

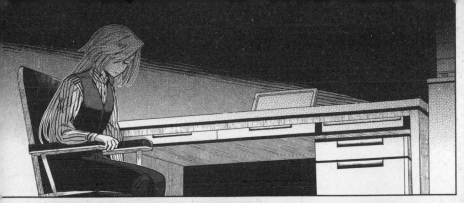

WELL, SHUCKS.

I DIDN'T EXPECT IT TO **ESCAPE**!

PUTTING IT UP FOR AUCTION WAS A TOTAL WASTE! BUT I SUPPOSE IT WAS ONLY **LUCK** THAT I GOT A SECOND ONE AT ALL.

SWIVEL

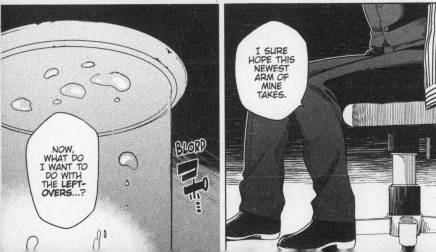

I SURE HOPE THIS NEWEST ARM OF MINE TAKES.

NOW, WHAT DO I WANT TO DO WITH THE LEFT-OVERS...?

BLORP

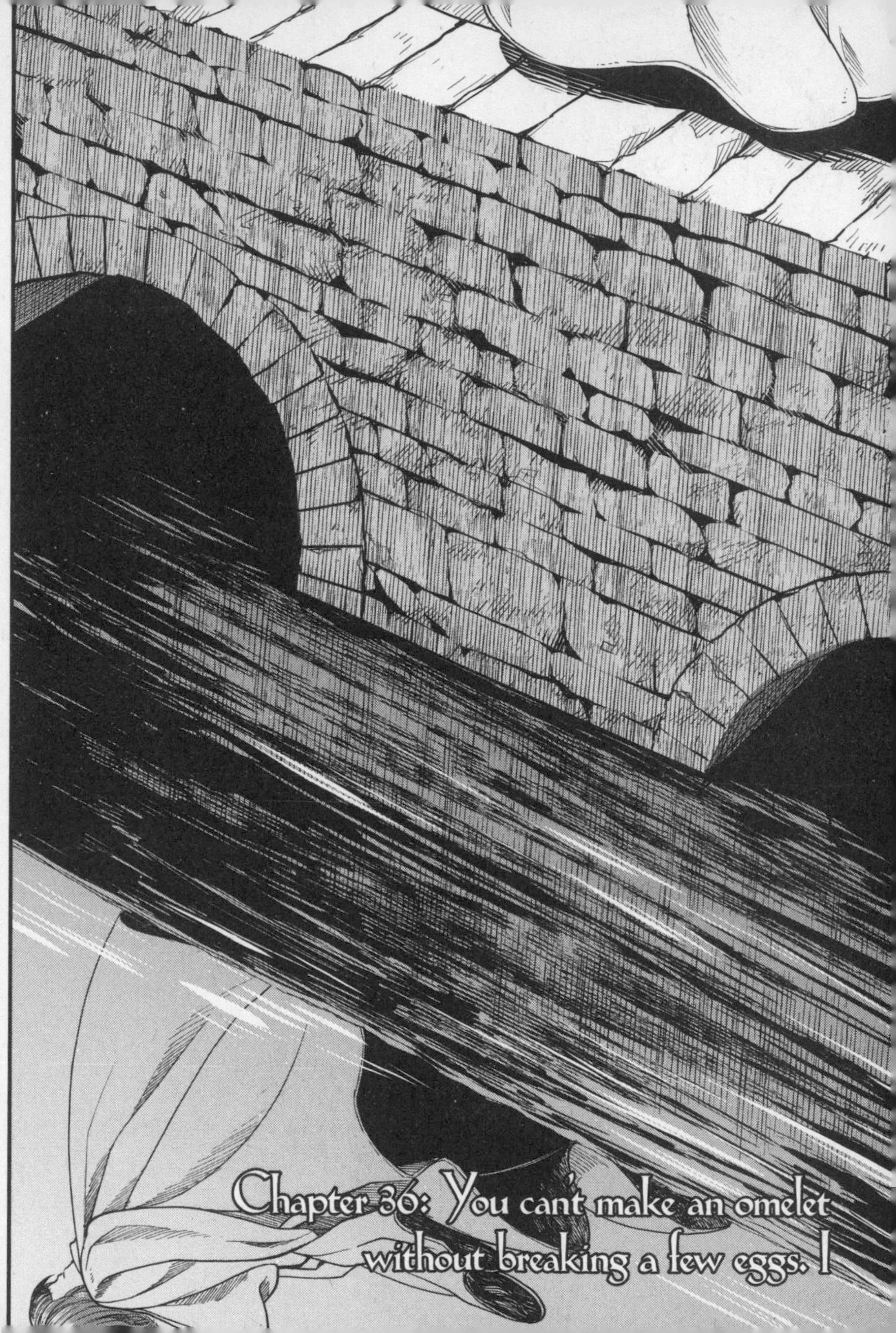

Chapter 36: You cant make an omelet without breaking a few eggs. I

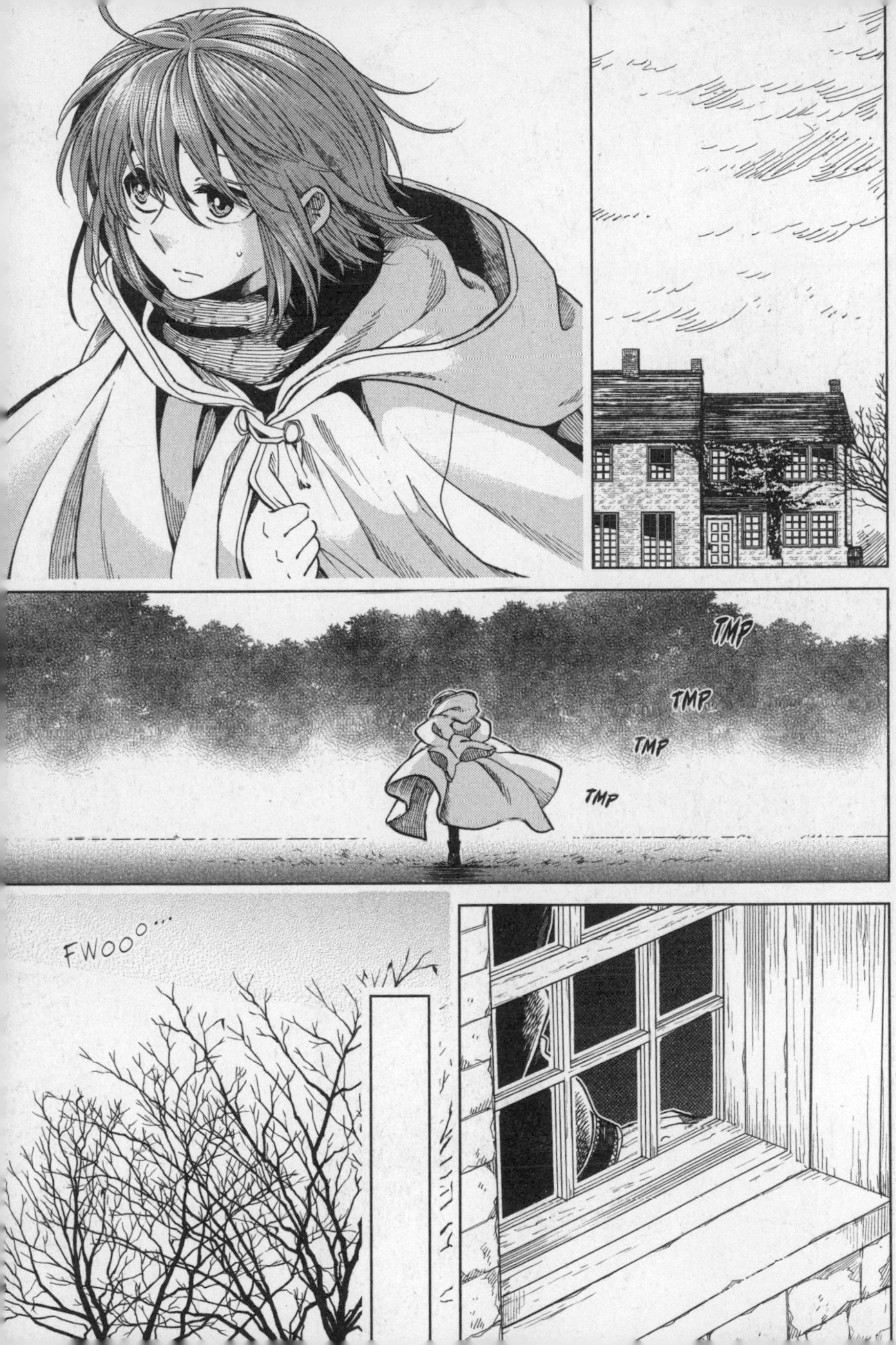
TMP
TMP
TMP
TMP
FWOOO...

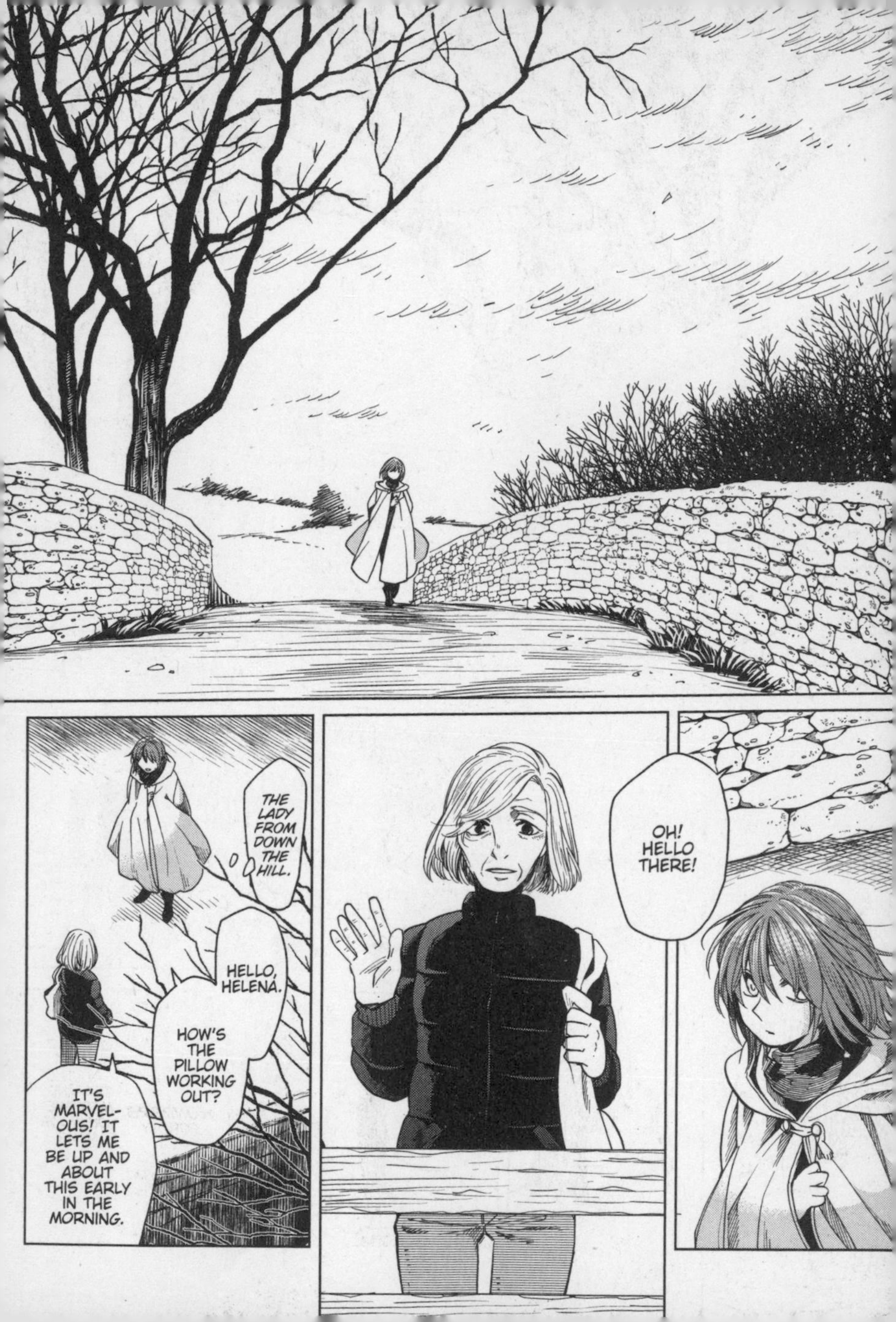
OH! HELLO THERE!
THE LADY FROM DOWN THE HILL.
HELLO, HELENA.
HOW'S THE PILLOW WORKING OUT?
IT'S MARVEL-OUS! IT LETS ME BE UP AND ABOUT THIS EARLY IN THE MORNING.

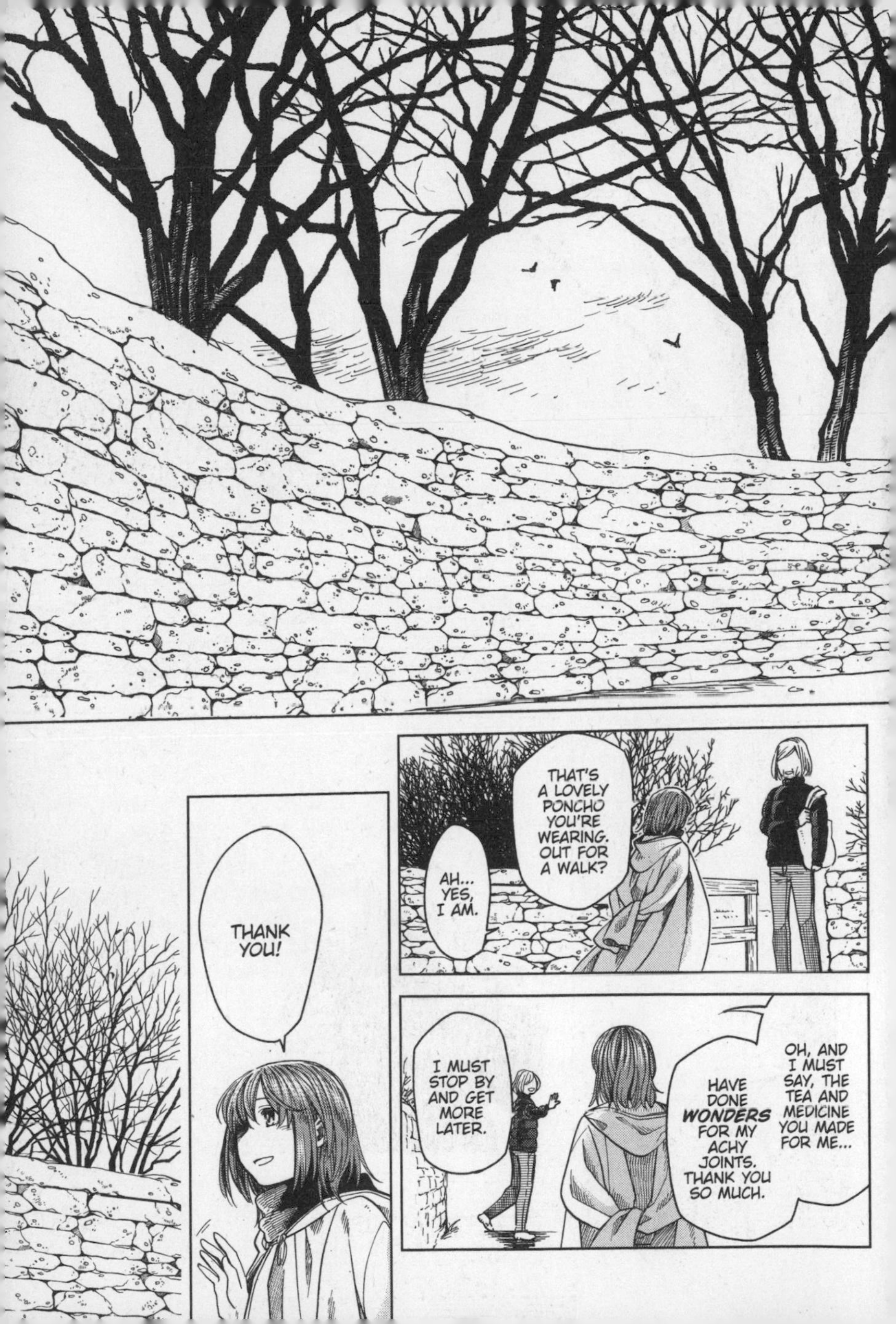
THAT'S A LOVELY PONCHO YOU'RE WEARING. OUT FOR A WALK?
AH... YES, I AM.
OH, AND I MUST SAY, THE TEA AND MEDICINE YOU MADE FOR ME...
HAVE DONE **WONDERS** FOR MY ACHY JOINTS. THANK YOU SO MUCH.
I MUST STOP BY AND GET MORE LATER.
THANK YOU!

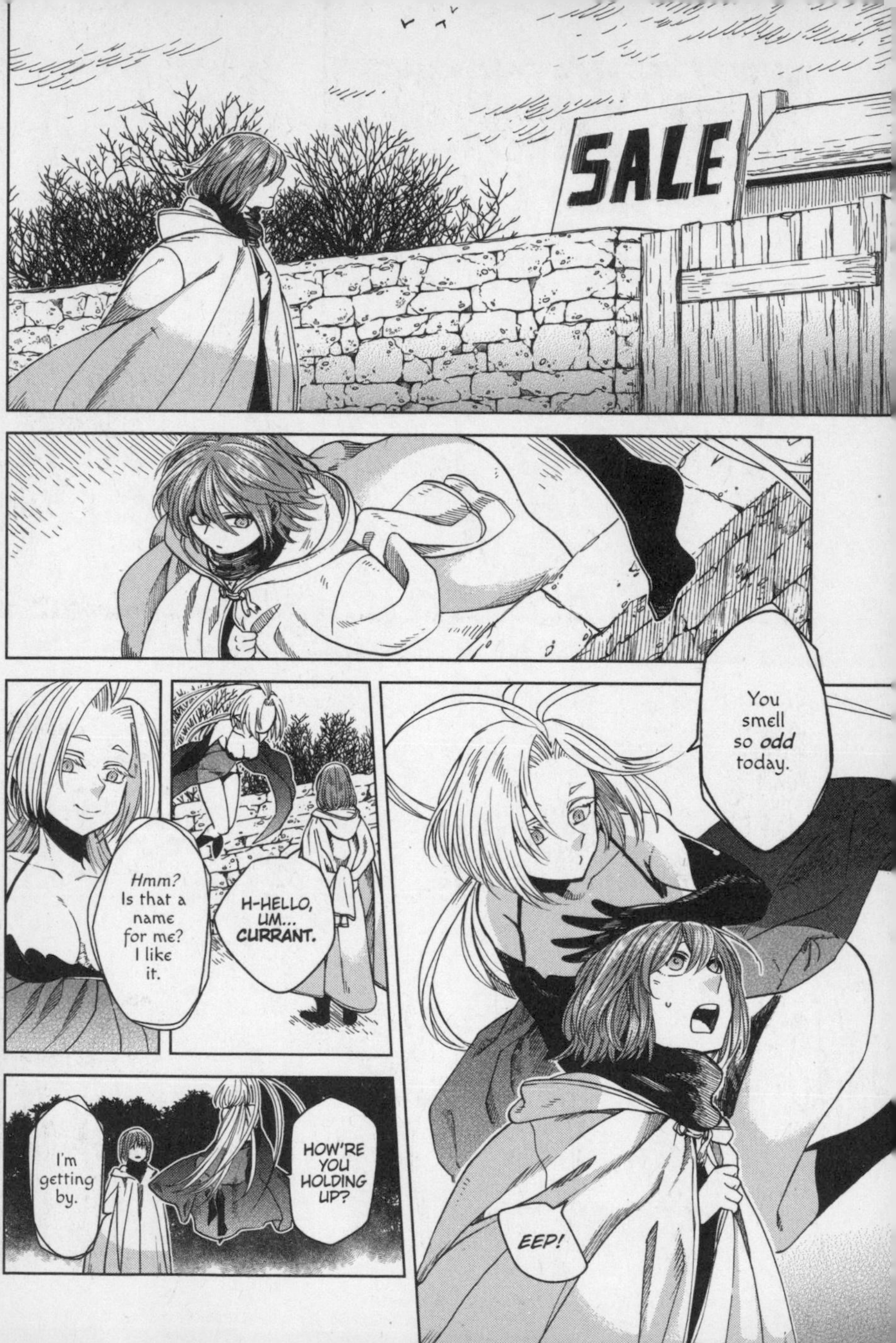
SALE
You smell so *odd* today.
EEP!
H-HELLO, UM... CURRANT.
Hmm? Is that a name for me? I like it.
HOW'RE YOU HOLDING UP?
I'm getting by.

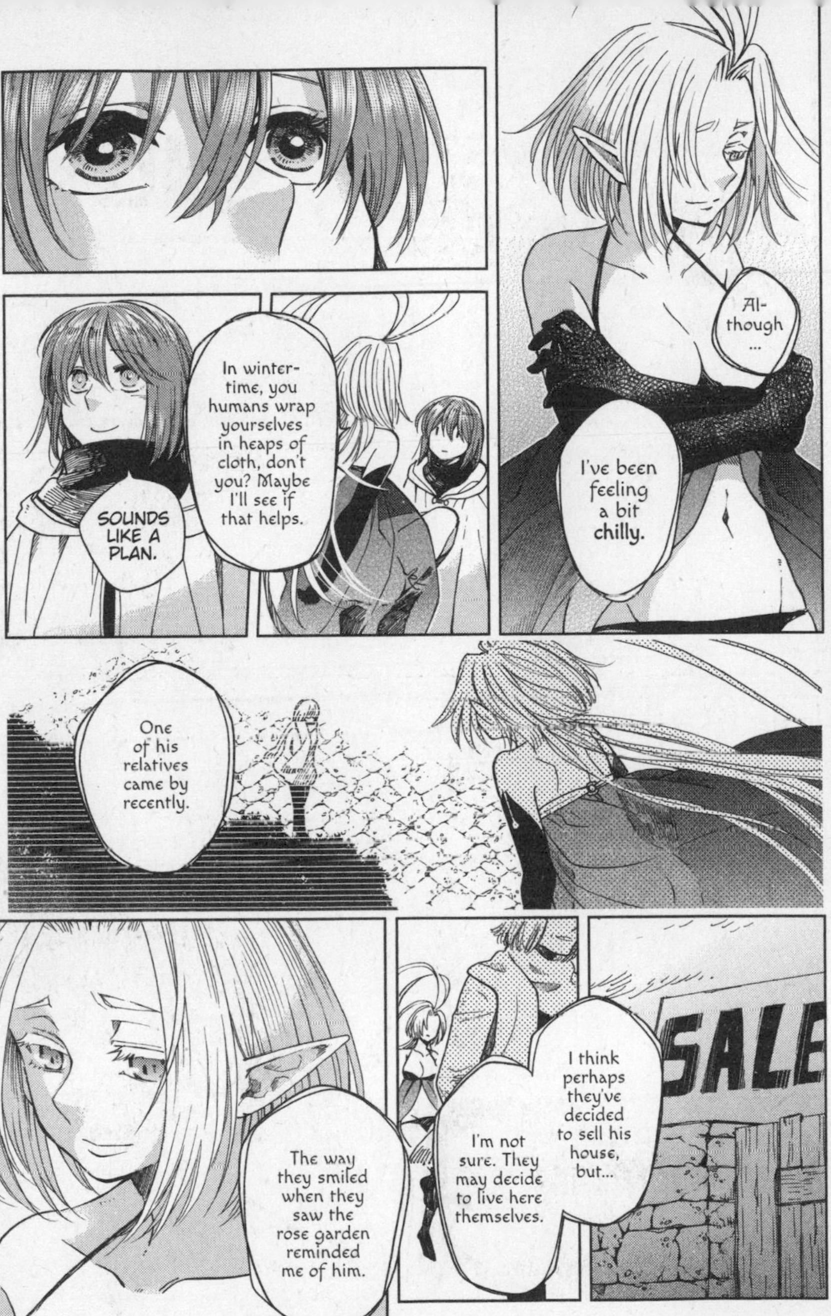
Al-though ...
I've been feeling a bit chilly.
In winter-time, you humans wrap yourselves in heaps of cloth, don't you? Maybe I'll see if that helps.
SOUNDS LIKE A PLAN.
One of his relatives came by recently.
SALE
I think perhaps they've decided to sell his house, but...
I'm not sure. They may decide to live here themselves.
The way they smiled when they saw the rose garden reminded me of him.

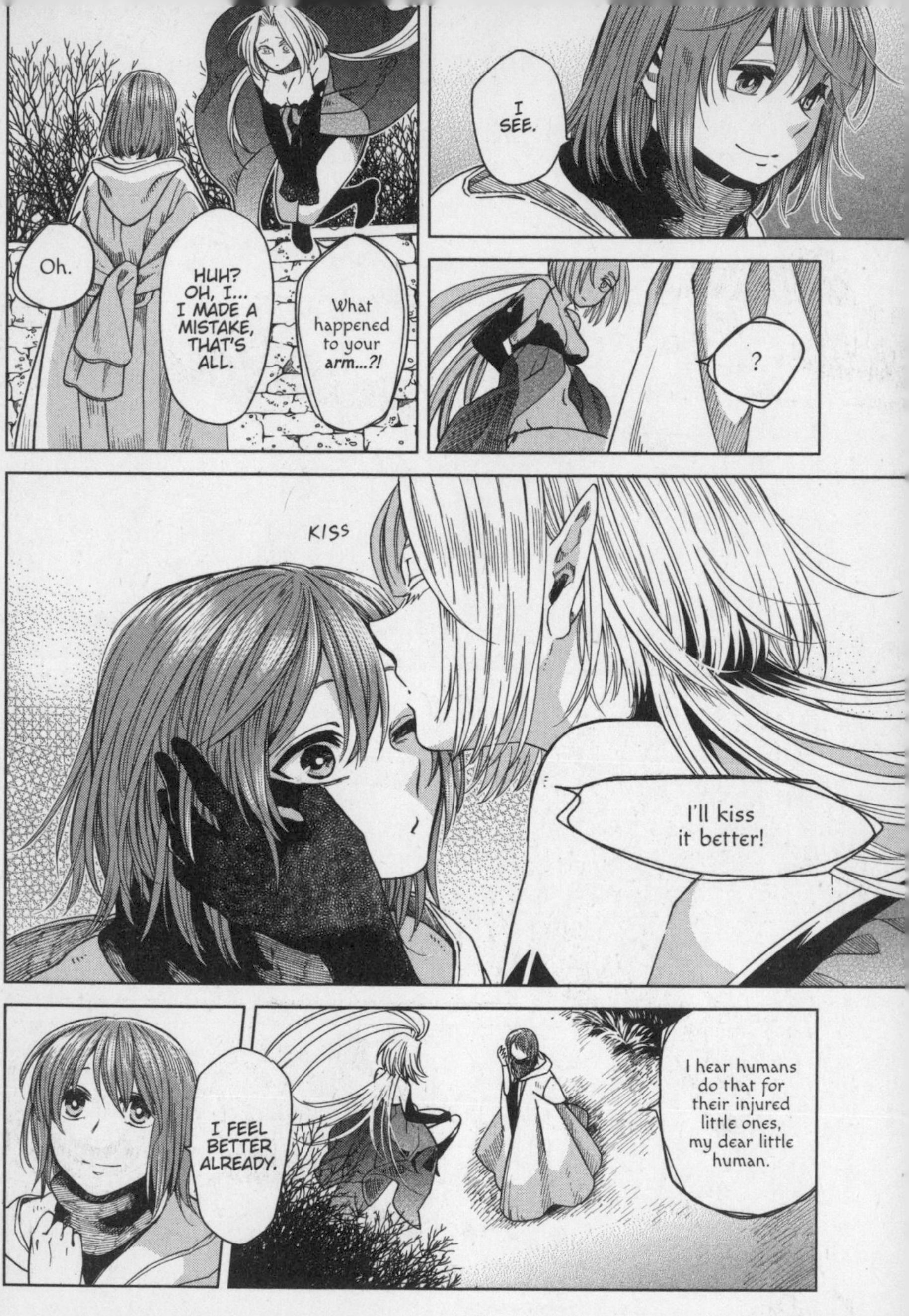
I SEE.
?
What happened to your arm...?!
HUH? OH, I... I MADE A MISTAKE, THAT'S ALL.
Oh.
KISS
I'll kiss it better!
I hear humans do that for their injured little ones, my dear little human.
I FEEL BETTER ALREADY.

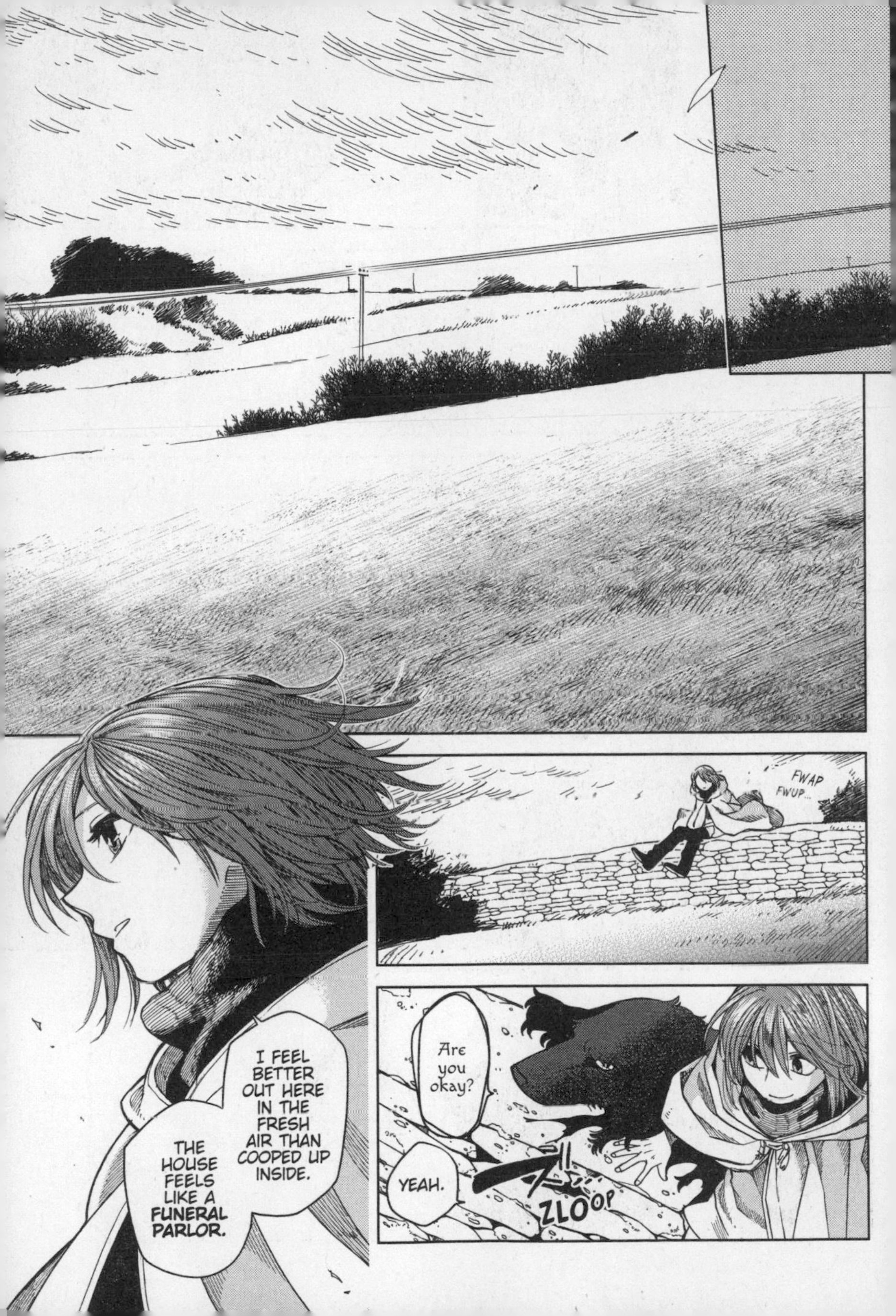
FWAP FWUP...
Are you okay?
YEAH.
ZLOOP
I FEEL BETTER OUT HERE IN THE FRESH AIR THAN COOPED UP INSIDE.
THE HOUSE FEELS LIKE A FUNERAL PARLOR.

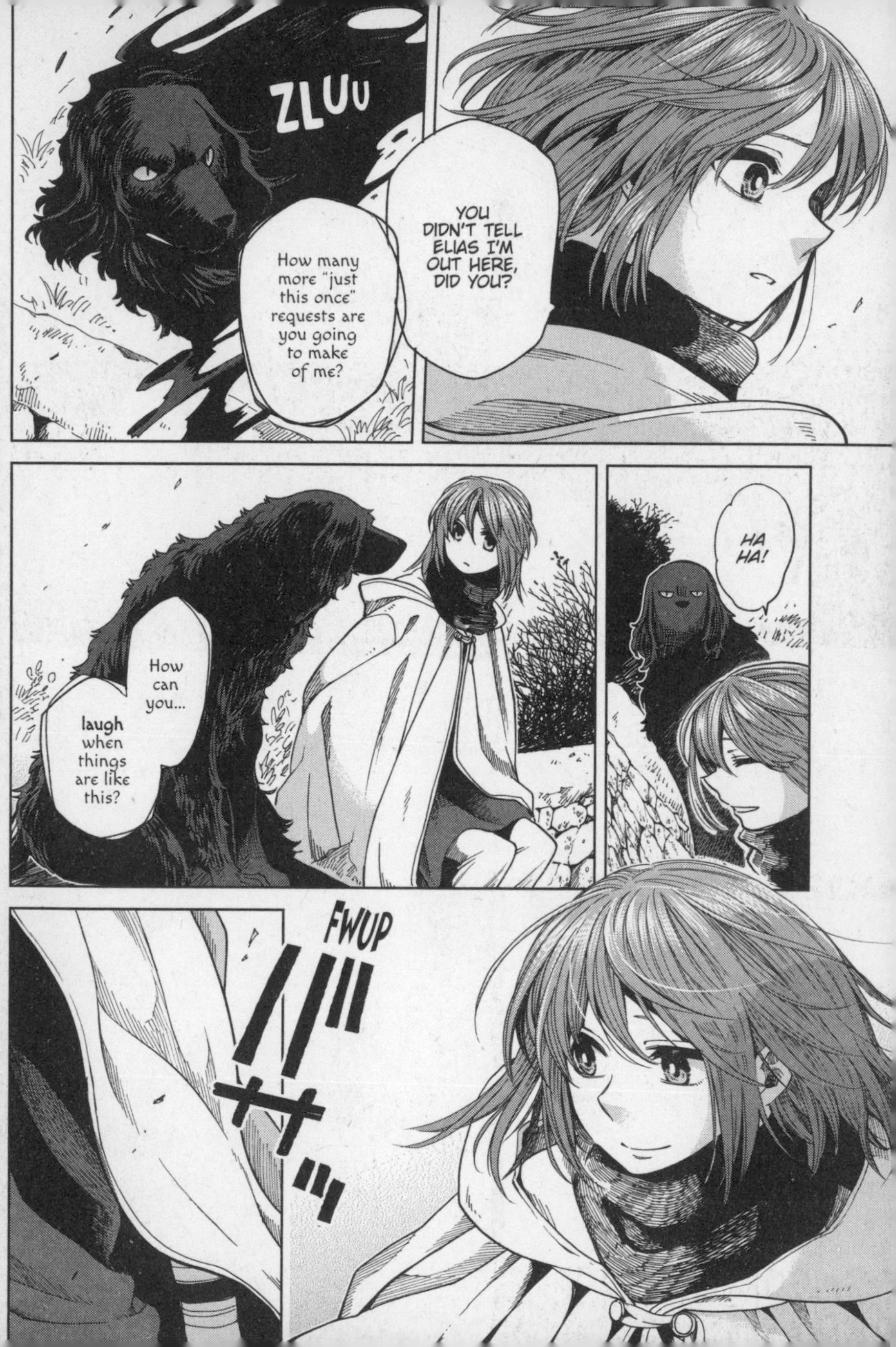
YOU DIDN'T TELL ELIAS I'M OUT HERE, DID YOU?
ZLUU
How many more "just this once" requests are you going to make of me?
HA HA!
How can you... laugh when things are like this?
FWUP

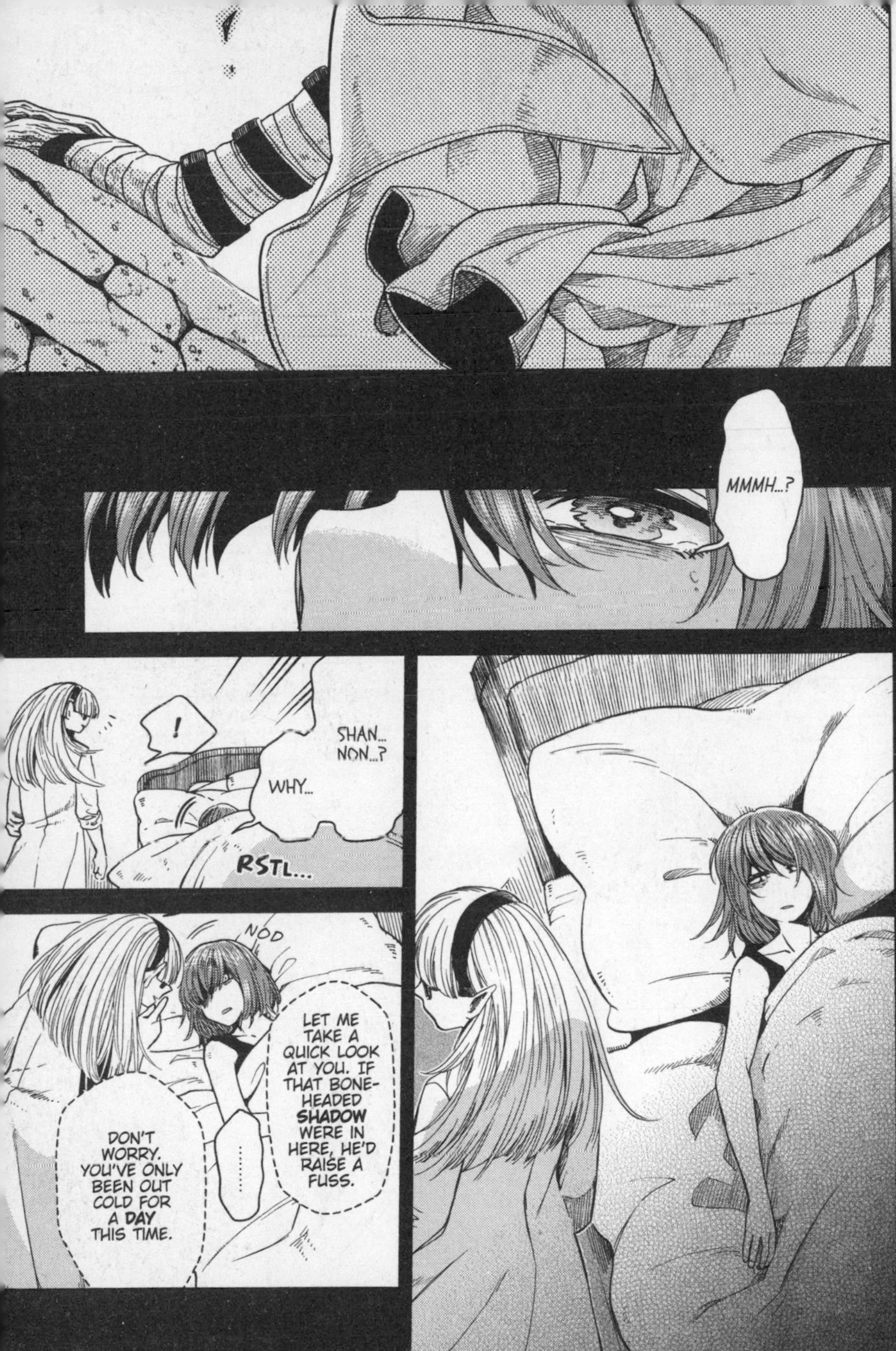
MMMH...?
SHAN... NON...?
WHY...
!
RSTL...
NOD
LET ME TAKE A QUICK LOOK AT YOU. IF THAT BONE-HEADED **SHADOW** WERE IN HERE, HE'D RAISE A FUSS.
......
DON'T WORRY. YOU'VE ONLY BEEN OUT COLD FOR A **DAY** THIS TIME.

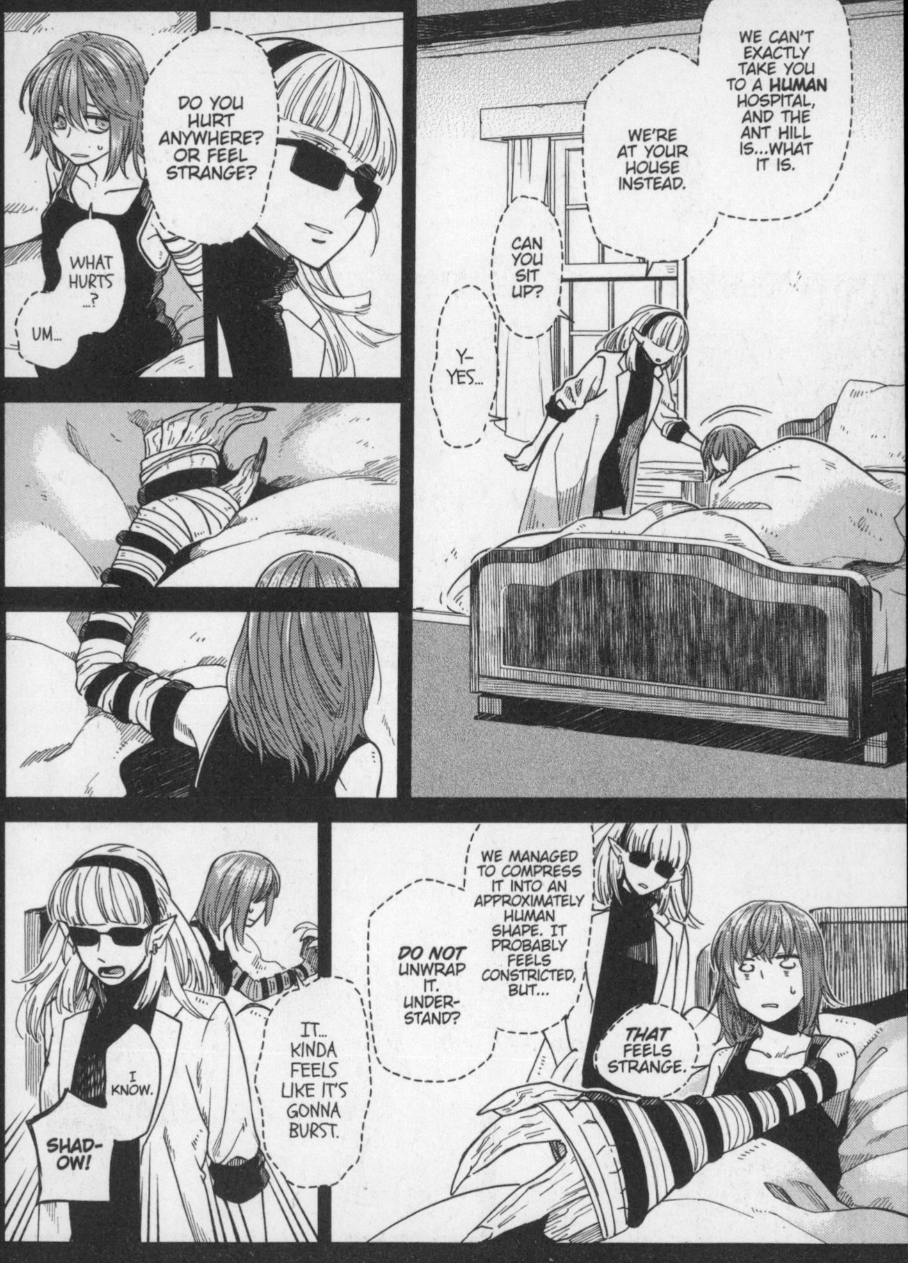
WE CAN'T EXACTLY TAKE YOU TO A **HUMAN** HOSPITAL, AND THE ANT HILL IS...WHAT IT IS.
WE'RE AT YOUR HOUSE INSTEAD.
CAN YOU SIT UP?
Y-YES...
DO YOU HURT ANYWHERE? OR FEEL STRANGE?
WHAT HURTS ...?
UM...
WE MANAGED TO COMPRESS IT INTO AN APPROXIMATELY HUMAN SHAPE. IT PROBABLY FEELS CONSTRICTED, BUT...
THAT FEELS STRANGE.
DO NOT UNWRAP IT. UNDER-STAND?
IT... KINDA FEELS LIKE IT'S GONNA BURST.
I KNOW.
SHAD-OW!

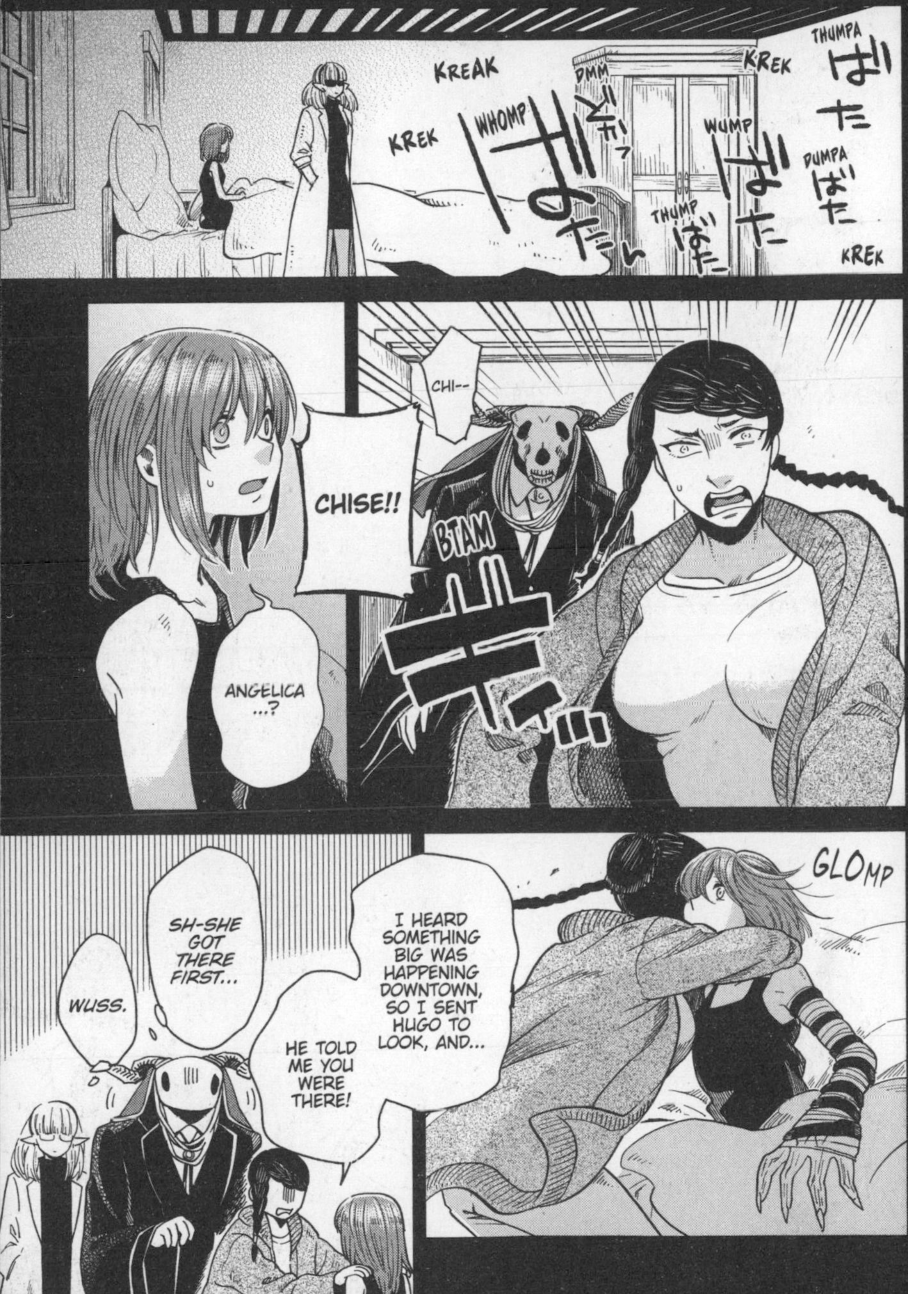
THUMPA
KREK
DMM
KREAK
WHOMP
WUMP
KREK
DUMPA
THUMP
KREK
CHI--
CHISE!!
BTAM
ANGELICA ...?
GLOMP
I HEARD SOMETHING BIG WAS HAPPENING DOWNTOWN, SO I SENT HUGO TO LOOK, AND...
HE TOLD ME YOU WERE THERE!
SH-SHE GOT THERE FIRST...
WUSS.

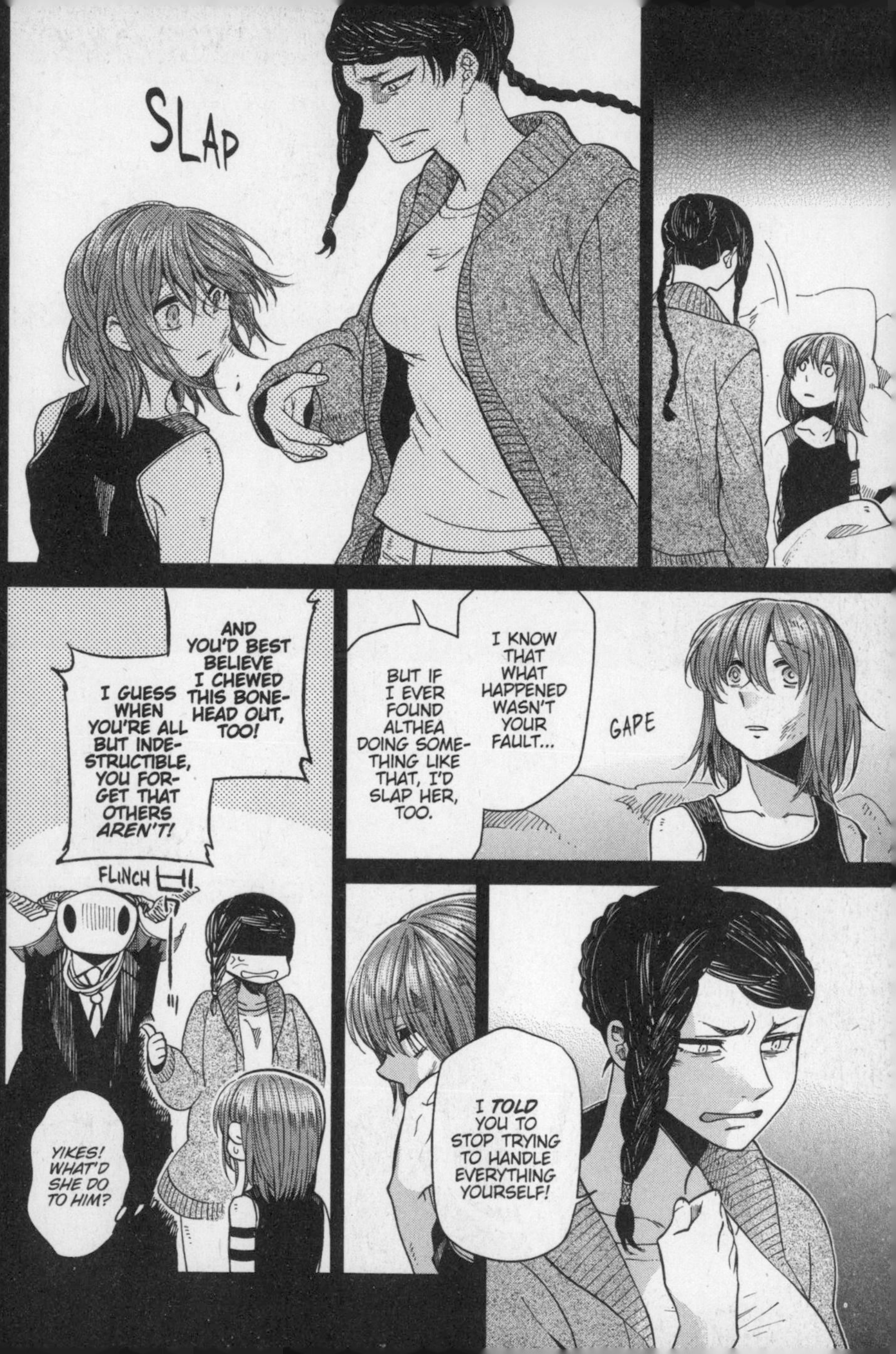
SLAP
GAPE
I KNOW THAT WHAT HAPPENED WASN'T YOUR FAULT...
BUT IF I EVER FOUND ALTHEA DOING SOMETHING LIKE THAT, I'D SLAP HER, TOO.
I GUESS WHEN YOU'RE ALL BUT INDESTRUCTIBLE, YOU FORGET THAT OTHERS AREN'T!
AND YOU'D BEST BELIEVE I CHEWED THIS BONEHEAD OUT, TOO!
I *TOLD* YOU TO STOP TRYING TO HANDLE EVERYTHING YOURSELF!
FLINCH
YIKES! WHAT'D SHE DO TO HIM?

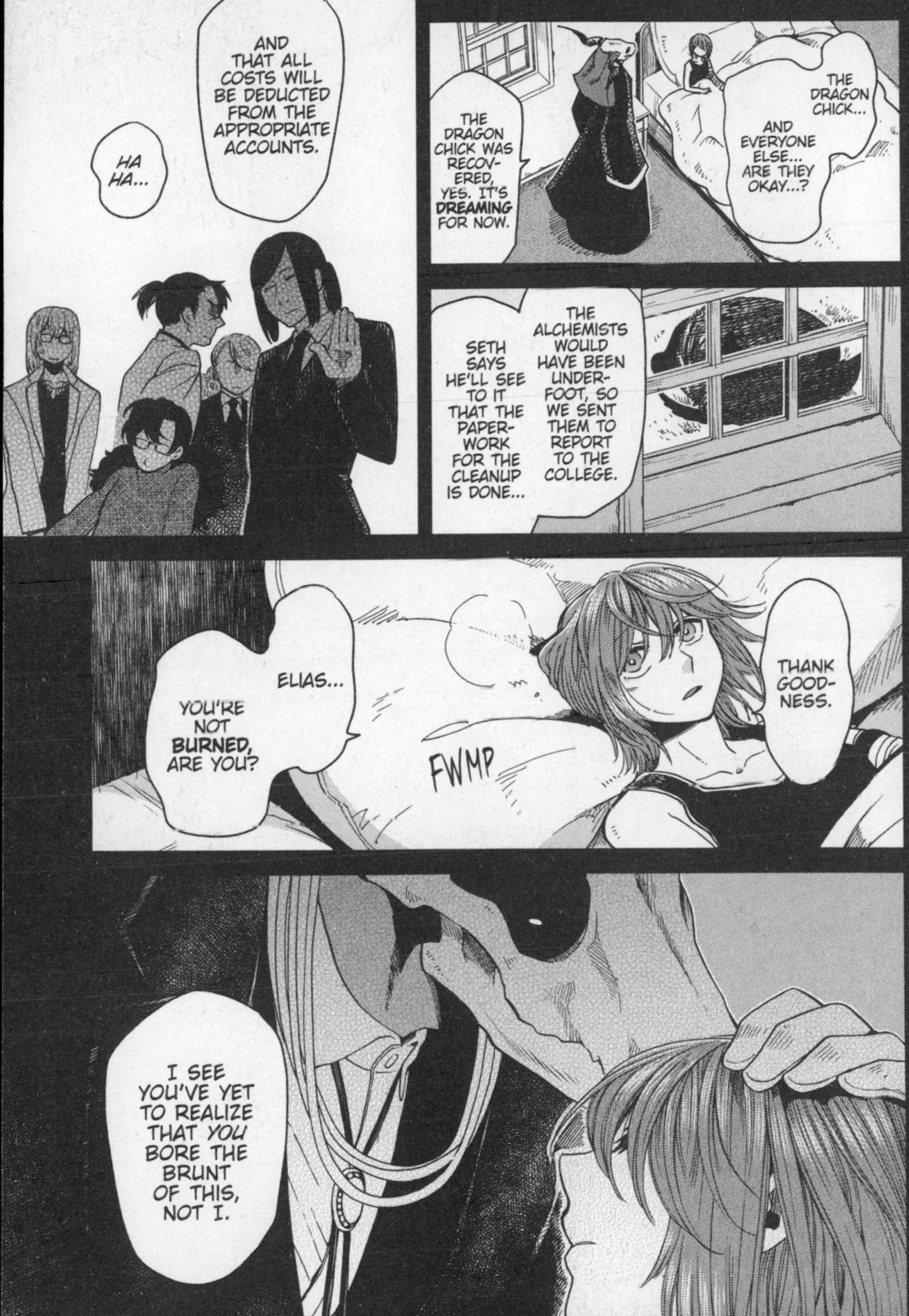
THE DRAGON CHICK...
AND EVERYONE ELSE... ARE THEY OKAY...?
THE DRAGON CHICK WAS RECOVERED, YES. IT'S **DREAMING** FOR NOW.
THE ALCHEMISTS WOULD HAVE BEEN UNDERFOOT, SO WE SENT THEM TO REPORT TO THE COLLEGE.
SETH SAYS HE'LL SEE TO IT THAT THE PAPERWORK FOR THE CLEANUP IS DONE...
AND THAT ALL COSTS WILL BE DEDUCTED FROM THE APPROPRIATE ACCOUNTS.
HA HA...
THANK GOODNESS.
ELIAS...
YOU'RE NOT **BURNED**, ARE YOU?
FWMP
I SEE YOU'VE YET TO REALIZE THAT *YOU* BORE THE BRUNT OF THIS, NOT I.

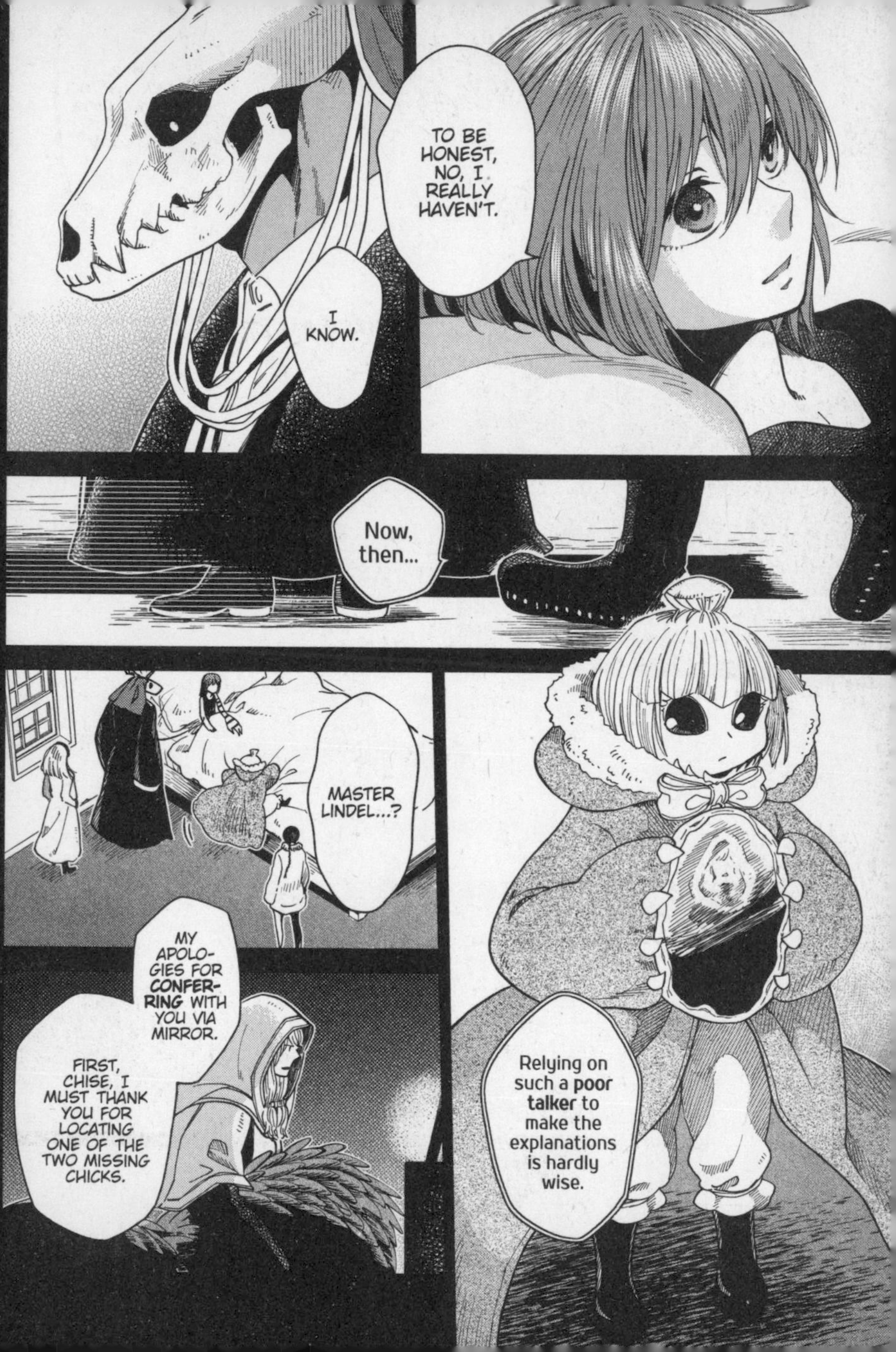
TO BE HONEST, NO, I REALLY HAVEN'T.
I KNOW.
Now, then...
Relying on such a **poor talker** to make the explanations is hardly wise.
MASTER LINDEL...?
MY APOLOGIES FOR **CONFERRING** WITH YOU VIA MIRROR.
FIRST, CHISE, I MUST THANK YOU FOR LOCATING ONE OF THE TWO MISSING CHICKS.

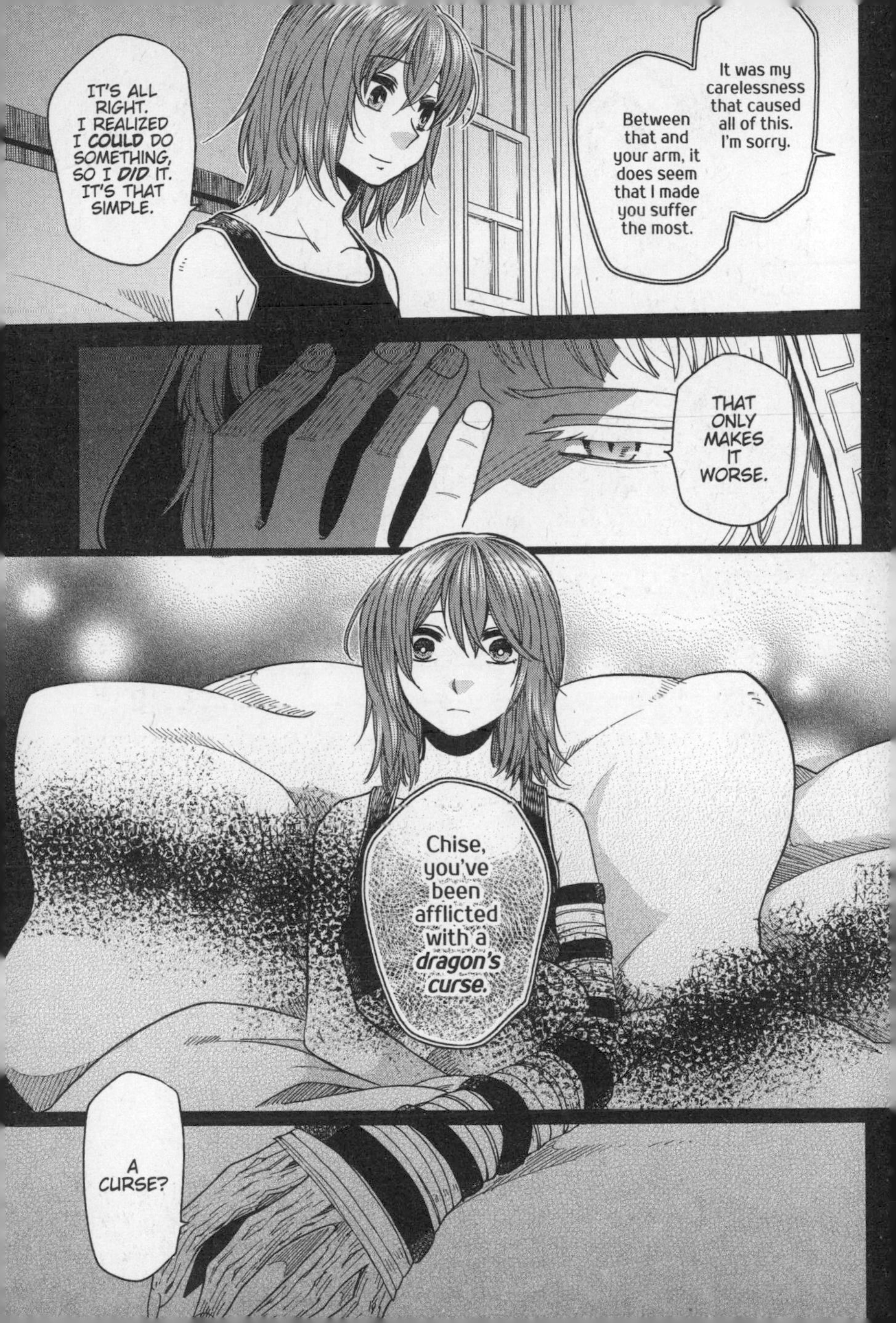
It was my carelessness that caused all of this. I'm sorry.
Between that and your arm, it does seem that I made you suffer the most.
IT'S ALL RIGHT. I REALIZED I COULD DO SOMETHING, SO I DID IT. IT'S THAT SIMPLE.
THAT ONLY MAKES IT WORSE.
Chise, you've been afflicted with a dragon's curse.
A CURSE?

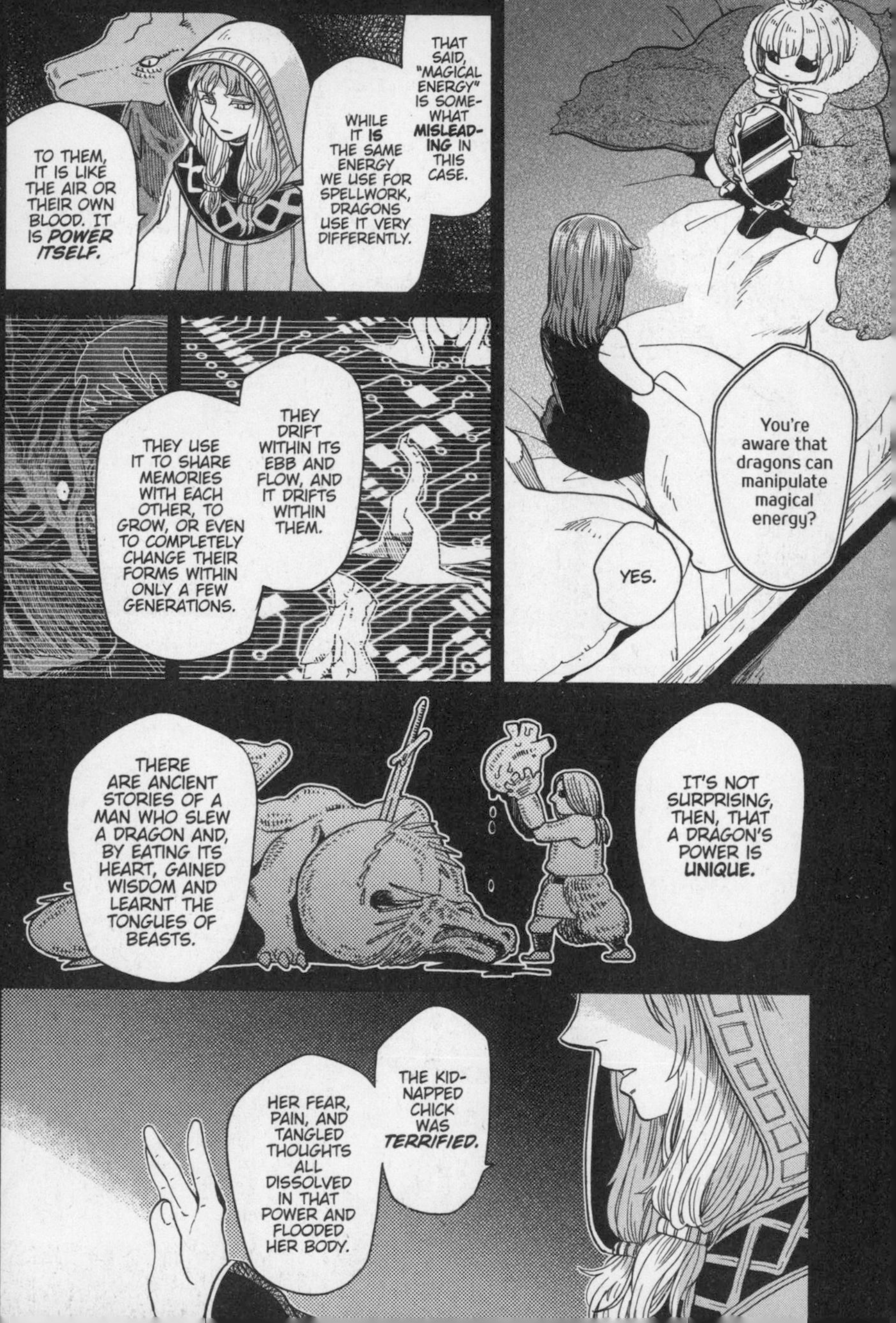
You're aware that dragons can manipulate magical energy?
YES.
THAT SAID, "MAGICAL ENERGY" IS SOMEWHAT MISLEADING IN THIS CASE.
WHILE IT IS THE SAME ENERGY WE USE FOR SPELLWORK, DRAGONS USE IT VERY DIFFERENTLY.
TO THEM, IT IS LIKE THE AIR OR THEIR OWN BLOOD. IT IS POWER ITSELF.
THEY DRIFT WITHIN ITS EBB AND FLOW, AND IT DRIFTS WITHIN THEM.
THEY USE IT TO SHARE MEMORIES WITH EACH OTHER, TO GROW, OR EVEN TO COMPLETELY CHANGE THEIR FORMS WITHIN ONLY A FEW GENERATIONS.
IT'S NOT SURPRISING, THEN, THAT A DRAGON'S POWER IS UNIQUE.
THERE ARE ANCIENT STORIES OF A MAN WHO SLEW A DRAGON AND, BY EATING ITS HEART, GAINED WISDOM AND LEARNT THE TONGUES OF BEASTS.
THE KIDNAPPED CHICK WAS TERRIFIED.
HER FEAR, PAIN, AND TANGLED THOUGHTS ALL DISSOLVED IN THAT POWER AND FLOODED HER BODY.

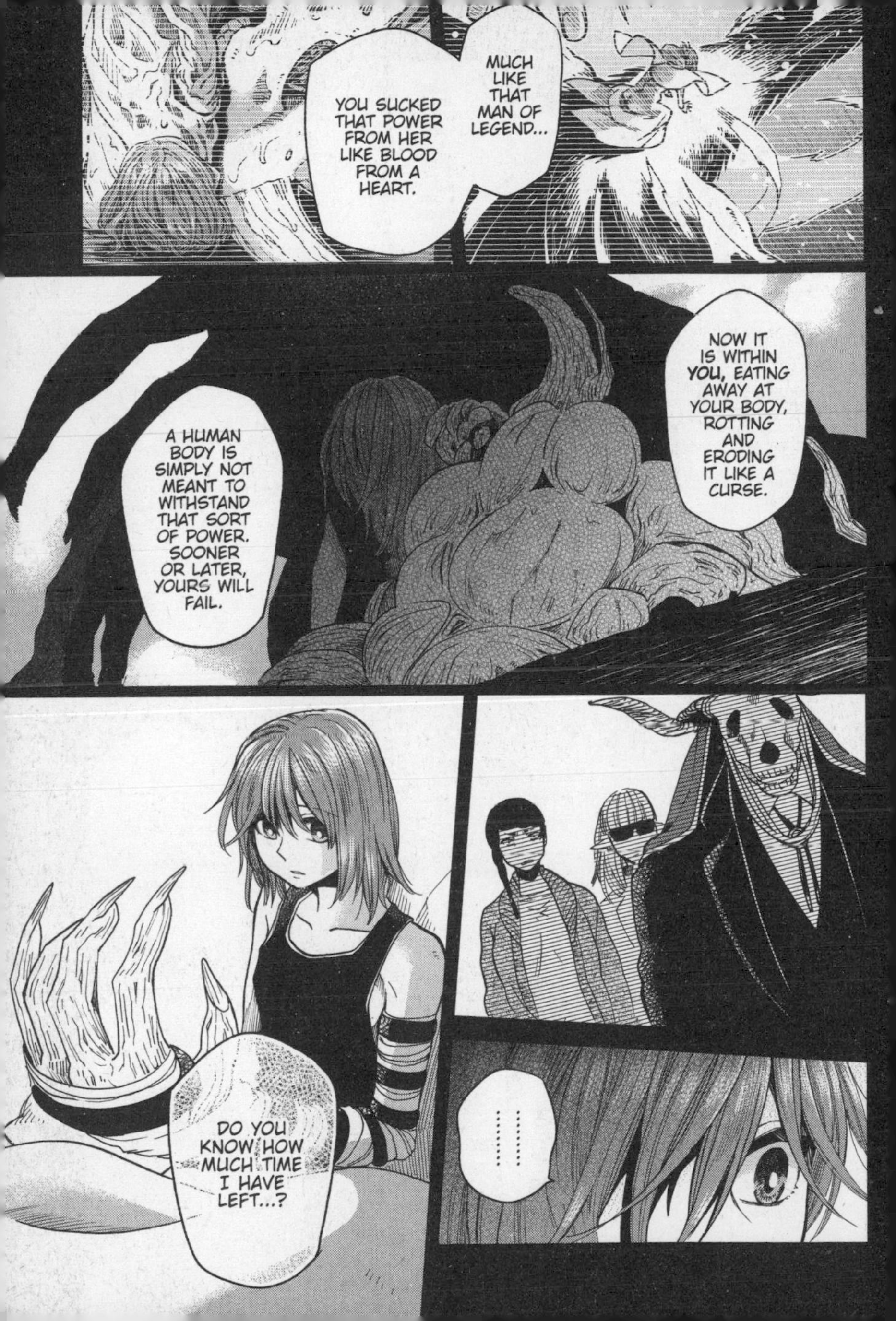
MUCH LIKE THAT MAN OF LEGEND...
YOU SUCKED THAT POWER FROM HER LIKE BLOOD FROM A HEART.
NOW IT IS WITHIN YOU, EATING AWAY AT YOUR BODY, ROTTING AND ERODING IT LIKE A CURSE.
A HUMAN BODY IS SIMPLY NOT MEANT TO WITHSTAND THAT SORT OF POWER. SOONER OR LATER, YOURS WILL FAIL.
......
DO YOU KNOW HOW MUCH TIME I HAVE LEFT...?

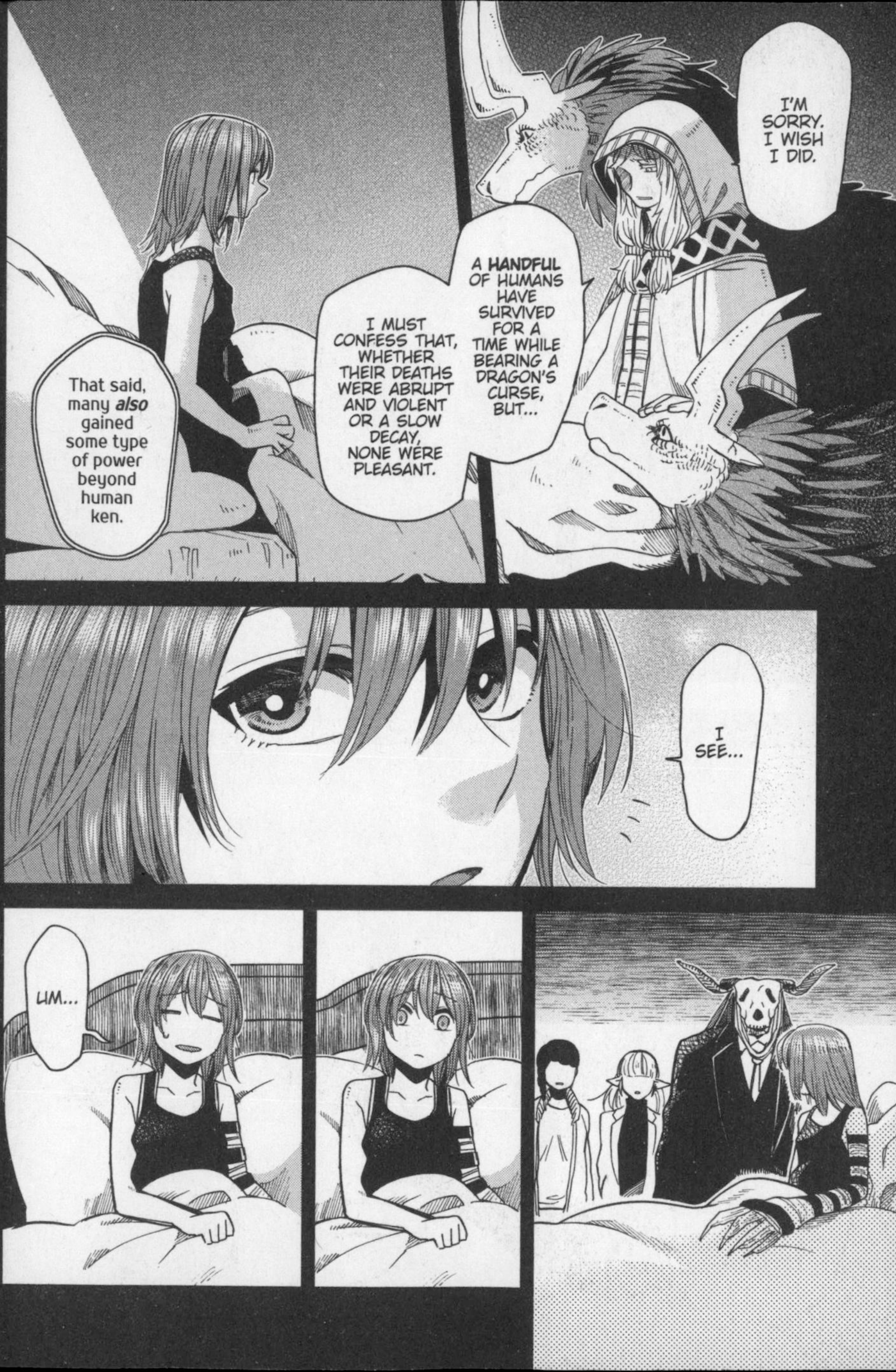
I'M SORRY. I WISH I DID.
A HANDFUL OF HUMANS HAVE SURVIVED FOR A TIME WHILE BEARING A DRAGON'S CURSE, BUT...
I MUST CONFESS THAT, WHETHER THEIR DEATHS WERE ABRUPT AND VIOLENT OR A SLOW DECAY, NONE WERE PLEASANT.
That said, many also gained some type of power beyond human ken.
I SEE...
UM...

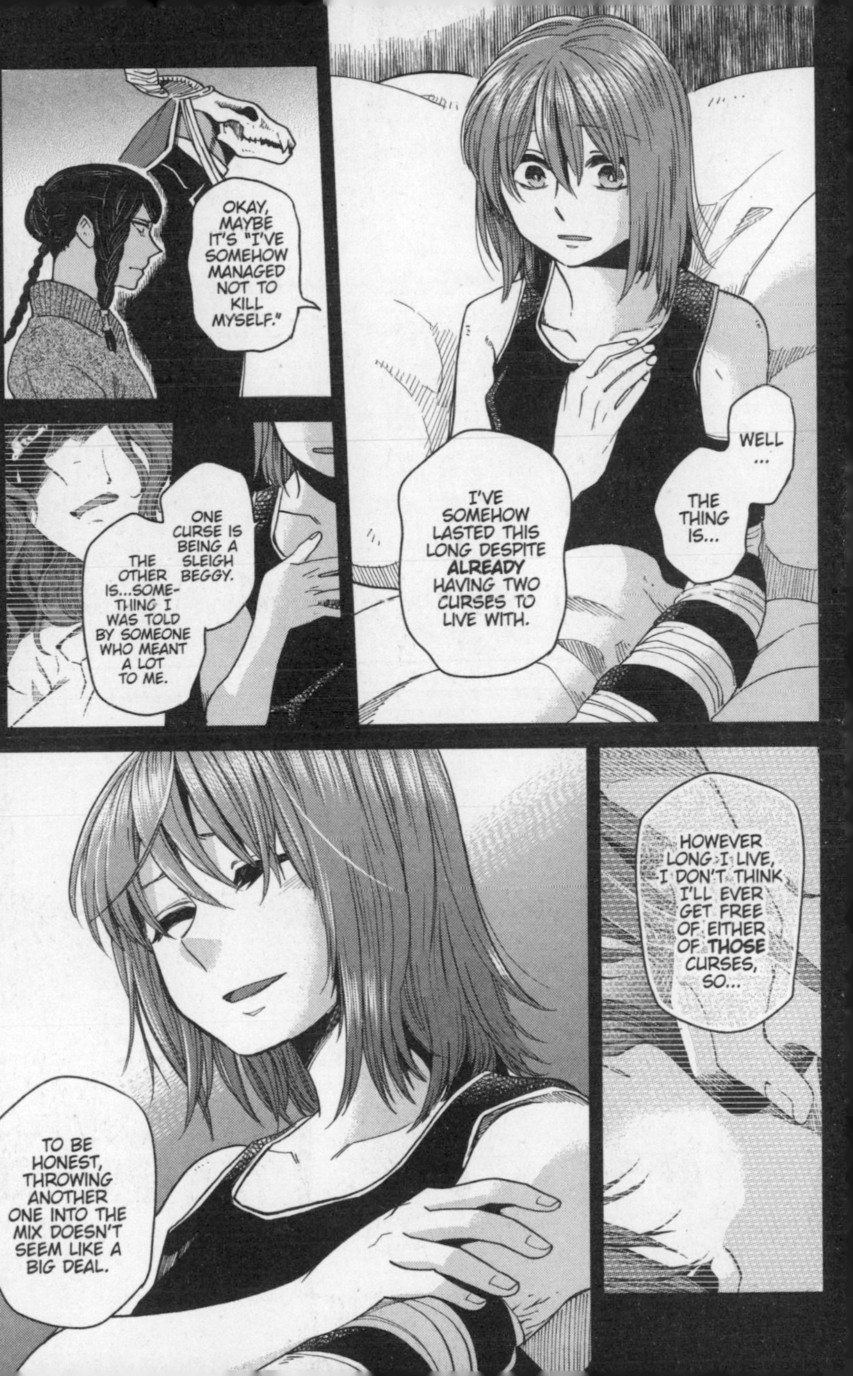
WELL...
THE THING IS...
I'VE SOMEHOW LASTED THIS LONG DESPITE **ALREADY** HAVING TWO CURSES TO LIVE WITH.
OKAY, MAYBE IT'S "I'VE SOMEHOW MANAGED NOT TO KILL MYSELF."
ONE CURSE IS BEING A SLEIGH BEGGY.
THE OTHER IS...SOMETHING I WAS TOLD BY SOMEONE WHO MEANT A LOT TO ME.
HOWEVER LONG I LIVE, I DON'T THINK I'LL EVER GET FREE OF EITHER OF **THOSE** CURSES, SO...
TO BE HONEST, THROWING ANOTHER ONE INTO THE MIX DOESN'T SEEM LIKE A BIG DEAL.

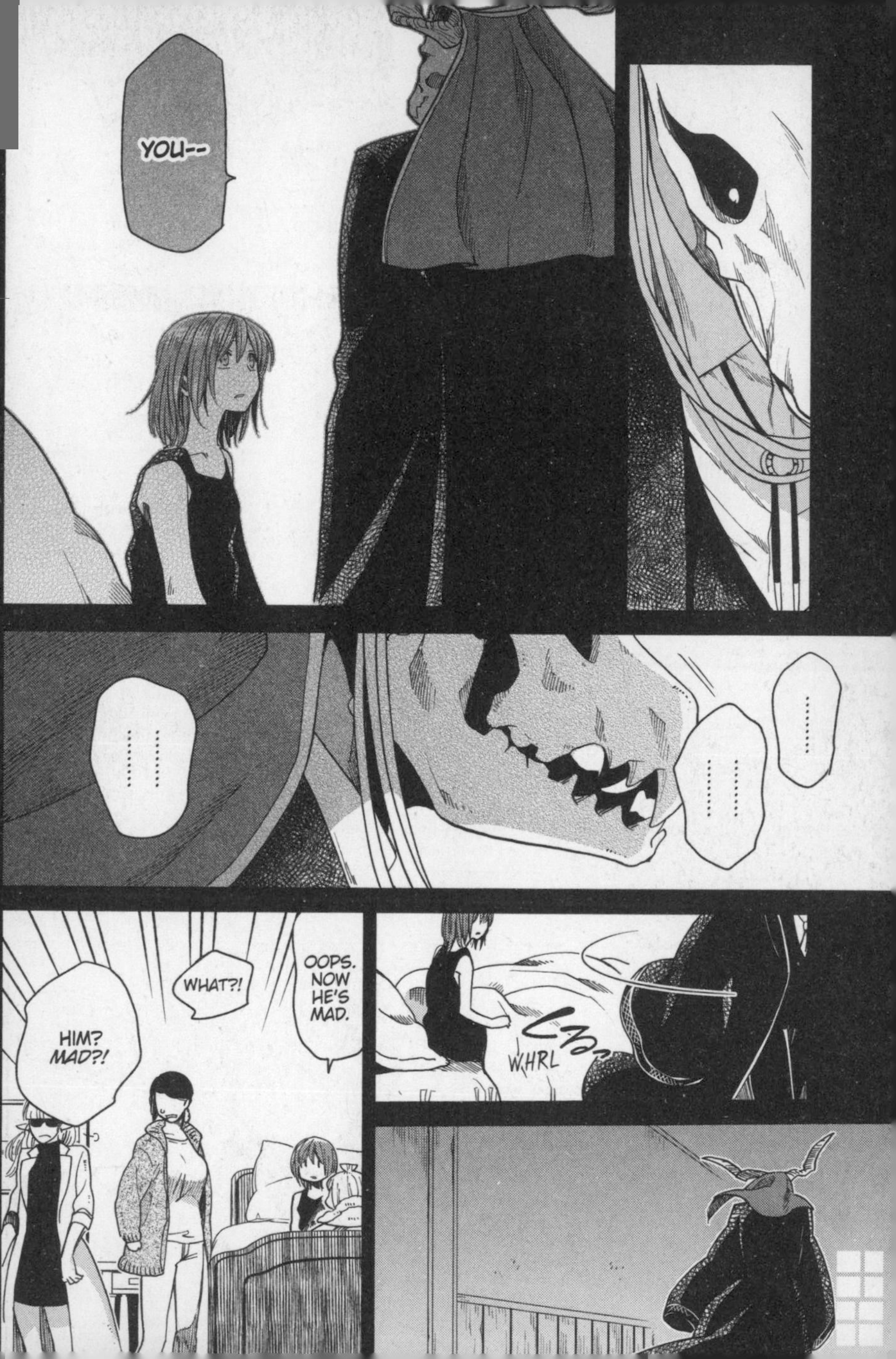
YOU--
......
......
......
......
WHIRL
OOPS. NOW HE'S MAD.
WHAT?!
HIM? MAD?!

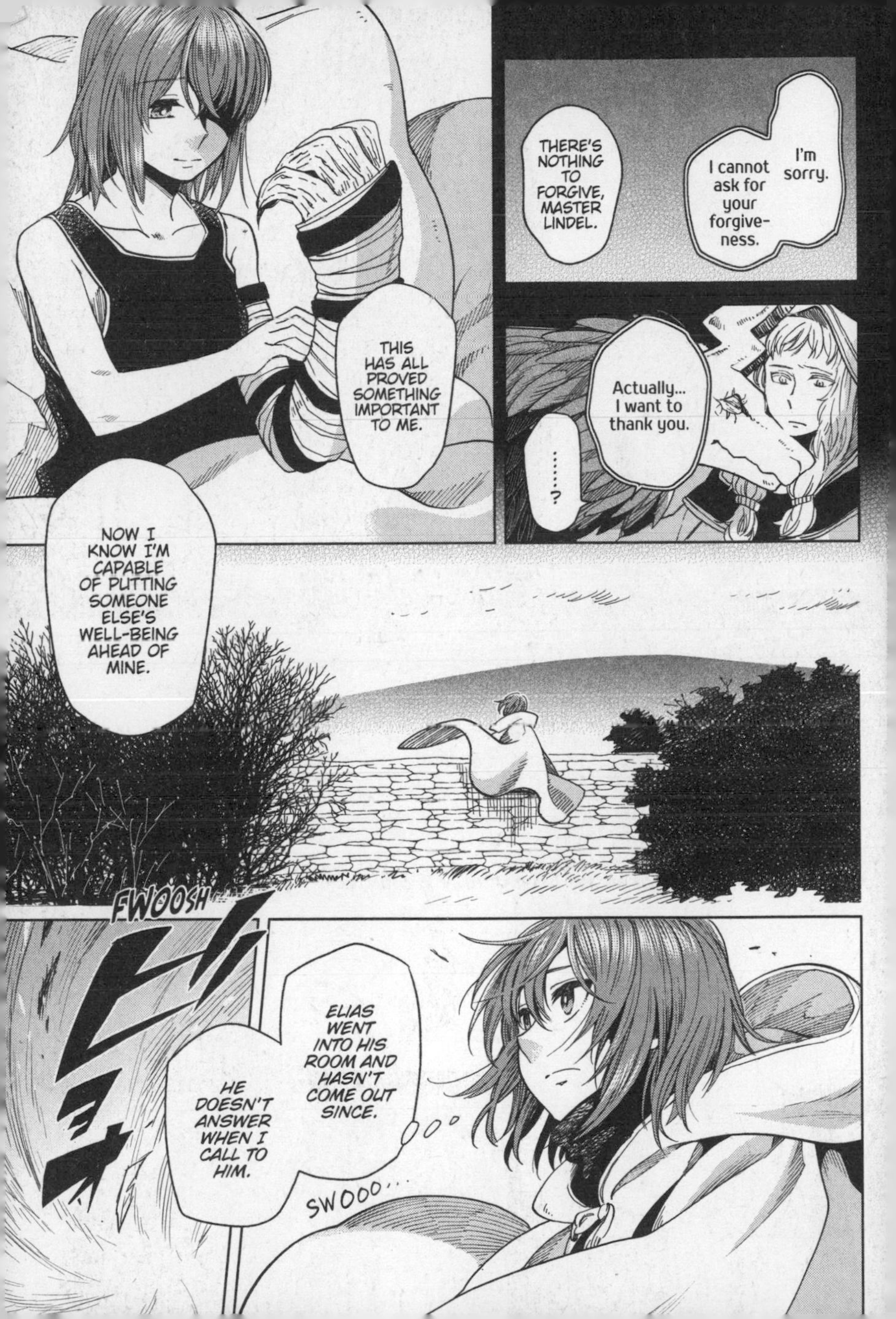

I'm sorry.
I cannot ask for your forgive-ness.
THERE'S NOTHING TO FORGIVE, MASTER LINDEL.
Actually... I want to thank you.
......?
THIS HAS ALL PROVED SOMETHING IMPORTANT TO ME.
NOW I KNOW I'M CAPABLE OF PUTTING SOMEONE ELSE'S WELL-BEING AHEAD OF MINE.
ELIAS WENT INTO HIS ROOM AND HASN'T COME OUT SINCE.
HE DOESN'T ANSWER WHEN I CALL TO HIM.
SWOOO...
FWOOSH

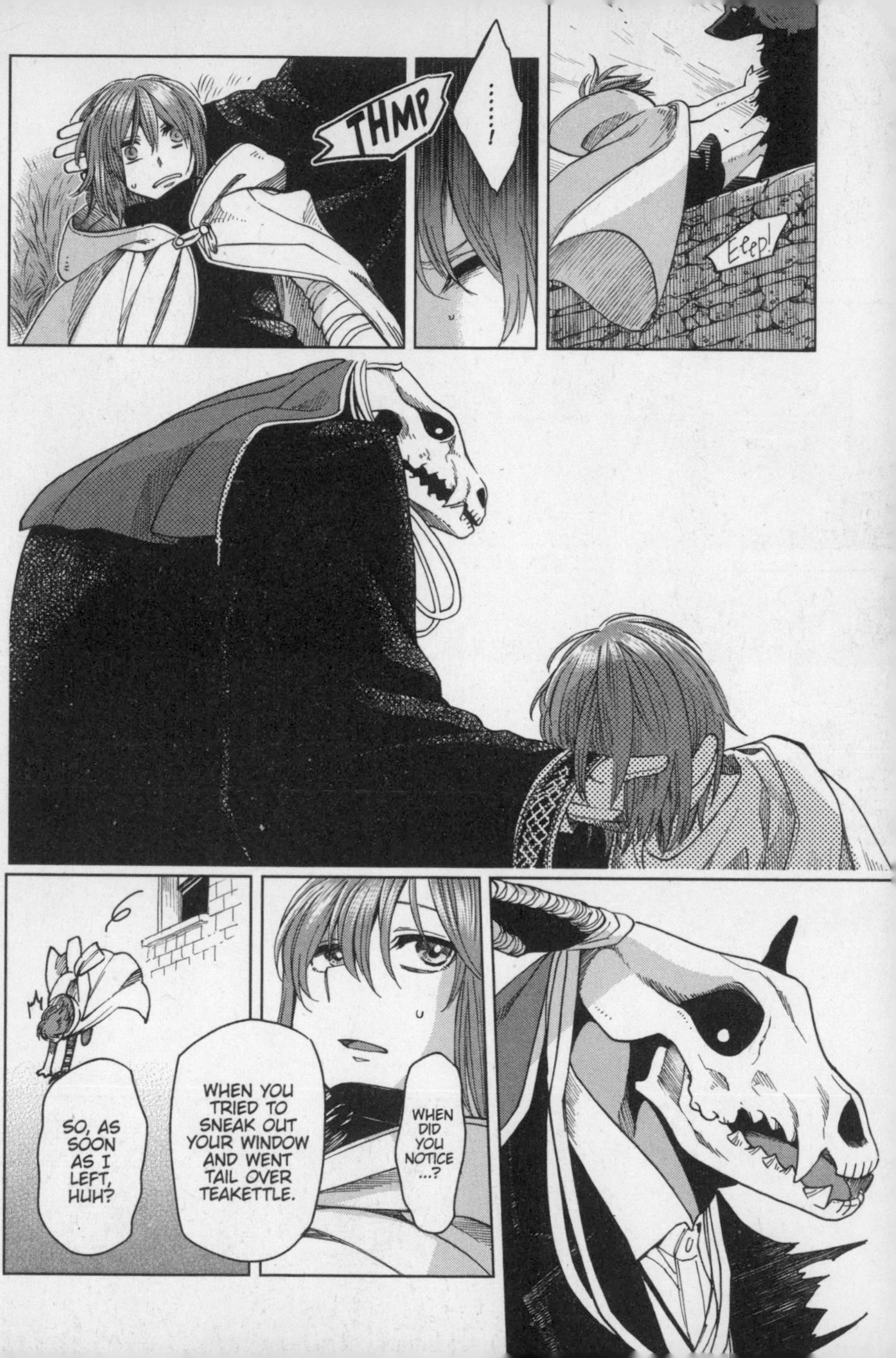
Eeep!
......!
THMP
WHEN DID YOU NOTICE ...?
WHEN YOU TRIED TO SNEAK OUT YOUR WINDOW AND WENT TAIL OVER TEAKETTLE.
SO, AS SOON AS I LEFT, HUH?

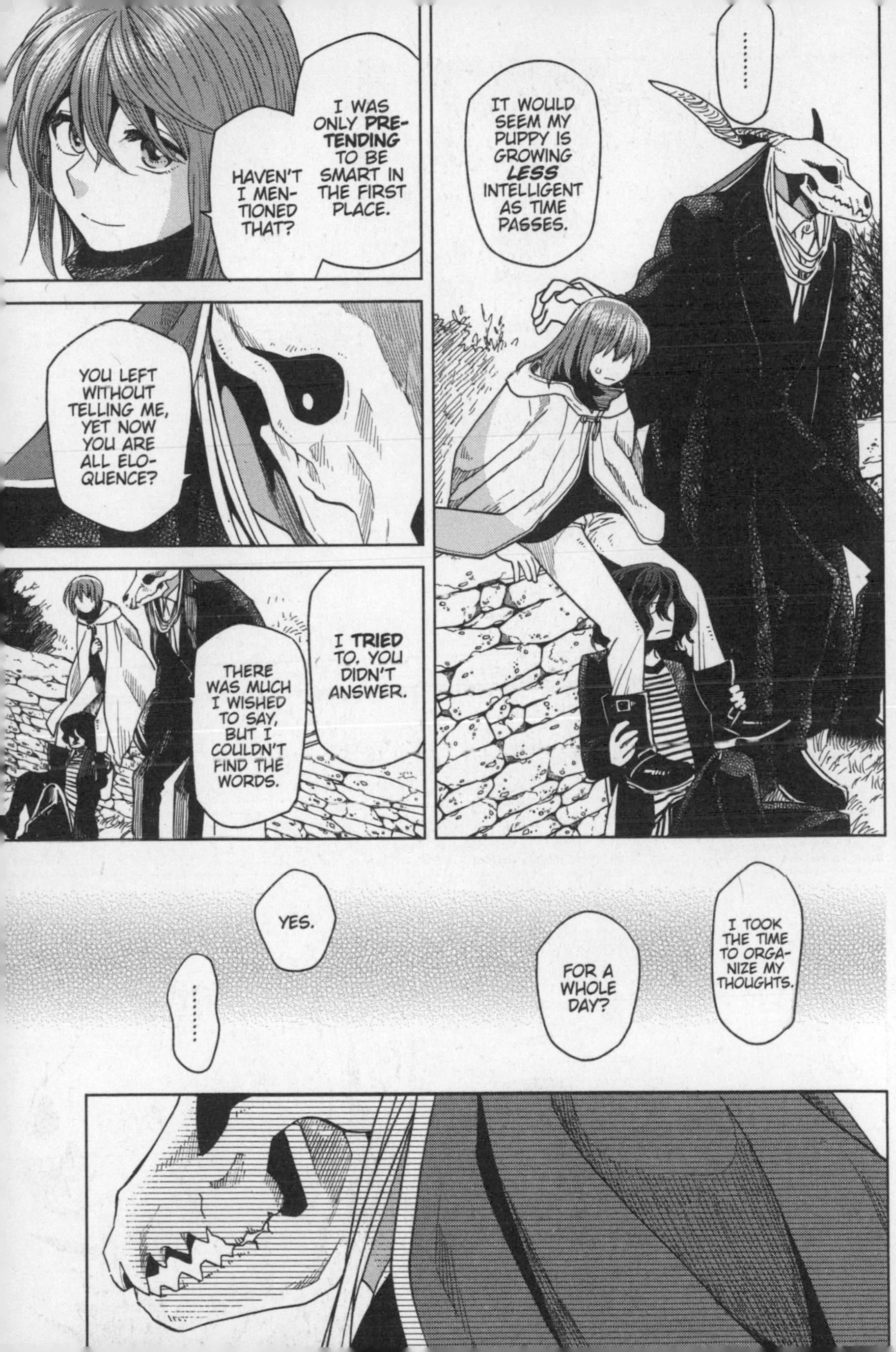
......
IT WOULD SEEM MY PUPPY IS GROWING LESS INTELLIGENT AS TIME PASSES.
I WAS ONLY PRETENDING TO BE SMART IN THE FIRST PLACE.
HAVEN'T I MENTIONED THAT?
YOU LEFT WITHOUT TELLING ME, YET NOW YOU ARE ALL ELOQUENCE?
I TRIED TO. YOU DIDN'T ANSWER.
THERE WAS MUCH I WISHED TO SAY, BUT I COULDN'T FIND THE WORDS.
I TOOK THE TIME TO ORGANIZE MY THOUGHTS.
FOR A WHOLE DAY?
YES.
......

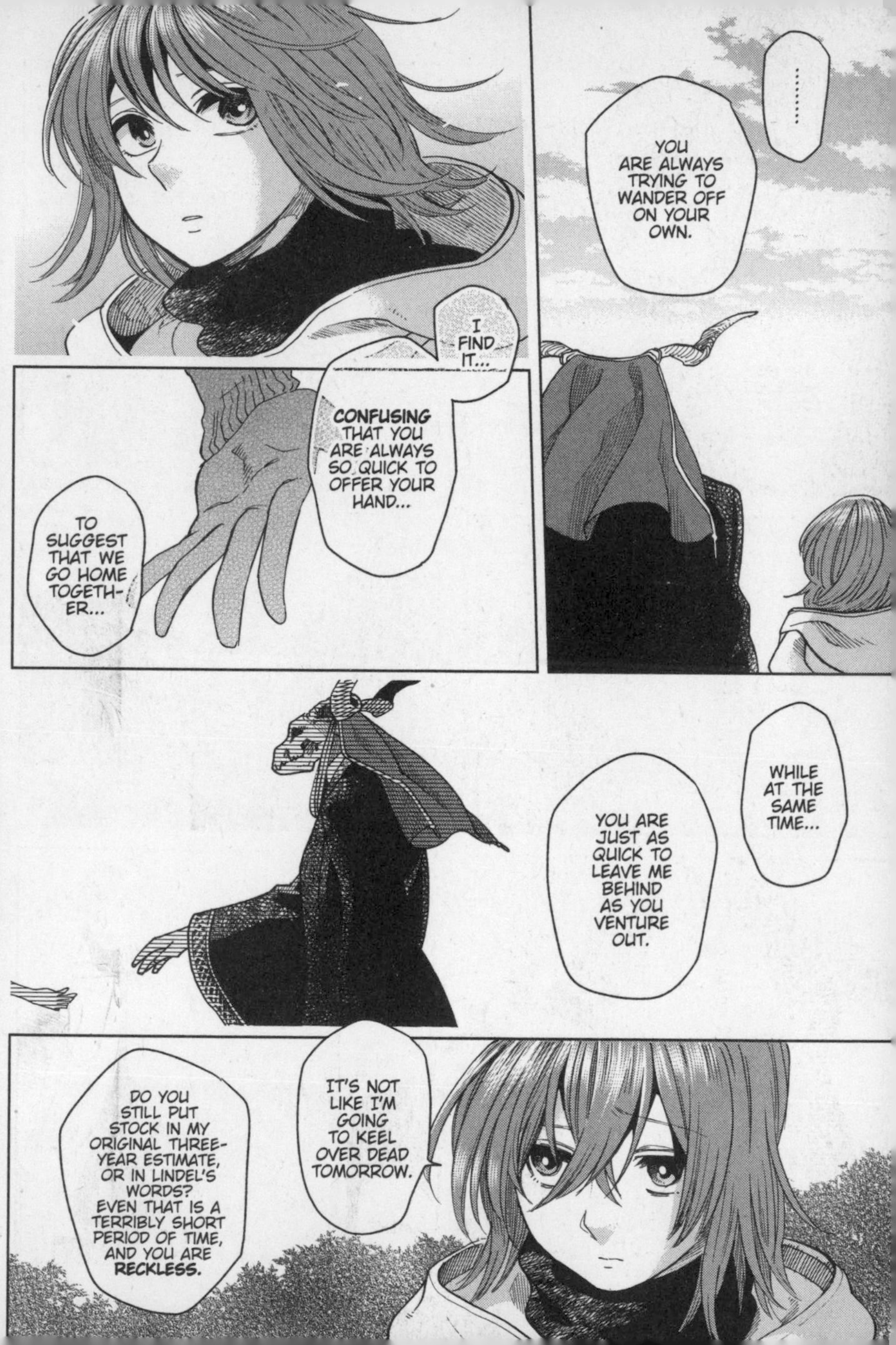
......
YOU ARE ALWAYS TRYING TO WANDER OFF ON YOUR OWN.
I FIND IT...
CONFUSING THAT YOU ARE ALWAYS SO QUICK TO OFFER YOUR HAND...
TO SUGGEST THAT WE GO HOME TOGETH-ER...
WHILE AT THE SAME TIME...
YOU ARE JUST AS QUICK TO LEAVE ME BEHIND AS YOU VENTURE OUT.
IT'S NOT LIKE I'M GOING TO KEEL OVER DEAD TOMORROW.
DO YOU STILL PUT STOCK IN MY ORIGINAL THREE-YEAR ESTIMATE, OR IN LINDEL'S WORDS? EVEN THAT IS A TERRIBLY SHORT PERIOD OF TIME, AND YOU ARE **RECKLESS.**

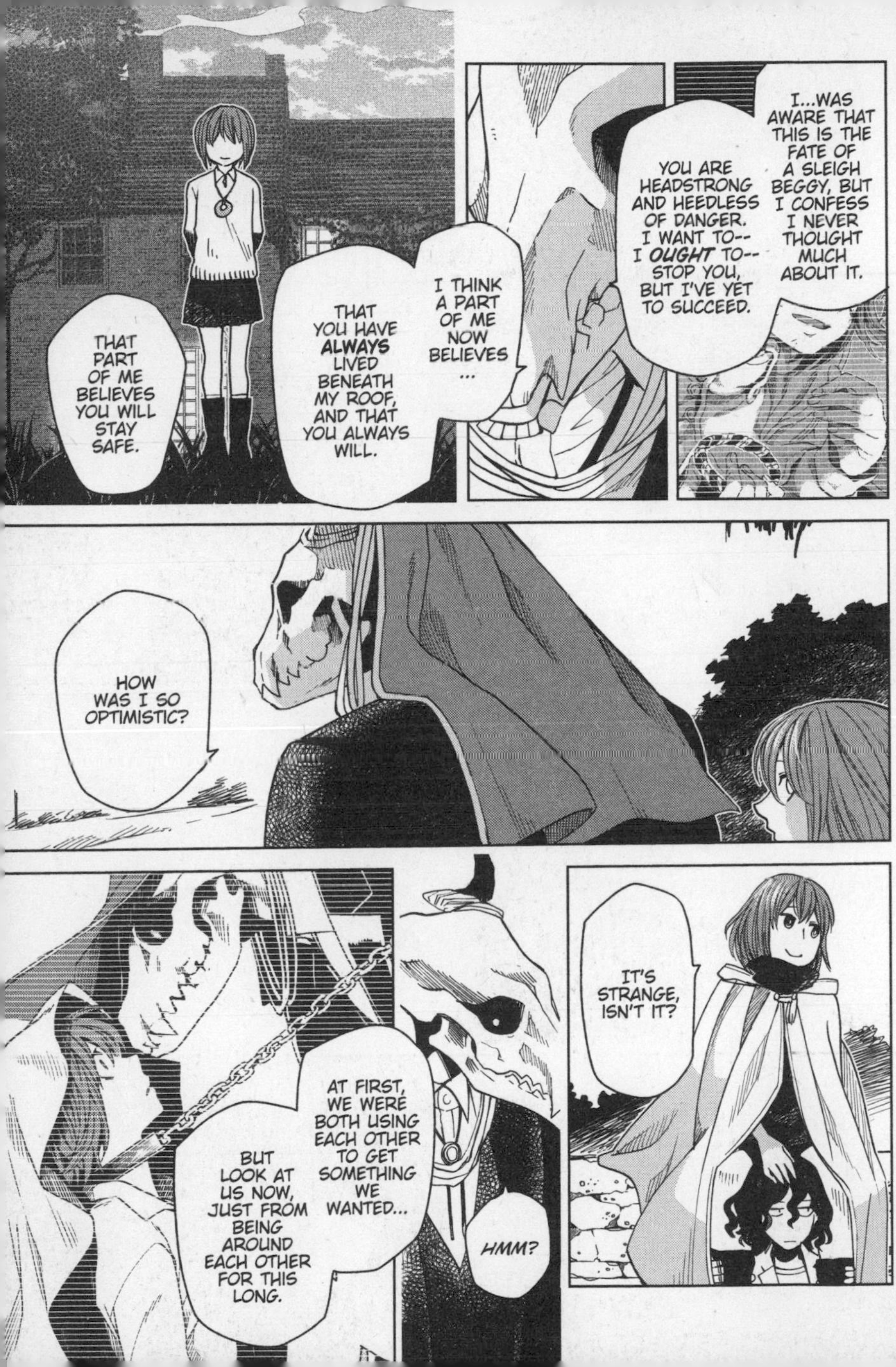
I...WAS AWARE THAT THIS IS THE FATE OF A SLEIGH BEGGY, BUT I CONFESS I NEVER THOUGHT MUCH ABOUT IT.
YOU ARE HEADSTRONG AND HEEDLESS OF DANGER. I WANT TO-- I *OUGHT* TO-- STOP YOU, BUT I'VE YET TO SUCCEED.
I THINK A PART OF ME NOW BELIEVES ...
THAT YOU HAVE **ALWAYS** LIVED BENEATH MY ROOF, AND THAT YOU ALWAYS WILL.
THAT PART OF ME BELIEVES YOU WILL STAY SAFE.
HOW WAS I SO OPTIMISTIC?
IT'S STRANGE, ISN'T IT?
HMM?
AT FIRST, WE WERE BOTH USING EACH OTHER TO GET SOMETHING WE WANTED...
BUT LOOK AT US NOW, JUST FROM BEING AROUND EACH OTHER FOR THIS LONG.

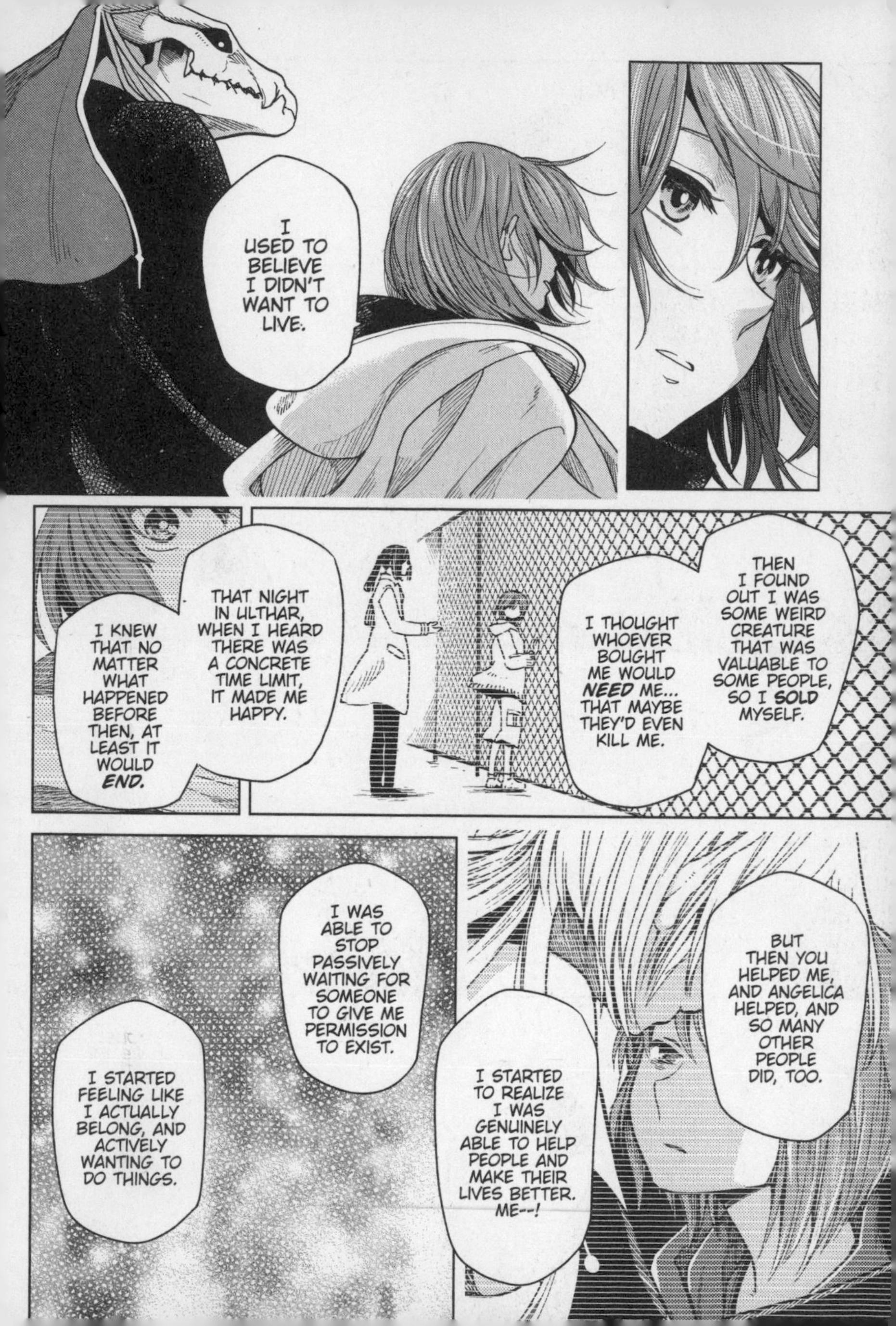
I USED TO BELIEVE I DIDN'T WANT TO LIVE.
THEN I FOUND OUT I WAS SOME WEIRD CREATURE THAT WAS VALUABLE TO SOME PEOPLE, SO I **SOLD** MYSELF.
I THOUGHT WHOEVER BOUGHT ME WOULD ***NEED*** ME... THAT MAYBE THEY'D EVEN KILL ME.
THAT NIGHT IN ULTHAR, WHEN I HEARD THERE WAS A CONCRETE TIME LIMIT, IT MADE ME HAPPY.
I KNEW THAT NO MATTER WHAT HAPPENED BEFORE THEN, AT LEAST IT WOULD ***END.***
BUT THEN YOU HELPED ME, AND ANGELICA HELPED, AND SO MANY OTHER PEOPLE DID, TOO.
I STARTED TO REALIZE I WAS GENUINELY ABLE TO HELP PEOPLE AND MAKE THEIR LIVES BETTER. ME--!
I WAS ABLE TO STOP PASSIVELY WAITING FOR SOMEONE TO GIVE ME PERMISSION TO EXIST.
I STARTED FEELING LIKE I ACTUALLY BELONG, AND ACTIVELY WANTING TO DO THINGS.

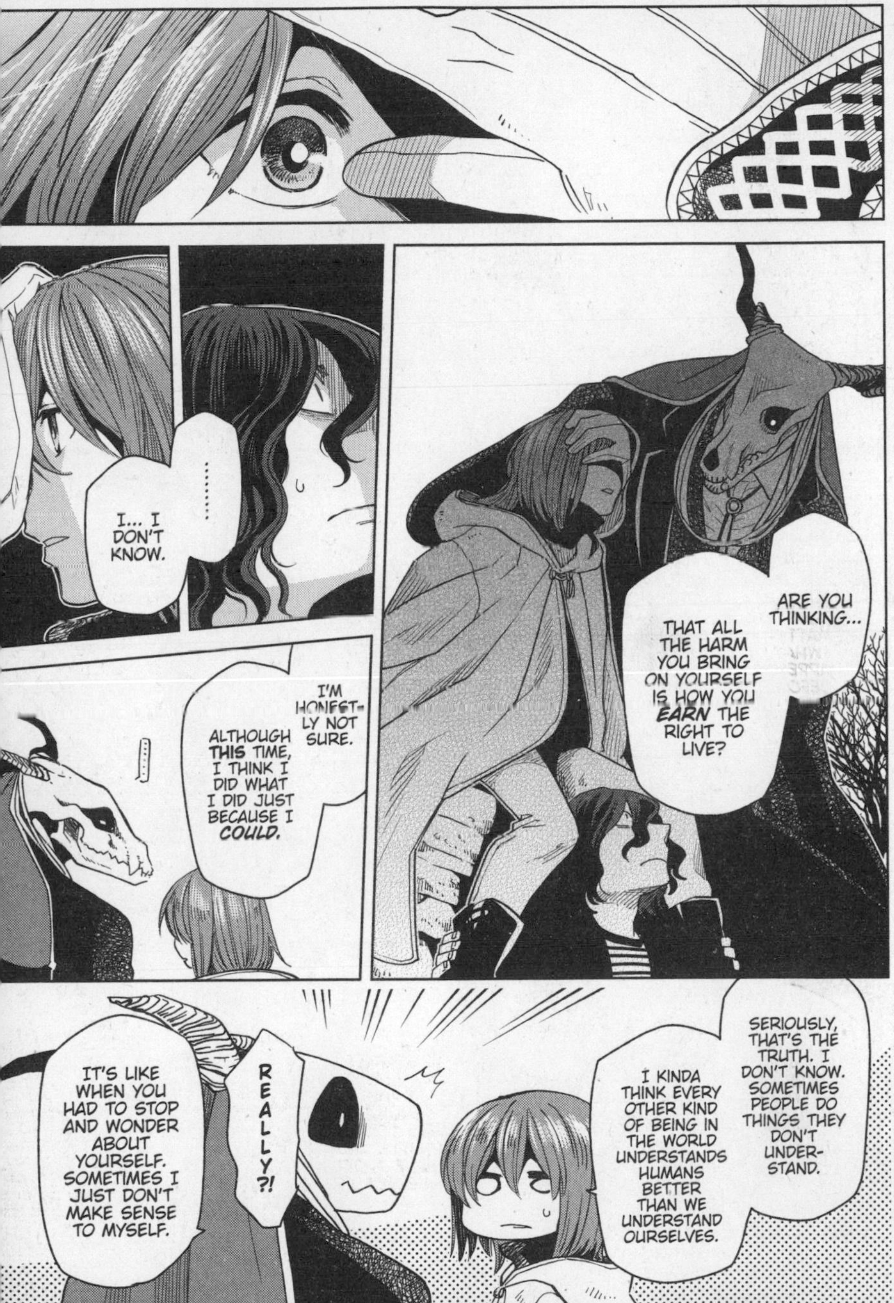
ARE YOU THINKING...
THAT ALL THE HARM YOU BRING ON YOURSELF IS HOW YOU **EARN** THE RIGHT TO LIVE?
......
I... I DON'T KNOW.
I'M HONESTLY NOT SURE.
ALTHOUGH **THIS** TIME, I THINK I DID WHAT I DID JUST BECAUSE I ***COULD.***
......
SERIOUSLY, THAT'S THE TRUTH. I DON'T KNOW. SOMETIMES PEOPLE DO THINGS THEY DON'T UNDERSTAND.
I KINDA THINK EVERY OTHER KIND OF BEING IN THE WORLD UNDERSTANDS HUMANS BETTER THAN WE UNDERSTAND OURSELVES.
REALLY?!
IT'S LIKE WHEN YOU HAD TO STOP AND WONDER ABOUT YOURSELF. SOMETIMES I JUST DON'T MAKE SENSE TO MYSELF.

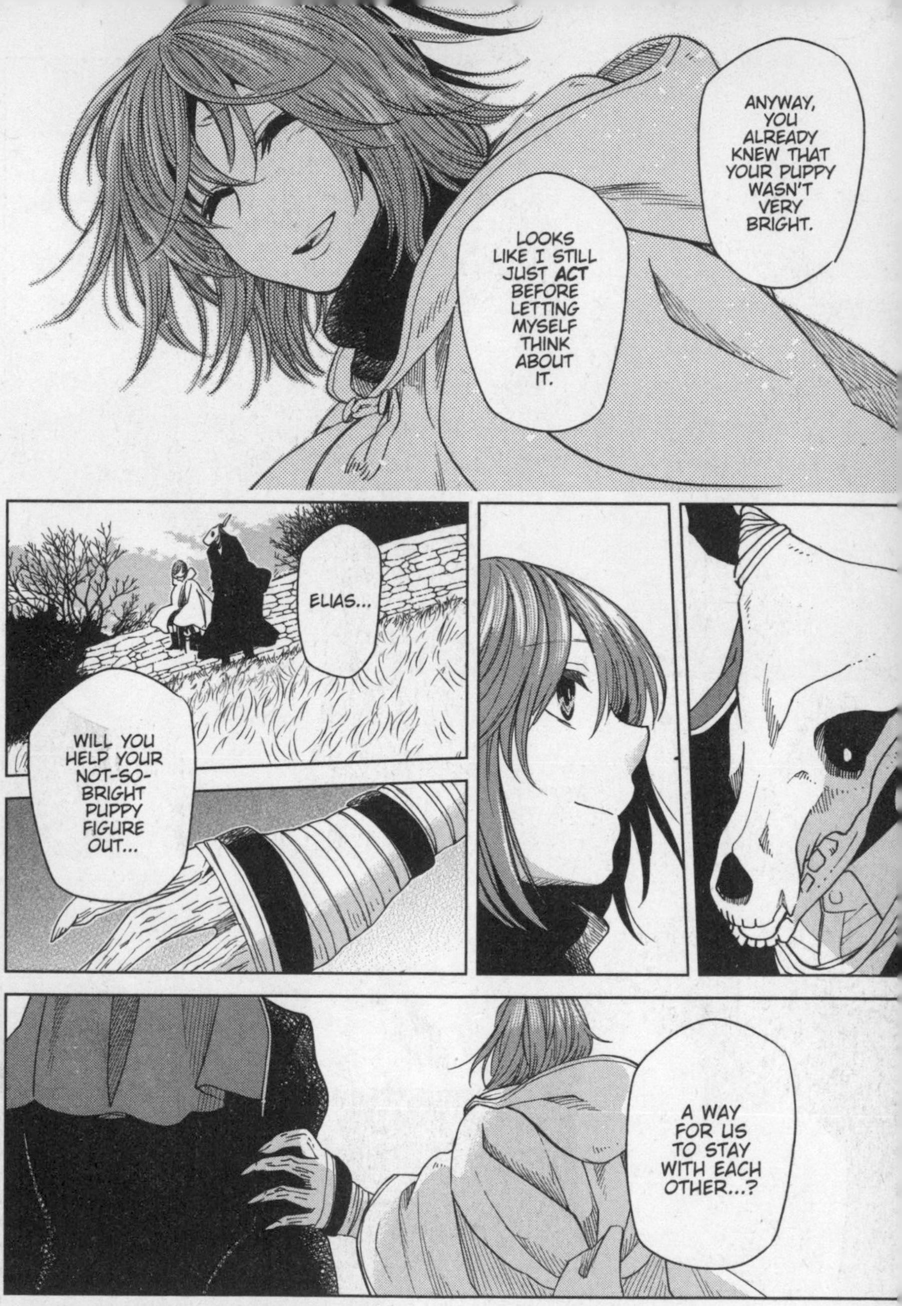
ANYWAY, YOU ALREADY KNEW THAT YOUR PUPPY WASN'T VERY BRIGHT.
LOOKS LIKE I STILL JUST **ACT** BEFORE LETTING MYSELF THINK ABOUT IT.
ELIAS...
WILL YOU HELP YOUR NOT-SO-BRIGHT PUPPY FIGURE OUT...
A WAY FOR US TO STAY WITH EACH OTHER...?

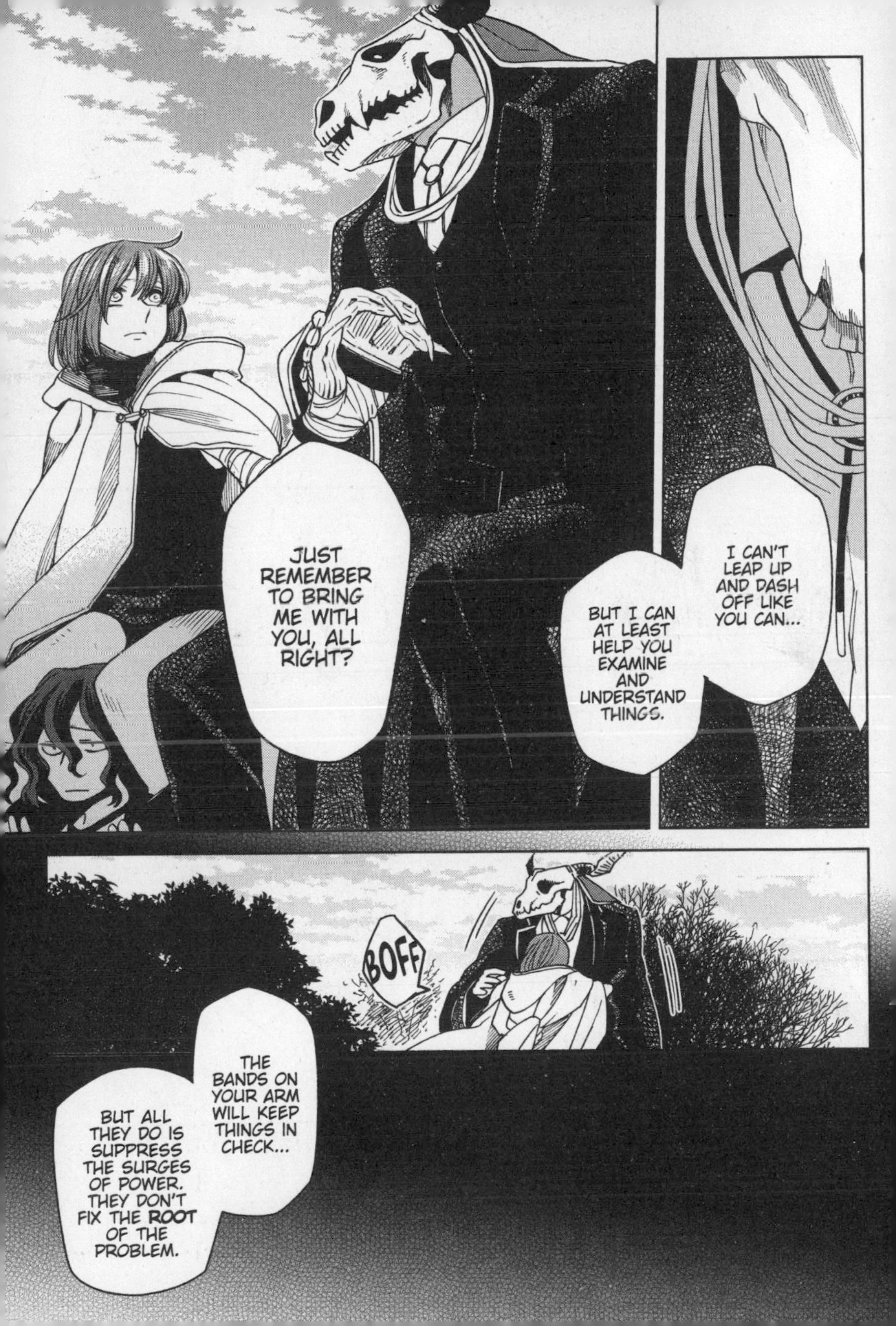
I CAN'T LEAP UP AND DASH OFF LIKE YOU CAN...
BUT I CAN AT LEAST HELP YOU EXAMINE AND UNDERSTAND THINGS.
JUST REMEMBER TO BRING ME WITH YOU, ALL RIGHT?
BOFF
THE BANDS ON YOUR ARM WILL KEEP THINGS IN CHECK...
BUT ALL THEY DO IS SUPPRESS THE SURGES OF POWER. THEY DON'T FIX THE **ROOT** OF THE PROBLEM.

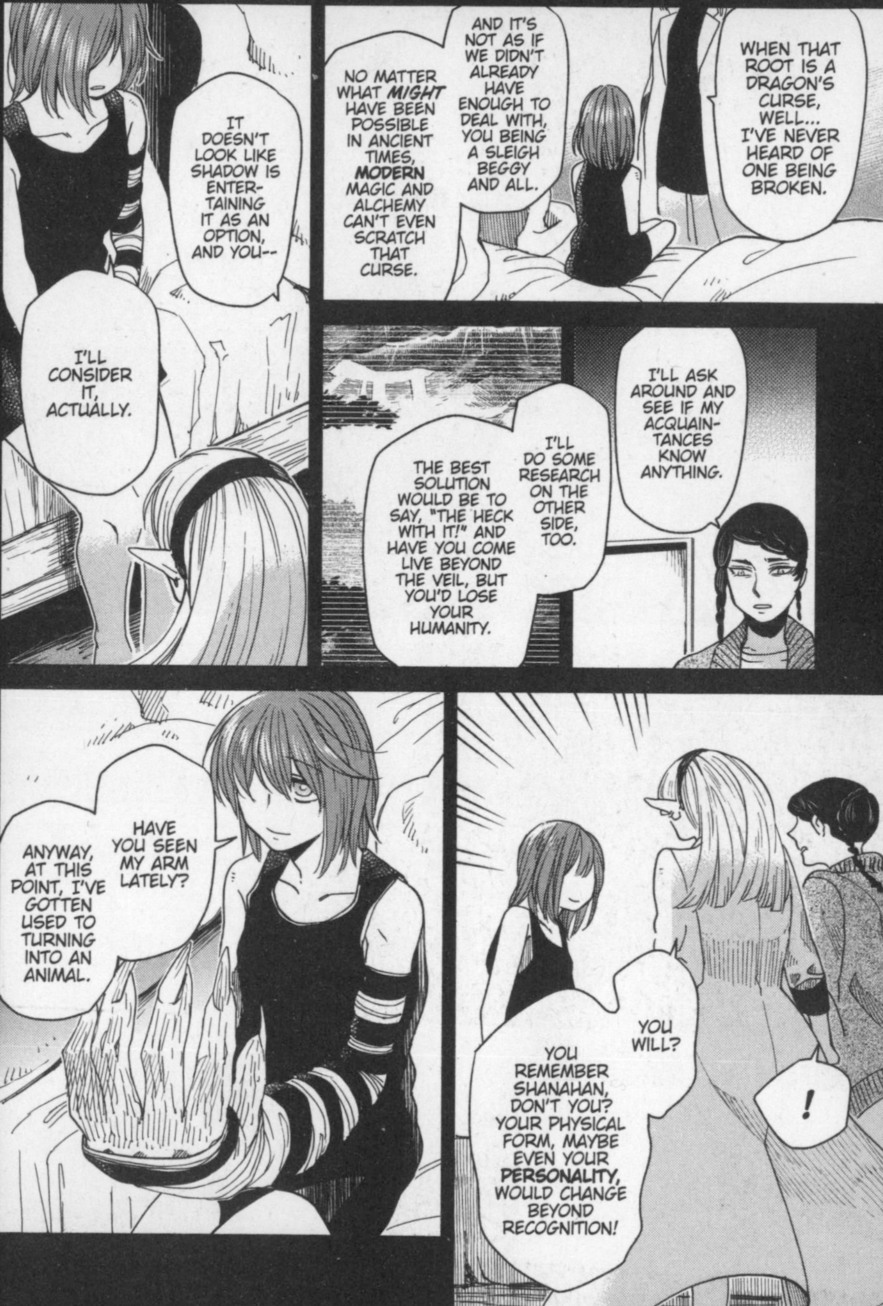
WHEN THAT ROOT IS A DRAGON'S CURSE, WELL... I'VE NEVER HEARD OF ONE BEING BROKEN.
AND IT'S NOT AS IF WE DIDN'T ALREADY HAVE ENOUGH TO DEAL WITH, YOU BEING A SLEIGH BEGGY AND ALL.
NO MATTER WHAT *MIGHT* HAVE BEEN POSSIBLE IN ANCIENT TIMES, **MODERN** MAGIC AND ALCHEMY CAN'T EVEN SCRATCH THAT CURSE.
I'LL ASK AROUND AND SEE IF MY ACQUAIN-TANCES KNOW ANYTHING.
I'LL DO SOME RESEARCH ON THE OTHER SIDE, TOO.
THE BEST SOLUTION WOULD BE TO SAY, "THE HECK WITH IT!" AND HAVE YOU COME LIVE BEYOND THE VEIL, BUT YOU'D LOSE YOUR HUMANITY.
IT DOESN'T LOOK LIKE SHADOW IS ENTER-TAINING IT AS AN OPTION, AND YOU--
I'LL CONSIDER IT, ACTUALLY.
YOU WILL?
!
YOU REMEMBER SHANAHAN, DON'T YOU? YOUR PHYSICAL FORM, MAYBE EVEN YOUR **PERSONALITY,** WOULD CHANGE BEYOND RECOGNITION!
HAVE YOU SEEN MY ARM LATELY?
ANYWAY, AT THIS POINT, I'VE GOTTEN USED TO TURNING INTO AN ANIMAL.

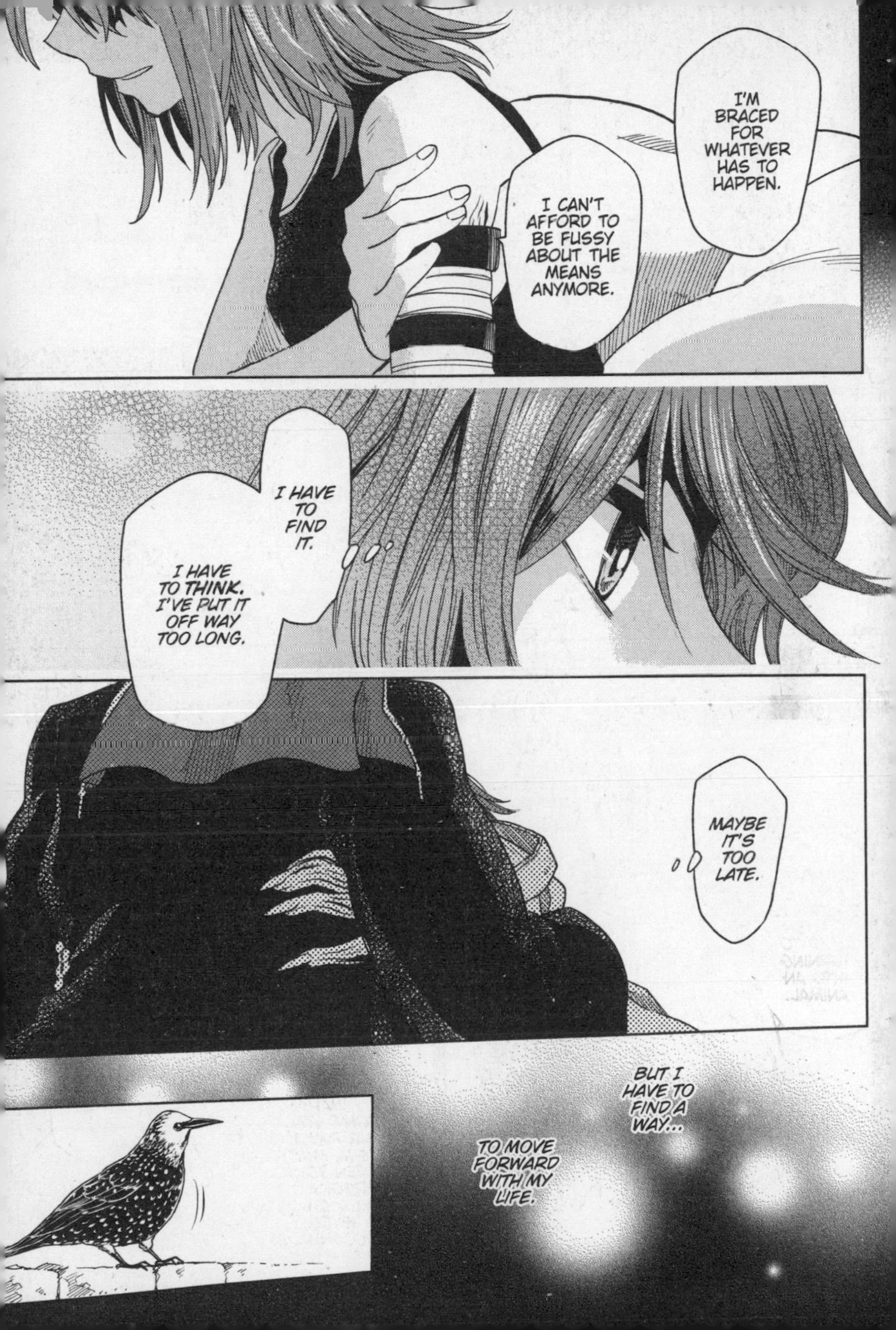
I'M BRACED FOR WHATEVER HAS TO HAPPEN.
I CAN'T AFFORD TO BE FUSSY ABOUT THE MEANS ANYMORE.
I HAVE TO FIND IT.
I HAVE TO THINK. I'VE PUT IT OFF WAY TOO LONG.
MAYBE IT'S TOO LATE.
BUT I HAVE TO FIND A WAY...
TO MOVE FORWARD WITH MY LIFE.

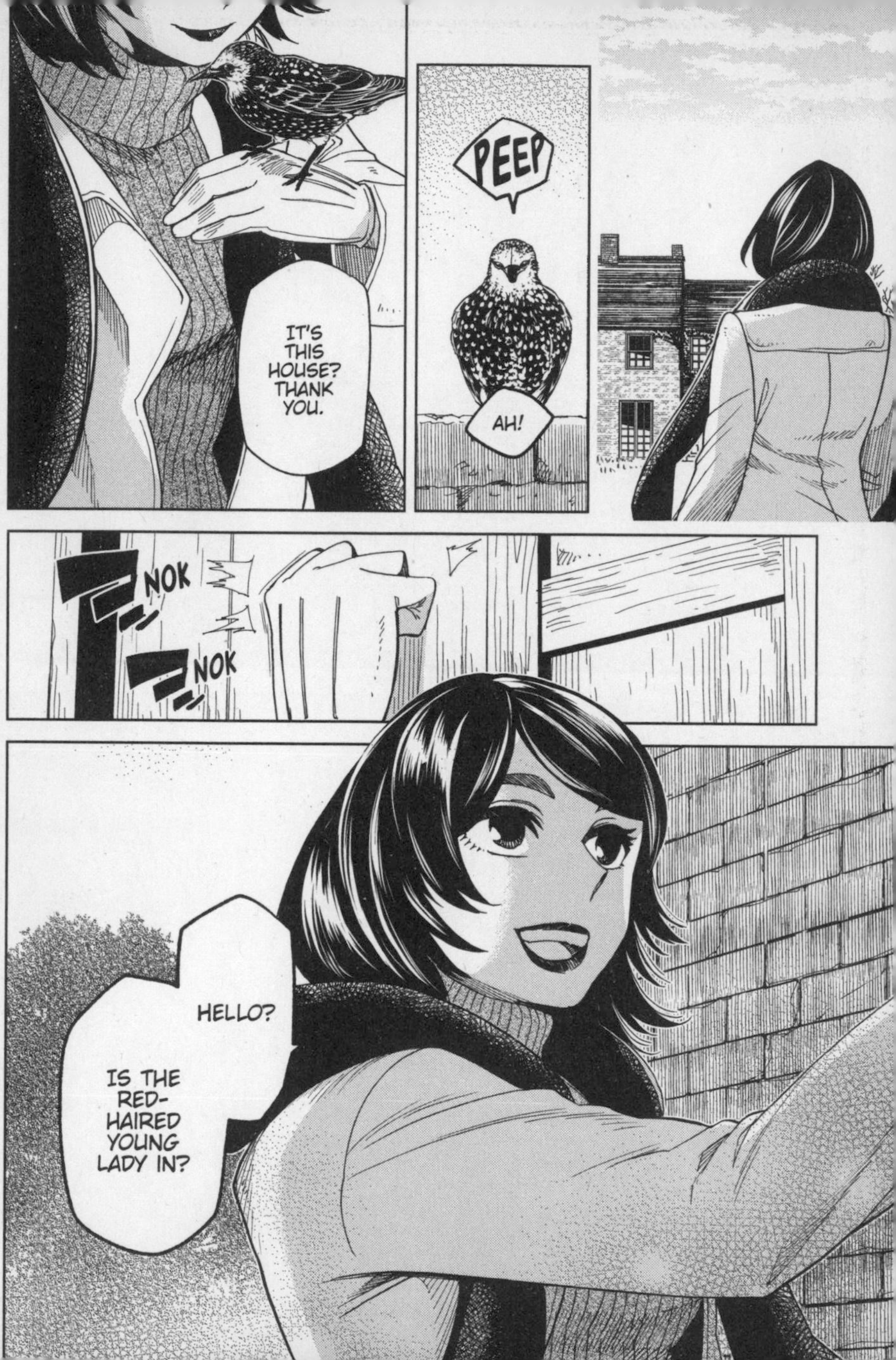
PEEP
AH!
IT'S THIS HOUSE? THANK YOU.
NOK
NOK
HELLO?
IS THE RED-HAIRED YOUNG LADY IN?

The Ancient Magus' Bride

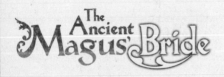

The Ancient Magus' Bride

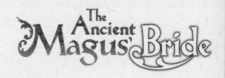

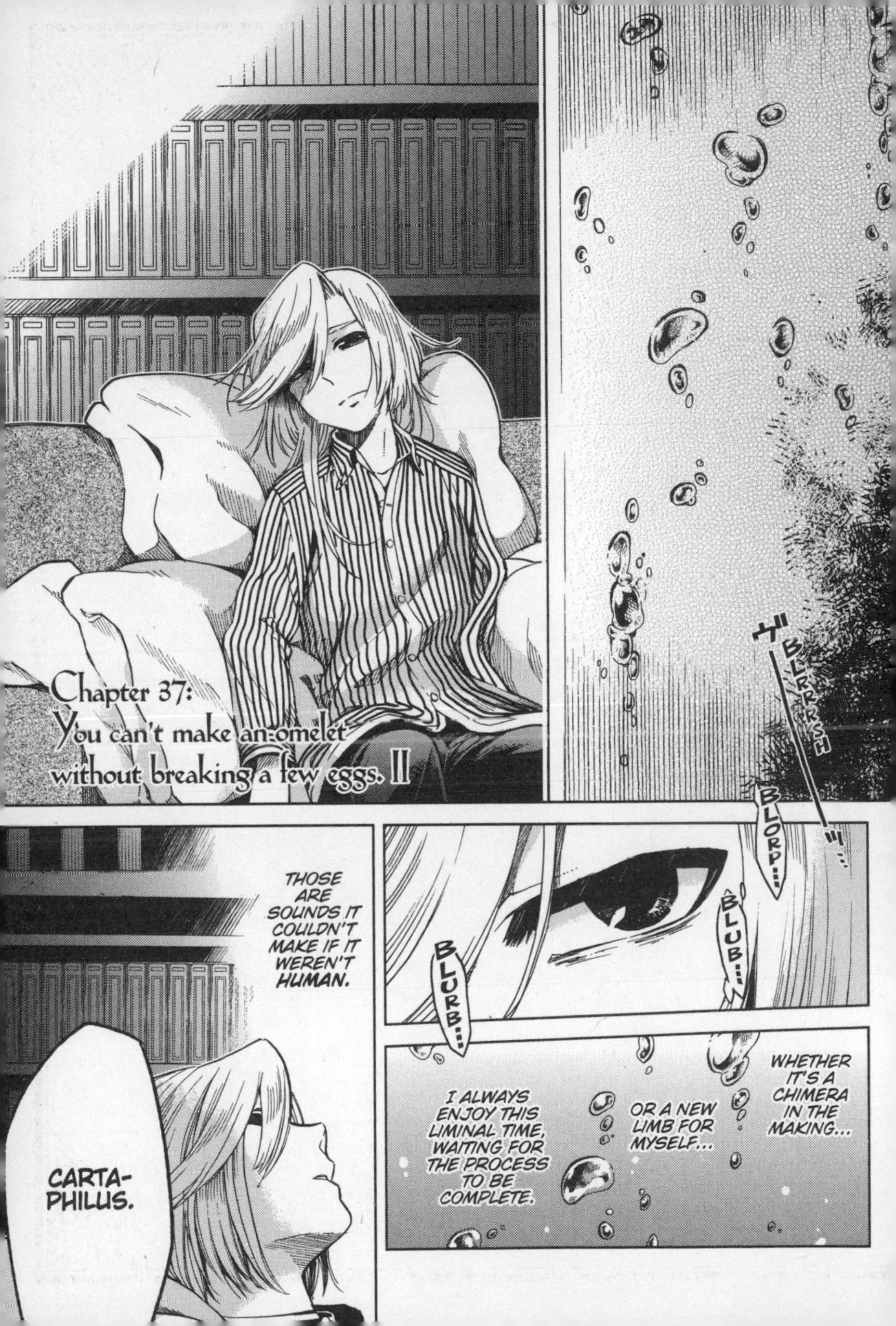
BLLRRRSH
Chapter 37:
You can't make an omelet without breaking a few eggs. II
BLORP...
BLUB...
BLURB...
WHETHER IT'S A CHIMERA IN THE MAKING...
OR A NEW LIMB FOR MYSELF...
I ALWAYS ENJOY THIS LIMINAL TIME, WAITING FOR THE PROCESS TO BE COMPLETE.
THOSE ARE SOUNDS IT COULDN'T MAKE IF IT WEREN'T HUMAN.
CARTA-PHILUS.

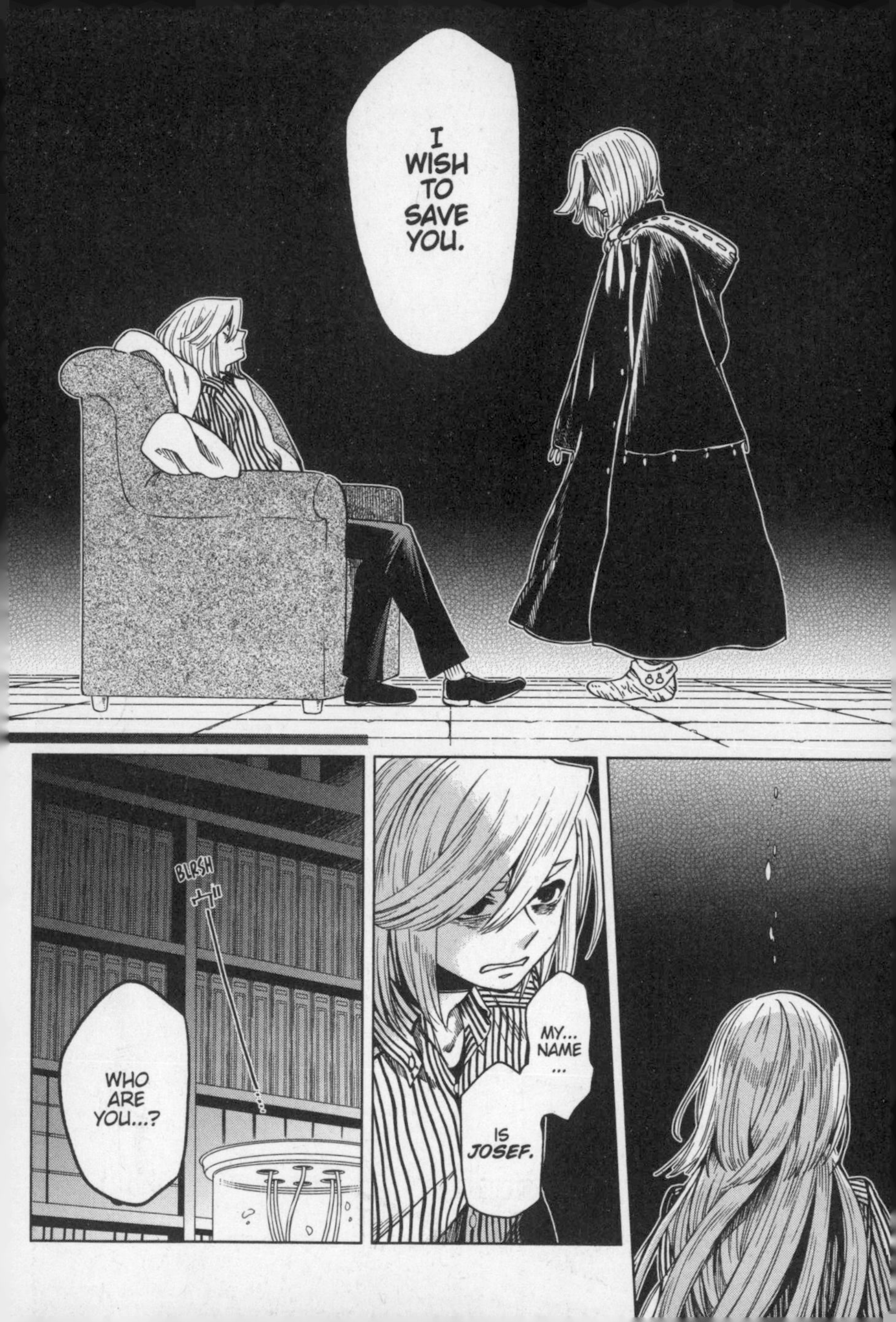
I WISH TO SAVE YOU.
MY... NAME ...
IS JOSEF.
BLRSH
WHO ARE YOU...?

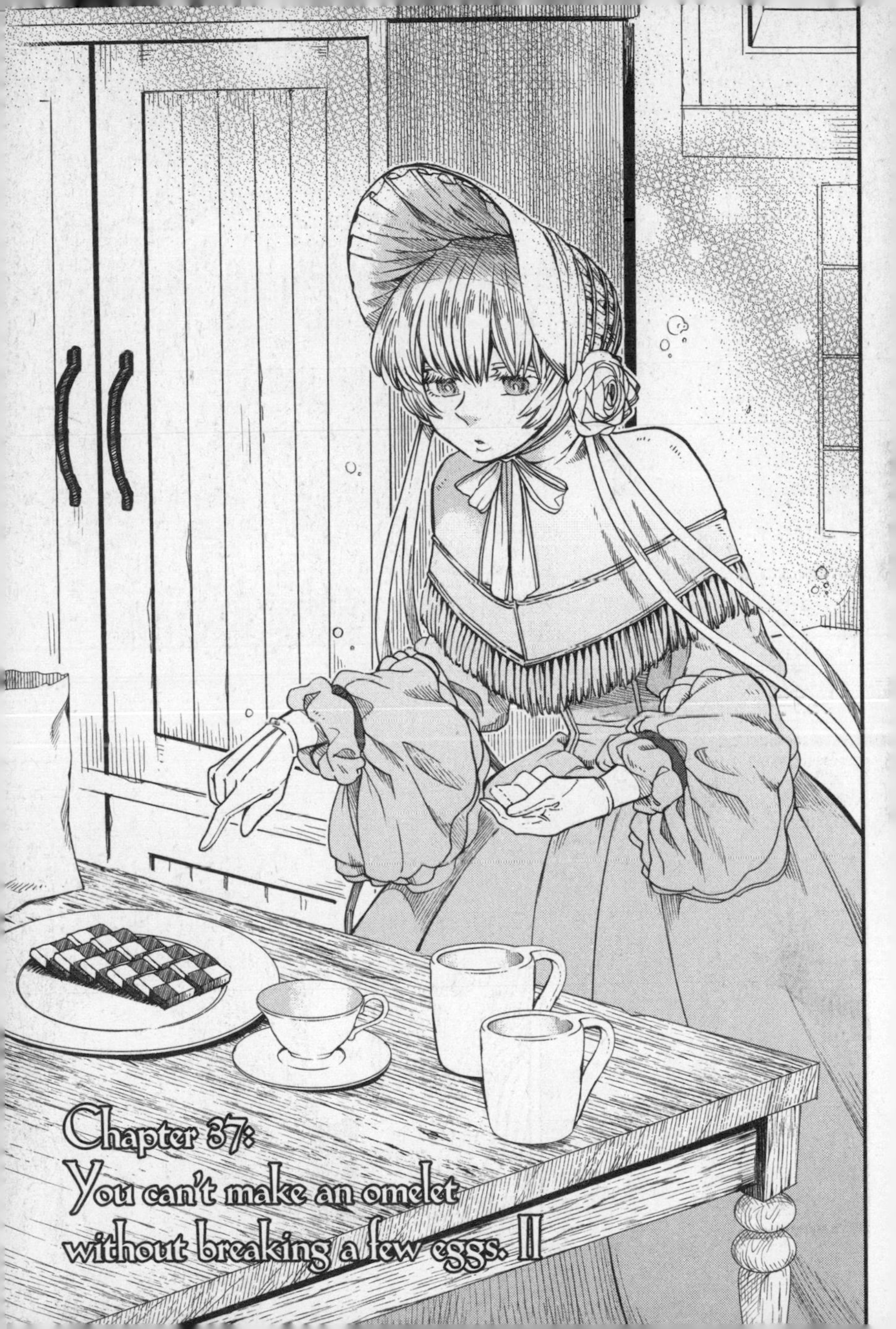
Chapter 37:
You can't make an omelet without breaking a few eggs. II

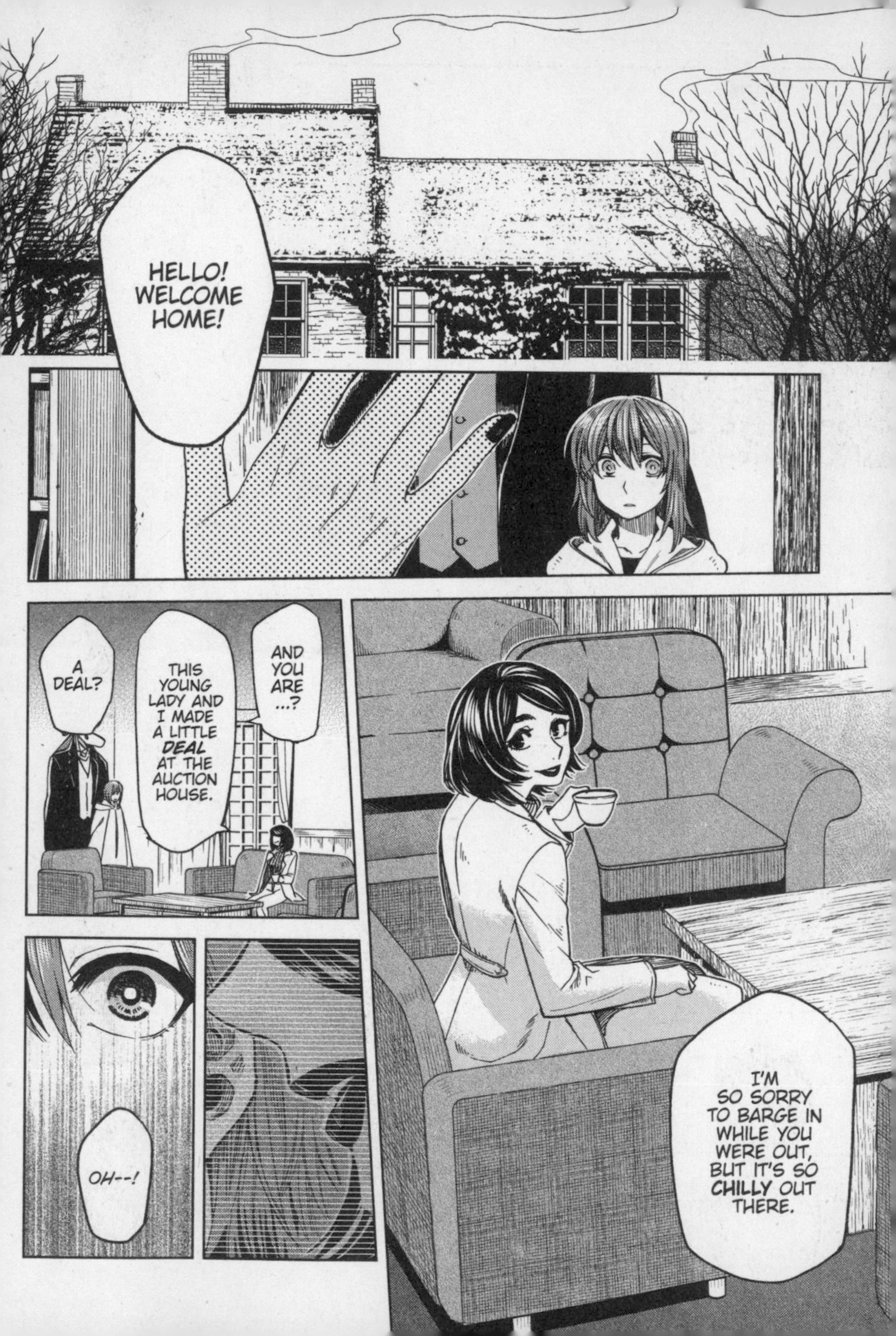
HELLO! WELCOME HOME!
I'M SO SORRY TO BARGE IN WHILE YOU WERE OUT, BUT IT'S SO CHILLY OUT THERE.
AND YOU ARE ...?
THIS YOUNG LADY AND I MADE A LITTLE DEAL AT THE AUCTION HOUSE.
A DEAL?
OH--!

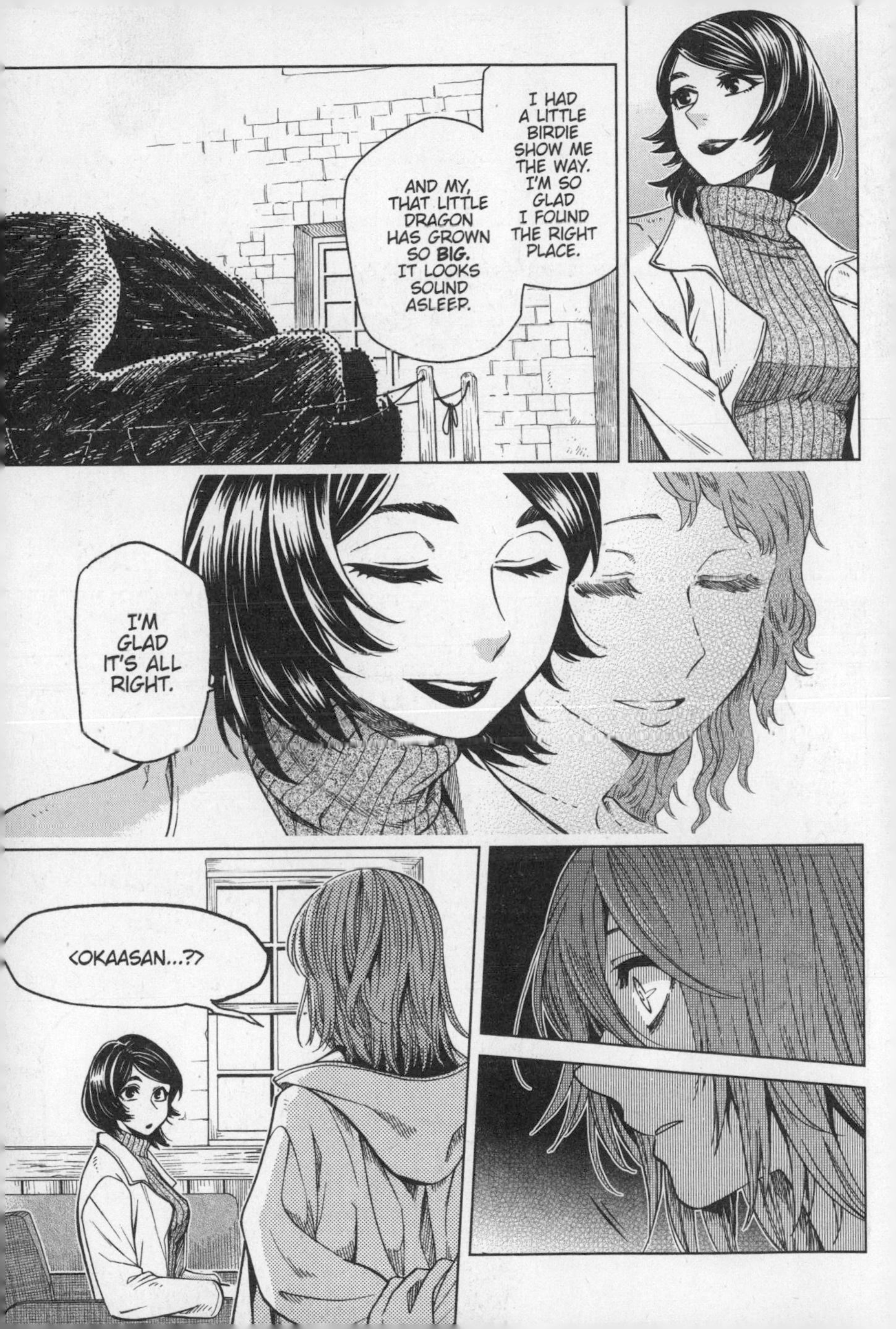
I HAD A LITTLE BIRDIE SHOW ME THE WAY. I'M SO GLAD I FOUND THE RIGHT PLACE.
AND MY, THAT LITTLE DRAGON HAS GROWN SO BIG. IT LOOKS SOUND ASLEEP.
I'M GLAD IT'S ALL RIGHT.
<OKAASAN...?>

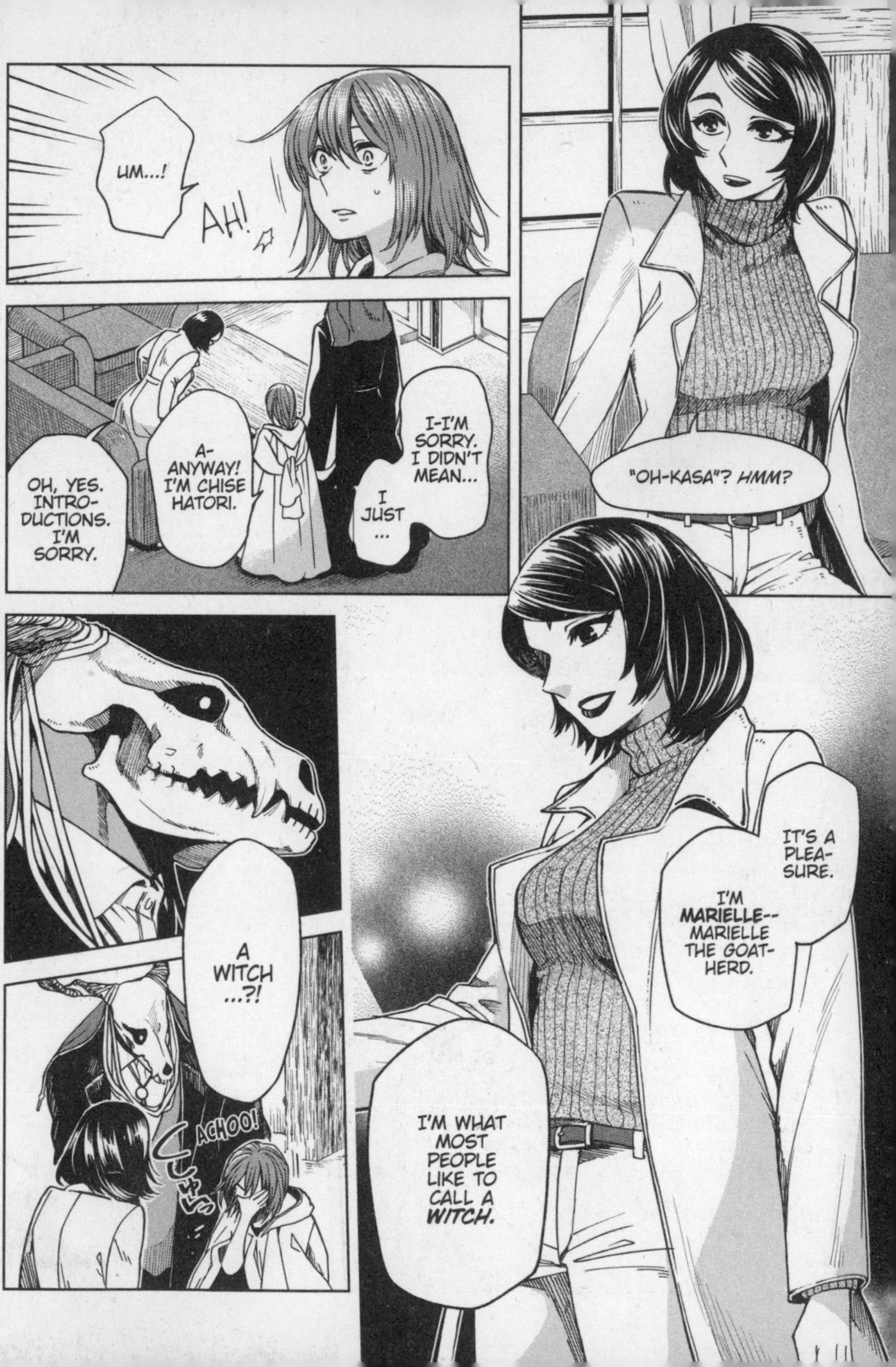
"OH-KASA"? HMM?
UM...!
AH!
I-I'M SORRY. I DIDN'T MEAN...
I JUST ...
A-ANYWAY! I'M CHISE HATORI.
OH, YES. INTRODUCTIONS. I'M SORRY.
IT'S A PLEASURE.
I'M MARIELLE-- MARIELLE THE GOAT-HERD.
I'M WHAT MOST PEOPLE LIKE TO CALL A WITCH.
A WITCH ...?!
ACHOO!

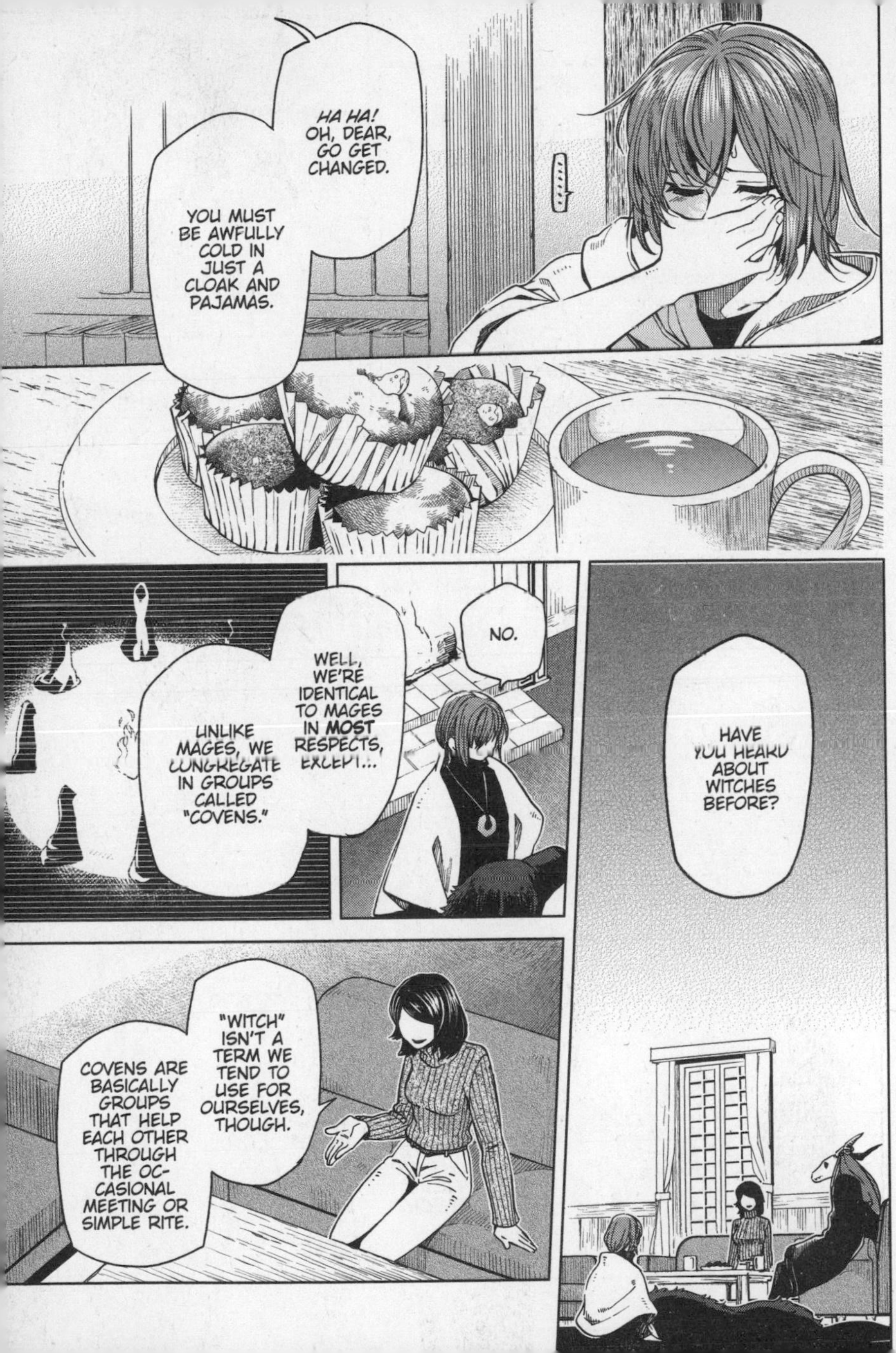
......
HA HA! OH, DEAR, GO GET CHANGED.
YOU MUST BE AWFULLY COLD IN JUST A CLOAK AND PAJAMAS.
HAVE YOU HEARD ABOUT WITCHES BEFORE?
NO.
WELL, WE'RE IDENTICAL TO MAGES IN **MOST** RESPECTS, EXCEPT...
UNLIKE MAGES, WE CONGREGATE IN GROUPS CALLED "COVENS."
"WITCH" ISN'T A TERM WE TEND TO USE FOR OURSELVES, THOUGH.
COVENS ARE BASICALLY GROUPS THAT HELP EACH OTHER THROUGH THE OC-CASIONAL MEETING OR SIMPLE RITE.

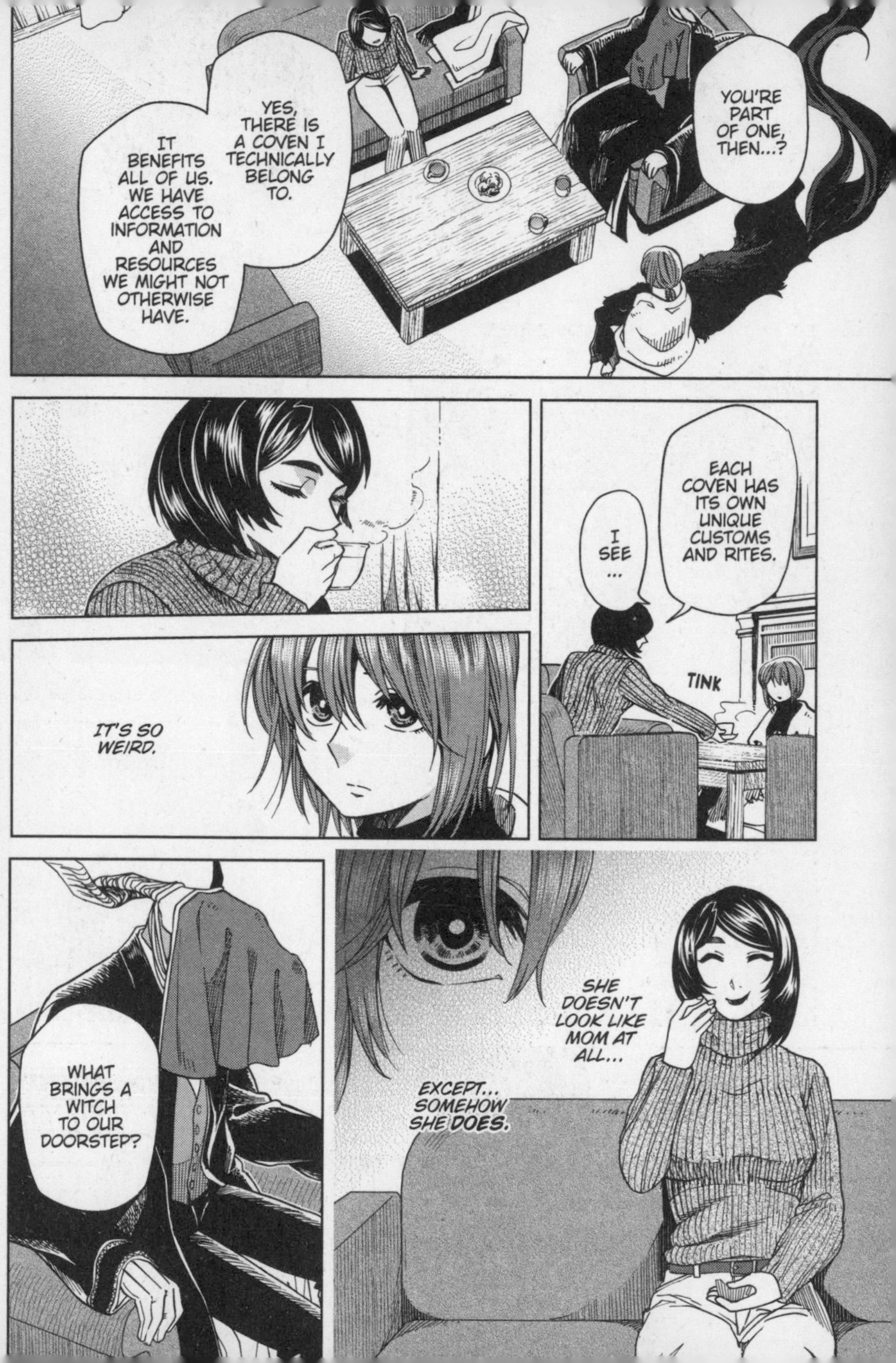
YOU'RE PART OF ONE, THEN...?
YES, THERE IS A COVEN I TECHNICALLY BELONG TO.
IT BENEFITS ALL OF US. WE HAVE ACCESS TO INFORMATION AND RESOURCES WE MIGHT NOT OTHERWISE HAVE.
EACH COVEN HAS ITS OWN UNIQUE CUSTOMS AND RITES.
I SEE...
TINK
IT'S SO WEIRD.
SHE DOESN'T LOOK LIKE MOM AT ALL...
EXCEPT... SOMEHOW SHE DOES.
WHAT BRINGS A WITCH TO OUR DOORSTEP?

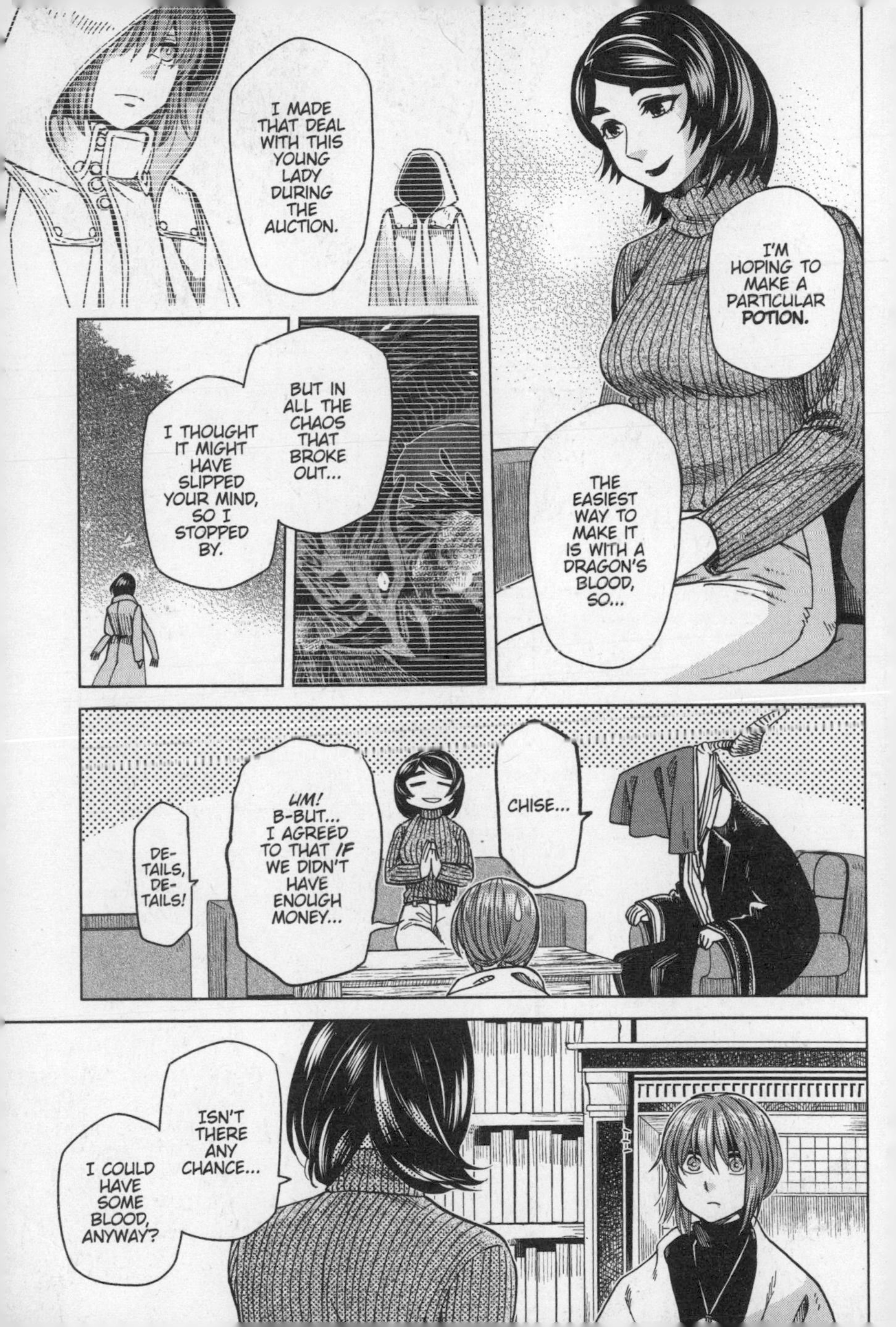
I'M HOPING TO MAKE A PARTICULAR **POTION.**
THE EASIEST WAY TO MAKE IT IS WITH A DRAGON'S BLOOD, SO...
I MADE THAT DEAL WITH THIS YOUNG LADY DURING THE AUCTION.
BUT IN ALL THE CHAOS THAT BROKE OUT...
I THOUGHT IT MIGHT HAVE SLIPPED YOUR MIND, SO I STOPPED BY.
CHISE...
UM! B-BUT... I AGREED TO THAT *IF* WE DIDN'T HAVE ENOUGH MONEY...
DE-TAILS, DE-TAILS!
ISN'T THERE ANY CHANCE...
I COULD HAVE SOME BLOOD, ANYWAY?

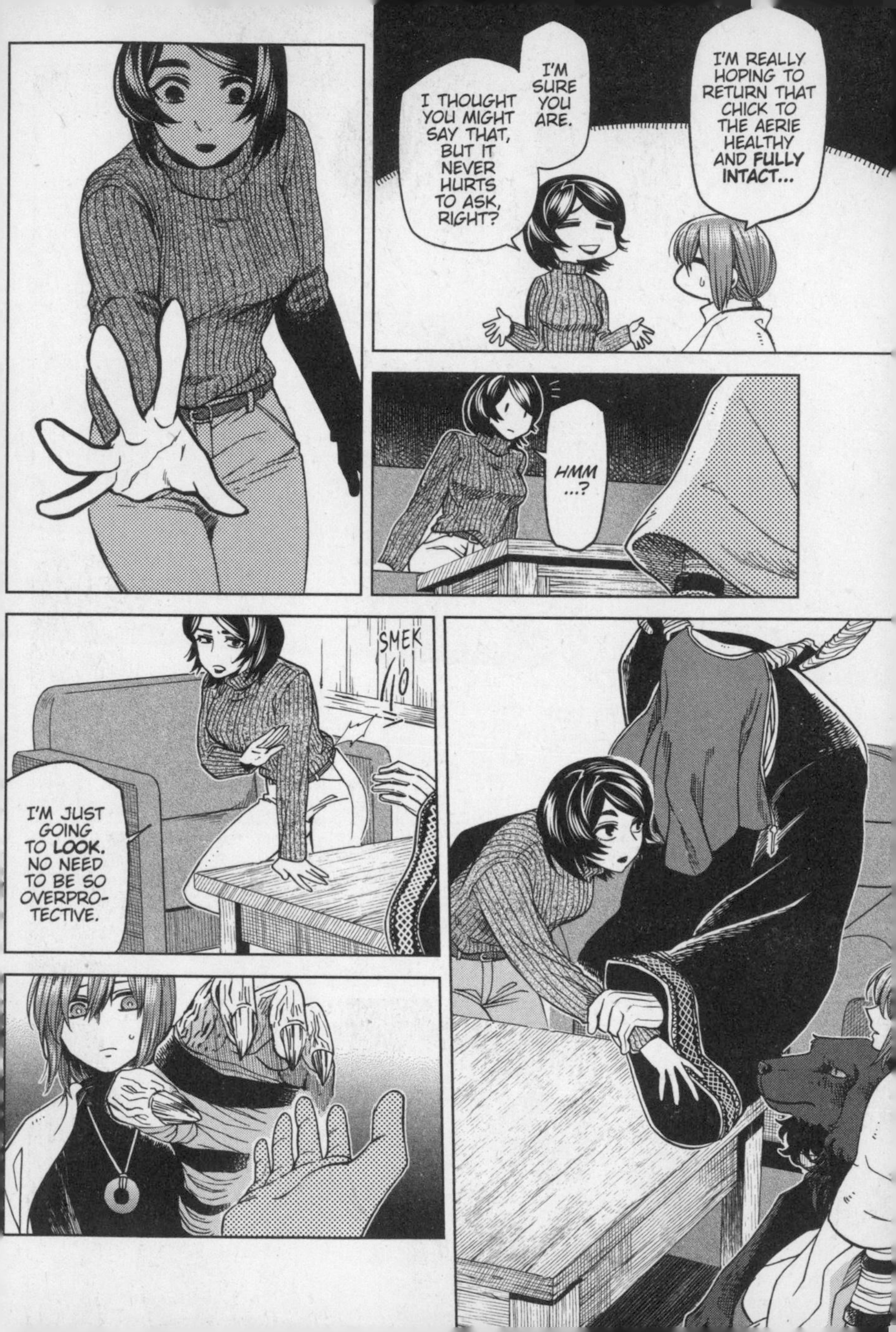
I'M REALLY HOPING TO RETURN THAT CHICK TO THE AERIE HEALTHY AND **FULLY INTACT...**
I'M SURE YOU ARE.
I THOUGHT YOU MIGHT SAY THAT, BUT IT NEVER HURTS TO ASK, RIGHT?
HMM ...?
SMEK
I'M JUST GOING TO **LOOK.** NO NEED TO BE SO OVERPROTECTIVE.

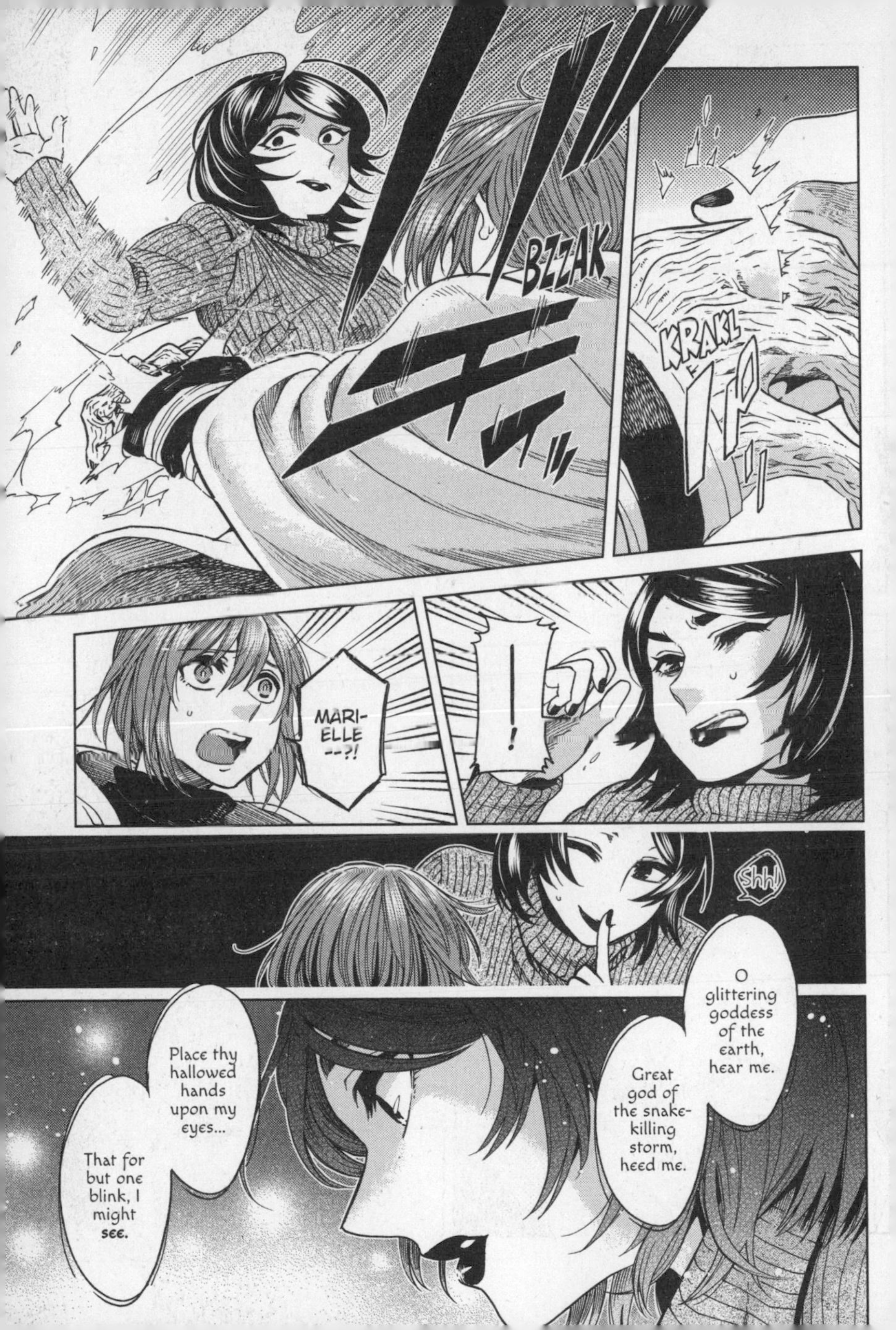
KRAKL
BZZAK
!
MARI-ELLE--?!
Shh!
O glittering goddess of the earth, hear me.
Great god of the snake-killing storm, heed me.
Place thy hallowed hands upon my eyes...
That for but one blink, I might see.

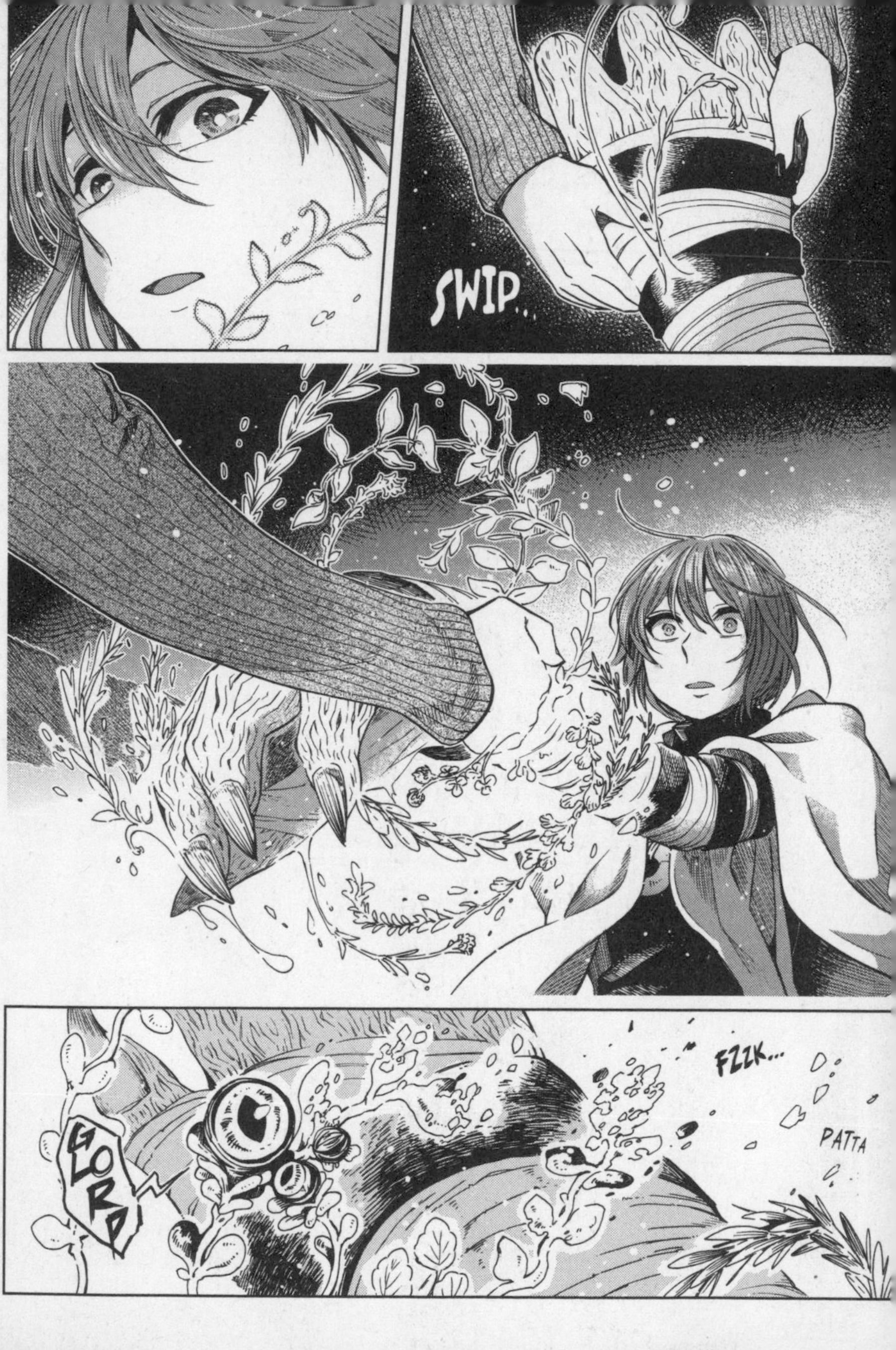
SWIP...
FZZK...
PATTA
GLORP

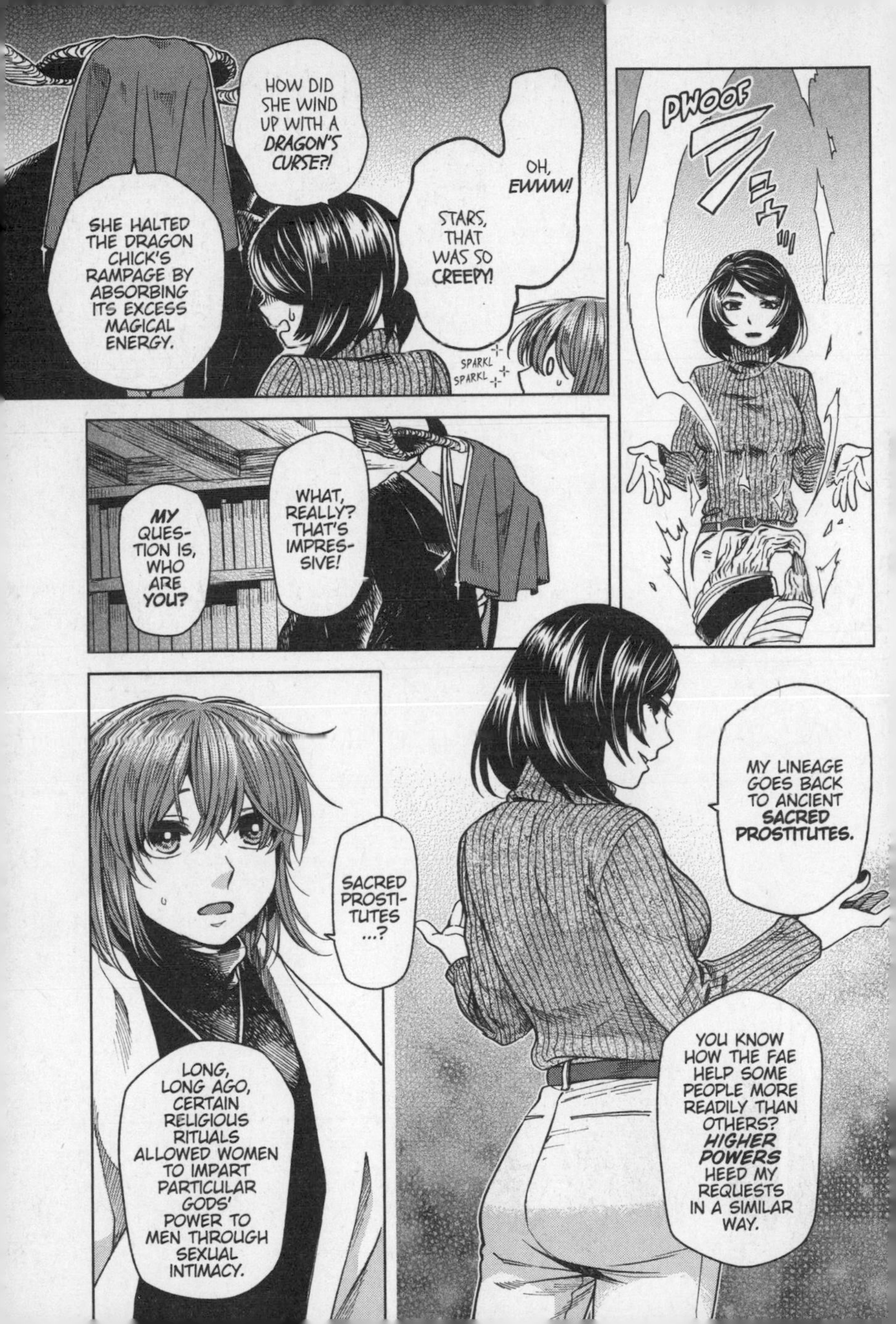
PWOOF
OH, EWWW!
STARS, THAT WAS SO CREEPY!
SPARKL SPARKL
HOW DID SHE WIND UP WITH A DRAGON'S CURSE?!
SHE HALTED THE DRAGON CHICK'S RAMPAGE BY ABSORBING ITS EXCESS MAGICAL ENERGY.
WHAT, REALLY? THAT'S IMPRES-SIVE!
MY QUES-TION IS, WHO ARE YOU?
MY LINEAGE GOES BACK TO ANCIENT SACRED PROSTITUTES.
SACRED PROSTI-TUTES ...?
LONG, LONG AGO, CERTAIN RELIGIOUS RITUALS ALLOWED WOMEN TO IMPART PARTICULAR GODS' POWER TO MEN THROUGH SEXUAL INTIMACY.
YOU KNOW HOW THE FAE HELP SOME PEOPLE MORE READILY THAN OTHERS? HIGHER POWERS HEED MY REQUESTS IN A SIMILAR WAY.

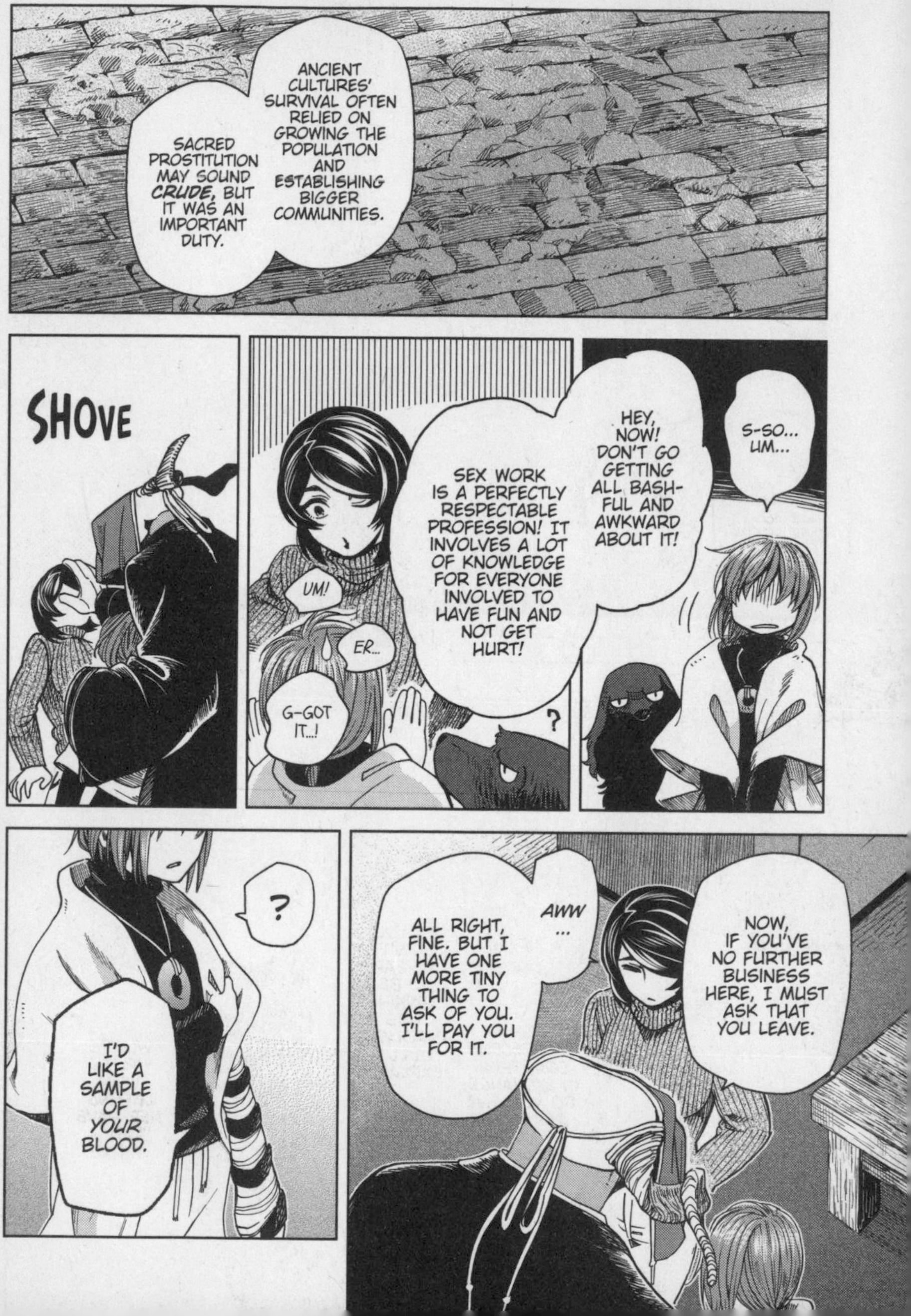
ANCIENT CULTURES' SURVIVAL OFTEN RELIED ON GROWING THE POPULATION AND ESTABLISHING BIGGER COMMUNITIES.
SACRED PROSTITUTION MAY SOUND CRUDE, BUT IT WAS AN IMPORTANT DUTY.
S-SO... UM...
HEY, NOW! DON'T GO GETTING ALL BASHFUL AND AWKWARD ABOUT IT!
SEX WORK IS A PERFECTLY RESPECTABLE PROFESSION! IT INVOLVES A LOT OF KNOWLEDGE FOR EVERYONE INVOLVED TO HAVE FUN AND NOT GET HURT!
UM!
ER...
G-GOT IT...!
?
SHOVE
NOW, IF YOU'VE NO FURTHER BUSINESS HERE, I MUST ASK THAT YOU LEAVE.
AWW ...
ALL RIGHT, FINE. BUT I HAVE ONE MORE TINY THING TO ASK OF YOU. I'LL PAY YOU FOR IT.
?
I'D LIKE A SAMPLE OF YOUR BLOOD.

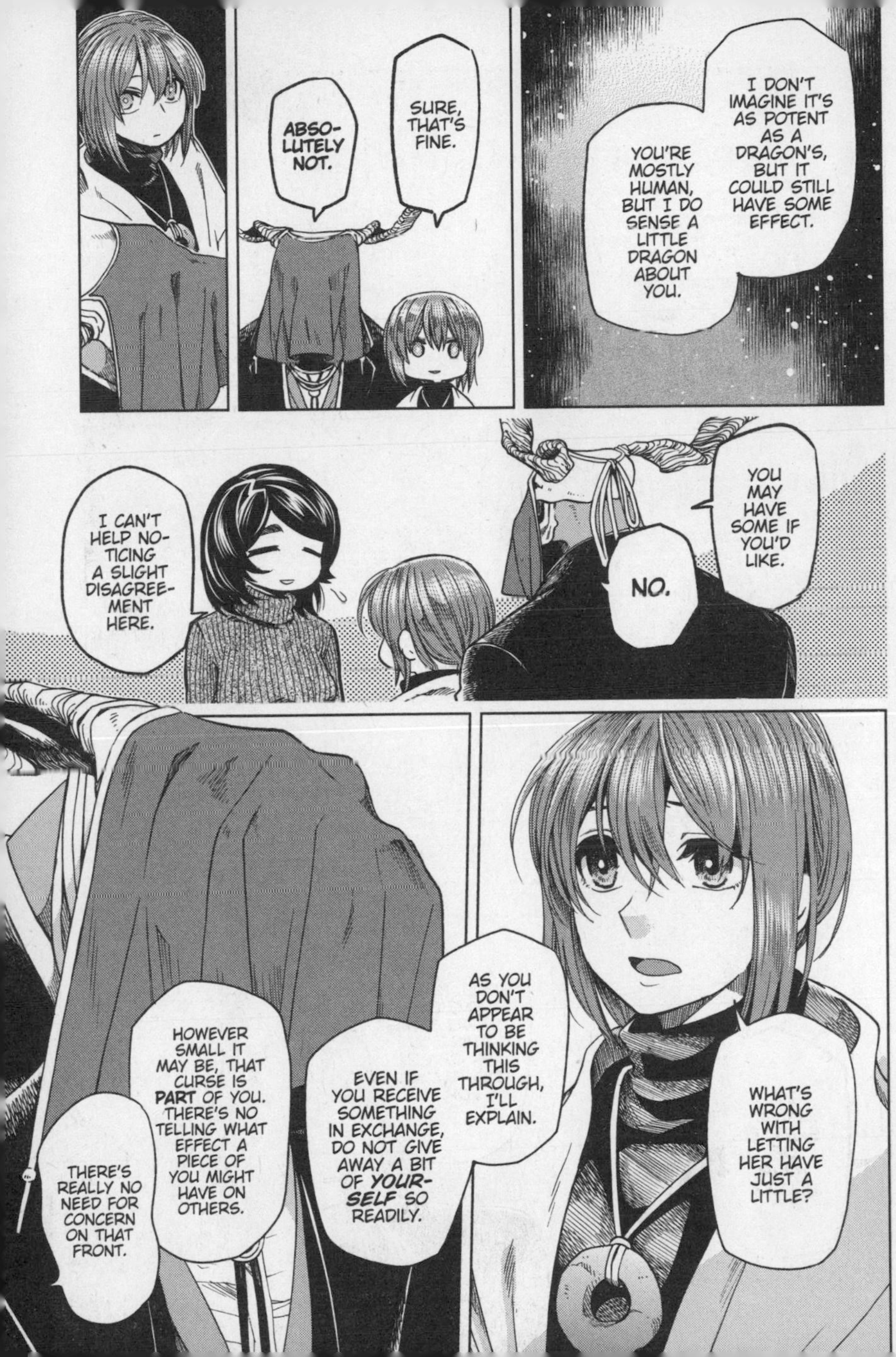
I DON'T IMAGINE IT'S AS POTENT AS A DRAGON'S, BUT IT COULD STILL HAVE SOME EFFECT.
YOU'RE MOSTLY HUMAN, BUT I DO SENSE A LITTLE DRAGON ABOUT YOU.
SURE, THAT'S FINE.
ABSO-LUTELY NOT.
YOU MAY HAVE SOME IF YOU'D LIKE.
NO.
I CAN'T HELP NO-TICING A SLIGHT DISAGREE-MENT HERE.
WHAT'S WRONG WITH LETTING HER HAVE JUST A LITTLE?
AS YOU DON'T APPEAR TO BE THINKING THIS THROUGH, I'LL EXPLAIN.
EVEN IF YOU RECEIVE SOMETHING IN EXCHANGE, DO NOT GIVE AWAY A BIT OF ***YOUR-SELF*** SO READILY.
HOWEVER SMALL IT MAY BE, THAT CURSE IS **PART** OF YOU. THERE'S NO TELLING WHAT EFFECT A PIECE OF YOU MIGHT HAVE ON OTHERS.
THERE'S REALLY NO NEED FOR CONCERN ON THAT FRONT.

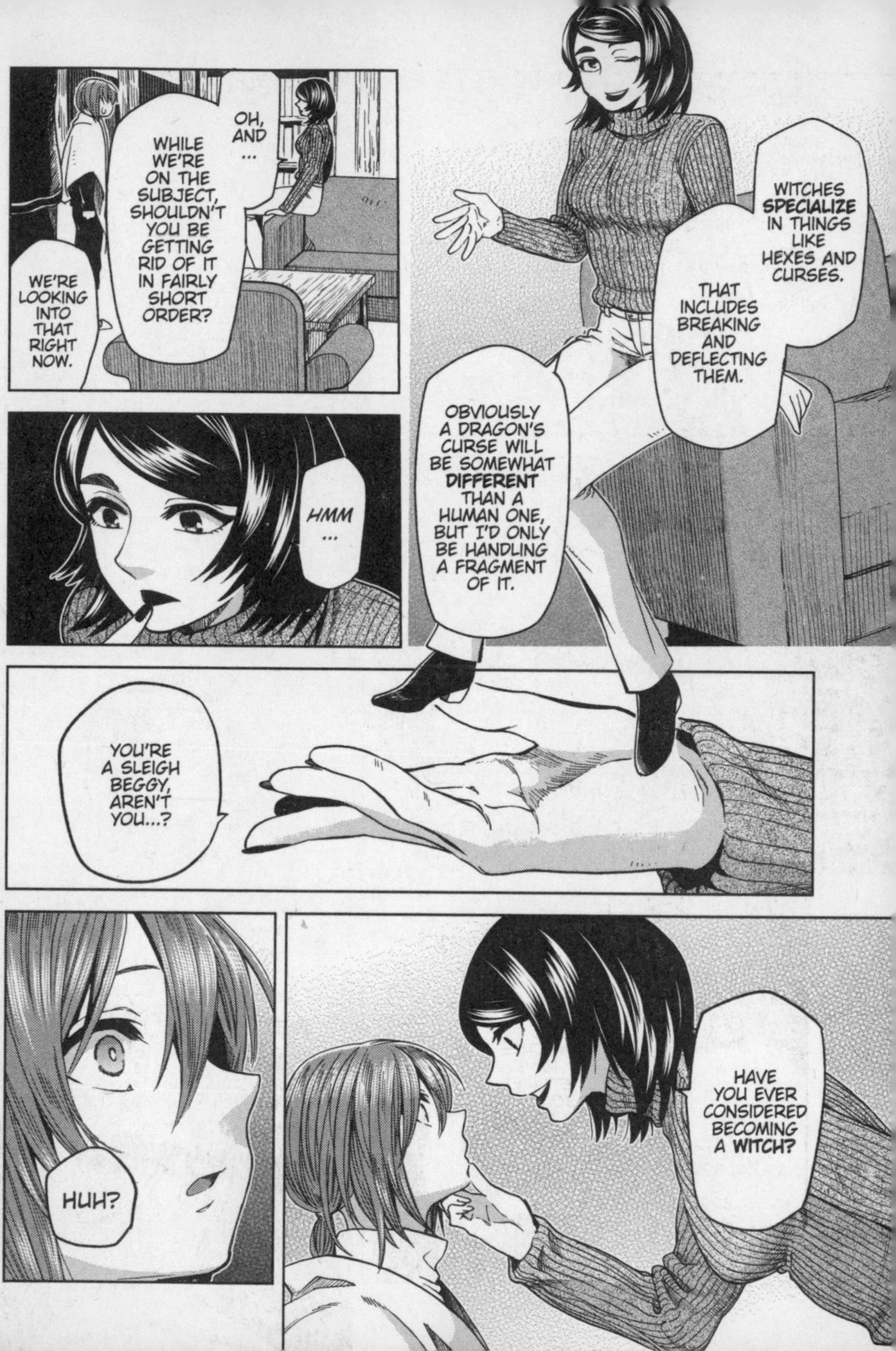
WITCHES SPECIALIZE IN THINGS LIKE HEXES AND CURSES.
THAT INCLUDES BREAKING AND DEFLECTING THEM.
OBVIOUSLY A DRAGON'S CURSE WILL BE SOMEWHAT DIFFERENT THAN A HUMAN ONE, BUT I'D ONLY BE HANDLING A FRAGMENT OF IT.
OH, AND ...
WHILE WE'RE ON THE SUBJECT, SHOULDN'T YOU BE GETTING RID OF IT IN FAIRLY SHORT ORDER?
WE'RE LOOKING INTO THAT RIGHT NOW.
HMM ...
YOU'RE A SLEIGH BEGGY, AREN'T YOU...?
HAVE YOU EVER CONSIDERED BECOMING A WITCH?
HUH?

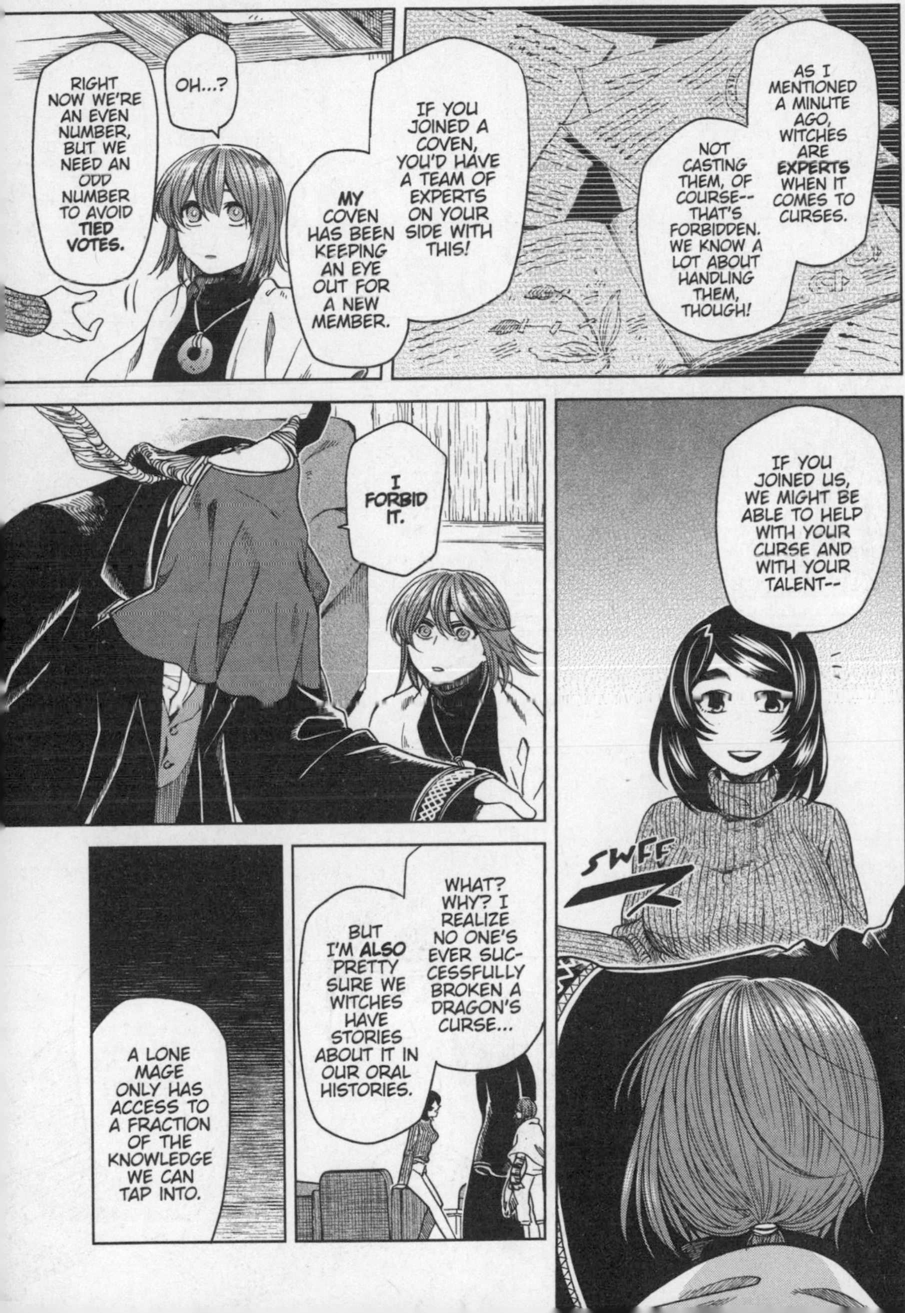
AS I MENTIONED A MINUTE AGO, WITCHES ARE **EXPERTS** WHEN IT COMES TO CURSES.
NOT CASTING THEM, OF COURSE--THAT'S FORBIDDEN. WE KNOW A LOT ABOUT HANDLING THEM, THOUGH!
IF YOU JOINED A COVEN, YOU'D HAVE A TEAM OF EXPERTS ON YOUR SIDE WITH THIS!
MY COVEN HAS BEEN KEEPING AN EYE OUT FOR A NEW MEMBER.
OH...?
RIGHT NOW WE'RE AN EVEN NUMBER, BUT WE NEED AN ODD NUMBER TO AVOID **TIED VOTES.**
IF YOU JOINED US, WE MIGHT BE ABLE TO HELP WITH YOUR CURSE AND WITH YOUR TALENT--
SWFF
I **FORBID** IT.
WHAT? WHY? I REALIZE NO ONE'S EVER SUCCESSFULLY BROKEN A DRAGON'S CURSE...
BUT I'M **ALSO** PRETTY SURE WE WITCHES HAVE STORIES ABOUT IT IN OUR ORAL HISTORIES.
A LONE MAGE ONLY HAS ACCESS TO A FRACTION OF THE KNOWLEDGE WE CAN TAP INTO.

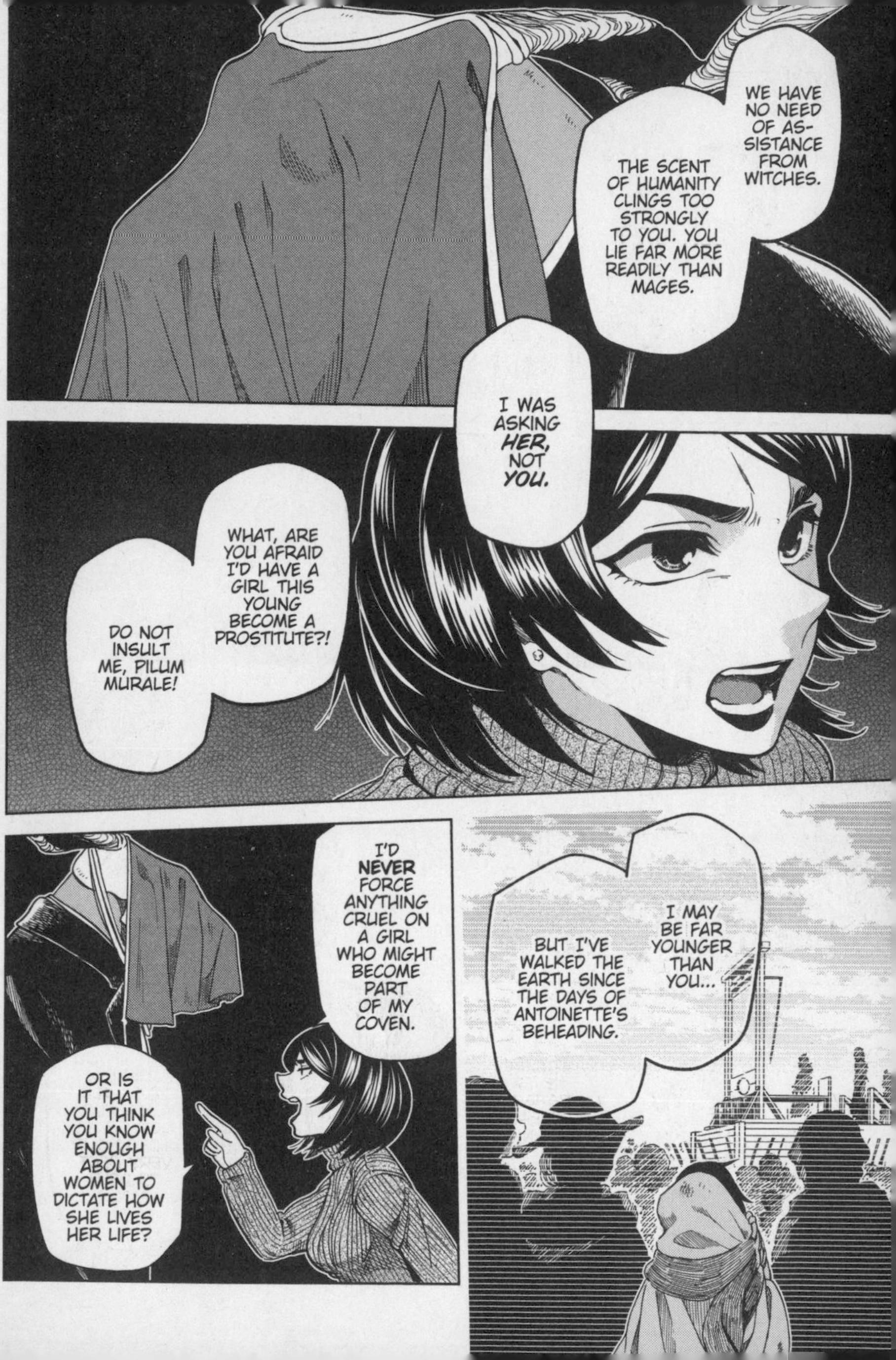
WE HAVE NO NEED OF ASSISTANCE FROM WITCHES.
THE SCENT OF HUMANITY CLINGS TOO STRONGLY TO YOU. YOU LIE FAR MORE READILY THAN MAGES.
I WAS ASKING *HER*, NOT *YOU*.
WHAT, ARE YOU AFRAID I'D HAVE A GIRL THIS YOUNG BECOME A PROSTITUTE?!
DO NOT INSULT ME, PILUM MURALE!
I MAY BE FAR YOUNGER THAN YOU...
BUT I'VE WALKED THE EARTH SINCE THE DAYS OF ANTOINETTE'S BEHEADING.
I'D **NEVER** FORCE ANYTHING CRUEL ON A GIRL WHO MIGHT BECOME PART OF MY COVEN.
OR IS IT THAT YOU THINK YOU KNOW ENOUGH ABOUT WOMEN TO DICTATE HOW SHE LIVES HER LIFE?

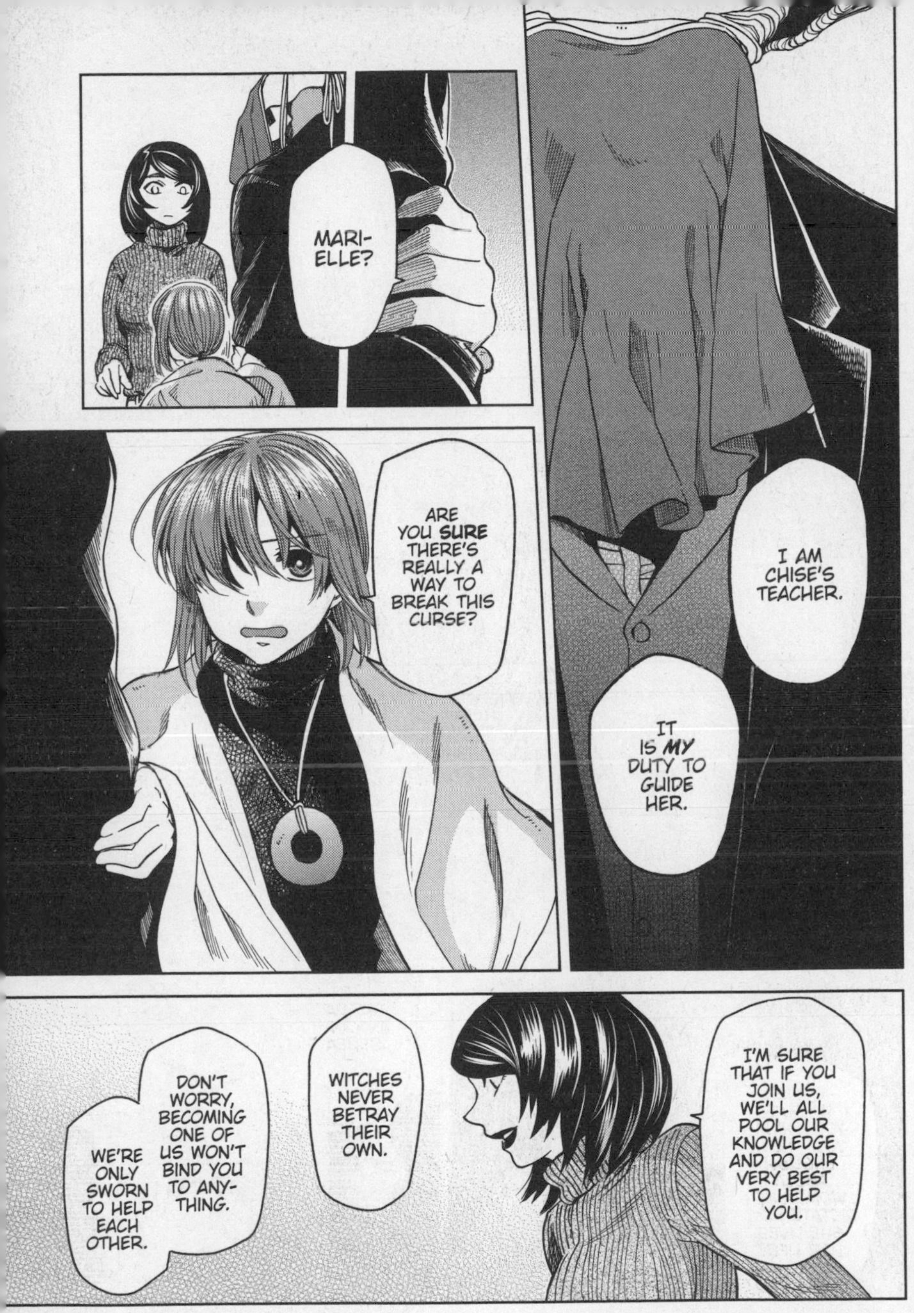
...
I AM CHISE'S TEACHER.
IT IS MY DUTY TO GUIDE HER.
MARI-ELLE?
ARE YOU SURE THERE'S REALLY A WAY TO BREAK THIS CURSE?
I'M SURE THAT IF YOU JOIN US, WE'LL ALL POOL OUR KNOWLEDGE AND DO OUR VERY BEST TO HELP YOU.
WITCHES NEVER BETRAY THEIR OWN.
DON'T WORRY, BECOMING ONE OF US WON'T BIND YOU TO ANY-THING.
WE'RE ONLY SWORN TO HELP EACH OTHER.

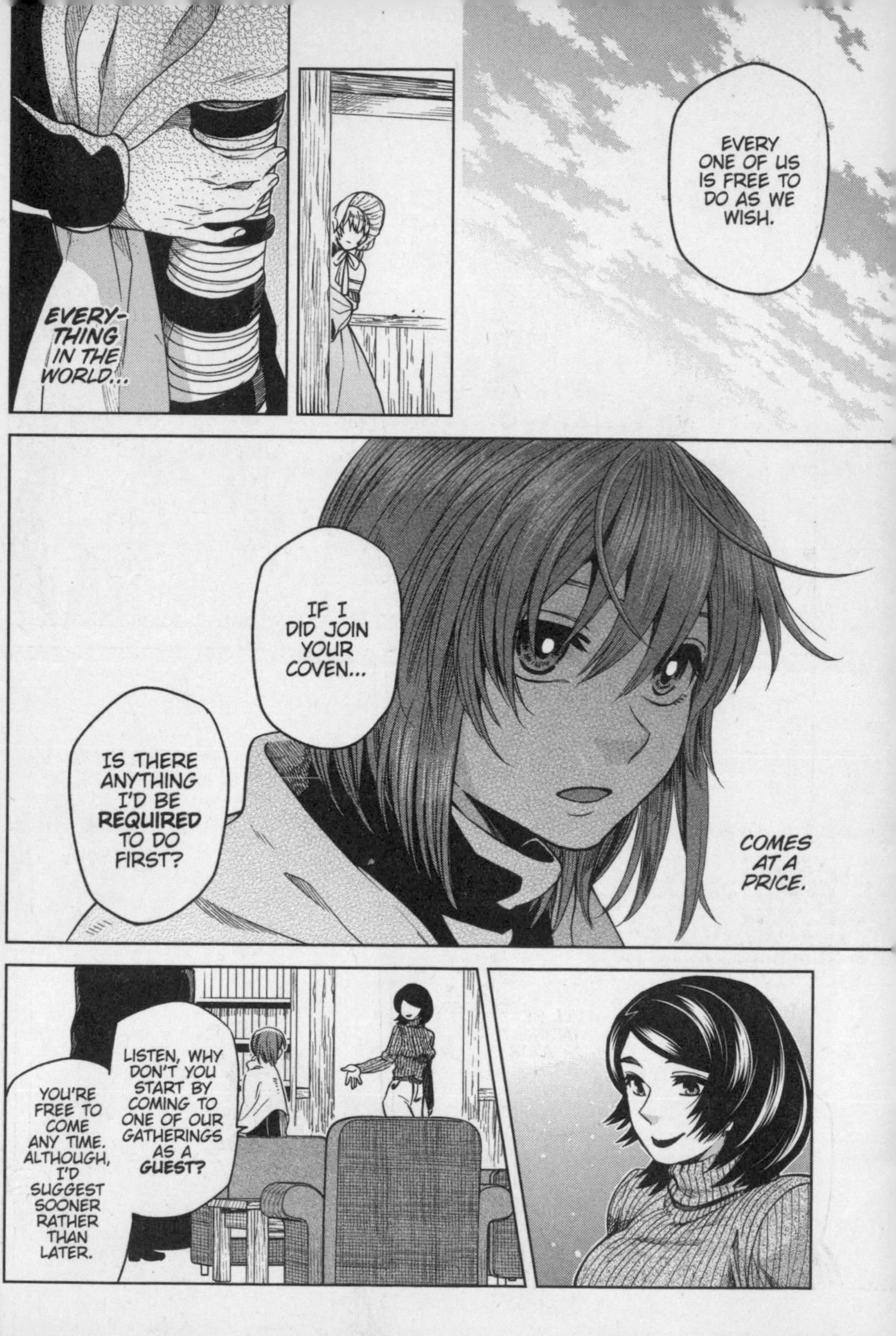
EVERY ONE OF US IS FREE TO DO AS WE WISH.
EVERY-THING IN THE WORLD...
IF I DID JOIN YOUR COVEN...
IS THERE ANYTHING I'D BE **REQUIRED** TO DO FIRST?
COMES AT A PRICE.
LISTEN, WHY DON'T YOU START BY COMING TO ONE OF OUR GATHERINGS AS A **GUEST**?
YOU'RE FREE TO COME ANY TIME. ALTHOUGH, I'D SUGGEST SOONER RATHER THAN LATER.

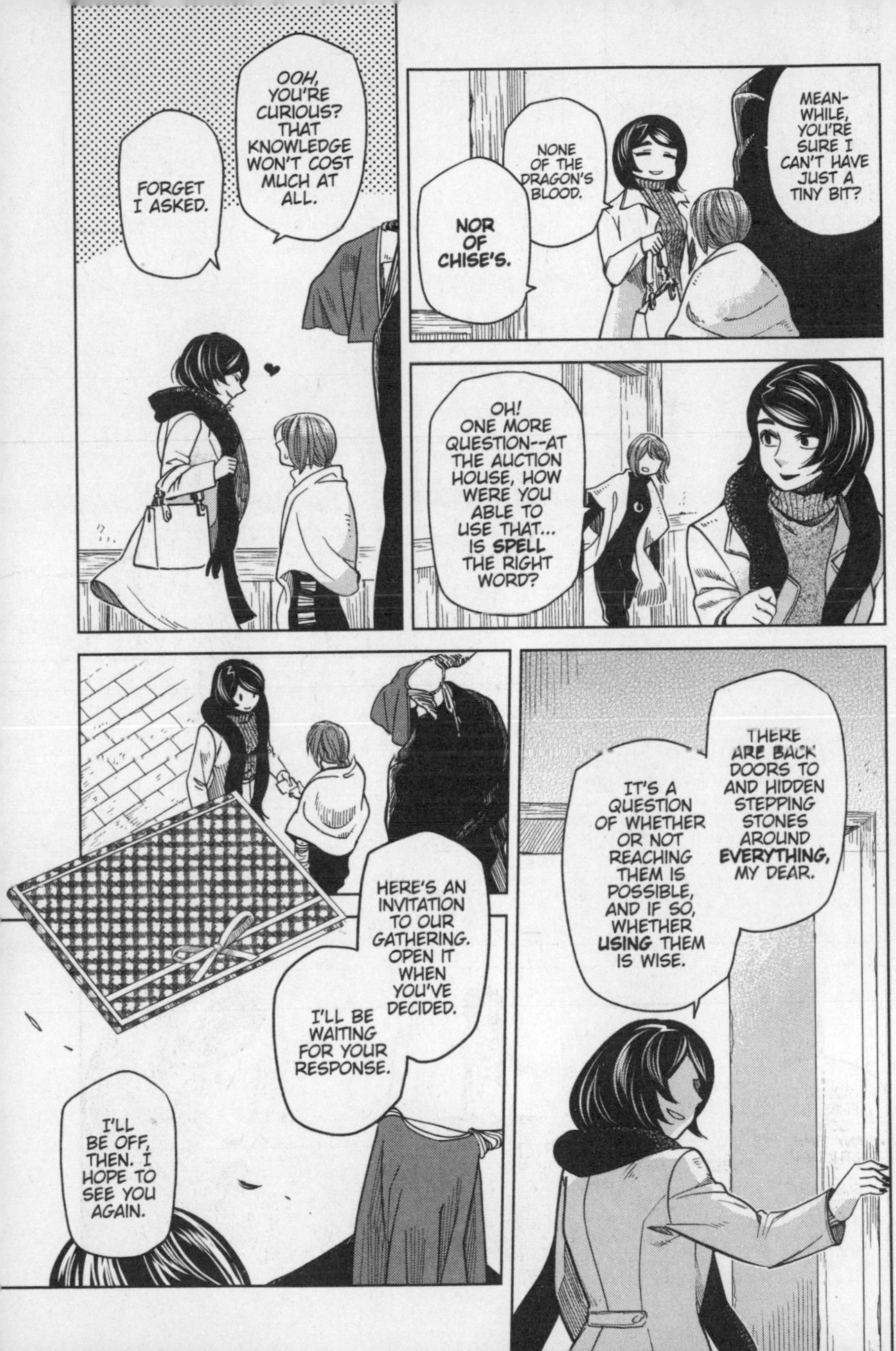
MEAN-WHILE, YOU'RE SURE I CAN'T HAVE JUST A TINY BIT?
NONE OF THE DRAGON'S BLOOD.
NOR OF CHISE'S.
OH! ONE MORE QUESTION--AT THE AUCTION HOUSE, HOW WERE YOU ABLE TO USE THAT... IS SPELL THE RIGHT WORD?
OOH, YOU'RE CURIOUS? THAT KNOWLEDGE WON'T COST MUCH AT ALL.
FORGET I ASKED.
THERE ARE BACK DOORS TO AND HIDDEN STEPPING STONES AROUND EVERYTHING, MY DEAR.
IT'S A QUESTION OF WHETHER OR NOT REACHING THEM IS POSSIBLE, AND IF SO, WHETHER USING THEM IS WISE.
HERE'S AN INVITATION TO OUR GATHERING. OPEN IT WHEN YOU'VE DECIDED.
I'LL BE WAITING FOR YOUR RESPONSE.
I'LL BE OFF, THEN. I HOPE TO SEE YOU AGAIN.

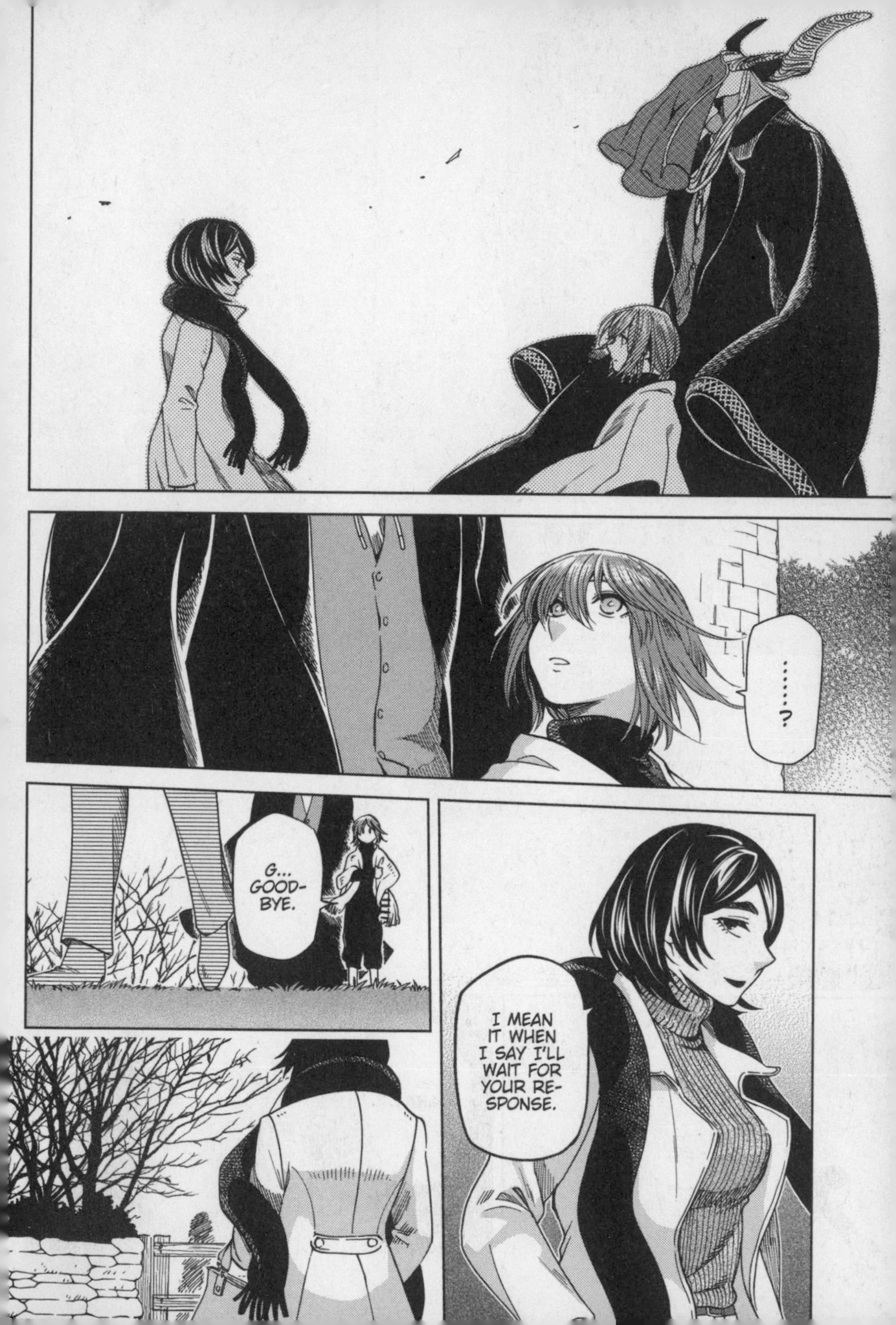
......?
I MEAN IT WHEN I SAY I'LL WAIT FOR YOUR RESPONSE.
G... GOODBYE.

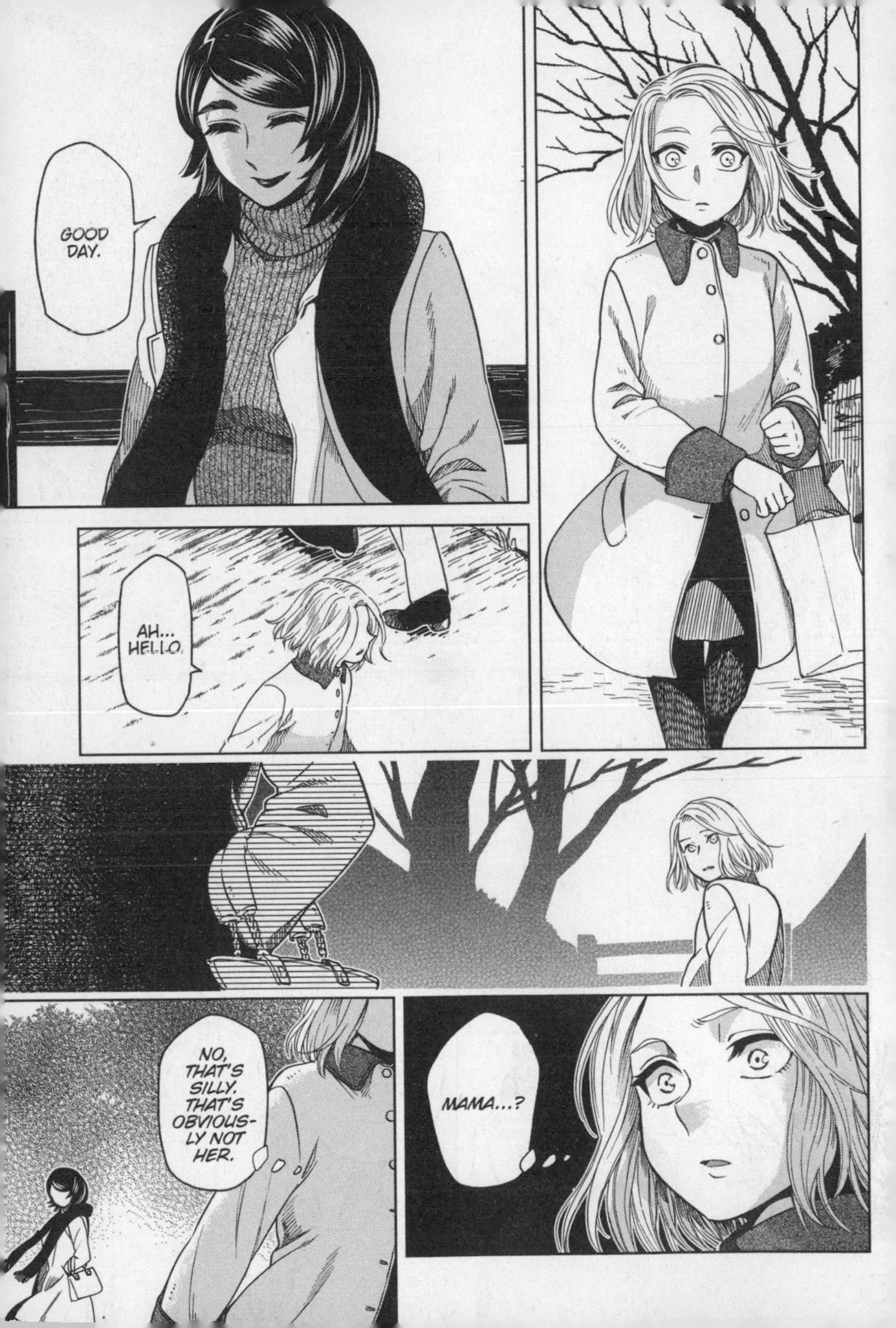
GOOD DAY.
AH... HELLO.
MAMA...?
NO, THAT'S SILLY. THAT'S OBVIOUSLY NOT HER.

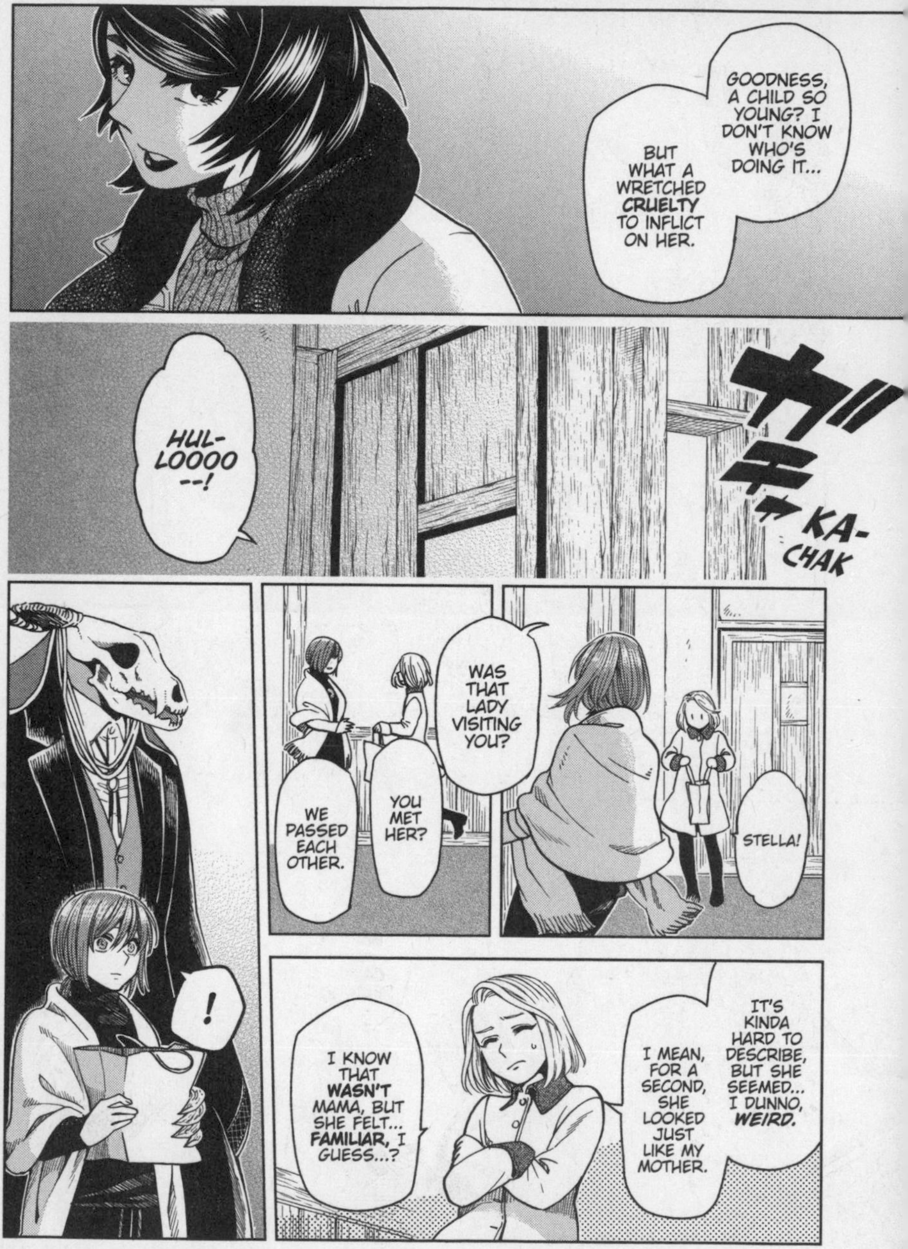
GOODNESS, A CHILD SO YOUNG? I DON'T KNOW WHO'S DOING IT...
BUT WHAT A WRETCHED CRUELTY TO INFLICT ON HER.
KA-CHAK
HUL-LOOOO--!
STELLA!
WAS THAT LADY VISITING YOU?
YOU MET HER?
WE PASSED EACH OTHER.
IT'S KINDA HARD TO DESCRIBE, BUT SHE SEEMED... I DUNNO, WEIRD.
I MEAN, FOR A SECOND, SHE LOOKED JUST LIKE MY MOTHER.
I KNOW THAT WASN'T MAMA, BUT SHE FELT... FAMILIAR, I GUESS...?
!

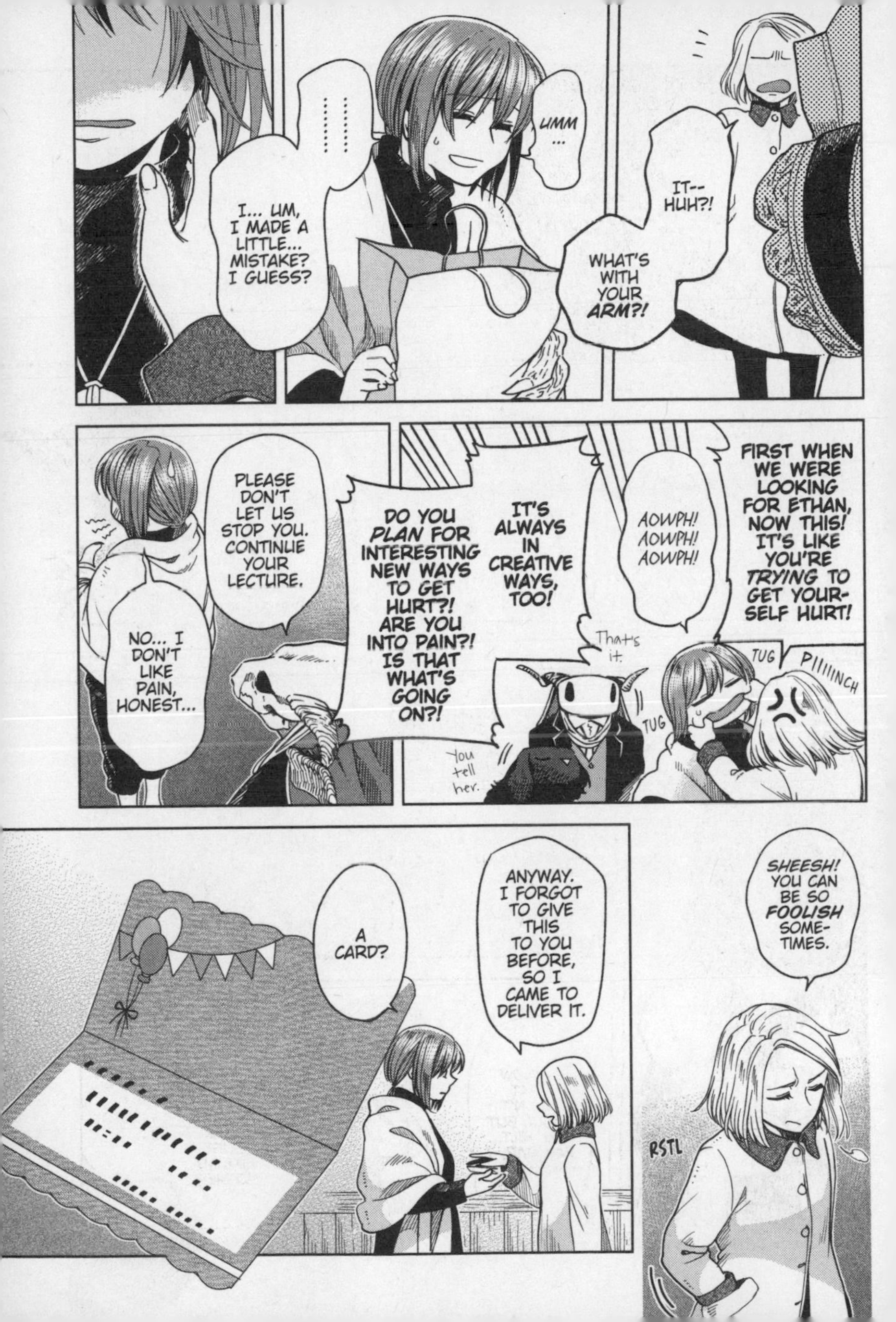
IT-- HUH?!
WHAT'S WITH YOUR *ARM?!*
UMM ...
......
I... UM, I MADE A LITTLE... MISTAKE? I GUESS?
FIRST WHEN WE WERE LOOKING FOR ETHAN, NOW THIS! IT'S LIKE YOU'RE *TRYING* TO GET YOUR-SELF HURT!
PIIIIINCH
TUG
AOWPH! AOWPH! AOWPH!
TUG
IT'S ALWAYS IN CREATIVE WAYS, TOO!
That's it.
DO YOU *PLAN* FOR INTERESTING NEW WAYS TO GET HURT?! ARE YOU INTO PAIN?! IS THAT WHAT'S GOING ON?!
You tell her.
PLEASE DON'T LET US STOP YOU. CONTINUE YOUR LECTURE.
NO... I DON'T LIKE PAIN, HONEST...
SHEESH! YOU CAN BE SO *FOOLISH* SOME-TIMES.
RSTL
ANYWAY. I FORGOT TO GIVE THIS TO YOU BEFORE, SO I CAME TO DELIVER IT.
A CARD?

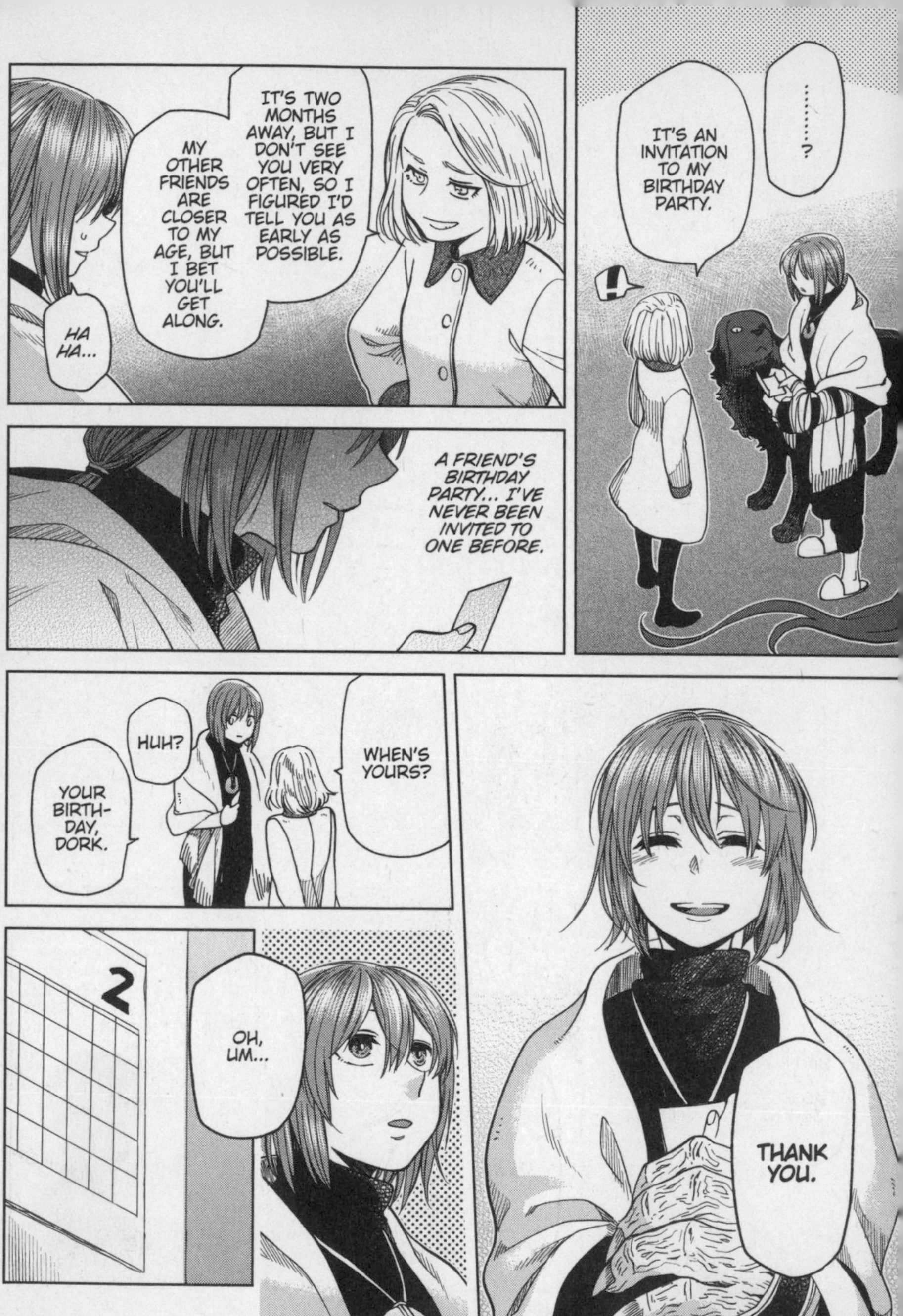
......?
IT'S AN INVITATION TO MY BIRTHDAY PARTY.
!
IT'S TWO MONTHS AWAY, BUT I DON'T SEE YOU VERY OFTEN, SO I FIGURED I'D TELL YOU AS EARLY AS POSSIBLE.
MY OTHER FRIENDS ARE CLOSER TO MY AGE, BUT I BET YOU'LL GET ALONG.
HA HA...
A FRIEND'S BIRTHDAY PARTY... I'VE NEVER BEEN INVITED TO ONE BEFORE.
THANK YOU.
WHEN'S YOURS?
HUH?
YOUR BIRTH-DAY, DORK.
2
OH, UM...

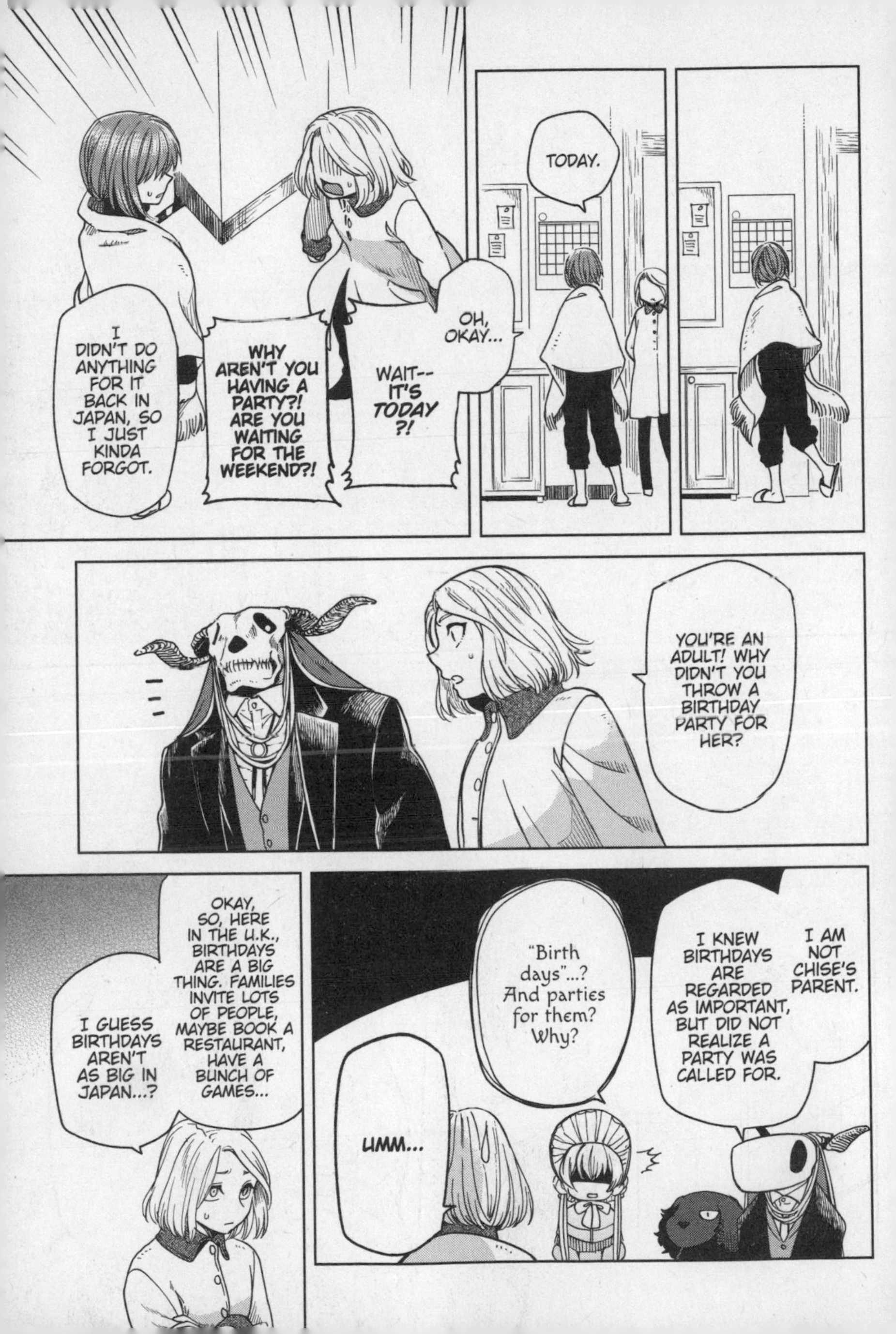
TODAY.
OH, OKAY...
WAIT-- IT'S TODAY?!
WHY AREN'T YOU HAVING A PARTY?! ARE YOU WAITING FOR THE WEEKEND?!
I DIDN'T DO ANYTHING FOR IT BACK IN JAPAN, SO I JUST KINDA FORGOT.
YOU'RE AN ADULT! WHY DIDN'T YOU THROW A BIRTHDAY PARTY FOR HER?
I AM NOT CHISE'S PARENT.
I KNEW BIRTHDAYS ARE REGARDED AS IMPORTANT, BUT DID NOT REALIZE A PARTY WAS CALLED FOR.
"Birth days"...? And parties for them? Why?
UMM...
OKAY, SO, HERE IN THE U.K., BIRTHDAYS ARE A BIG THING. FAMILIES INVITE LOTS OF PEOPLE, MAYBE BOOK A RESTAURANT, HAVE A BUNCH OF GAMES...
I GUESS BIRTHDAYS AREN'T AS BIG IN JAPAN...?

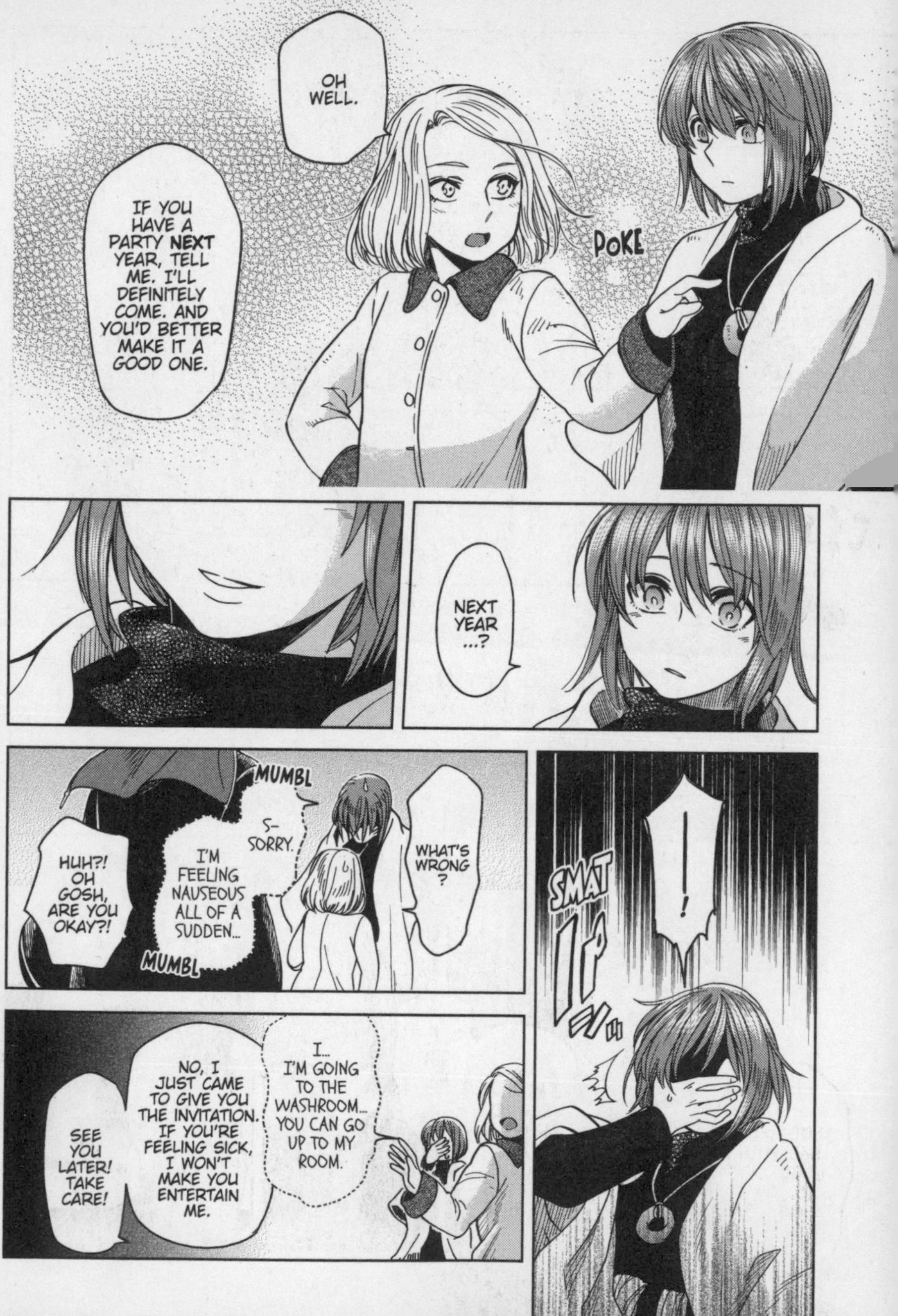

OH WELL.
POKE
IF YOU HAVE A PARTY NEXT YEAR, TELL ME. I'LL DEFINITELY COME. AND YOU'D BETTER MAKE IT A GOOD ONE.
NEXT YEAR ...?
!
SMAT
WHAT'S WRONG ?
S-SORRY.
MUMBL
I'M FEELING NAUSEOUS ALL OF A SUDDEN...
MUMBL
HUH?! OH GOSH, ARE YOU OKAY?!
I... I'M GOING TO THE WASHROOM... YOU CAN GO UP TO MY ROOM.
NO, I JUST CAME TO GIVE YOU THE INVITATION. IF YOU'RE FEELING SICK, I WON'T MAKE YOU ENTERTAIN ME.
SEE YOU LATER! TAKE CARE!

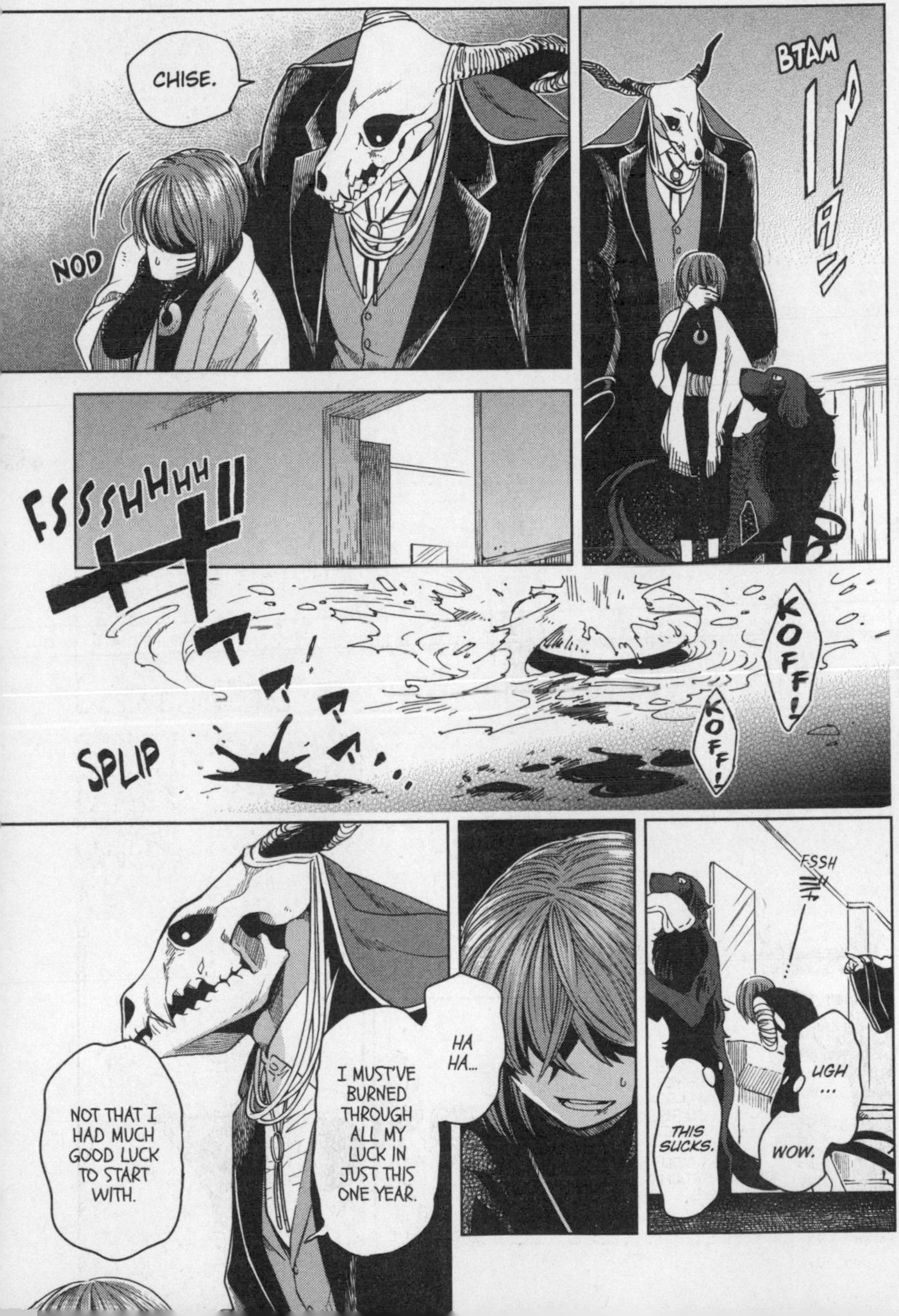
BTAM
CHISE.
NOD
FSSHHHH
KOFF!
KOFF!
SPLIP
FSSH
UGH...
THIS SUCKS.
WOW.
HA HA...
I MUST'VE BURNED THROUGH ALL MY LUCK IN JUST THIS ONE YEAR.
NOT THAT I HAD MUCH GOOD LUCK TO START WITH.

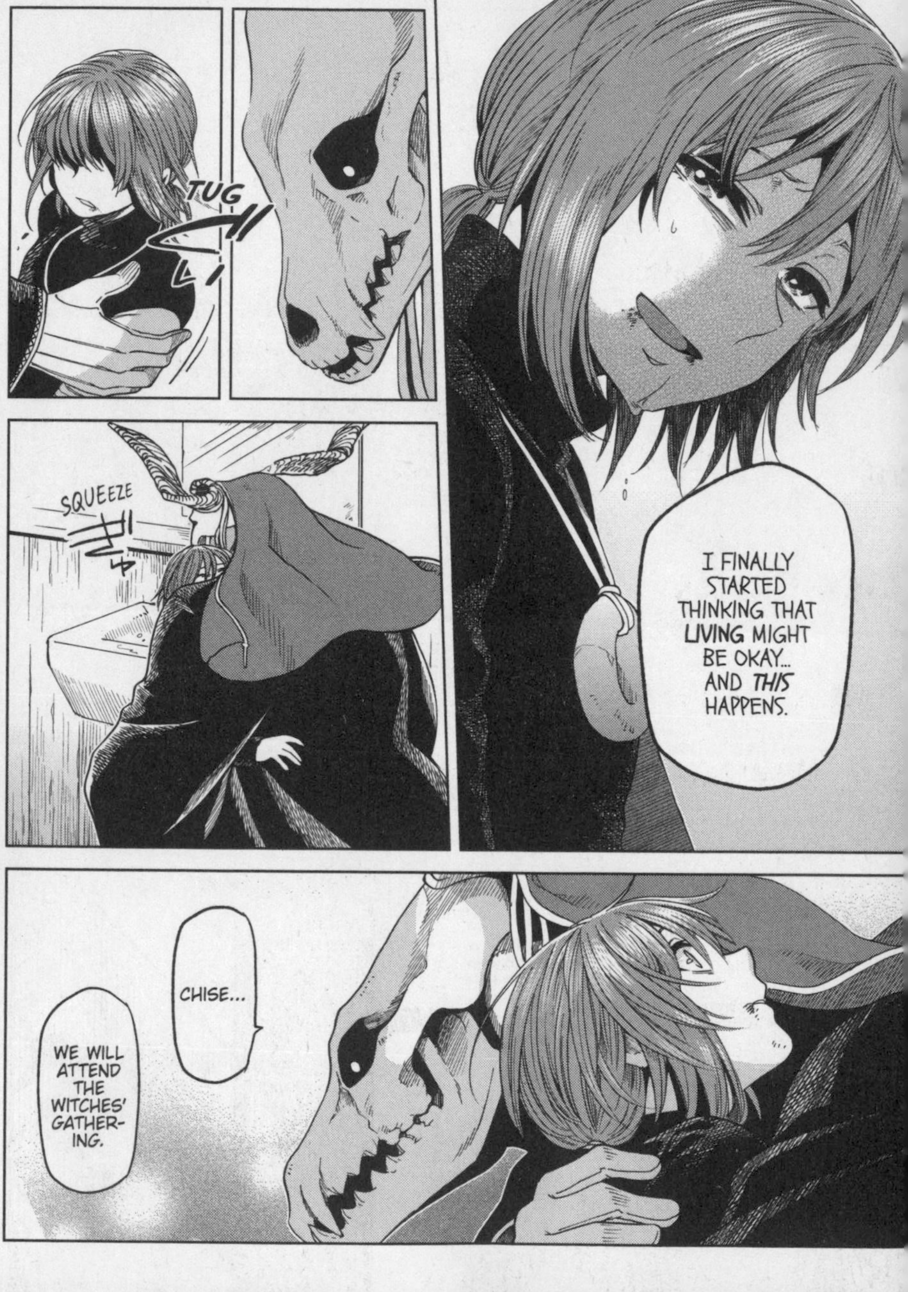
I FINALLY STARTED THINKING THAT LIVING MIGHT BE OKAY... AND THIS HAPPENS.
TUG
SQUEEZE
CHISE...
WE WILL ATTEND THE WITCHES' GATHERING.

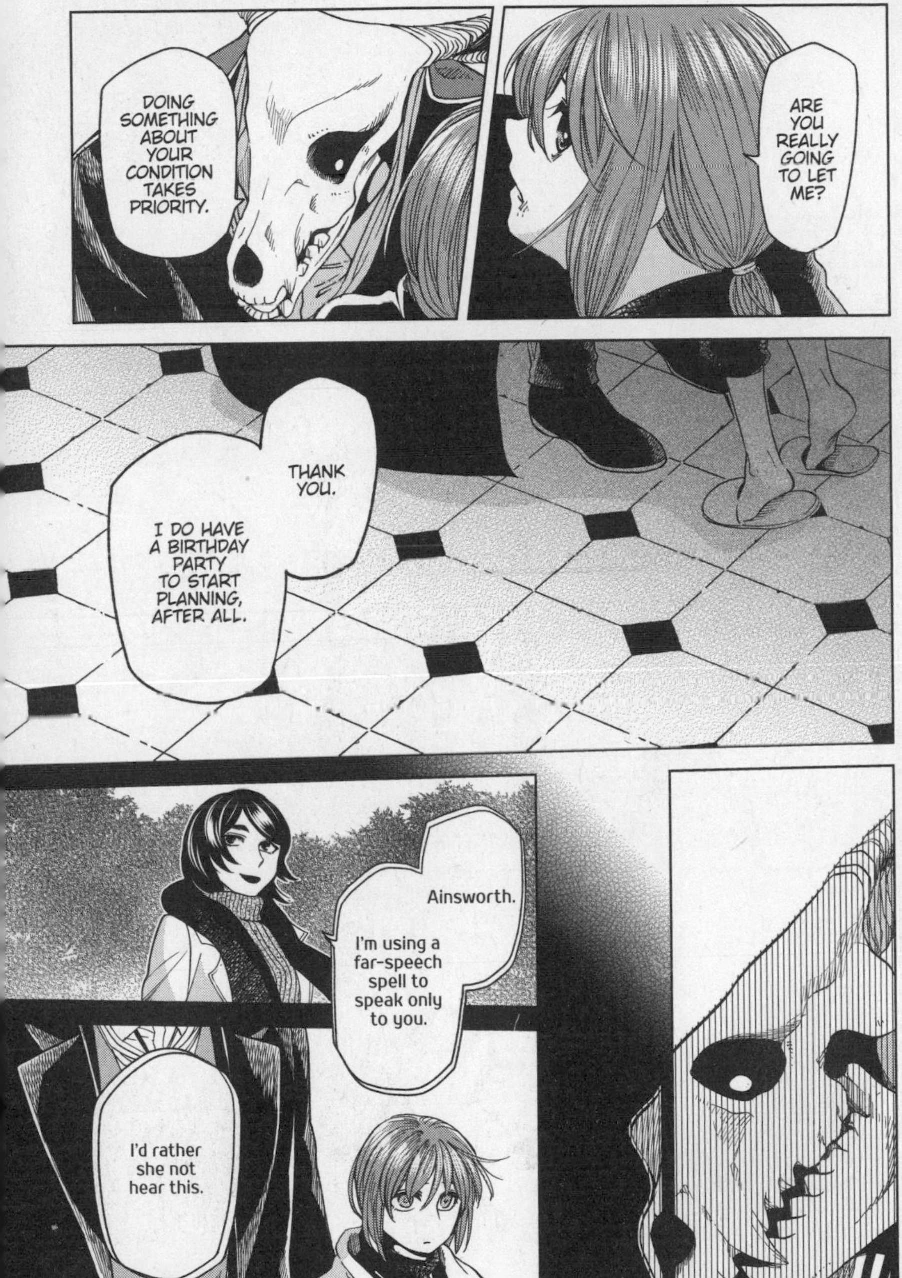
ARE YOU REALLY GOING TO LET ME?
DOING SOMETHING ABOUT YOUR CONDITION TAKES PRIORITY.
THANK YOU.
I DO HAVE A BIRTHDAY PARTY TO START PLANNING, AFTER ALL.
Ainsworth.
I'm using a far-speech spell to speak only to you.
I'd rather she not hear this.

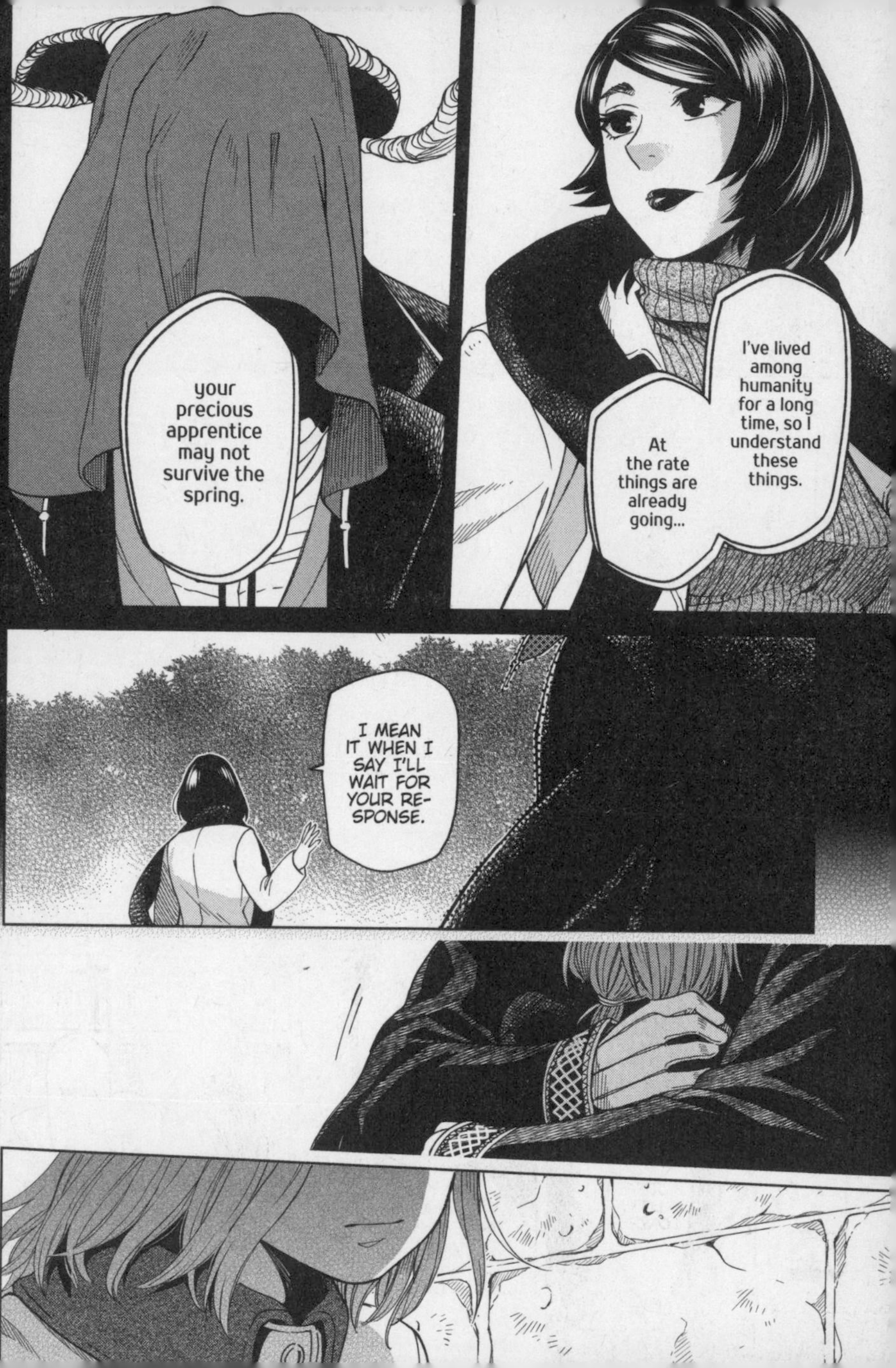
I've lived among humanity for a long time, so I understand these things.
At the rate things are already going...
your precious apprentice may not survive the spring.
I MEAN IT WHEN I SAY I'LL WAIT FOR YOUR RESPONSE.

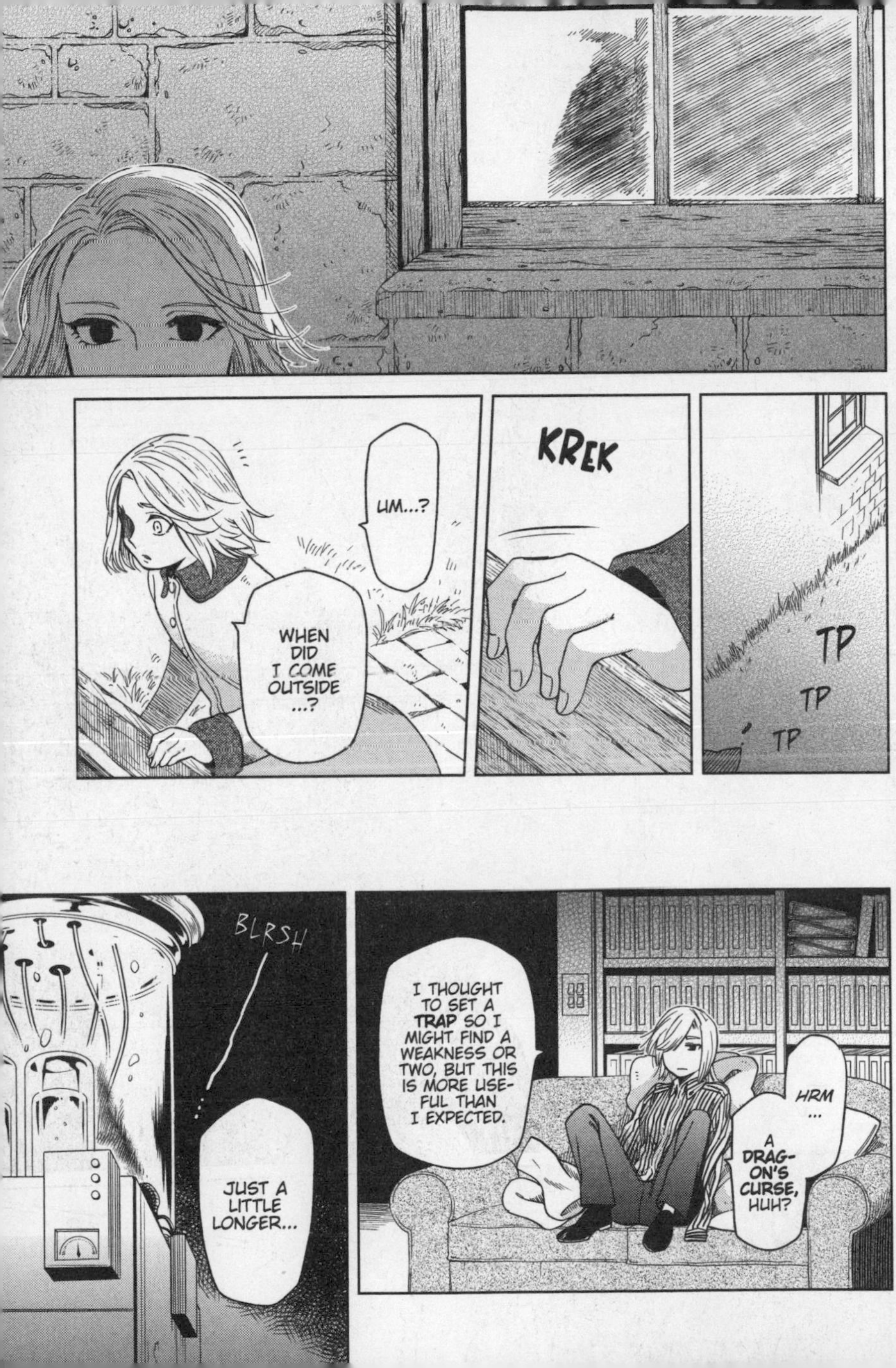
TP
TP
TP
KREK
UM...?
WHEN DID I COME OUTSIDE...?
HRM...
A DRAGON'S CURSE, HUH?
I THOUGHT TO SET A TRAP SO I MIGHT FIND A WEAKNESS OR TWO, BUT THIS IS MORE USEFUL THAN I EXPECTED.
BLRSH
JUST A LITTLE LONGER...

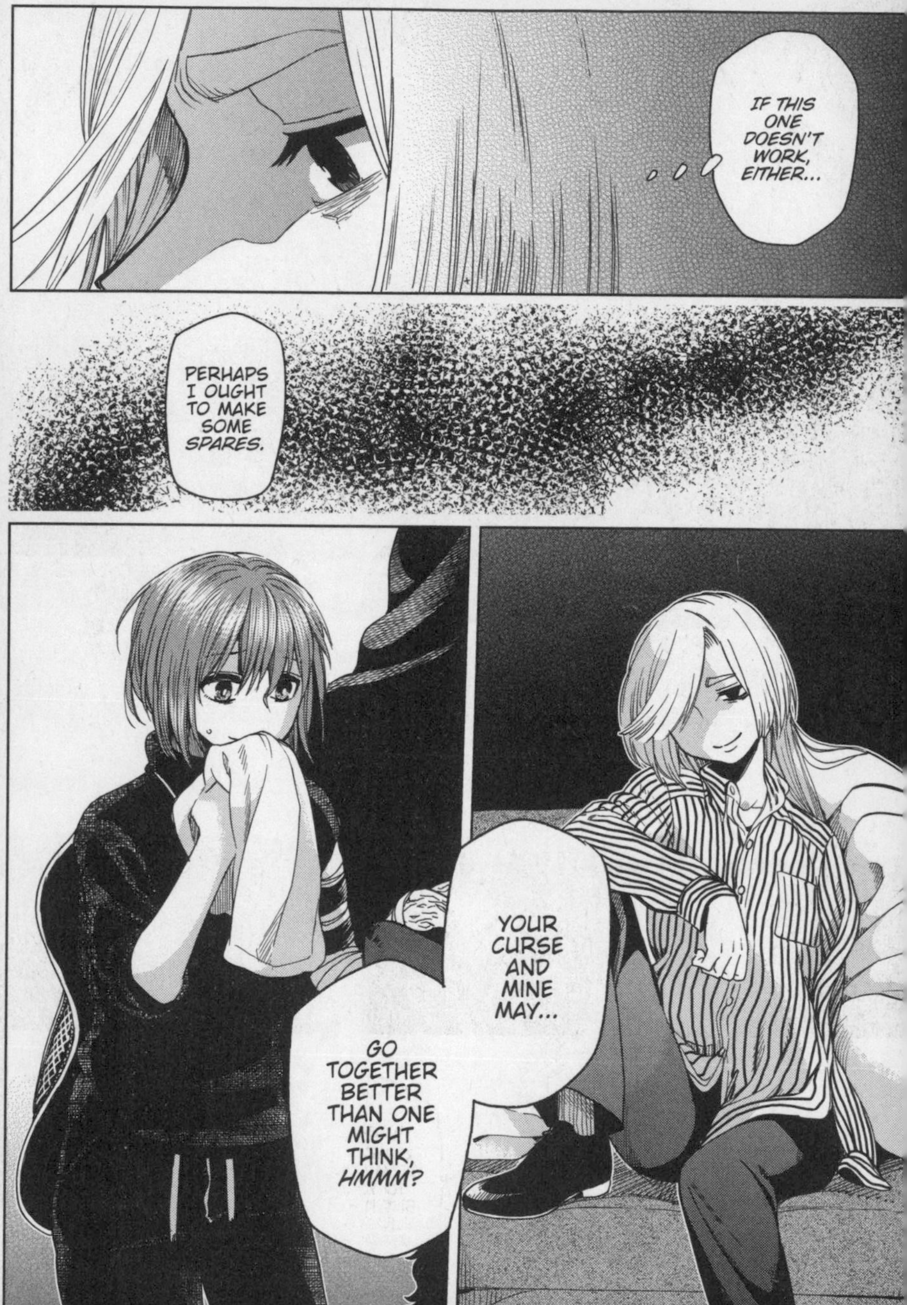
IF THIS ONE DOESN'T WORK, EITHER...
PERHAPS I OUGHT TO MAKE SOME SPARES.
YOUR CURSE AND MINE MAY...
GO TOGETHER BETTER THAN ONE MIGHT THINK, HMMM?

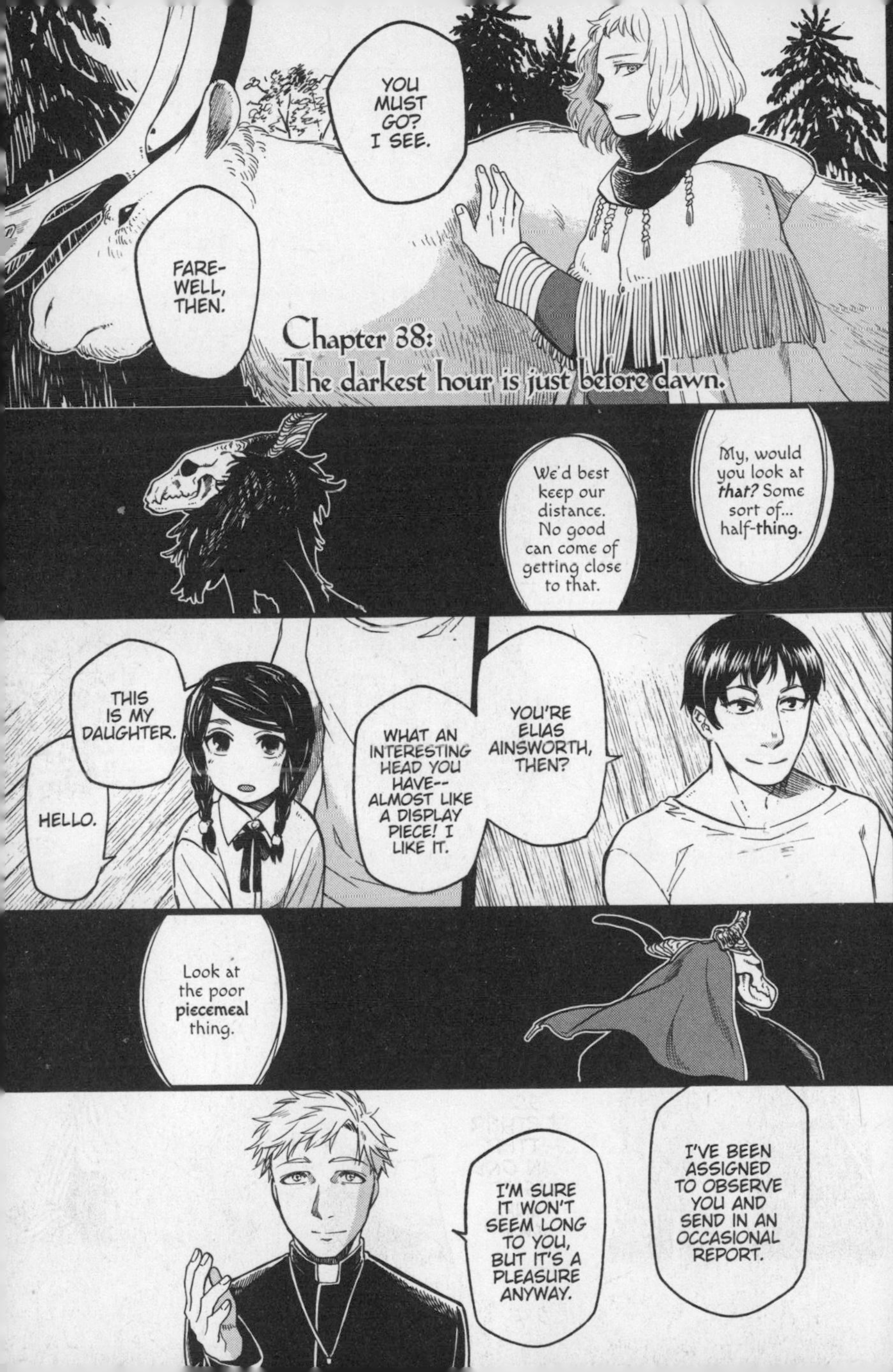
YOU MUST GO? I SEE.
FARE-WELL, THEN.
Chapter 38: The darkest hour is just before dawn.
My, would you look at *that?* Some sort of... half-**thing**.
We'd best keep our distance. No good can come of getting close to that.
YOU'RE ELIAS AINSWORTH, THEN?
WHAT AN INTERESTING HEAD YOU HAVE-- ALMOST LIKE A DISPLAY PIECE! I LIKE IT.
THIS IS MY DAUGHTER.
HELLO.
Look at the poor **piecemeal** thing.
I'VE BEEN ASSIGNED TO OBSERVE YOU AND SEND IN AN OCCASIONAL REPORT.
I'M SURE IT WON'T SEEM LONG TO YOU, BUT IT'S A PLEASURE ANYWAY.

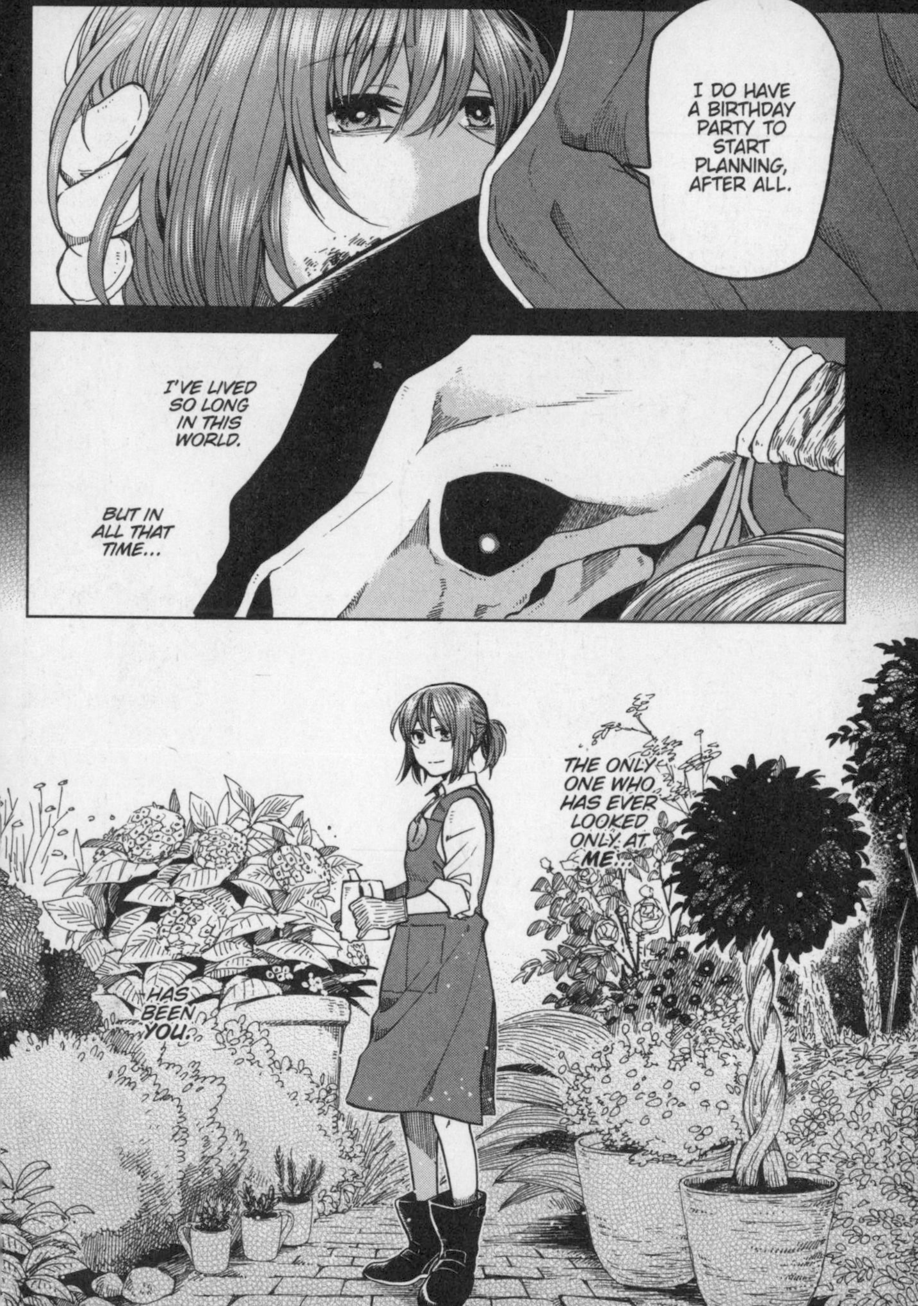
I DO HAVE A BIRTHDAY PARTY TO START PLANNING, AFTER ALL.
I'VE LIVED SO LONG IN THIS WORLD.
BUT IN ALL THAT TIME...
THE ONLY ONE WHO HAS EVER LOOKED ONLY AT ME...
HAS BEEN YOU.

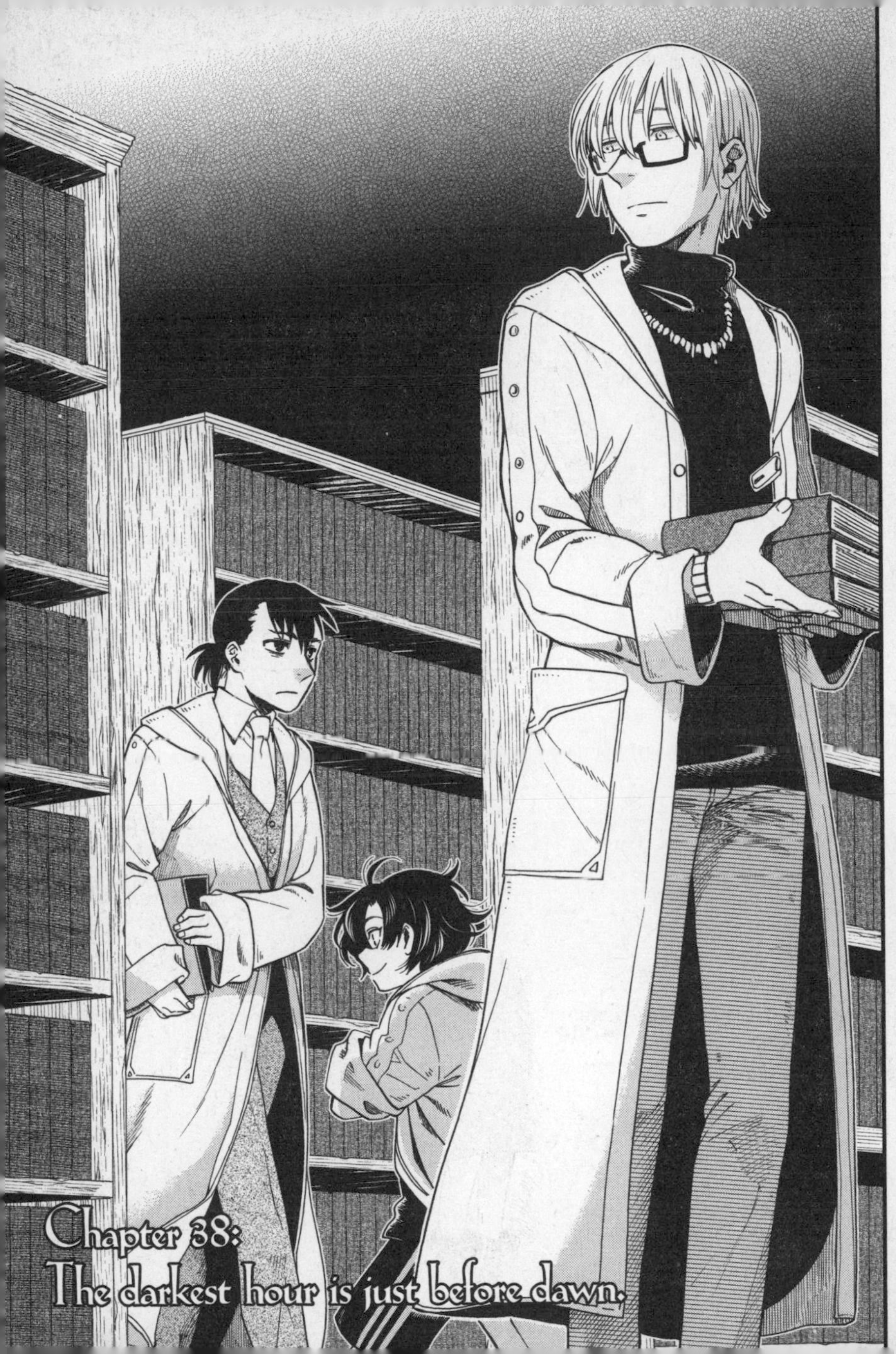
Chapter 38:
The darkest hour is just before dawn.

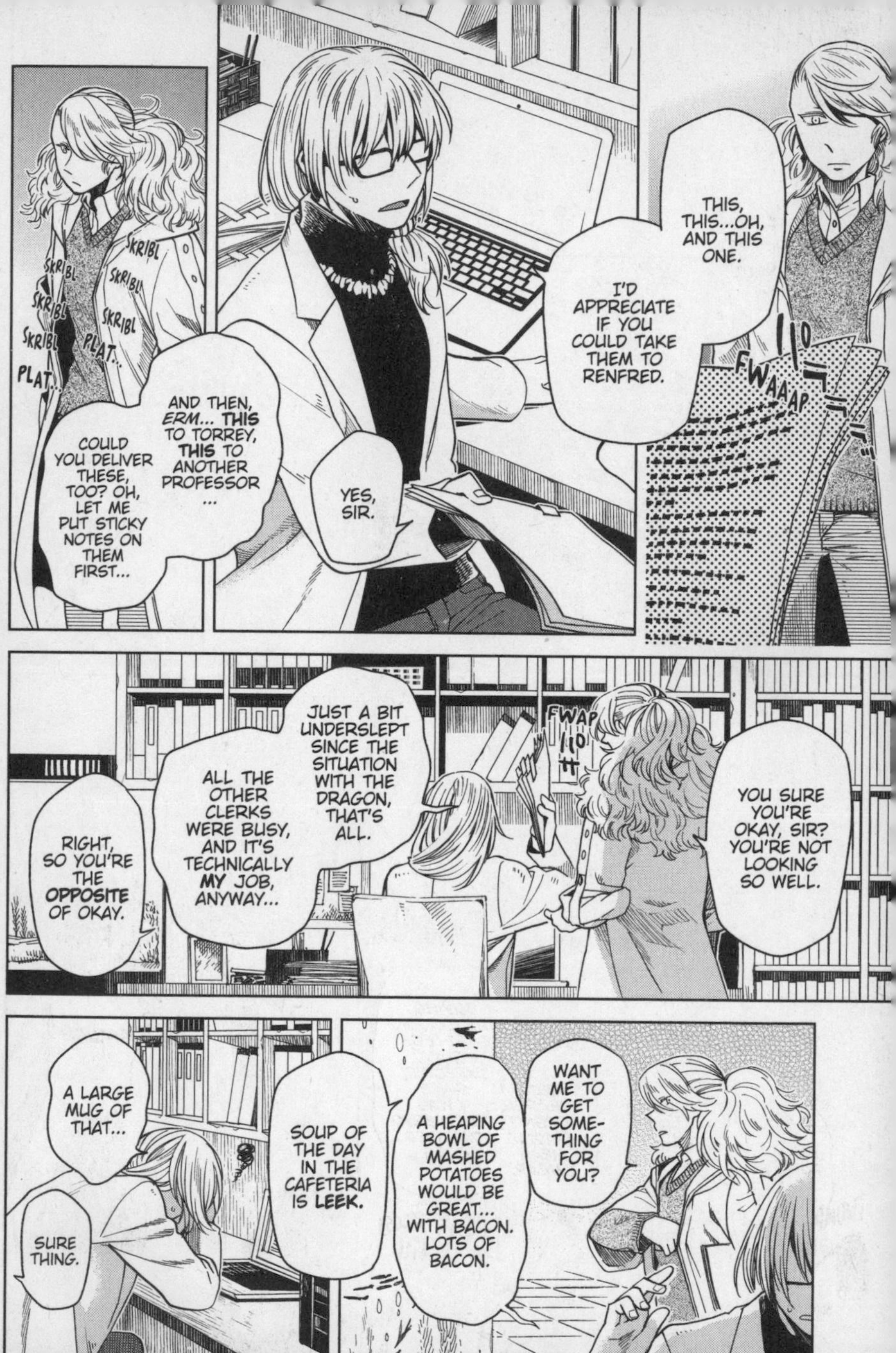
THIS, THIS...OH, AND THIS ONE.
I'D APPRECIATE IF YOU COULD TAKE THEM TO RENFRED.
FWAAAP
YES, SIR.
AND THEN, *ERM*... **THIS** TO TORREY, **THIS** TO ANOTHER PROFESSOR ...
COULD YOU DELIVER THESE, TOO? OH, LET ME PUT STICKY NOTES ON THEM FIRST...
SKRIBL SKRIBL SKRIBL SKRIBL SKRIBL SKRIBL
PLAT... PLAT...
YOU SURE YOU'RE OKAY, SIR? YOU'RE NOT LOOKING SO WELL.
FWAP
JUST A BIT UNDERSLEPT SINCE THE SITUATION WITH THE DRAGON, THAT'S ALL.
ALL THE OTHER CLERKS WERE BUSY, AND IT'S TECHNICALLY **MY** JOB, ANYWAY...
RIGHT, SO YOU'RE THE **OPPOSITE** OF OKAY.
WANT ME TO GET SOME-THING FOR YOU?
A HEAPING BOWL OF MASHED POTATOES WOULD BE GREAT... WITH BACON. LOTS OF BACON.
SOUP OF THE DAY IN THE CAFETERIA IS **LEEK.**
A LARGE MUG OF THAT...
SURE THING.

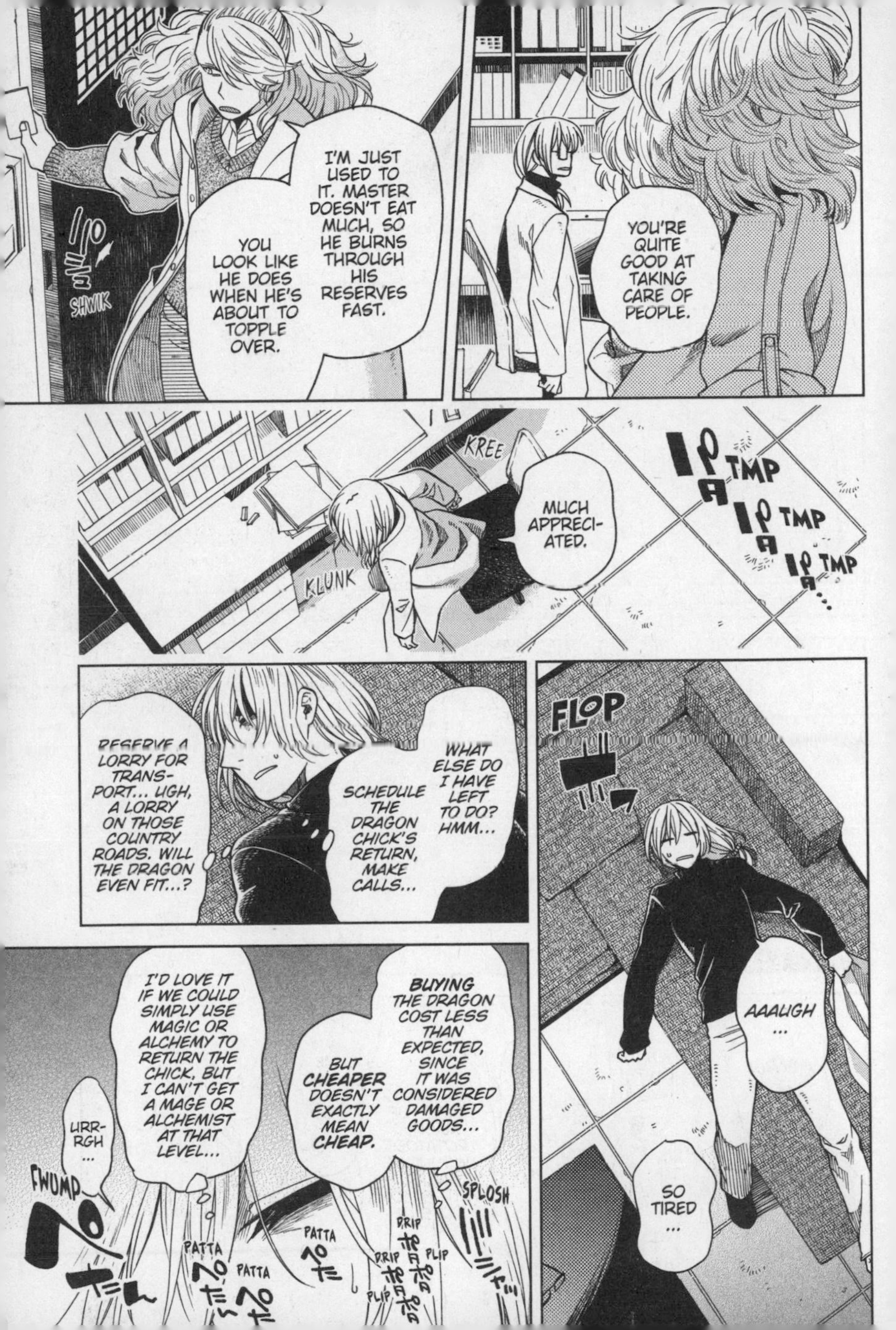
YOU'RE QUITE GOOD AT TAKING CARE OF PEOPLE.
I'M JUST USED TO IT. MASTER DOESN'T EAT MUCH, SO HE BURNS THROUGH HIS RESERVES FAST.
YOU LOOK LIKE HE DOES WHEN HE'S ABOUT TO TOPPLE OVER.
SHWIK
TMP TMP TMP...
KREE
MUCH APPRECIATED.
KLUNK
FLOP
AAAUGH...
SO TIRED...
WHAT ELSE DO I HAVE LEFT TO DO? HMM...
SCHEDULE THE DRAGON CHICK'S RETURN, MAKE CALLS...
RESERVE A LORRY FOR TRANSPORT... UGH, A LORRY ON THOSE COUNTRY ROADS. WILL THE DRAGON EVEN FIT...?
SPLOSH
BUYING THE DRAGON COST LESS THAN EXPECTED, SINCE IT WAS CONSIDERED DAMAGED GOODS...
BUT CHEAPER DOESN'T EXACTLY MEAN CHEAP.
DRIP DRIP PLIP PLIP PLIP
PATTA
I'D LOVE IT IF WE COULD SIMPLY USE MAGIC OR ALCHEMY TO RETURN THE CHICK, BUT I CAN'T GET A MAGE OR ALCHEMIST AT THAT LEVEL...
PATTA PATTA
URR-RGH...
FWUMP

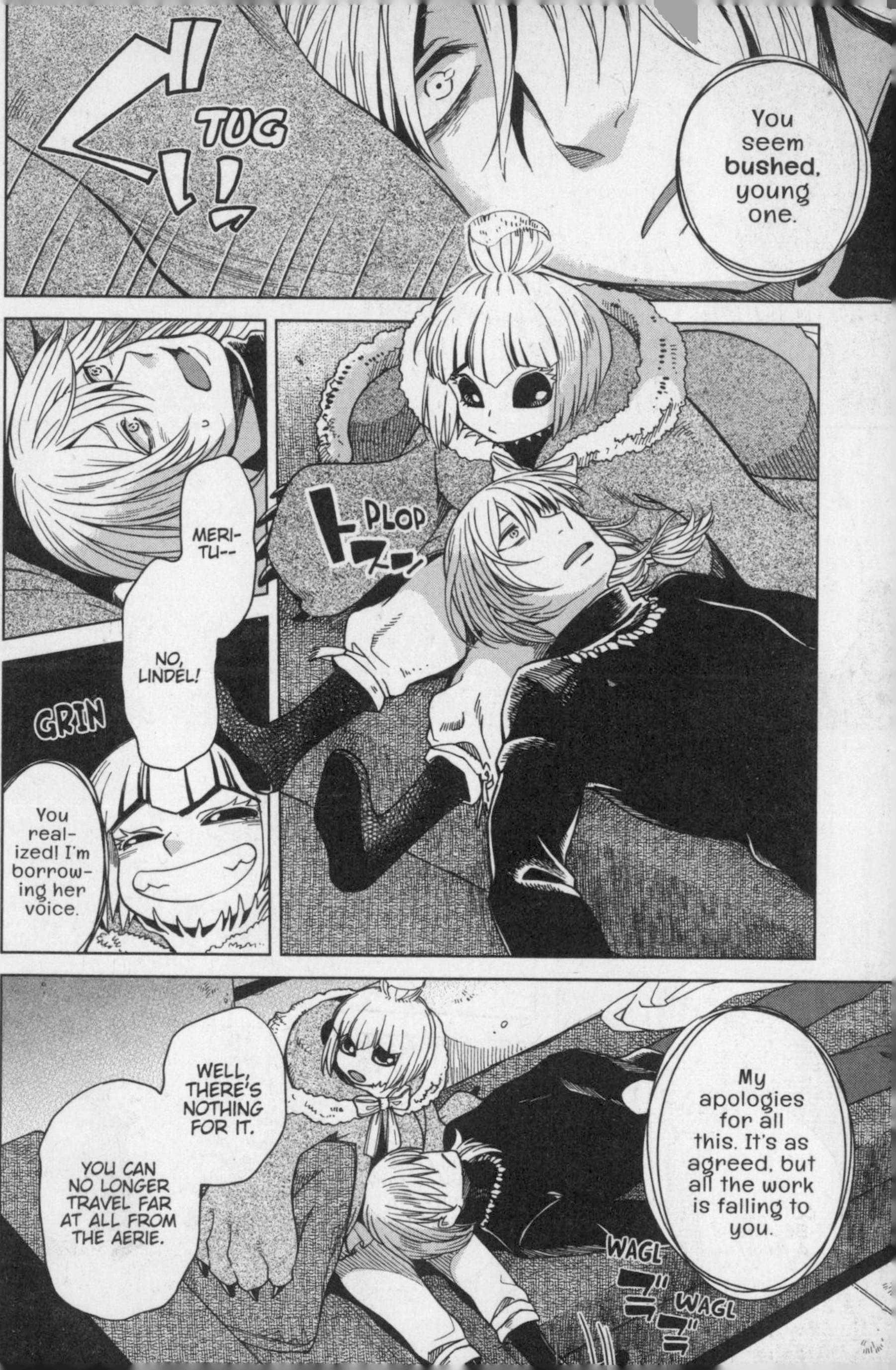

You seem bushed, young one.
TUG
PLOP
MERI-TU--
NO, LINDEL!
GRIN
You realized! I'm borrowing her voice.
My apologies for all this. It's as agreed, but all the work is falling to you.
WAGL
WAGL
WELL, THERE'S NOTHING FOR IT.
YOU CAN NO LONGER TRAVEL FAR AT ALL FROM THE AERIE.

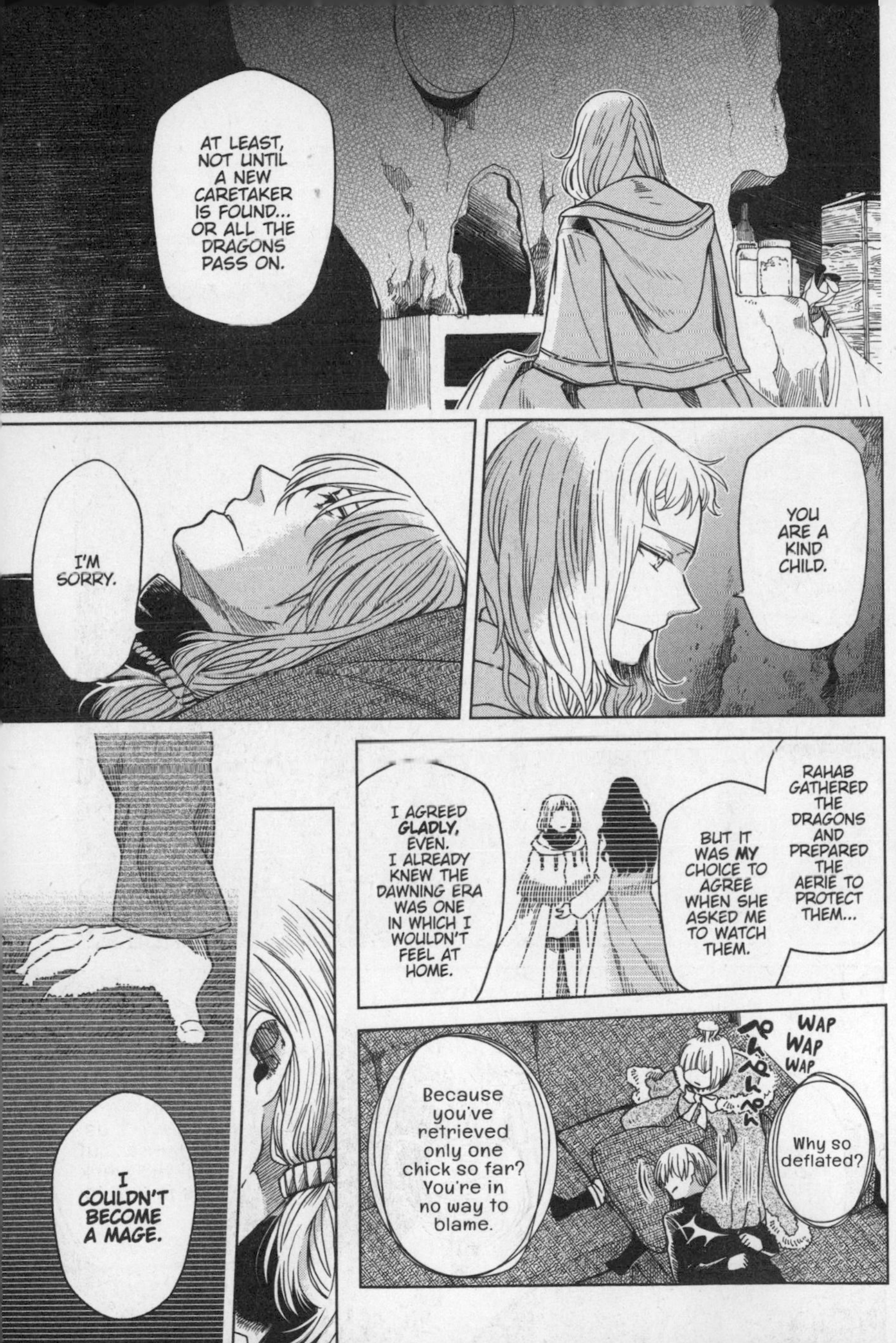
AT LEAST, NOT UNTIL A NEW CARETAKER IS FOUND... OR ALL THE DRAGONS PASS ON.
YOU ARE A KIND CHILD.
I'M SORRY.
RAHAB GATHERED THE DRAGONS AND PREPARED THE AERIE TO PROTECT THEM...
BUT IT WAS MY CHOICE TO AGREE WHEN SHE ASKED ME TO WATCH THEM.
I AGREED GLADLY, EVEN. I ALREADY KNEW THE DAWNING ERA WAS ONE IN WHICH I WOULDN'T FEEL AT HOME.
WAP WAP WAP
Why so deflated?
Because you've retrieved only one chick so far? You're in no way to blame.
I COULDN'T BECOME A MAGE.

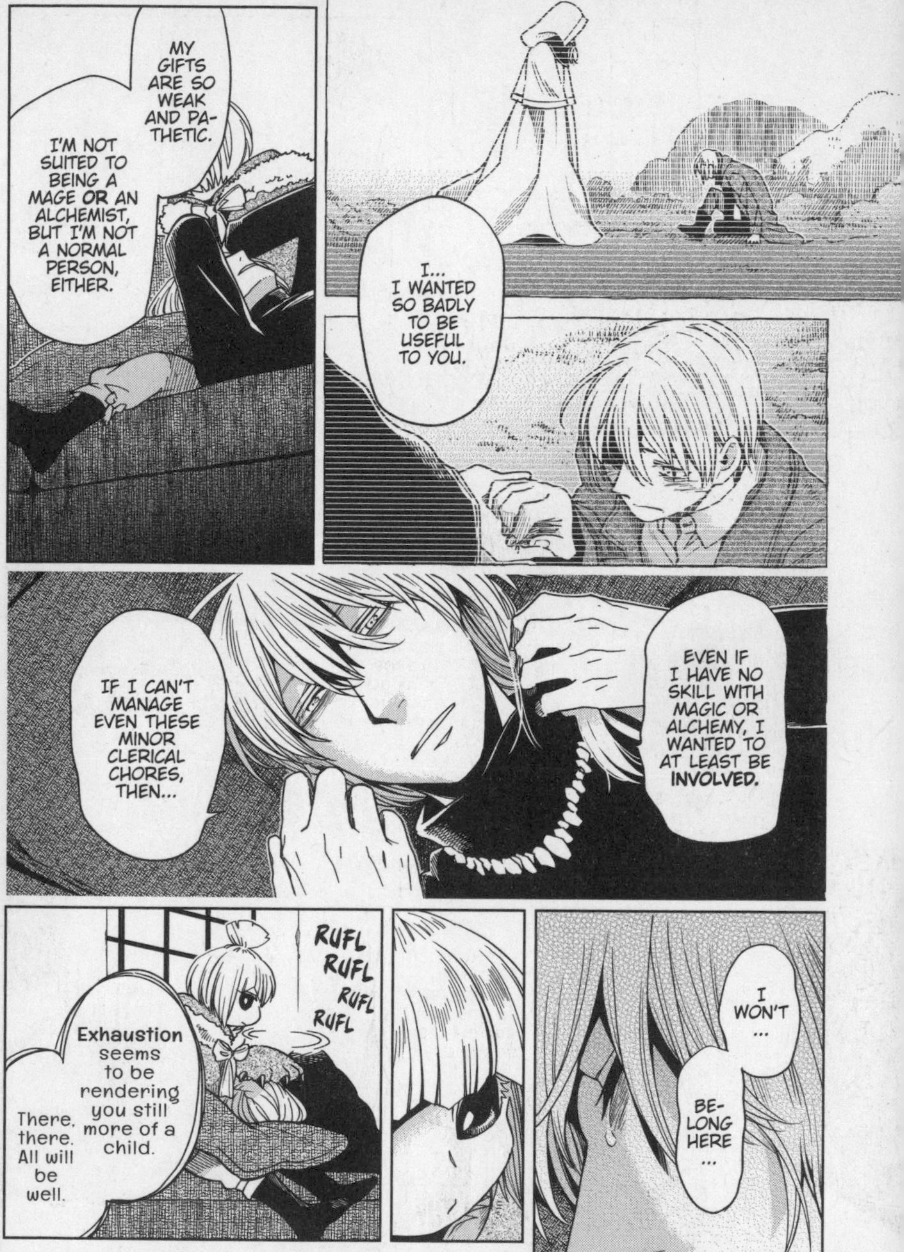
I... I WANTED SO BADLY TO BE USEFUL TO YOU.
MY GIFTS ARE SO WEAK AND PA-THETIC.
I'M NOT SUITED TO BEING A MAGE **OR** AN ALCHEMIST, BUT I'M NOT A NORMAL PERSON, EITHER.
EVEN IF I HAVE NO SKILL WITH MAGIC OR ALCHEMY, I WANTED TO AT LEAST BE **INVOLVED.**
IF I CAN'T MANAGE EVEN THESE MINOR CLERICAL CHORES, THEN...
I WON'T ...
BE-LONG HERE ...
RUFL RUFL RUFL RUFL
Exhaustion seems to be rendering you still more of a child.
There, there. All will be well.

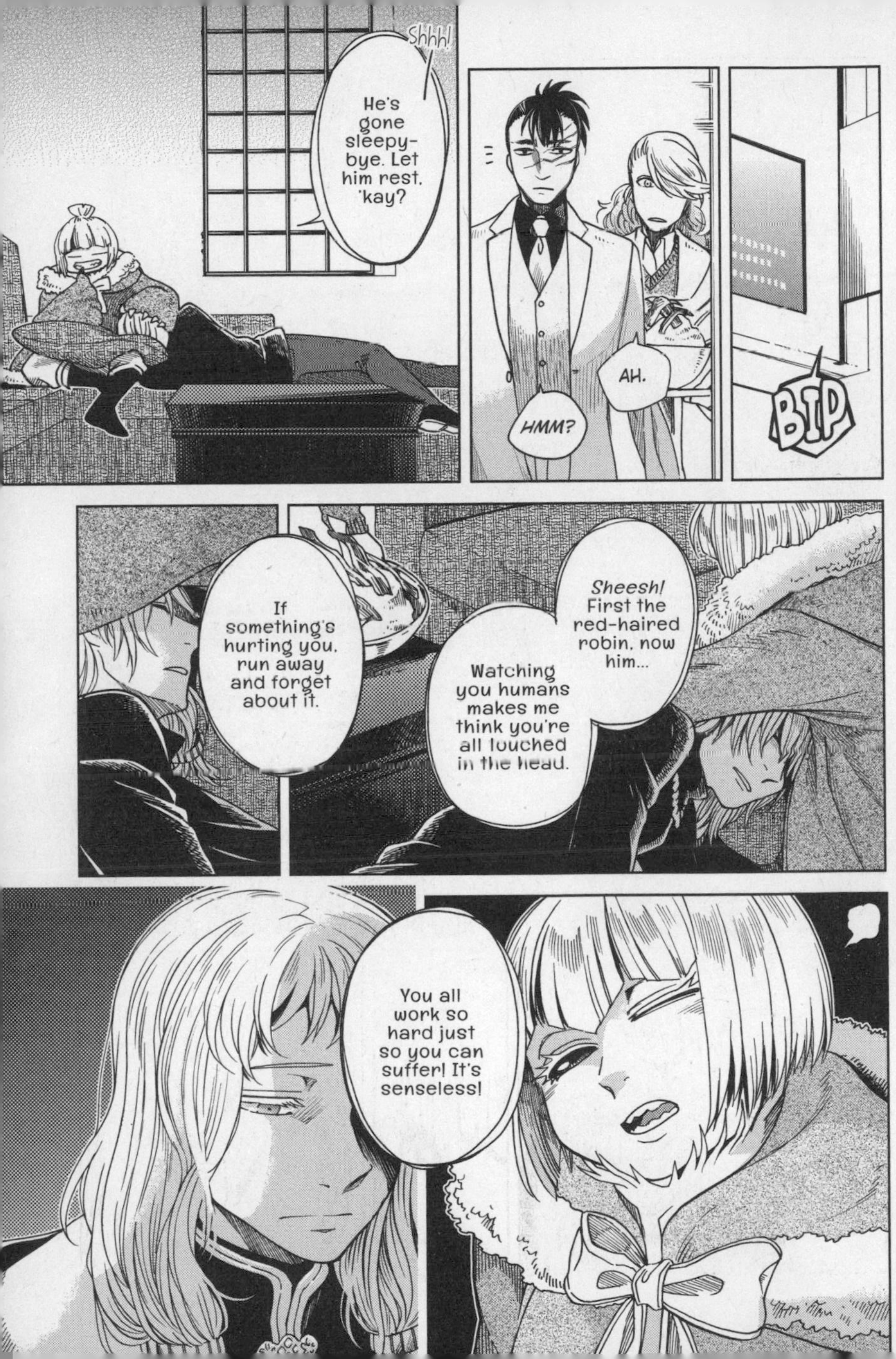
BIP
AH.
HMM?
Shhh!
He's gone sleepy-bye. Let him rest, 'kay?
Sheesh! First the red-haired robin, now him...
Watching you humans makes me think you're all touched in the head.
If something's hurting you, run away and forget about it.
You all work so hard just so you can suffer! It's senseless!

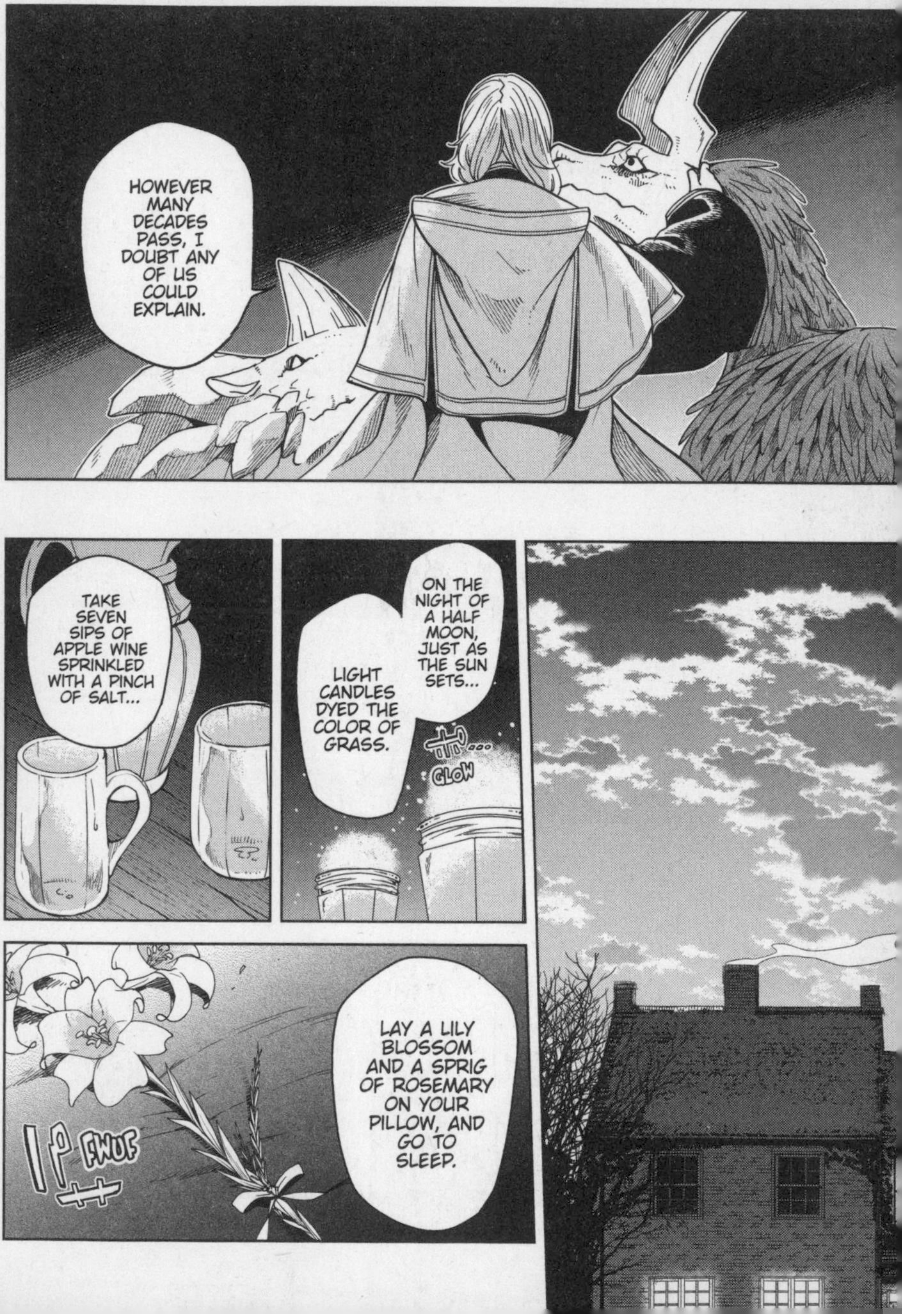
HOWEVER MANY DECADES PASS, I DOUBT ANY OF US COULD EXPLAIN.
ON THE NIGHT OF A HALF MOON, JUST AS THE SUN SETS...
LIGHT CANDLES DYED THE COLOR OF GRASS.
GLOW
TAKE SEVEN SIPS OF APPLE WINE SPRINKLED WITH A PINCH OF SALT...
LAY A LILY BLOSSOM AND A SPRIG OF ROSEMARY ON YOUR PILLOW, AND GO TO SLEEP.
FWUF

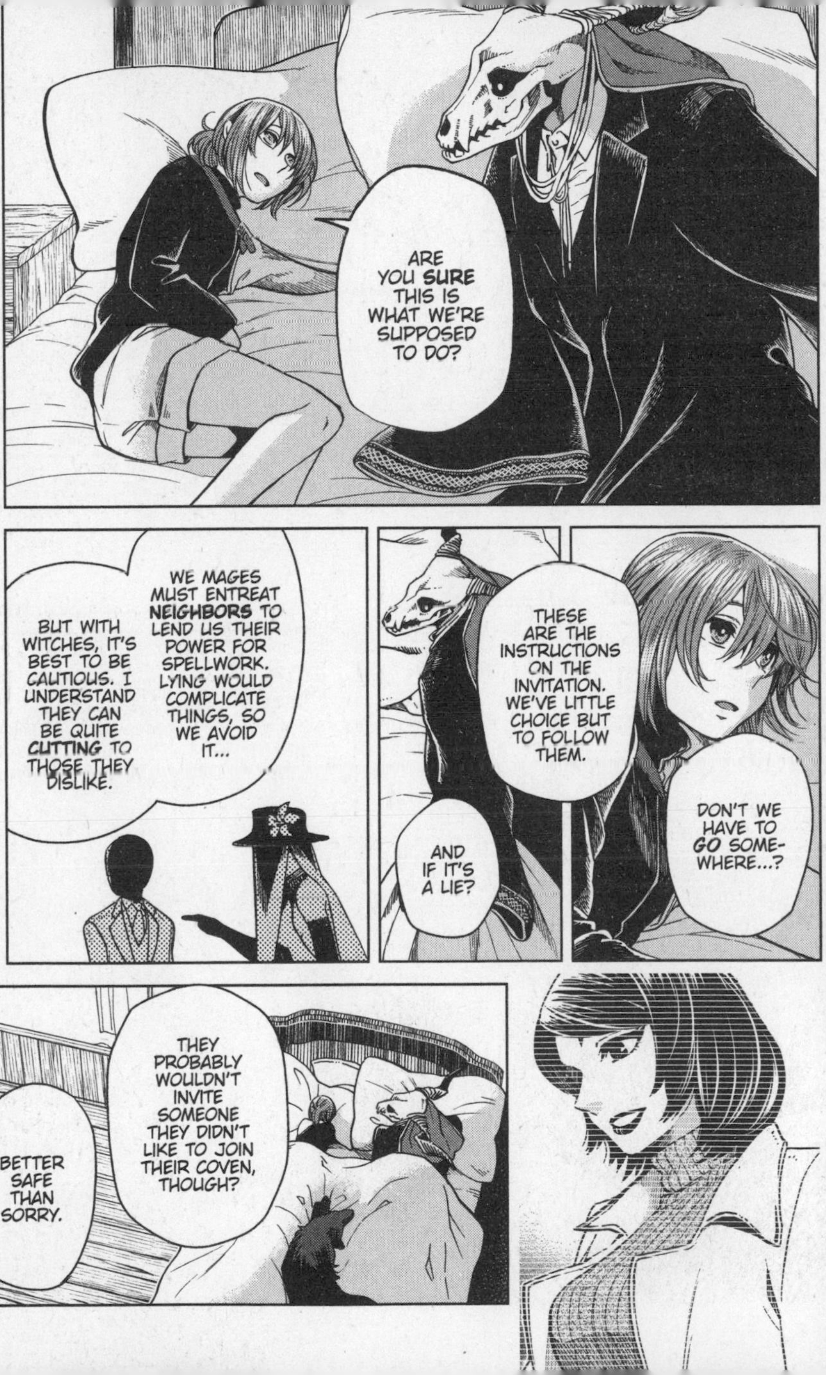
ARE YOU SURE THIS IS WHAT WE'RE SUPPOSED TO DO?
DON'T WE HAVE TO GO SOMEWHERE...?
THESE ARE THE INSTRUCTIONS ON THE INVITATION. WE'VE LITTLE CHOICE BUT TO FOLLOW THEM.
AND IF IT'S A LIE?
WE MAGES MUST ENTREAT NEIGHBORS TO LEND US THEIR POWER FOR SPELLWORK. LYING WOULD COMPLICATE THINGS, SO WE AVOID IT...
BUT WITH WITCHES, IT'S BEST TO BE CAUTIOUS. I UNDERSTAND THEY CAN BE QUITE CUTTING TO THOSE THEY DISLIKE.
THEY PROBABLY WOULDN'T INVITE SOMEONE THEY DIDN'T LIKE TO JOIN THEIR COVEN, THOUGH?
BETTER SAFE THAN SORRY.

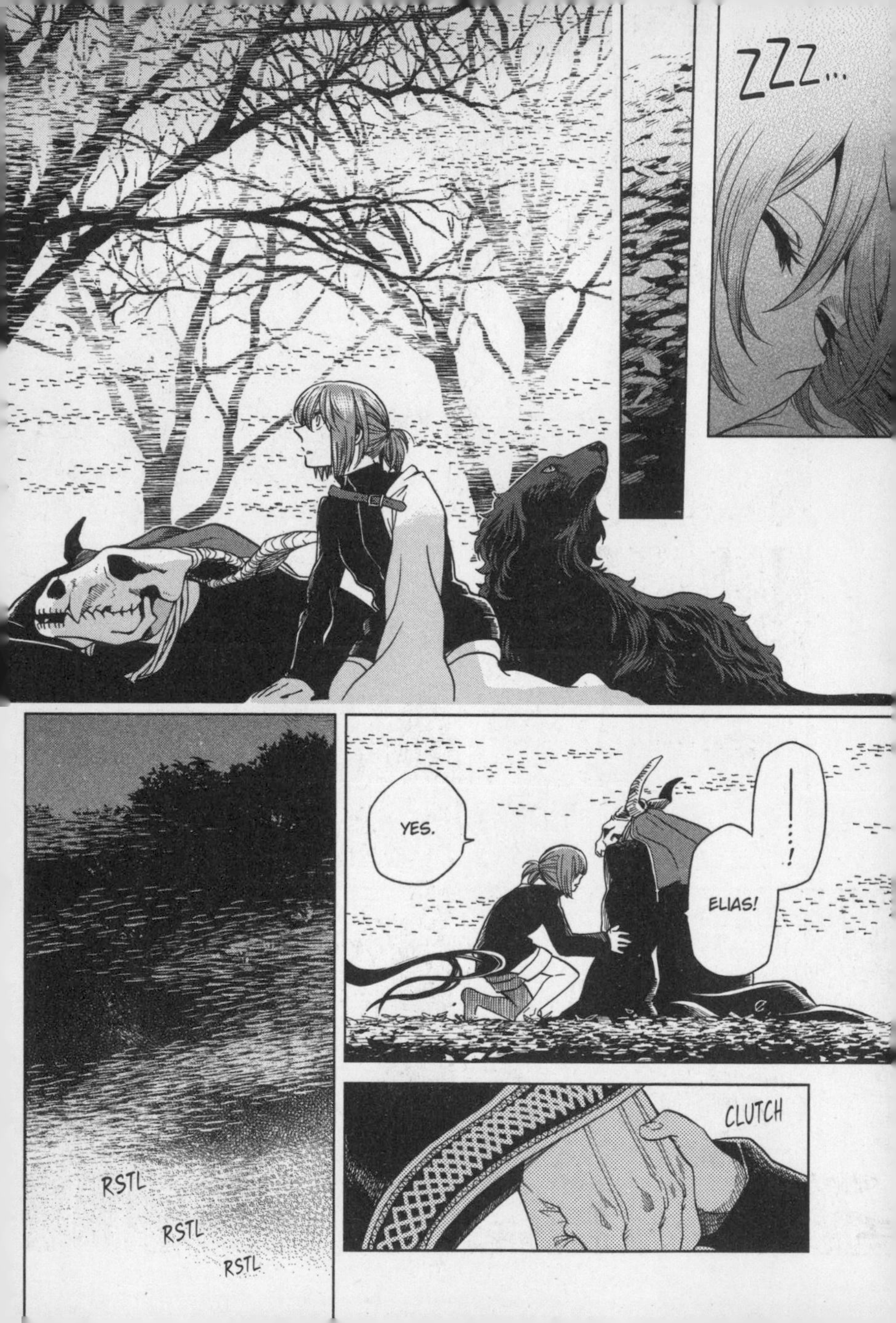
ZZZ...
...!
ELIAS!
YES.
CLUTCH
RSTL
RSTL
RSTL

IF I SAID THAT THE WORLD IS *LAYERED*, LIKE THE STRATA OF THE EARTH...

WOULD THAT METAPHOR MAKE SENSE TO YOU?

EARTH STRATA...?

YOU MIGHT ALSO CALL THEM *FREQUENCIES*.

LET US SUPPOSE A PERSON DIGS A HOLE IN A HILLSIDE.

A NORMAL HUMAN'S EYES WOULD PERCEIVE ONLY THE LAYERS OF SOIL AND ROCK...

WHILE WE, AND THOSE WITH EYES LIKE OURS, MIGHT SEE A DOOR INTO THE FAERIE REALM.

DIFFERENT CREATURES CAN SEE, AND RESIDE IN, DIFFERENT LAYERS...

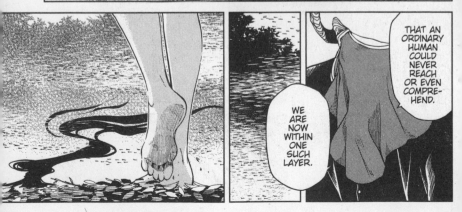

THAT AN ORDINARY HUMAN COULD NEVER REACH OR EVEN COMPREHEND.

WE ARE NOW WITHIN ONE SUCH LAYER.

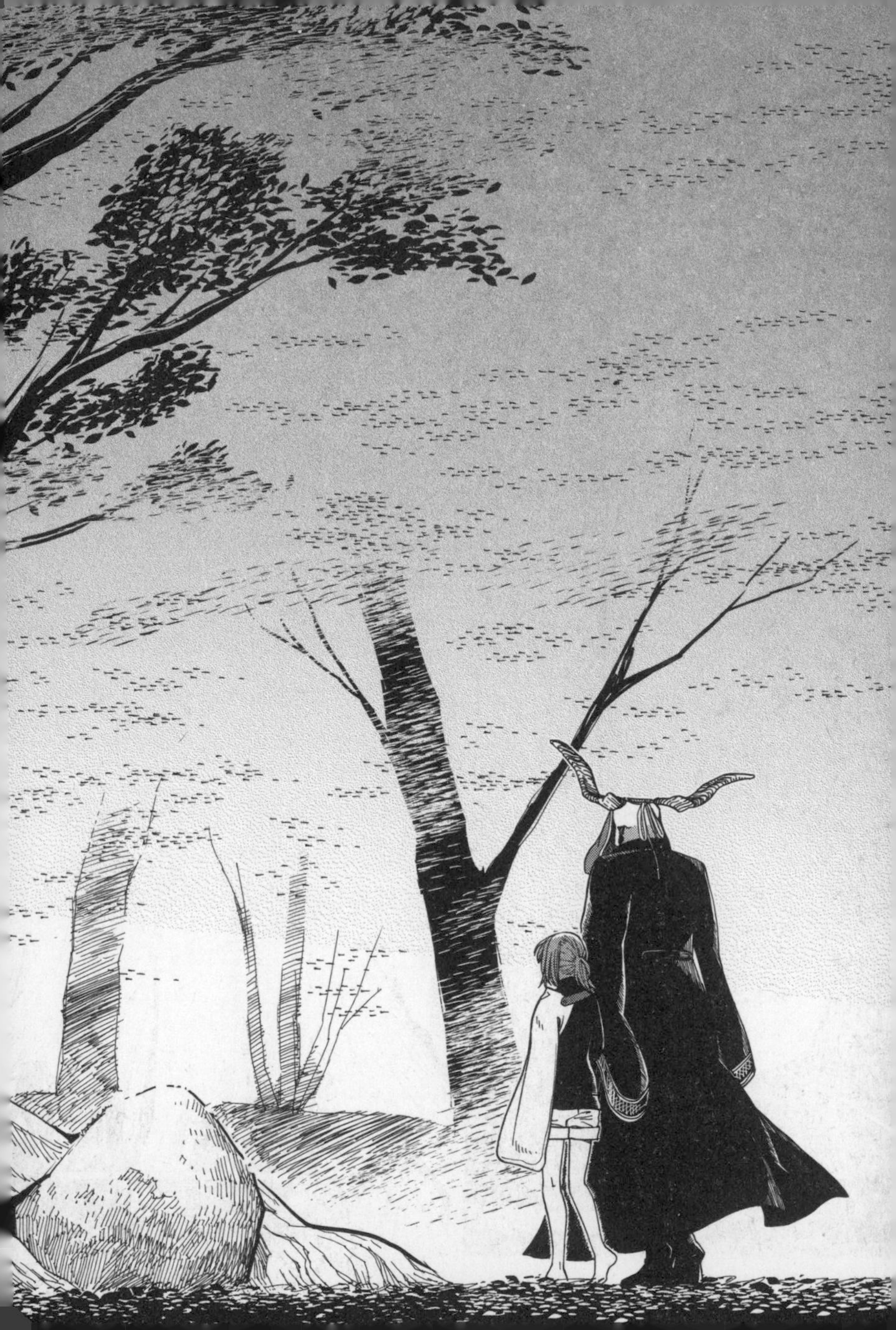

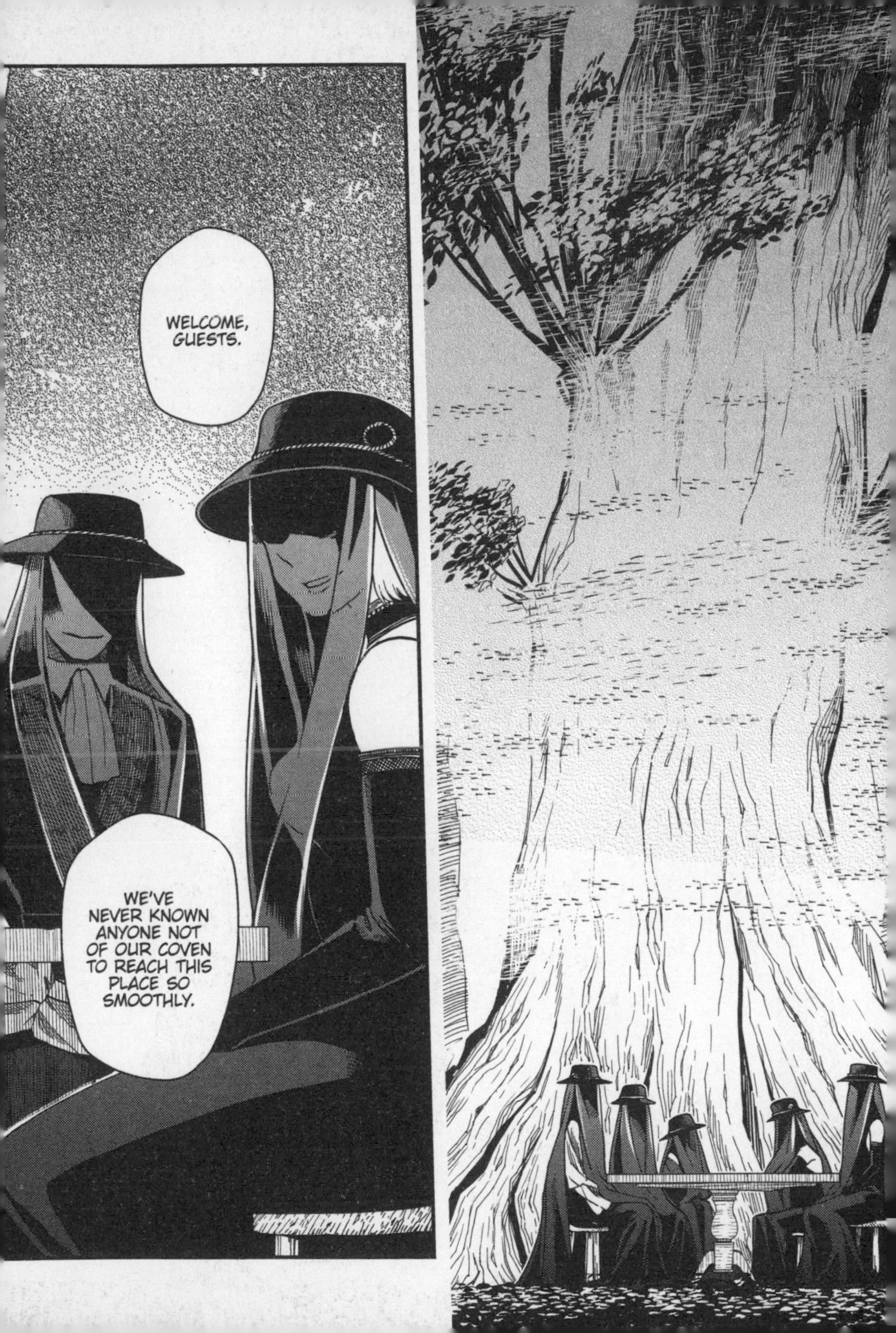
WELCOME, GUESTS.
WE'VE NEVER KNOWN ANYONE NOT OF OUR COVEN TO REACH THIS PLACE SO SMOOTHLY.

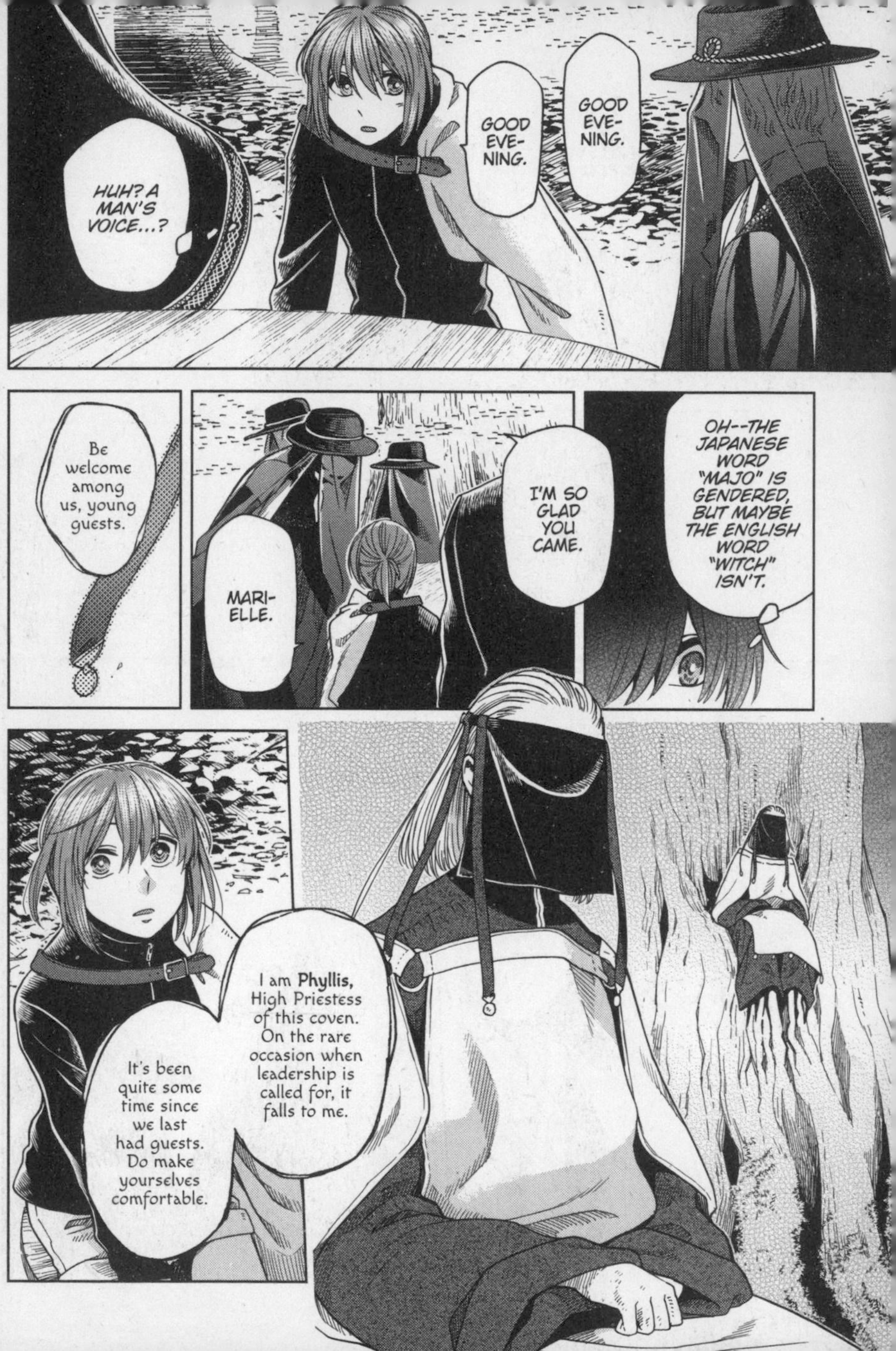
GOOD EVE- NING.
GOOD EVE- NING.
HUH? A MAN'S VOICE...?
OH--THE JAPANESE WORD "MAJO" IS GENDERED, BUT MAYBE THE ENGLISH WORD "WITCH" ISN'T.
I'M SO GLAD YOU CAME.
MARI- ELLE.
Be welcome among us, young guests.
I am **Phyllis**, High Priestess of this coven. On the rare occasion when leadership is called for, it falls to me.
It's been quite some time since we last had guests. Do make yourselves comfortable.

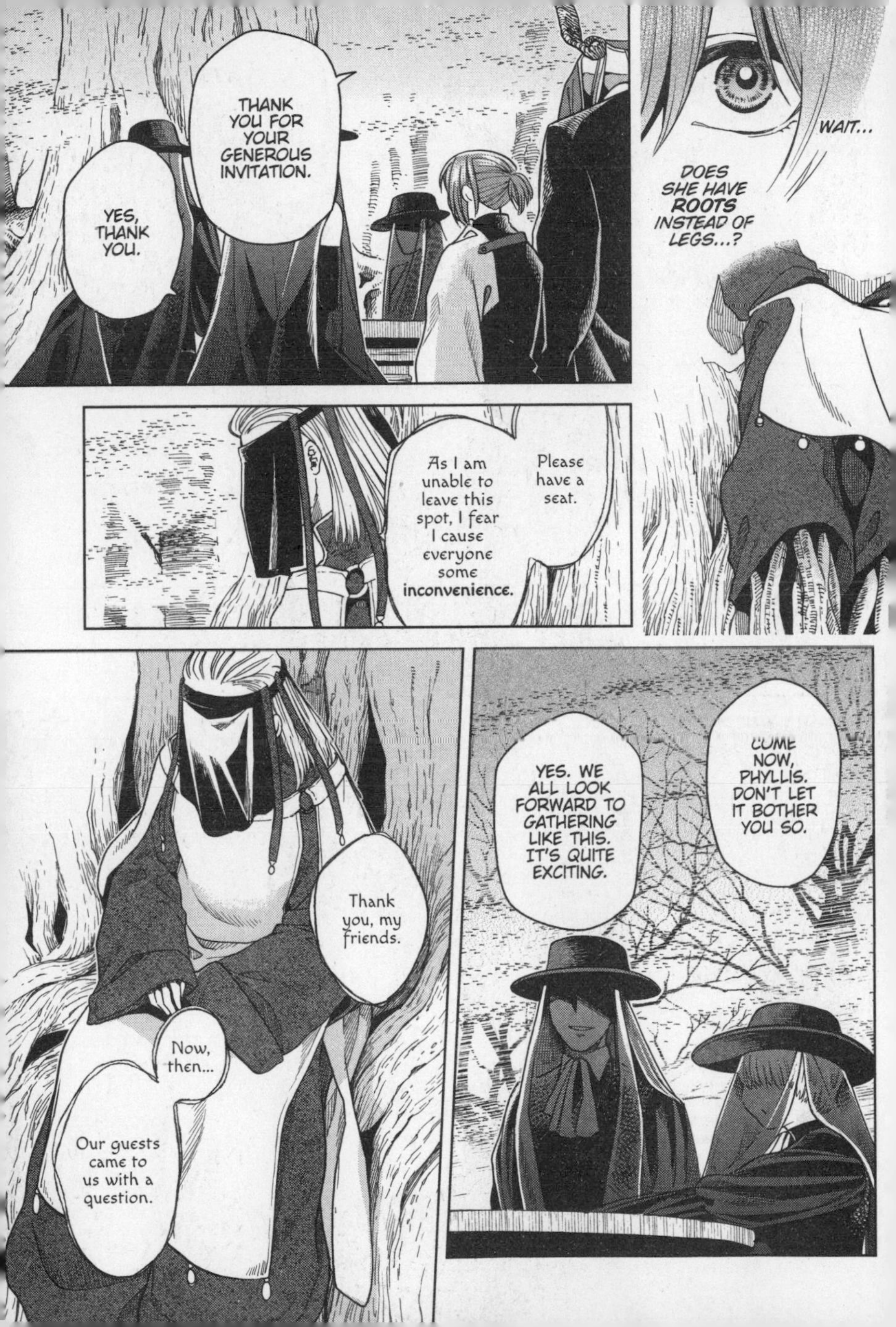
WAIT...
DOES SHE HAVE **ROOTS** INSTEAD OF LEGS...?
THANK YOU FOR YOUR GENEROUS INVITATION.
YES, THANK YOU.
Please have a seat.
As I am unable to leave this spot, I fear I cause everyone some **inconvenience.**
COME NOW, PHYLLIS. DON'T LET IT BOTHER YOU SO.
YES. WE ALL LOOK FORWARD TO GATHERING LIKE THIS. IT'S QUITE EXCITING.
Thank you, my friends.
Now, then...
Our guests came to us with a question.

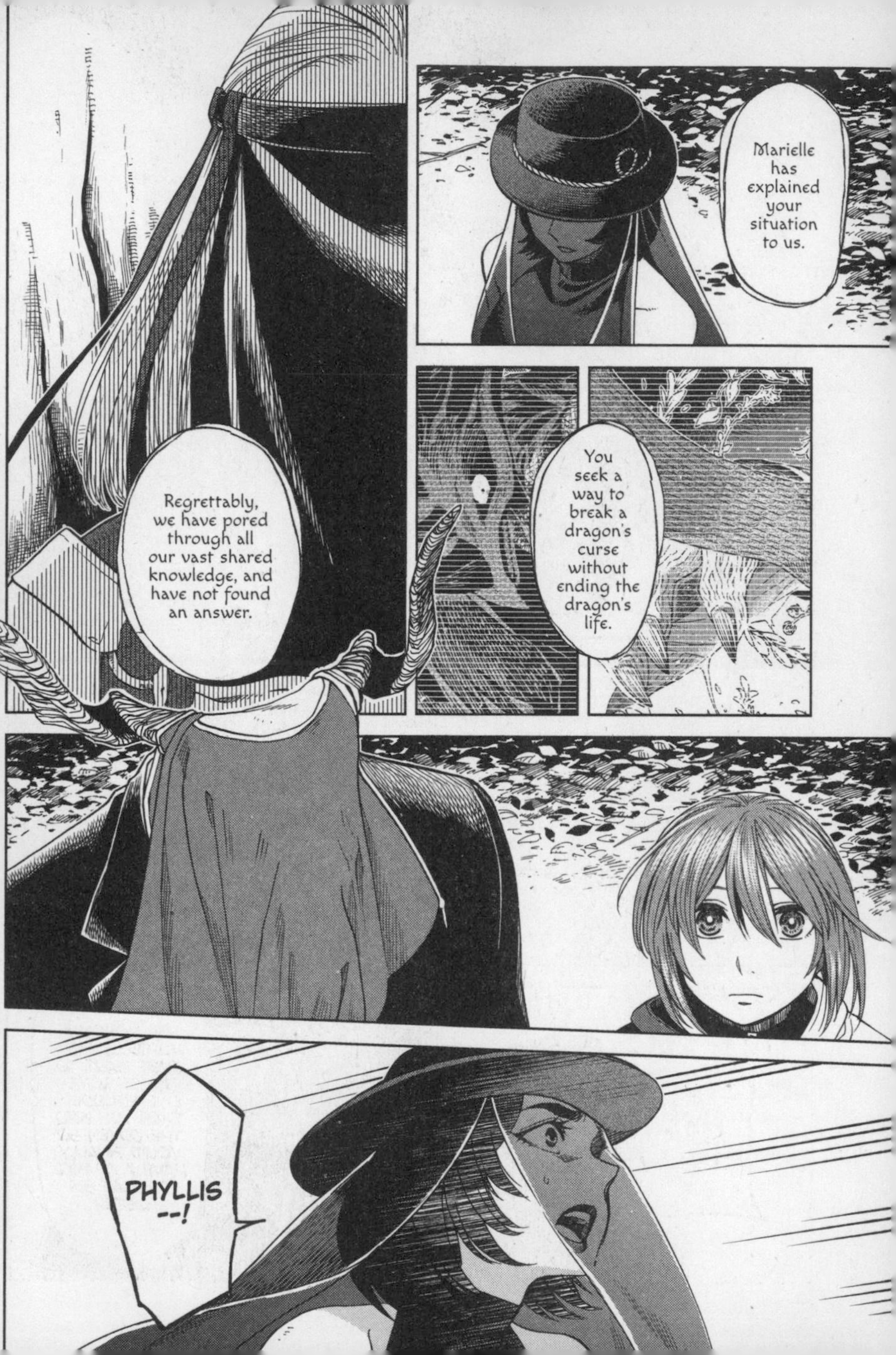
Marielle has explained your situation to us.
You seek a way to break a dragon's curse without ending the dragon's life.
Regrettably, we have pored through all our vast shared knowledge, and have not found an answer.
PHYLLIS --!

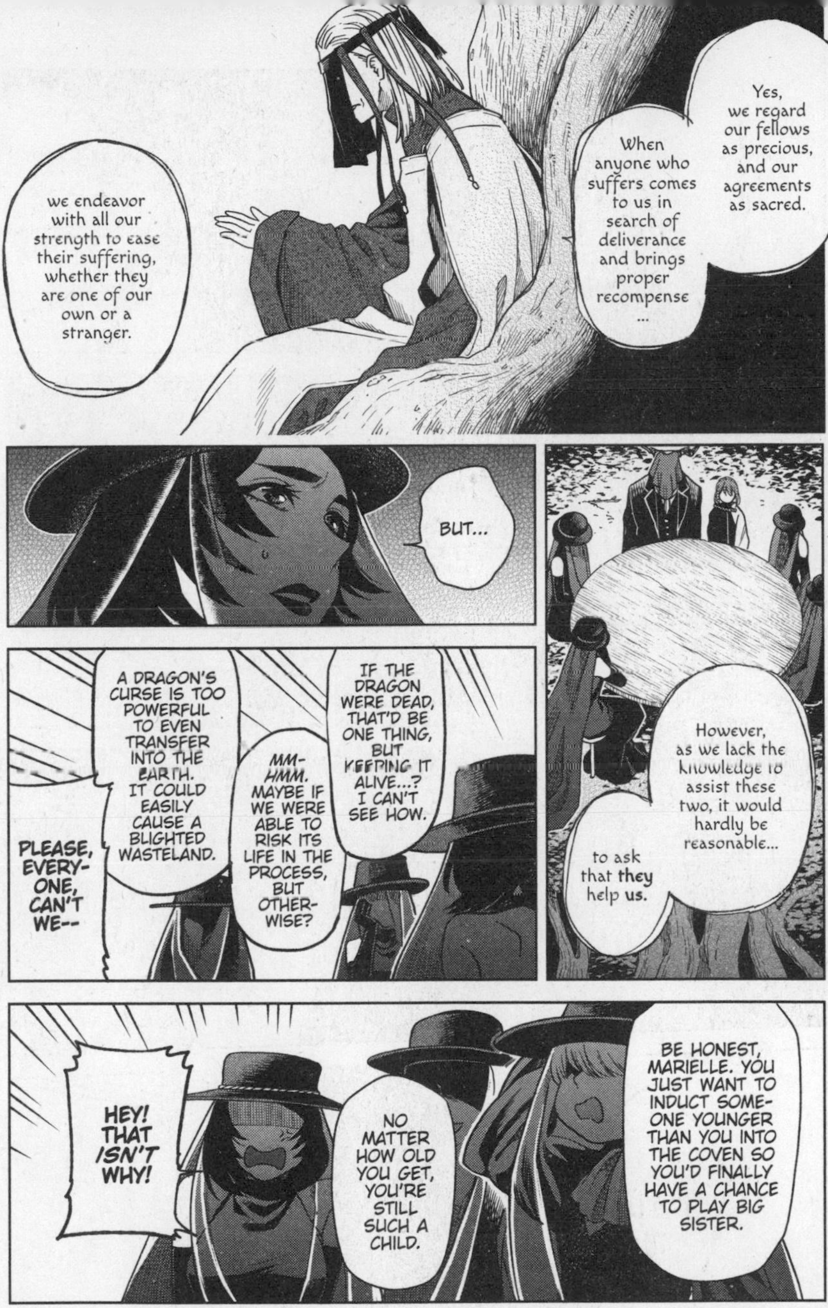
Yes, we regard our fellows as precious, and our agreements as sacred.
When anyone who suffers comes to us in search of deliverance and brings proper recompense ...
we endeavor with all our strength to ease their suffering, whether they are one of our own or a stranger.
However, as we lack the knowledge to assist these two, it would hardly be reasonable...
to ask that they help us.
BUT...
IF THE DRAGON WERE DEAD, THAT'D BE ONE THING, BUT KEEPING IT ALIVE...? I CAN'T SEE HOW.
A DRAGON'S CURSE IS TOO POWERFUL TO EVEN TRANSFER INTO THE EARTH. IT COULD EASILY CAUSE A BLIGHTED WASTELAND.
MM-HMM. MAYBE IF WE WERE ABLE TO RISK ITS LIFE IN THE PROCESS, BUT OTHERWISE?
PLEASE, EVERYONE, CAN'T WE--
BE HONEST, MARIELLE. YOU JUST WANT TO INDUCT SOMEONE YOUNGER THAN YOU INTO THE COVEN SO YOU'D FINALLY HAVE A CHANCE TO PLAY BIG SISTER.
NO MATTER HOW OLD YOU GET, YOU'RE STILL SUCH A CHILD.
HEY! THAT ISN'T WHY!

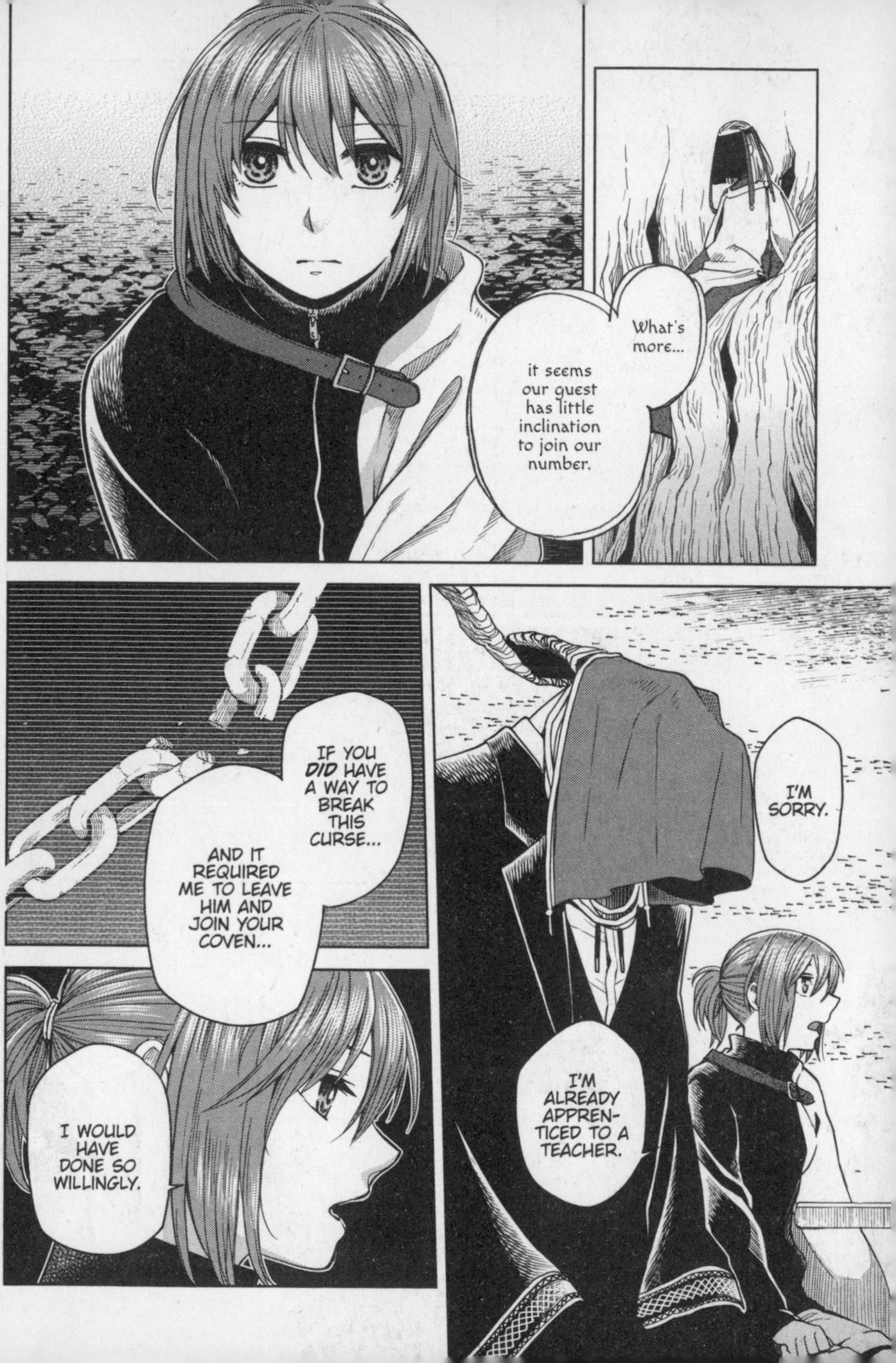
What's more...
it seems our guest has little inclination to join our number.
I'M SORRY.
I'M ALREADY APPREN-TICED TO A TEACHER.
IF YOU ***DID*** HAVE A WAY TO BREAK THIS CURSE...
AND IT REQUIRED ME TO LEAVE HIM AND JOIN YOUR COVEN...
I WOULD HAVE DONE SO WILLINGLY.

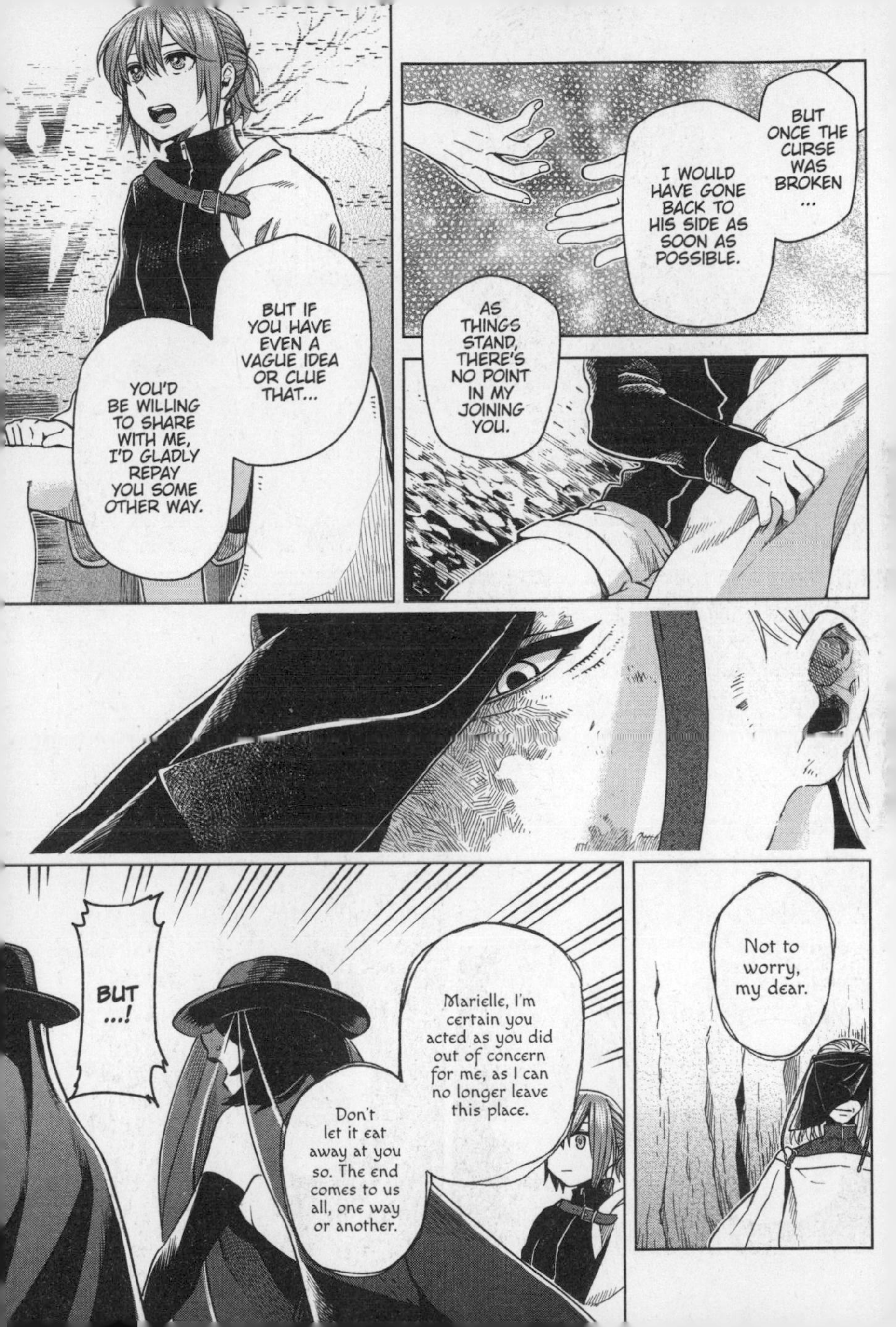
BUT ONCE THE CURSE WAS BROKEN ...
I WOULD HAVE GONE BACK TO HIS SIDE AS SOON AS POSSIBLE.
AS THINGS STAND, THERE'S NO POINT IN MY JOINING YOU.
BUT IF YOU HAVE EVEN A VAGUE IDEA OR CLUE THAT...
YOU'D BE WILLING TO SHARE WITH ME, I'D GLADLY REPAY YOU SOME OTHER WAY.
Not to worry, my dear.
Marielle, I'm certain you acted as you did out of concern for me, as I can no longer leave this place.
Don't let it eat away at you so. The end comes to us all, one way or another.
BUT ...!

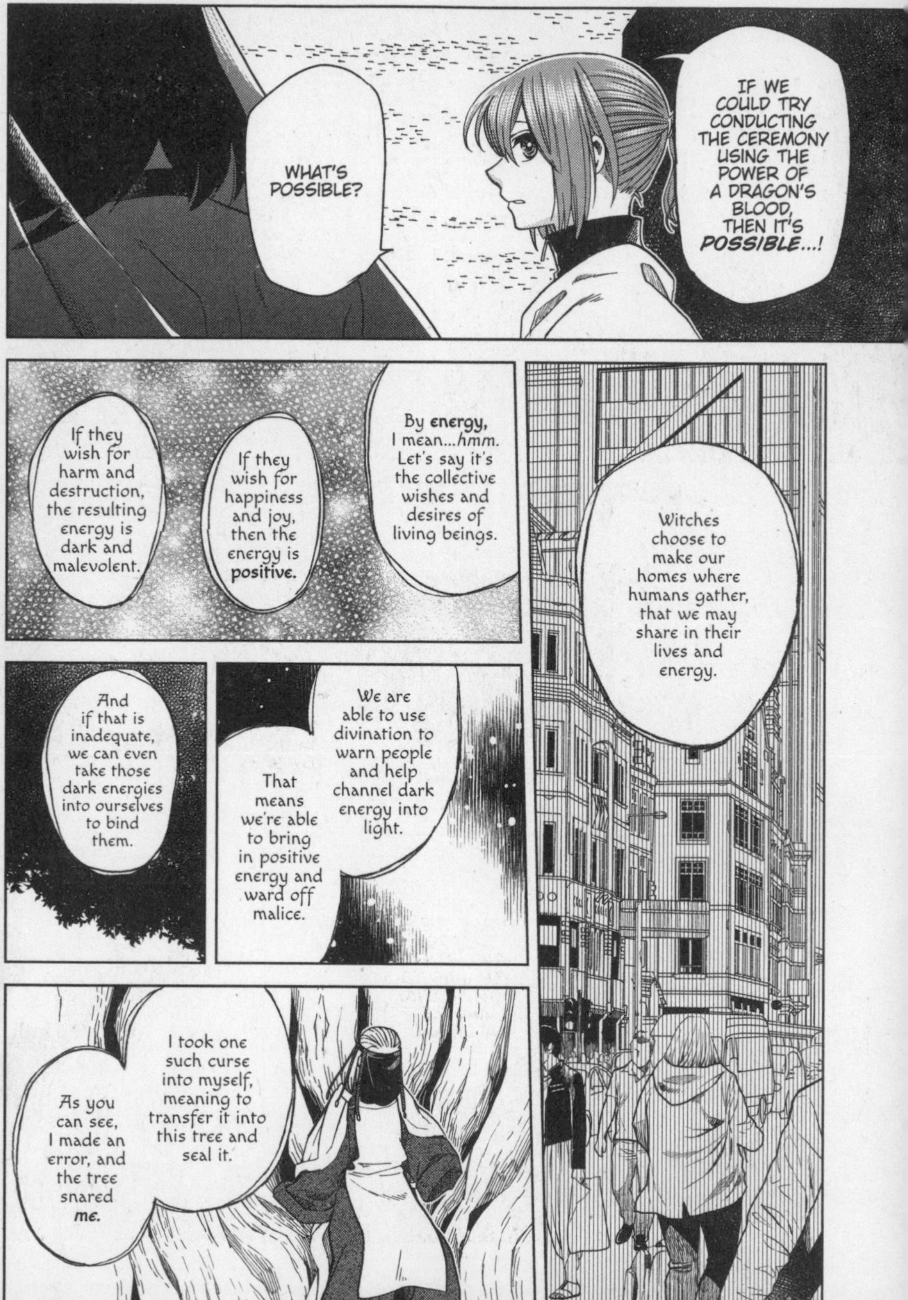
IF WE COULD TRY CONDUCTING THE CEREMONY USING THE POWER OF A DRAGON'S BLOOD, THEN IT'S POSSIBLE...!
WHAT'S POSSIBLE?
Witches choose to make our homes where humans gather, that we may share in their lives and energy.
By energy, I mean...hmm. Let's say it's the collective wishes and desires of living beings.
If they wish for happiness and joy, then the energy is positive.
If they wish for harm and destruction, the resulting energy is dark and malevolent.
We are able to use divination to warn people and help channel dark energy into light.
That means we're able to bring in positive energy and ward off malice.
And if that is inadequate, we can even take those dark energies into ourselves to bind them.
I took one such curse into myself, meaning to transfer it into this tree and seal it.
As you can see, I made an error, and the tree snared me.

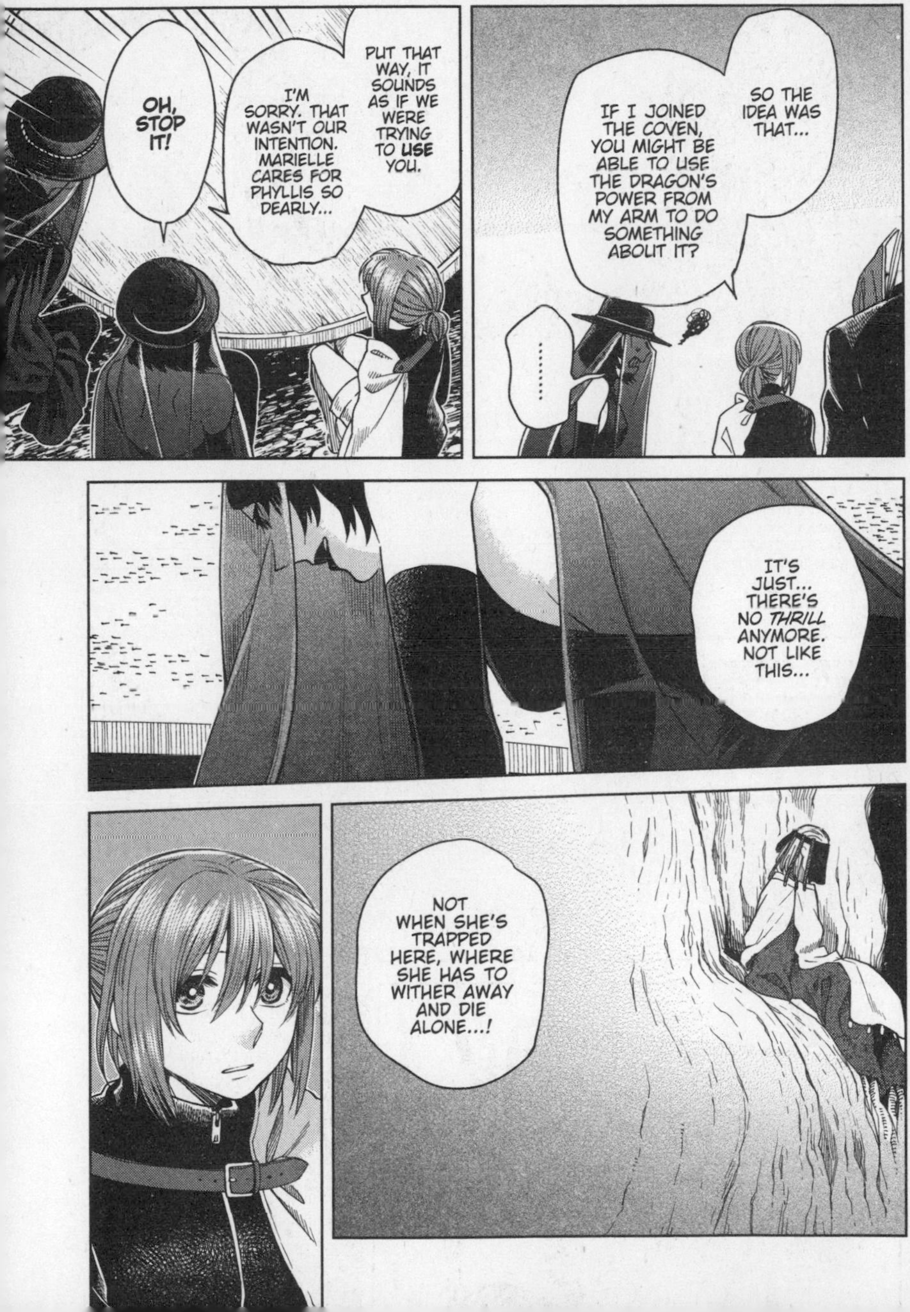
SO THE IDEA WAS THAT...
IF I JOINED THE COVEN, YOU MIGHT BE ABLE TO USE THE DRAGON'S POWER FROM MY ARM TO DO SOMETHING ABOUT IT?
......
PUT THAT WAY, IT SOUNDS AS IF WE WERE TRYING TO USE YOU.
I'M SORRY. THAT WASN'T OUR INTENTION. MARIELLE CARES FOR PHYLLIS SO DEARLY...
OH, STOP IT!
IT'S JUST... THERE'S NO THRILL ANYMORE. NOT LIKE THIS...
NOT WHEN SHE'S TRAPPED HERE, WHERE SHE HAS TO WITHER AWAY AND DIE ALONE...!

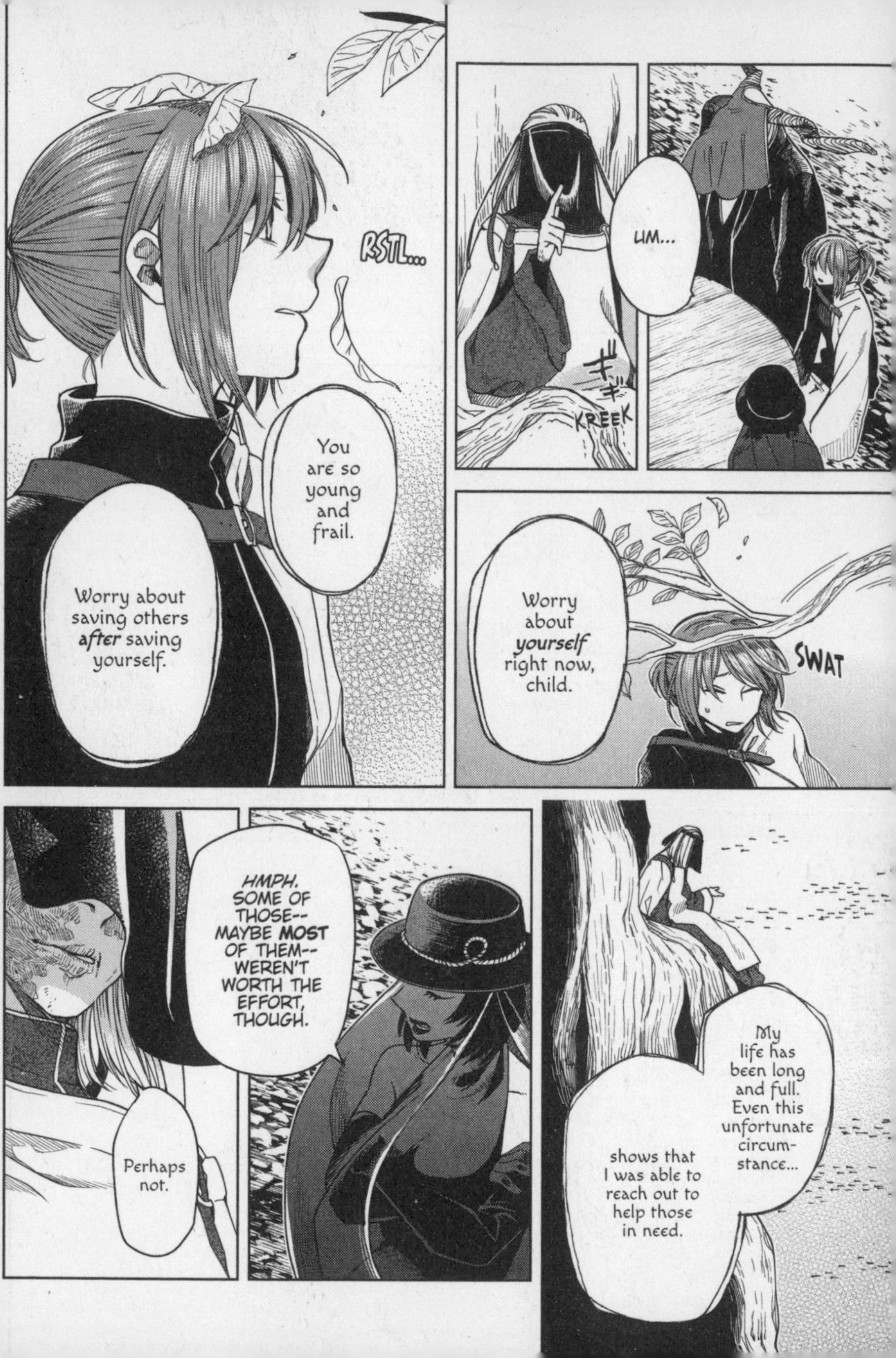
UM...
ギギ
KREEK
Worry about *yourself* right now, child.
SWAT
RSTL...
You are so young and frail.
Worry about saving others *after* saving yourself.
My life has been long and full. Even this unfortunate circumstance...
shows that I was able to reach out to help those in need.
HMPH. SOME OF THOSE-- MAYBE **MOST** OF THEM-- WEREN'T WORTH THE EFFORT, THOUGH.
Perhaps not.

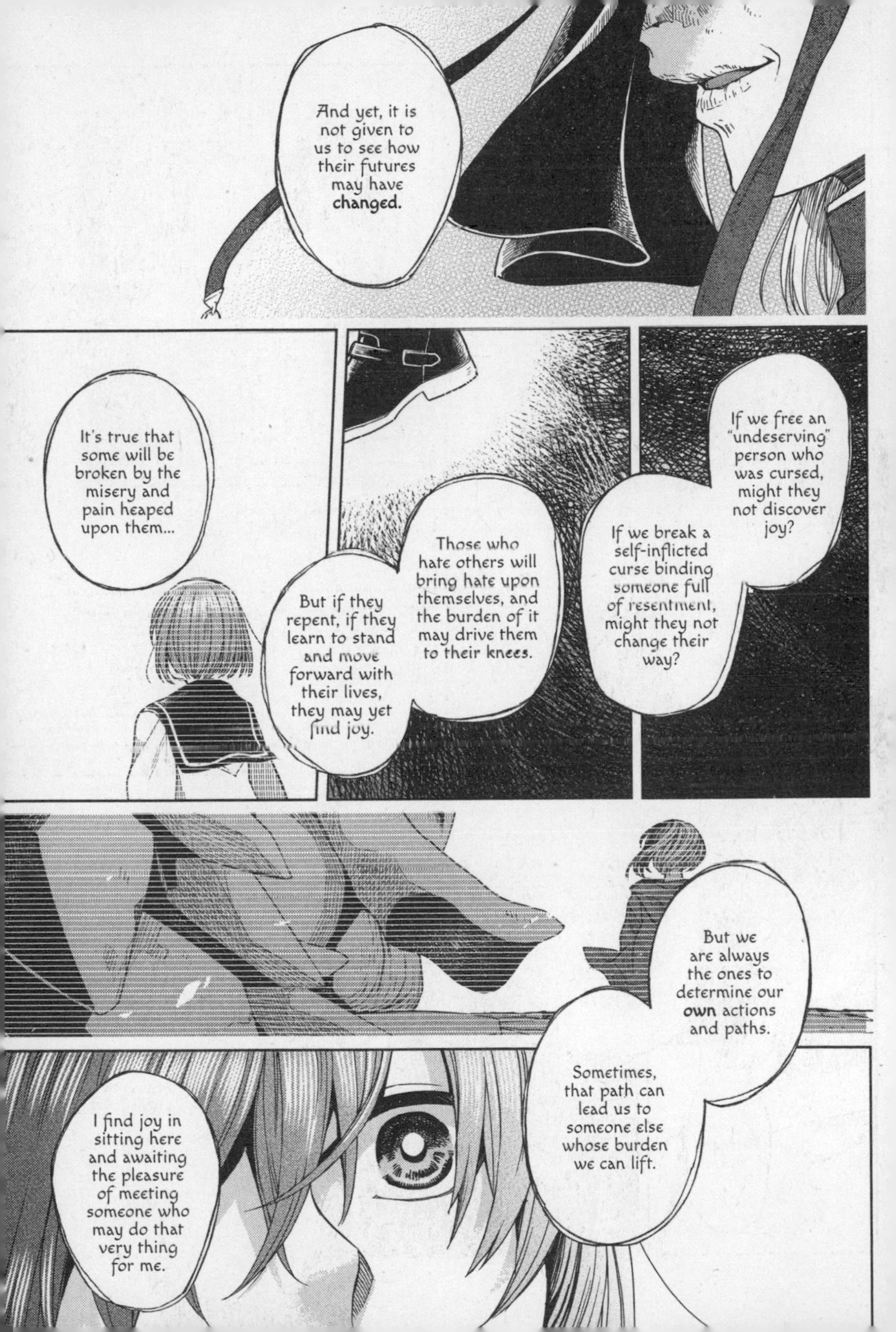
And yet, it is not given to us to see how their futures may have **changed.**
If we free an "undeserving" person who was cursed, might they not discover joy?
If we break a self-inflicted curse binding someone full of resentment, might they not change their way?
Those who hate others will bring hate upon themselves, and the burden of it may drive them to their knees.
But if they repent, if they learn to stand and move forward with their lives, they may yet find joy.
It's true that some will be broken by the misery and pain heaped upon them...
But we are always the ones to determine our **own** actions and paths.
Sometimes, that path can lead us to someone else whose burden we can lift.
I find joy in sitting here and awaiting the pleasure of meeting someone who may do that very thing for me.

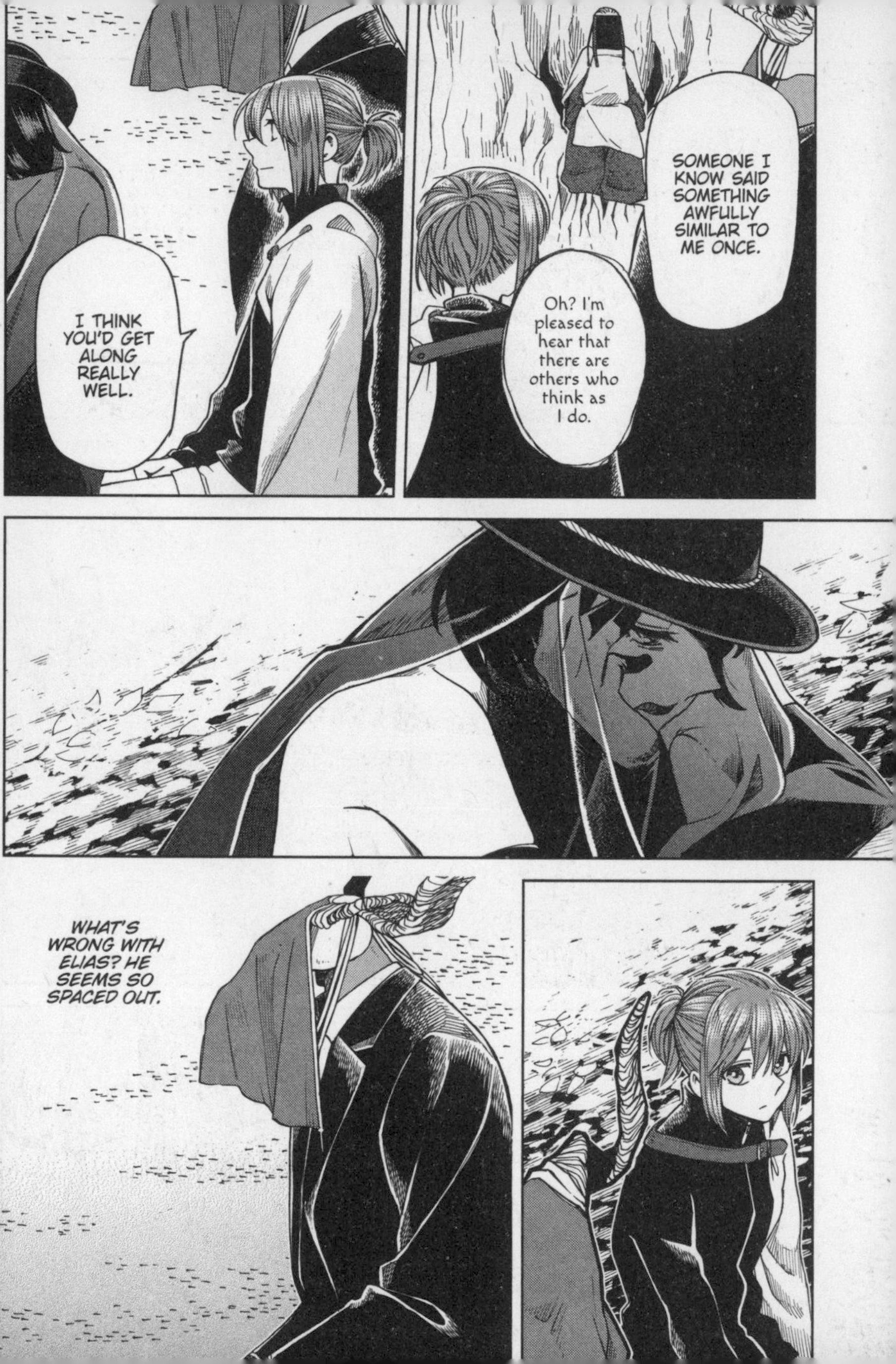
SOMEONE I KNOW SAID SOMETHING AWFULLY SIMILAR TO ME ONCE.
Oh? I'm pleased to hear that there are others who think as I do.
I THINK YOU'D GET ALONG REALLY WELL.
WHAT'S WRONG WITH ELIAS? HE SEEMS SO SPACED OUT.

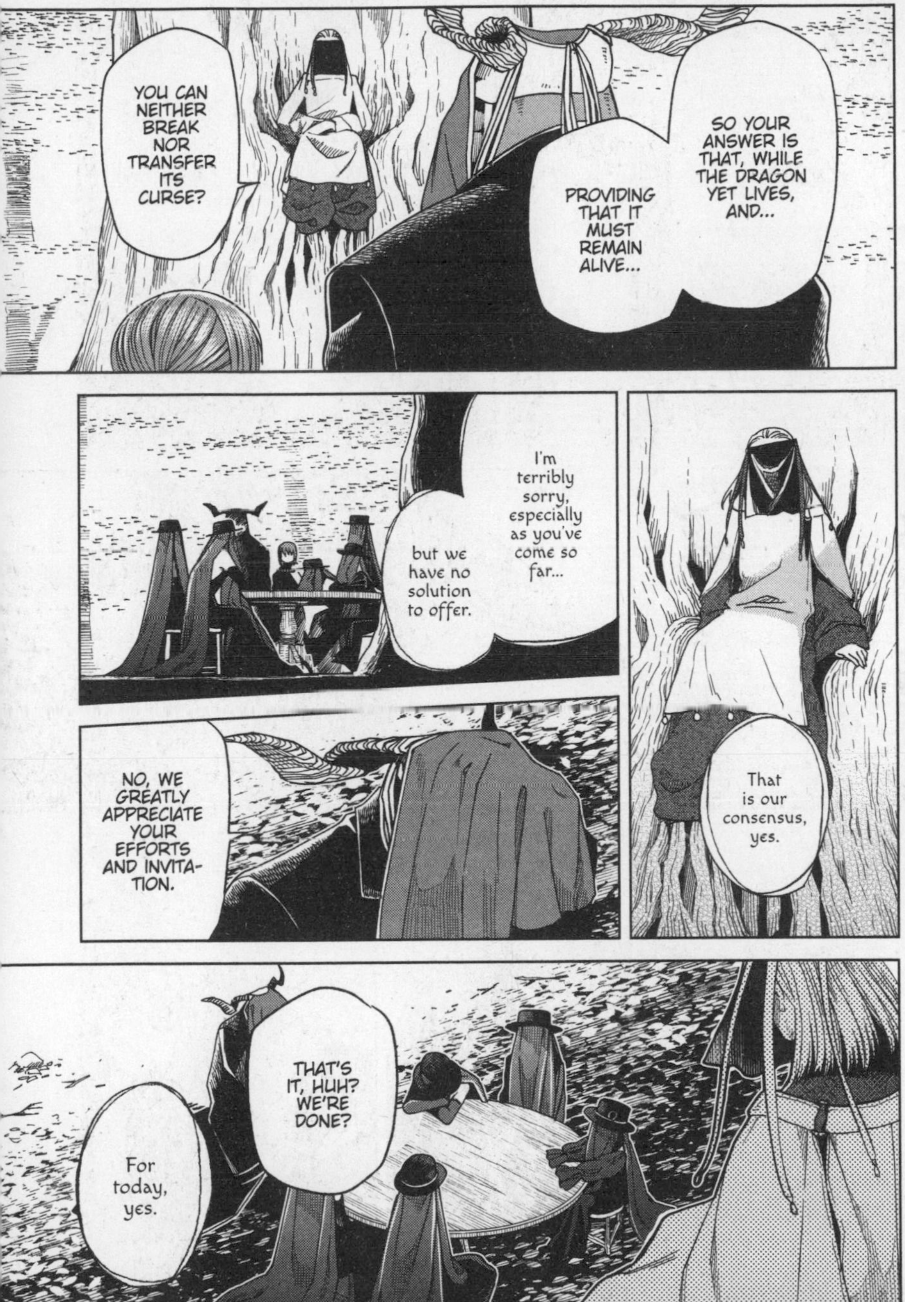
SO YOUR ANSWER IS THAT, WHILE THE DRAGON YET LIVES, AND...
PROVIDING THAT IT MUST REMAIN ALIVE...
YOU CAN NEITHER BREAK NOR TRANSFER ITS CURSE?
That is our consensus, yes.
I'm terribly sorry, especially as you've come so far...
but we have no solution to offer.
NO, WE GREATLY APPRECIATE YOUR EFFORTS AND INVITA-TION.
THAT'S IT, HUH? WE'RE DONE?
For today, yes.

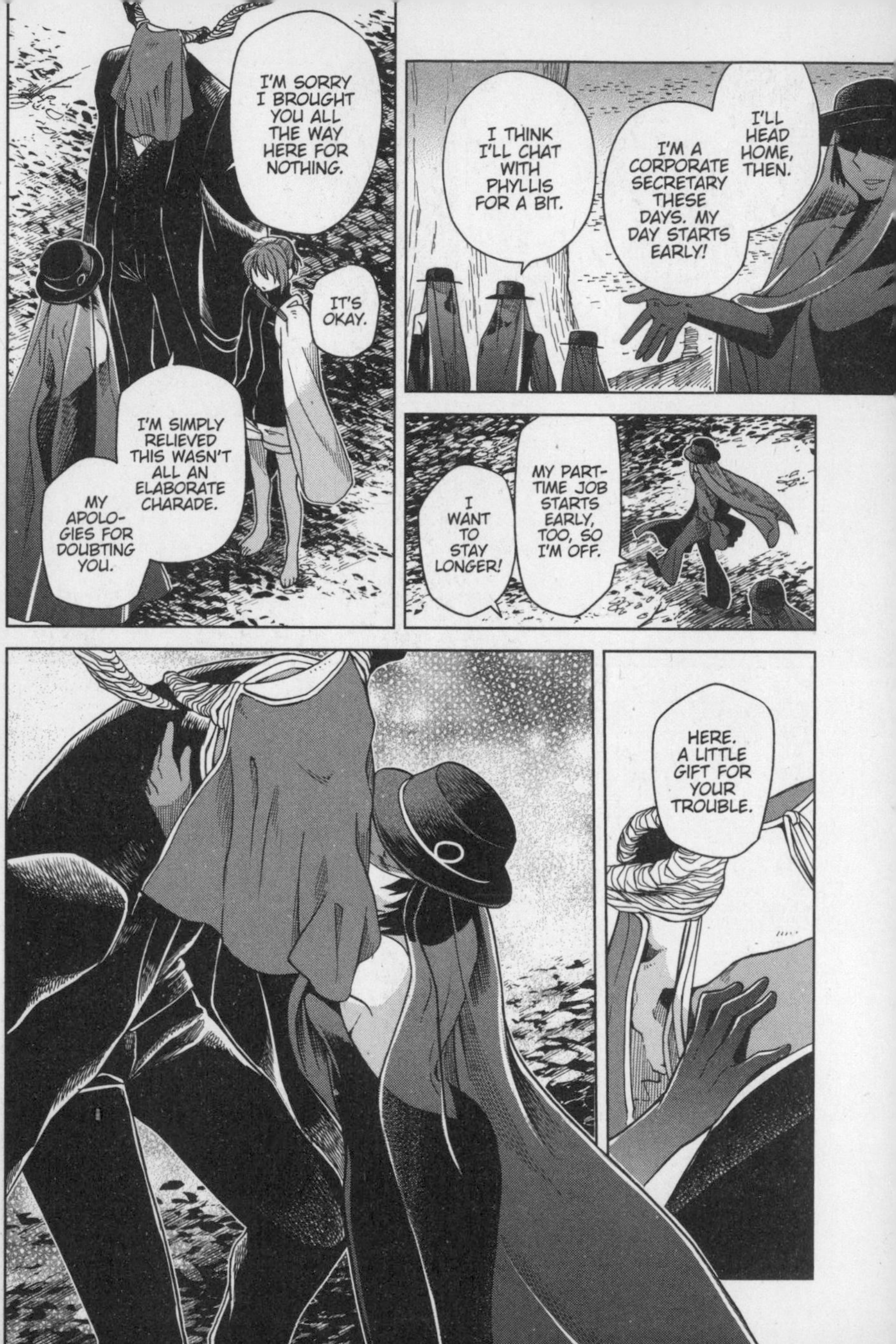
I'LL HEAD HOME, THEN.
I'M A CORPORATE SECRETARY THESE DAYS. MY DAY STARTS EARLY!
I THINK I'LL CHAT WITH PHYLLIS FOR A BIT.
MY PART-TIME JOB STARTS EARLY, TOO, SO I'M OFF.
I WANT TO STAY LONGER!
I'M SORRY I BROUGHT YOU ALL THE WAY HERE FOR NOTHING.
IT'S OKAY.
I'M SIMPLY RELIEVED THIS WASN'T ALL AN ELABORATE CHARADE.
MY APOLOGIES FOR DOUBTING YOU.
HERE. A LITTLE GIFT FOR YOUR TROUBLE.

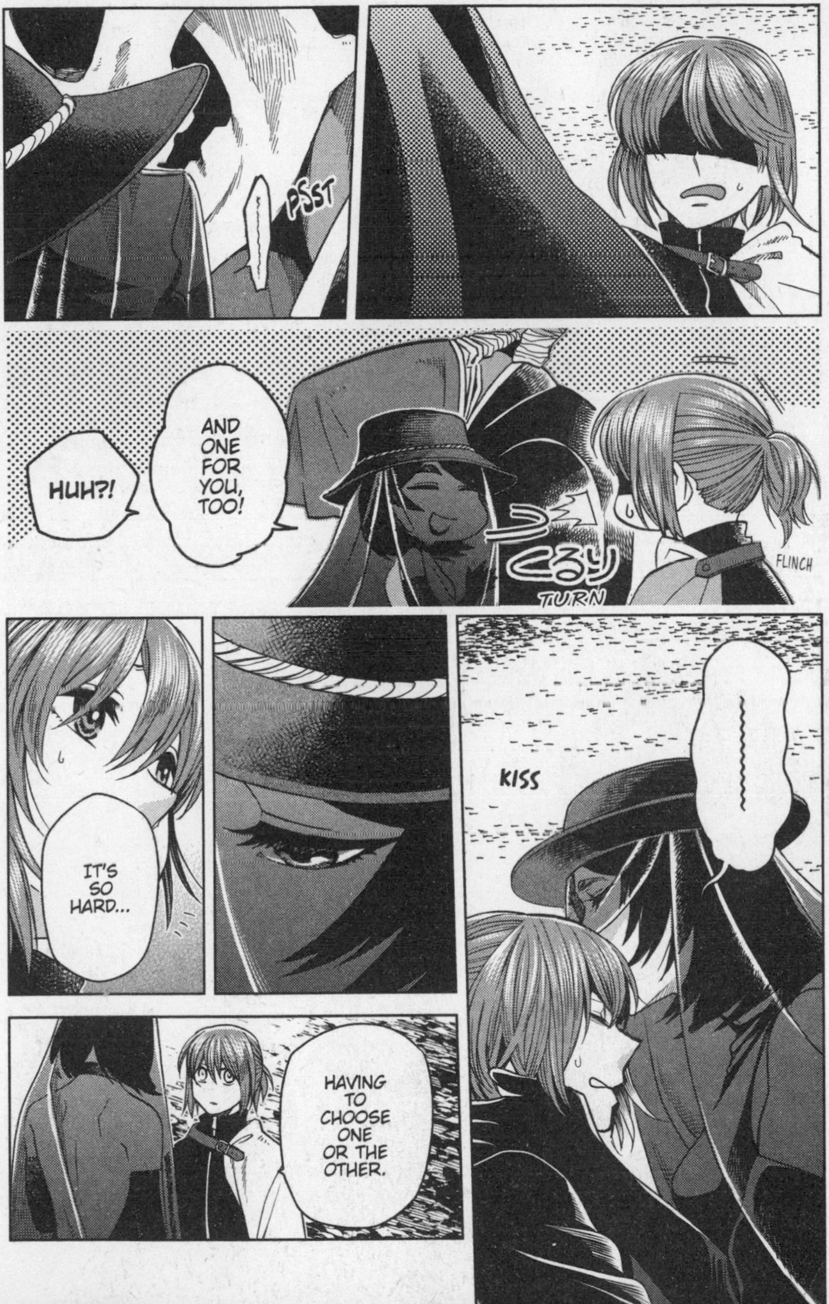
PSST
FLINCH
くるり
TURN
AND ONE FOR YOU, TOO!
HUH?!
KISS
IT'S SO HARD...
HAVING TO CHOOSE ONE OR THE OTHER.

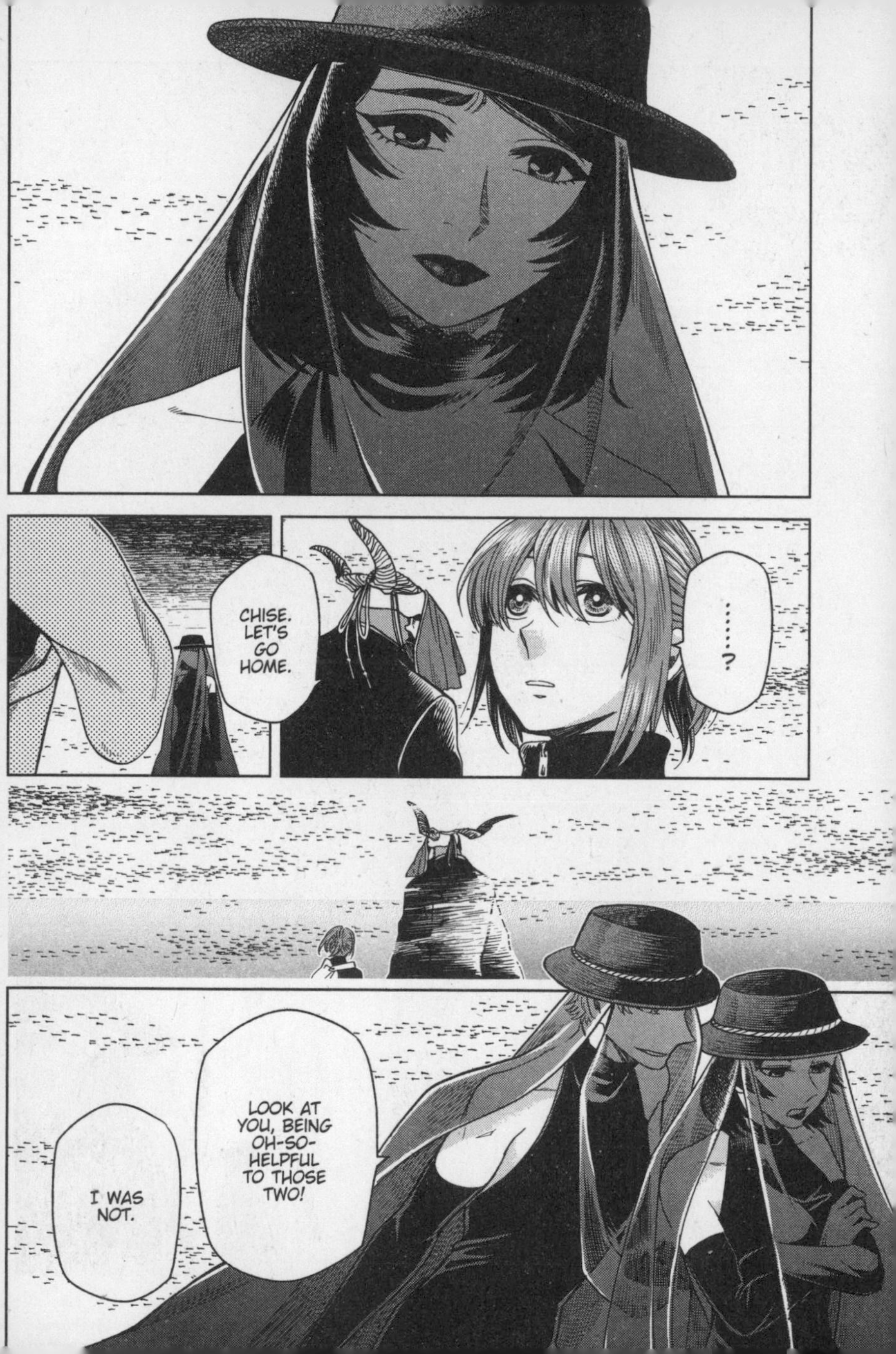
......?
CHISE. LET'S GO HOME.
LOOK AT YOU, BEING OH-SO-HELPFUL TO THOSE TWO!
I WAS NOT.

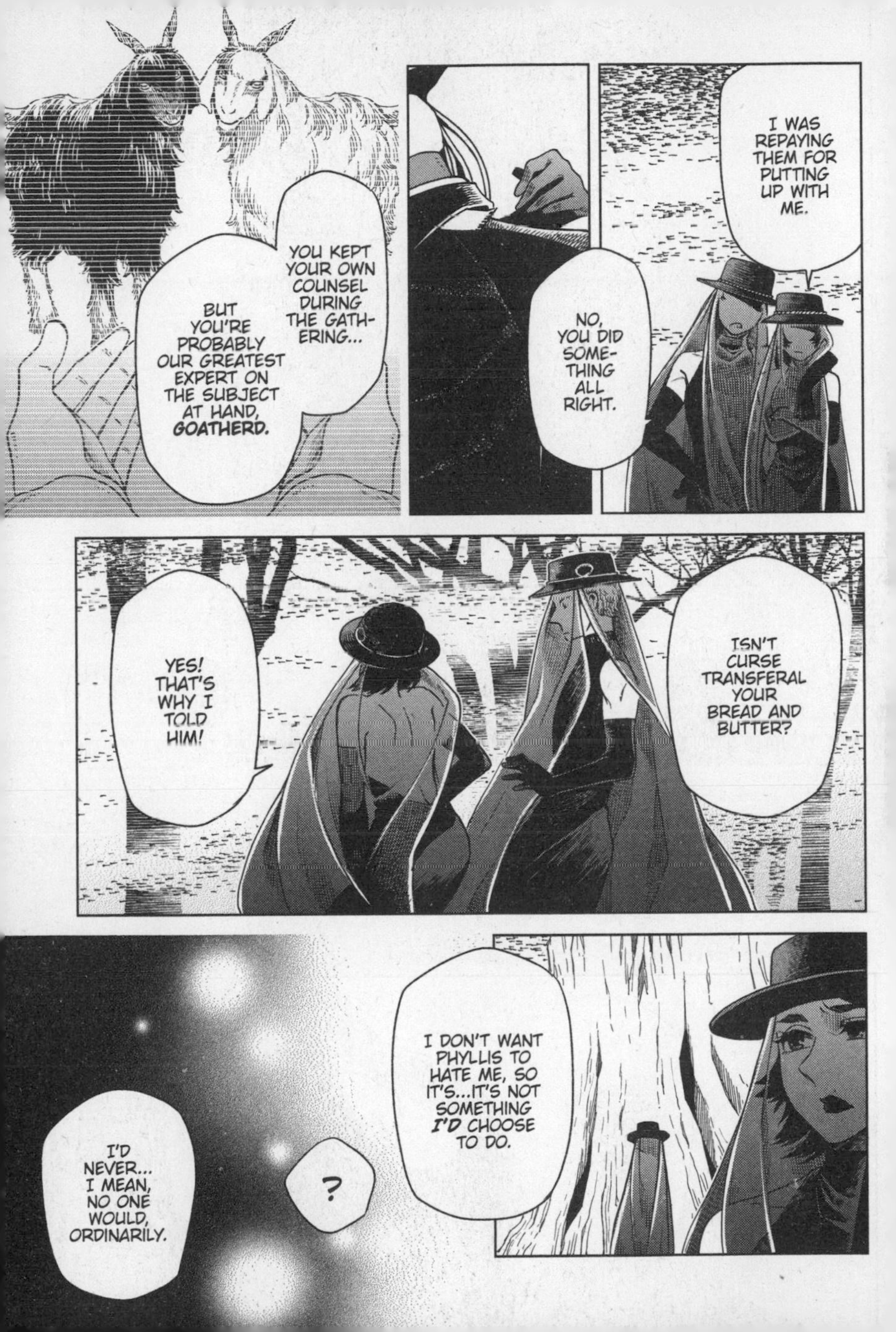
I WAS REPAYING THEM FOR PUTTING UP WITH ME.
NO, YOU DID SOMETHING ALL RIGHT.
YOU KEPT YOUR OWN COUNSEL DURING THE GATHERING...
BUT YOU'RE PROBABLY OUR GREATEST EXPERT ON THE SUBJECT AT HAND, **GOATHERD.**
ISN'T CURSE TRANSFERAL YOUR BREAD AND BUTTER?
YES! THAT'S WHY I TOLD HIM!
I DON'T WANT PHYLLIS TO HATE ME, SO IT'S...IT'S NOT SOMETHING ***I'D*** CHOOSE TO DO.
?
I'D NEVER... I MEAN, NO ONE WOULD, ORDINARILY.

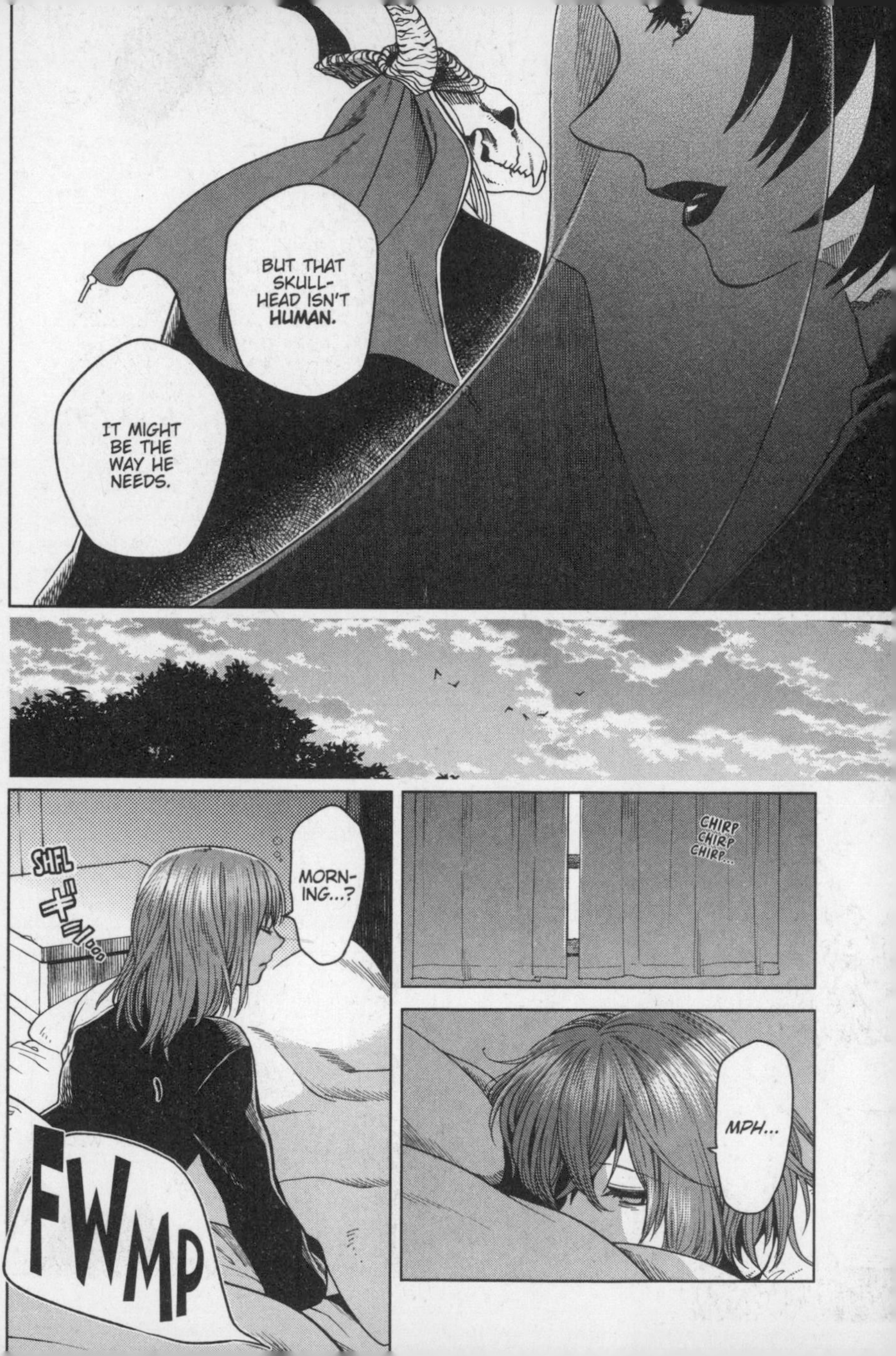
BUT THAT SKULL-HEAD ISN'T HUMAN.
IT MIGHT BE THE WAY HE NEEDS.
CHIRP CHIRP CHIRP...
MPH...
MORNING...?
SHFL
FWMP

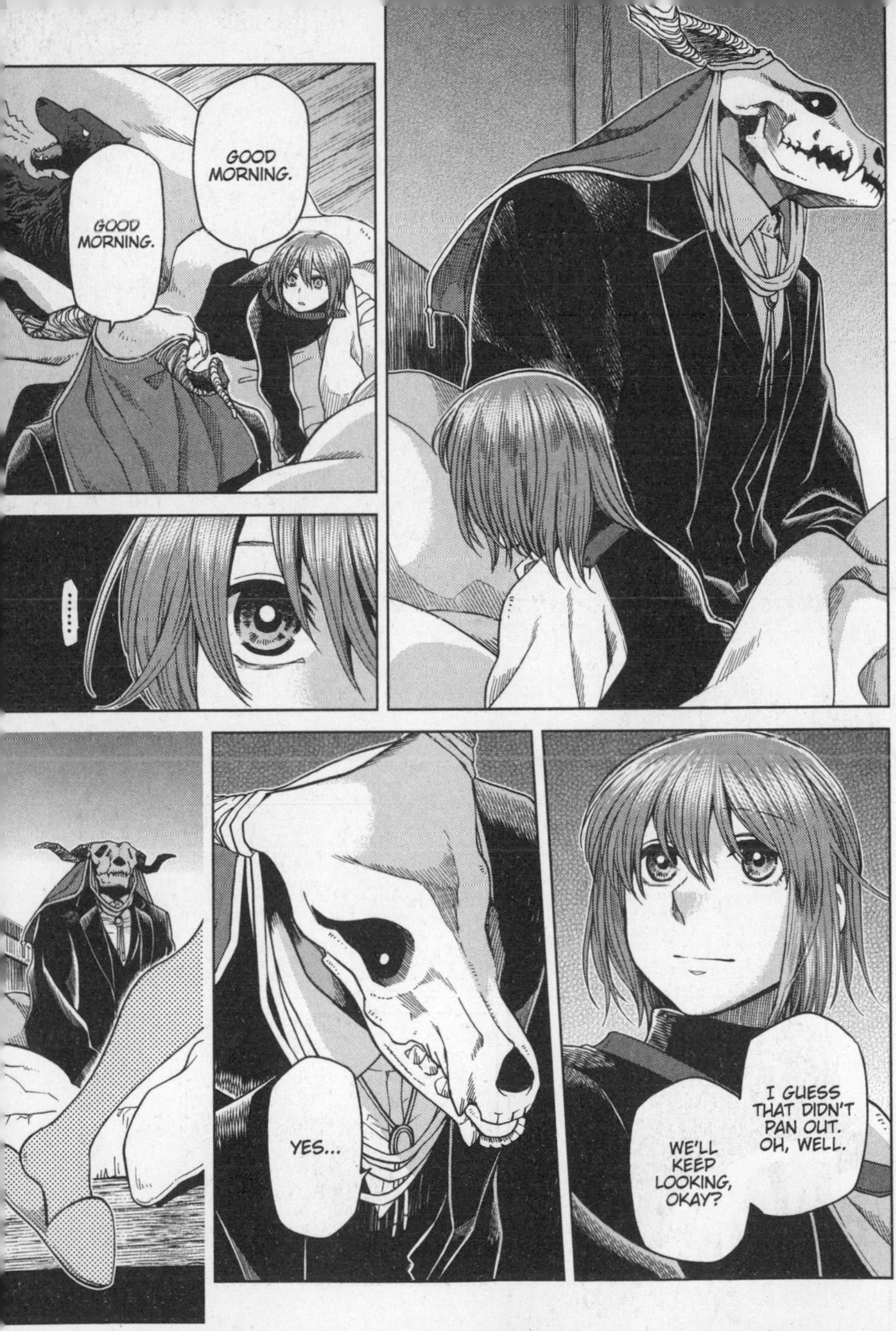
GOOD MORNING.
GOOD MORNING.
......
I GUESS THAT DIDN'T PAN OUT. OH, WELL.
WE'LL KEEP LOOKING, OKAY?
YES...

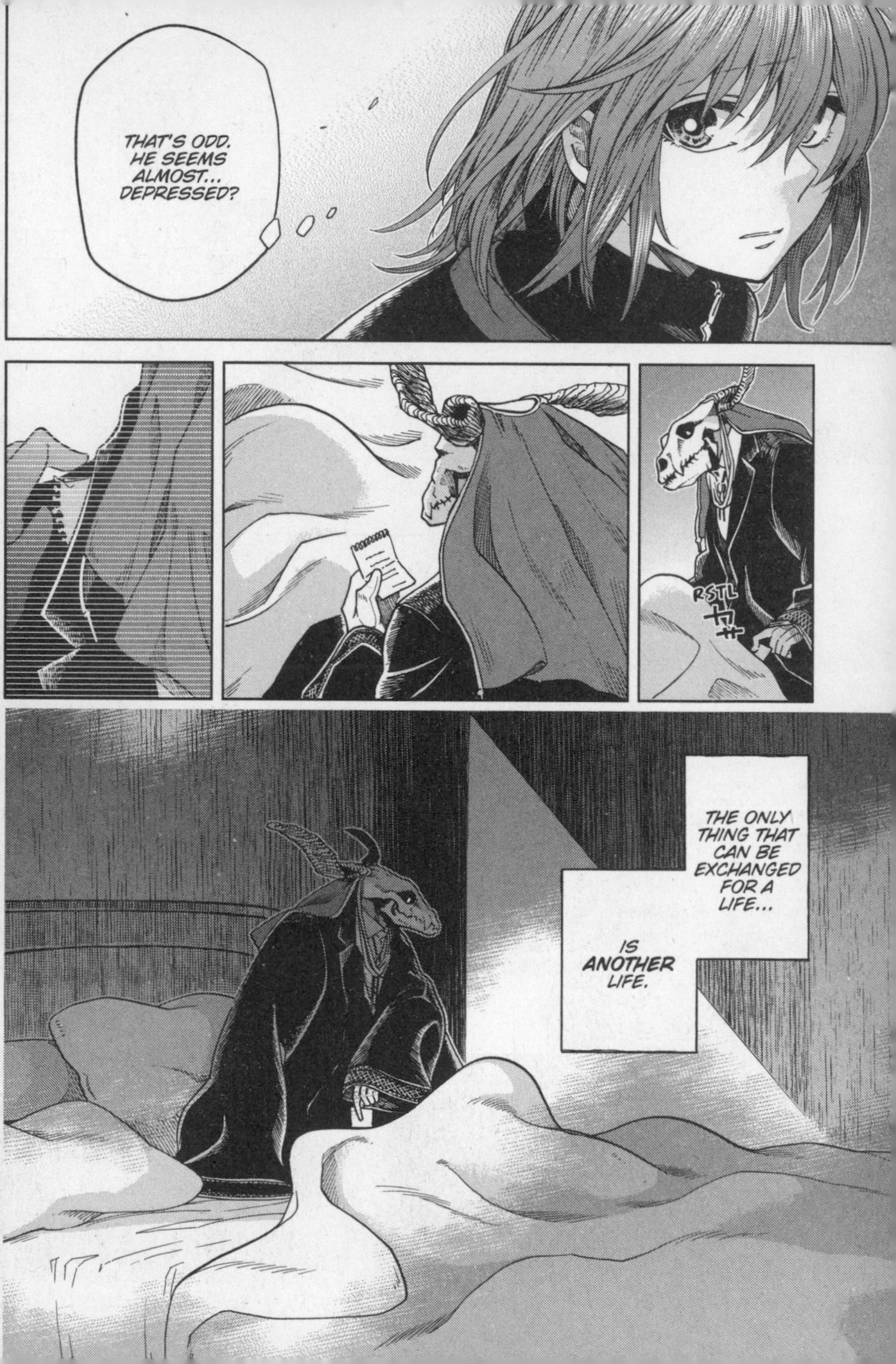
THAT'S ODD. HE SEEMS ALMOST... DEPRESSED?
RSTL
THE ONLY THING THAT CAN BE EXCHANGED FOR A LIFE...
IS ANOTHER LIFE.

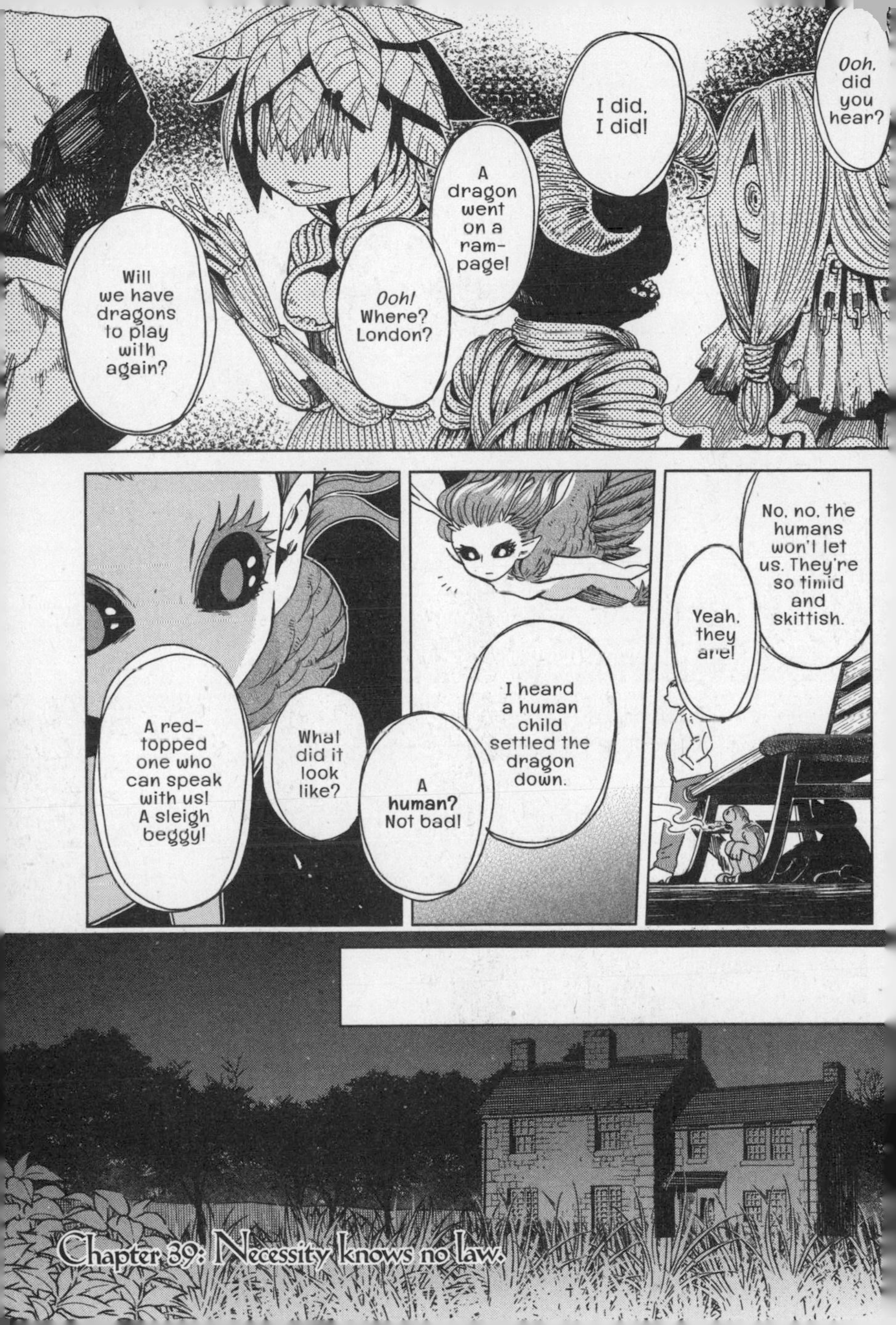

Ooh, did you hear?
I did, I did!
A dragon went on a ram-page!
Ooh! Where? London?
Will we have dragons to play with again?
No, no, the humans won't let us. They're so timid and skittish.
Yeah, they are!
I heard a human child settled the dragon down.
A human? Not bad!
What did it look like?
A red-topped one who can speak with us! A sleigh beggy!
Chapter 39: Necessity knows no law.

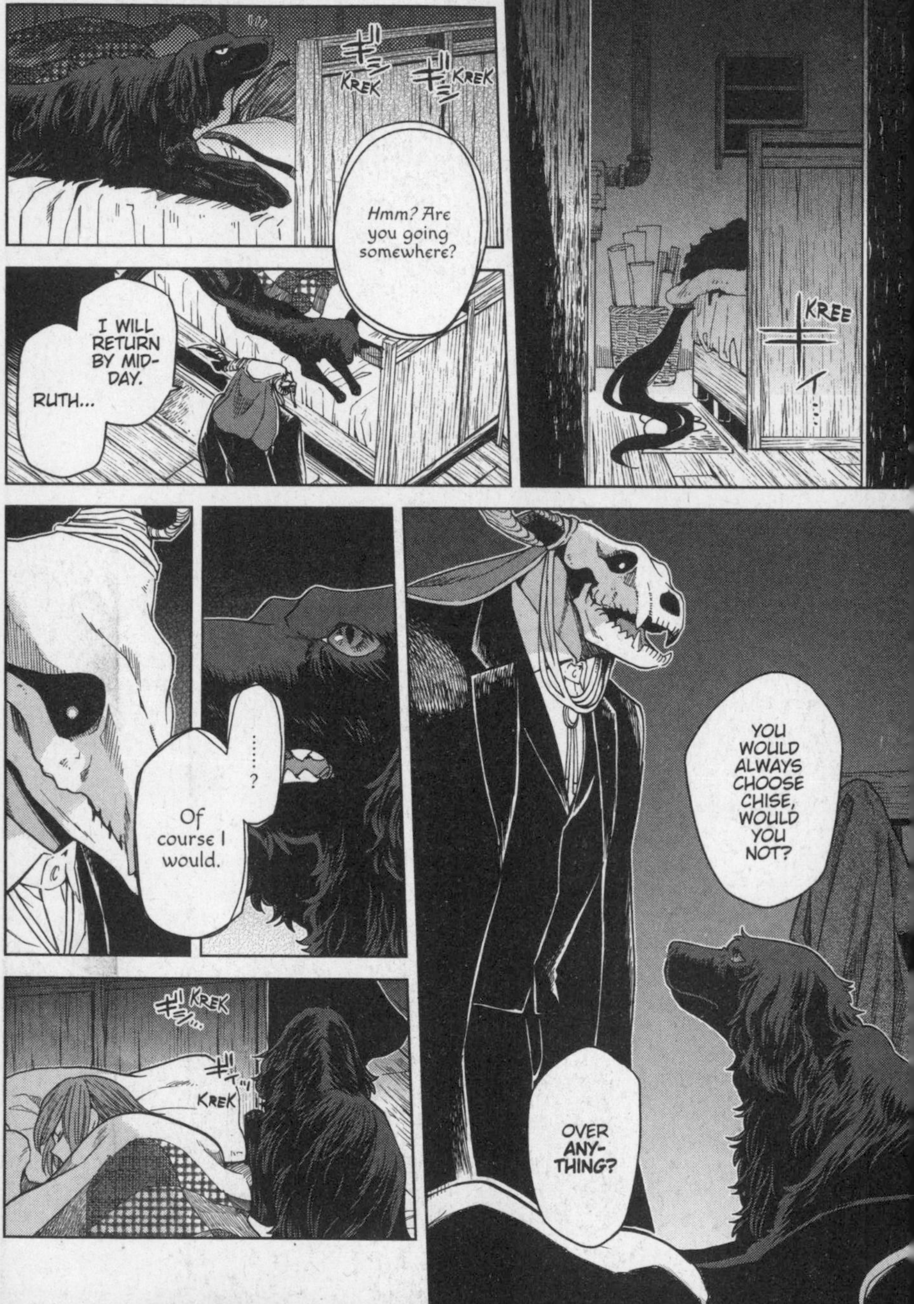
KREE
KREK
KREK
Hmm? Are you going somewhere?
I WILL RETURN BY MID-DAY.
RUTH...
YOU WOULD ALWAYS CHOOSE CHISE, WOULD YOU NOT?
OVER ANY-THING?
......?
Of course I would.
KREK
KREK

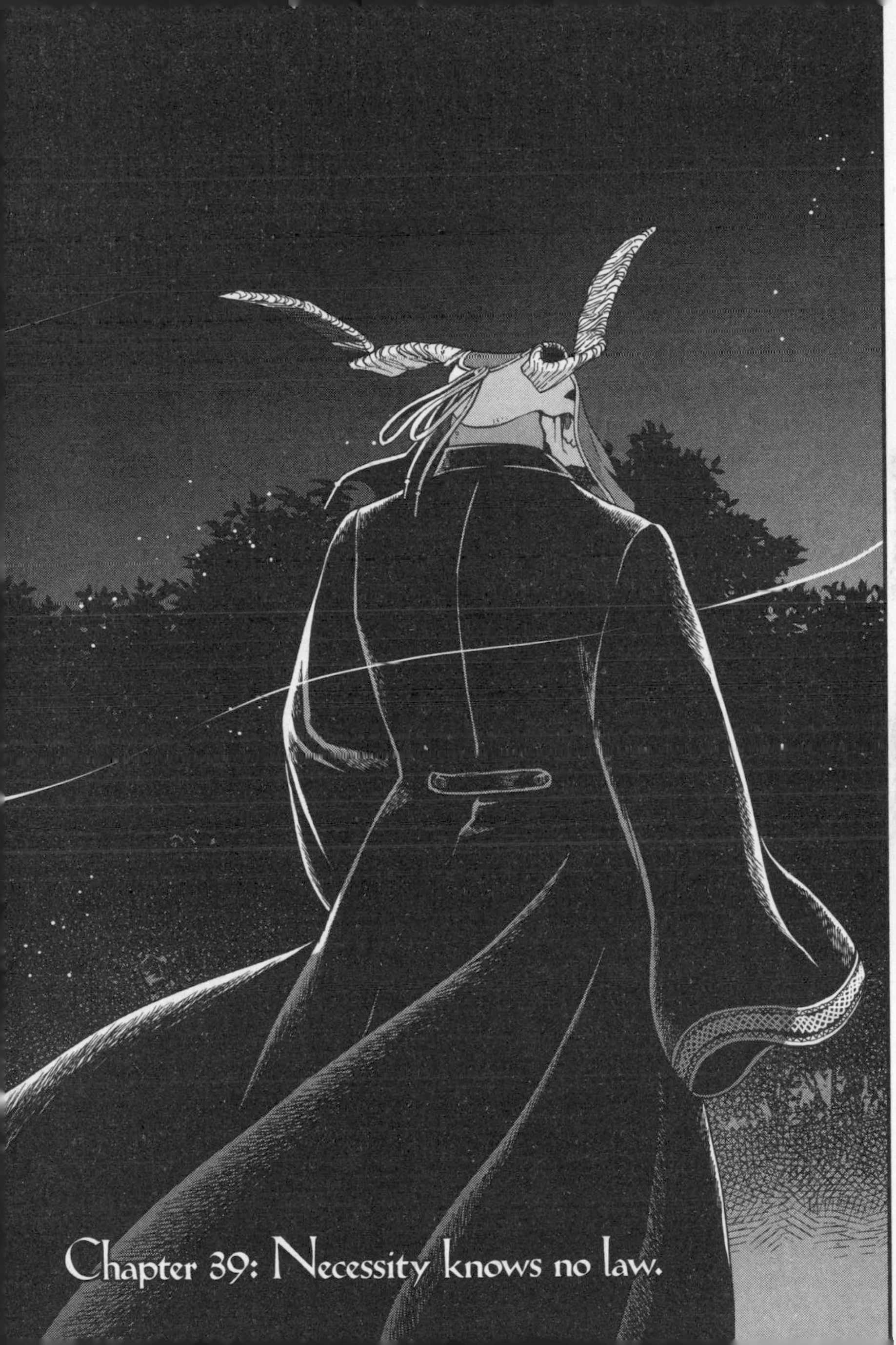
Chapter 39: Necessity knows no law.

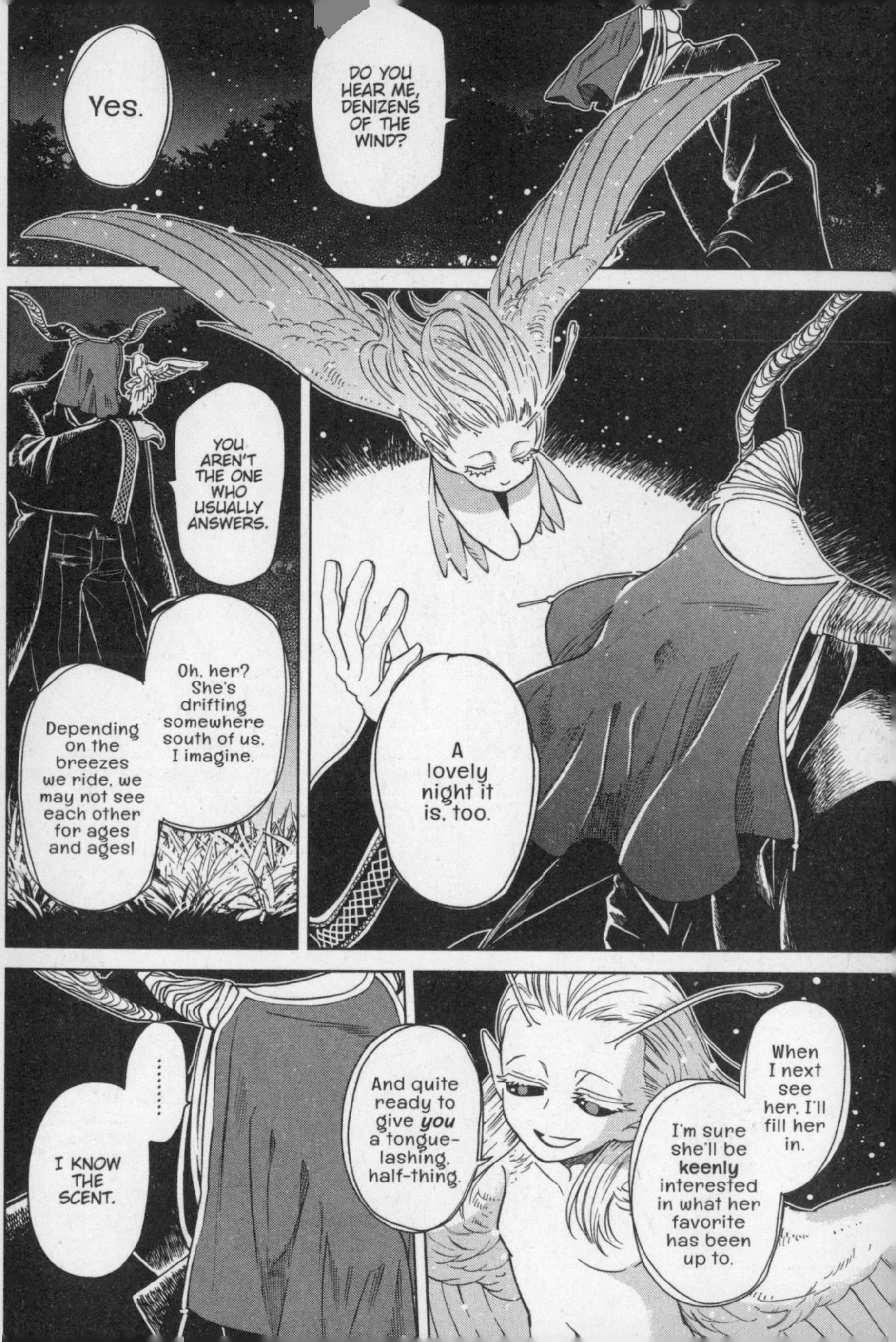

DO YOU HEAR ME, DENIZENS OF THE WIND?
Yes.
A lovely night it is, too.
YOU AREN'T THE ONE WHO USUALLY ANSWERS.
Oh, her? She's drifting somewhere south of us, I imagine.
Depending on the breezes we ride, we may not see each other for ages and ages!
When I next see her, I'll fill her in.
I'm sure she'll be **keenly** interested in what her favorite has been up to.
And quite ready to give ***you*** a tongue-lashing, half-thing.
......
I KNOW THE SCENT.

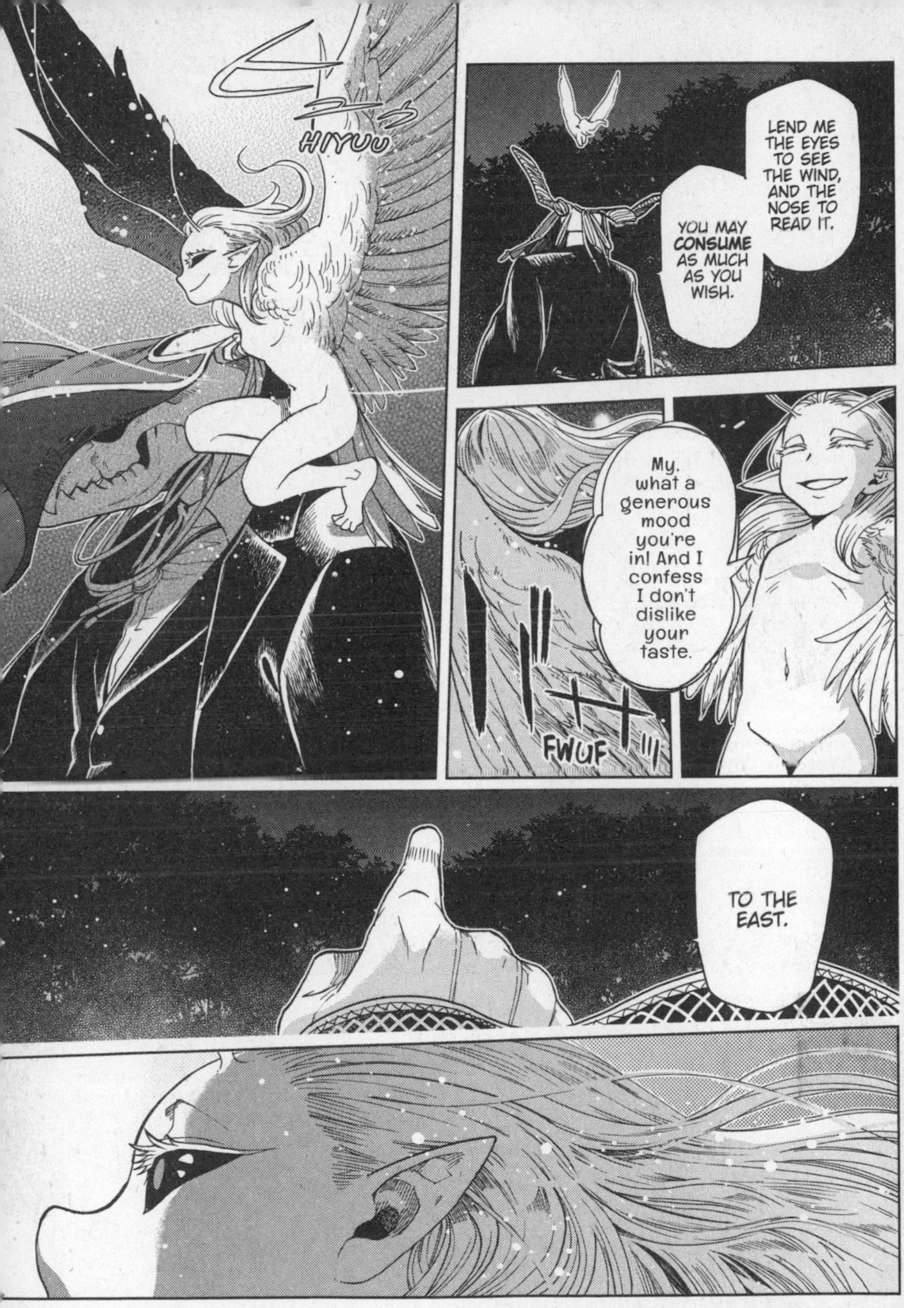
LEND ME THE EYES TO SEE THE WIND, AND THE NOSE TO READ IT.
YOU MAY CONSUME AS MUCH AS YOU WISH.
My, what a generous mood you're in! And I confess I don't dislike your taste.
FWUF
HIYUU
TO THE EAST.

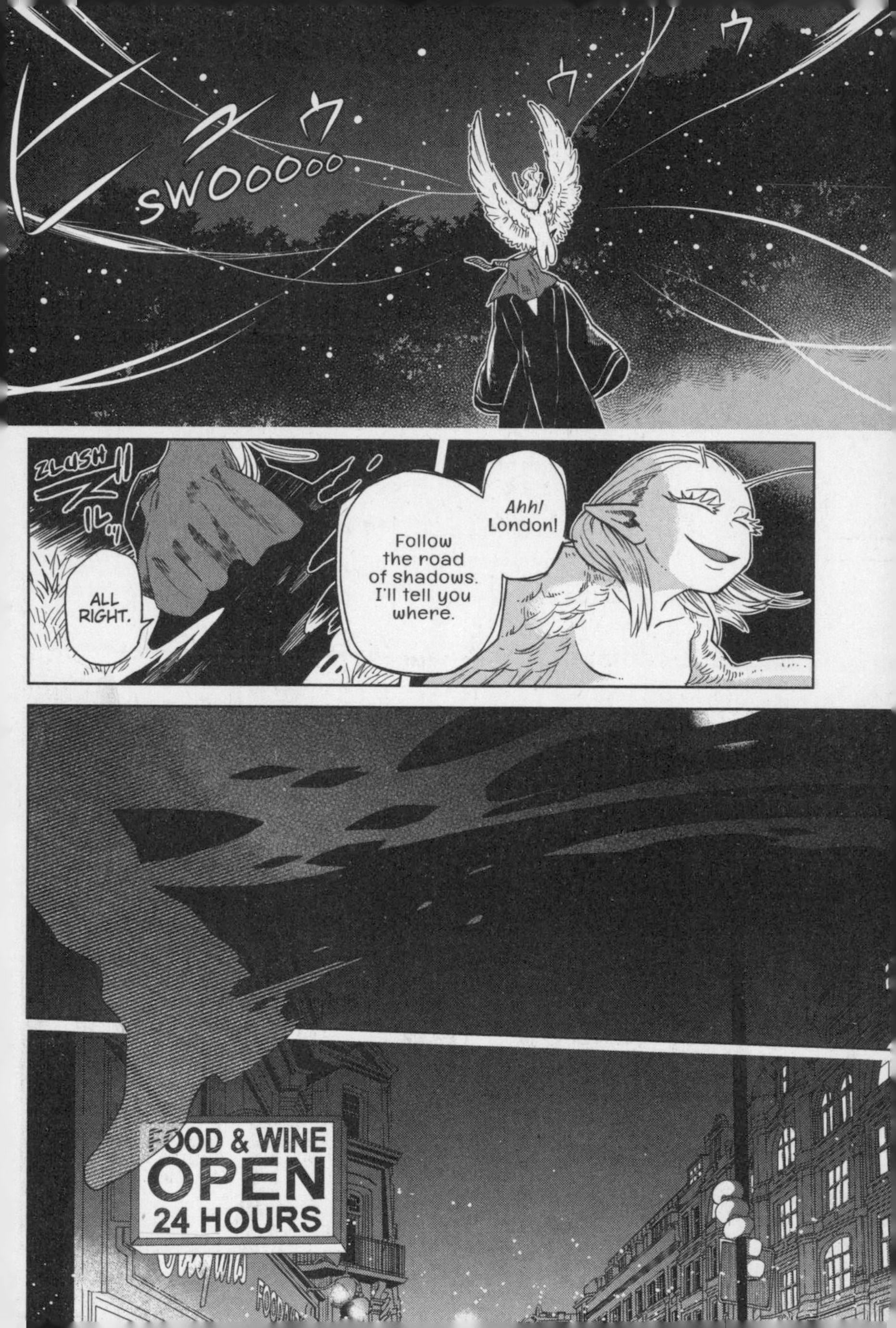
SWOOOOO
Ahh! London!
Follow the road of shadows. I'll tell you where.
ZLUSH
ALL RIGHT.
FOOD & WINE
OPEN
24 HOURS

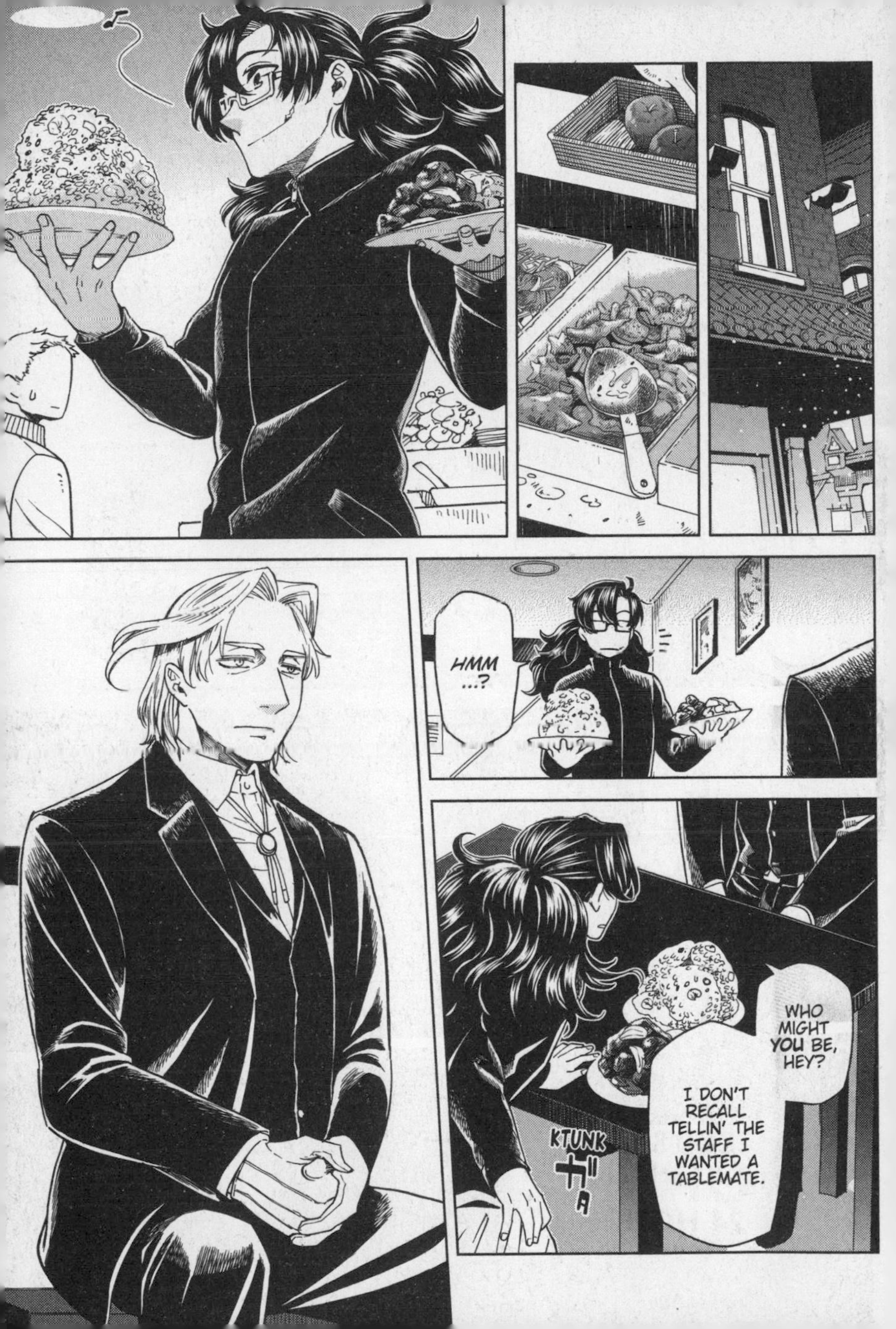

HMM ...?
WHO MIGHT YOU BE, HEY?
I DON'T RECALL TELLIN' THE STAFF I WANTED A TABLEMATE.
KTUNK

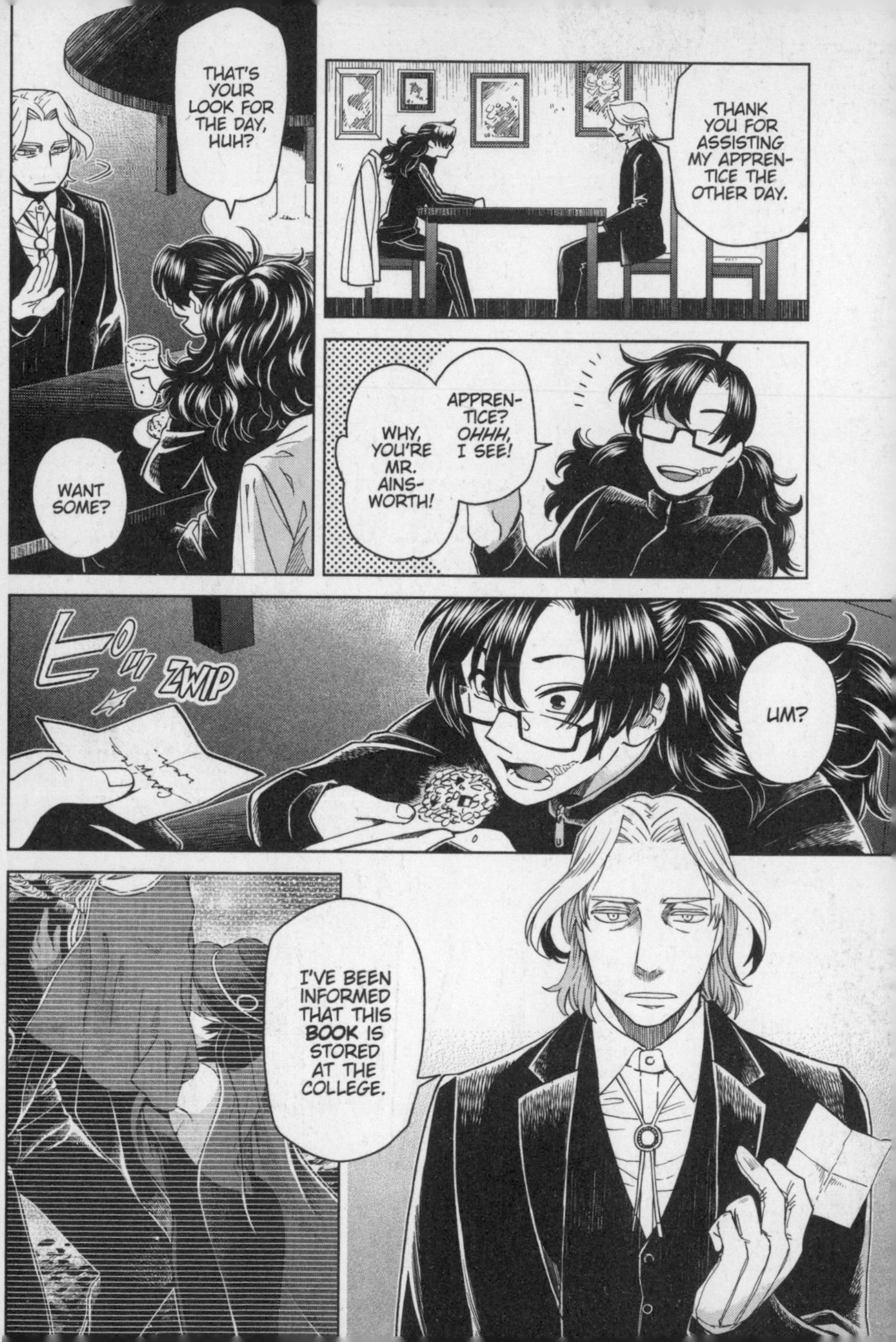
THANK YOU FOR ASSISTING MY APPRENTICE THE OTHER DAY.
APPRENTICE? OHHH, I SEE!
WHY, YOU'RE MR. AINSWORTH!
THAT'S YOUR LOOK FOR THE DAY, HUH?
WANT SOME?
UM?
ZWIP
I'VE BEEN INFORMED THAT THIS BOOK IS STORED AT THE COLLEGE.

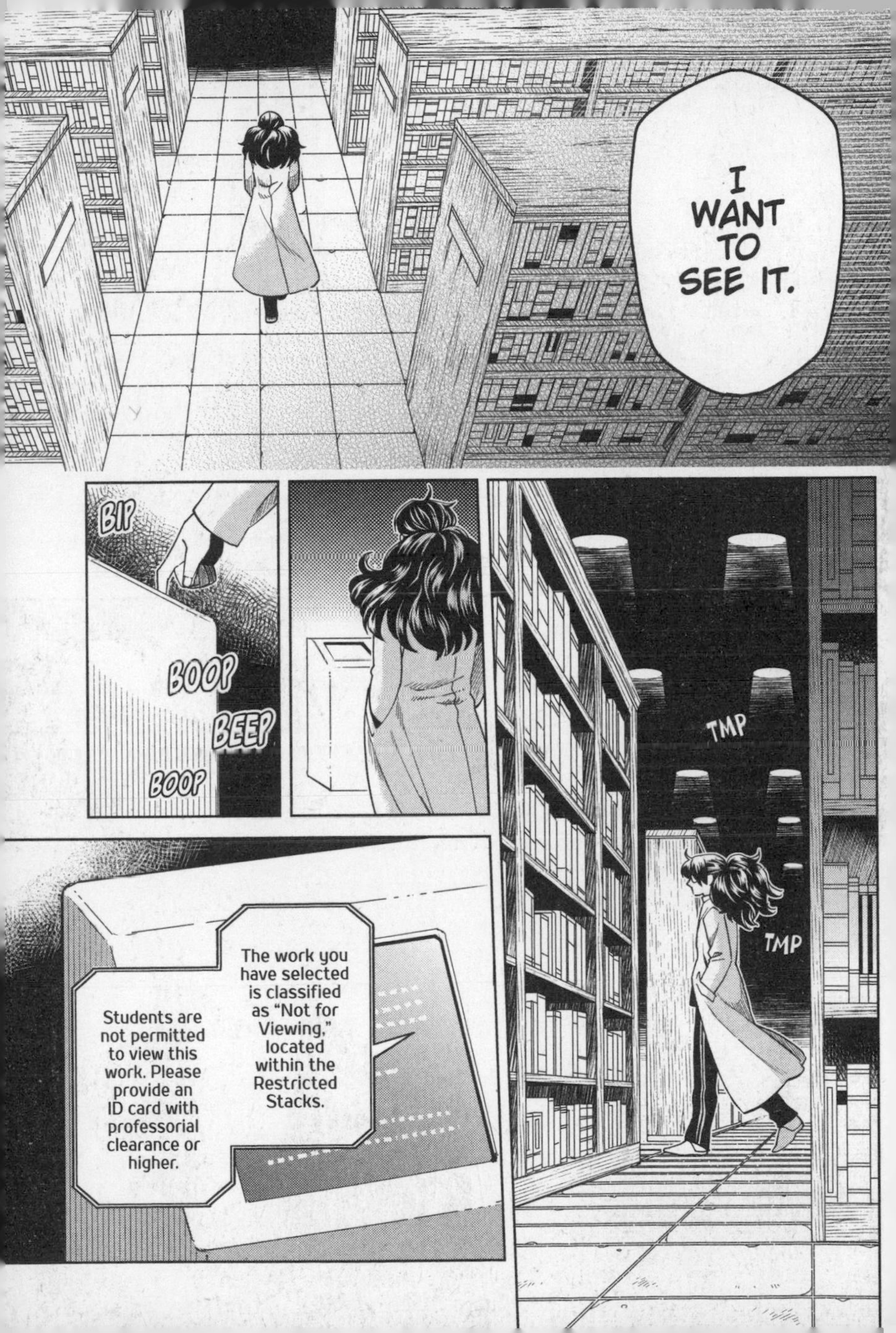
I WANT TO SEE IT.
TMP
TMP
BIP
BOOP
BEEP
BOOP
The work you have selected is classified as "Not for Viewing," located within the Restricted Stacks.
Students are not permitted to view this work. Please provide an ID card with professorial clearance or higher.

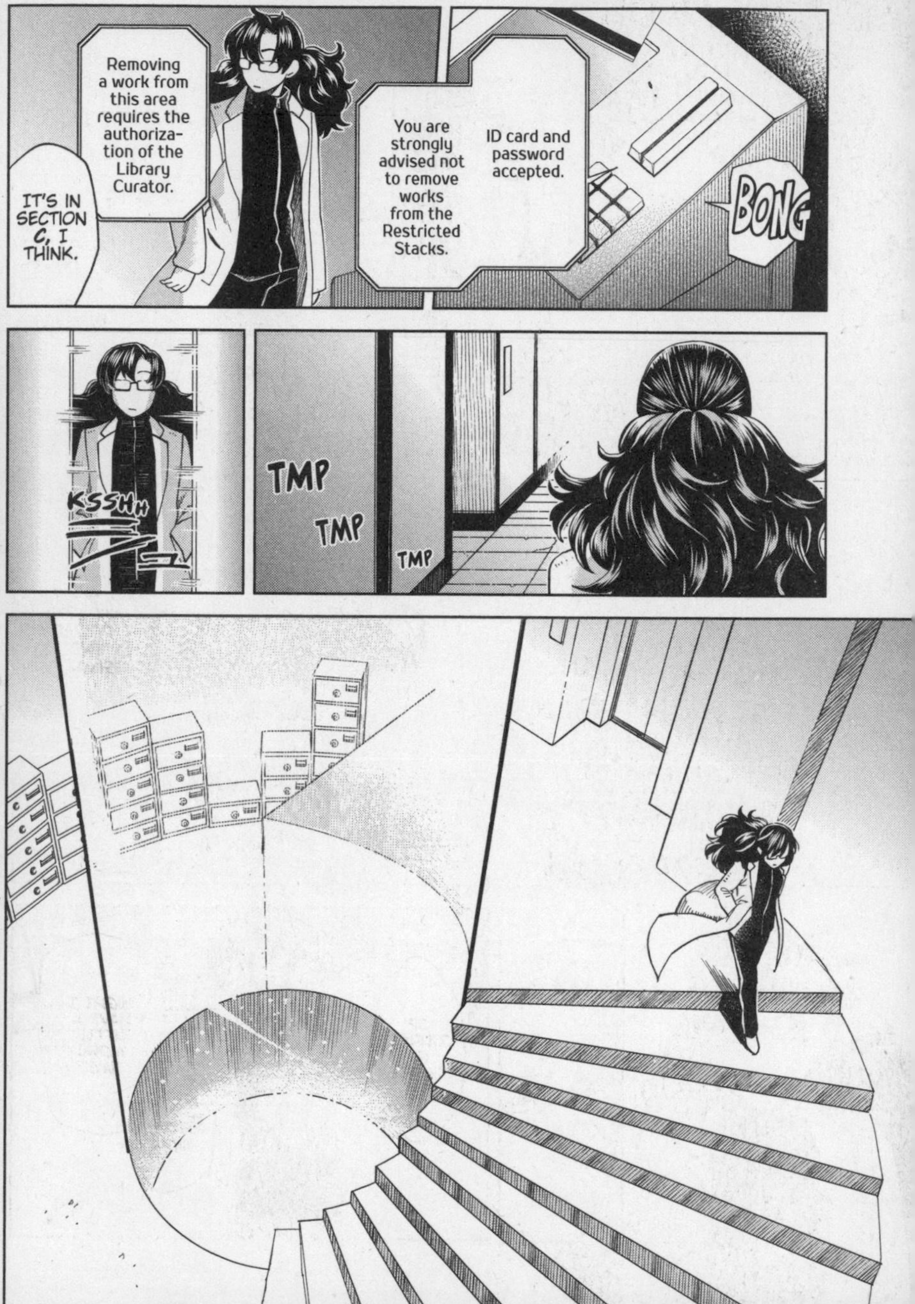
BONG
ID card and password accepted.
You are strongly advised not to remove works from the Restricted Stacks.
Removing a work from this area requires the authorization of the Library Curator.
IT'S IN SECTION C, I THINK.
TMP
TMP
TMP
KSSHH

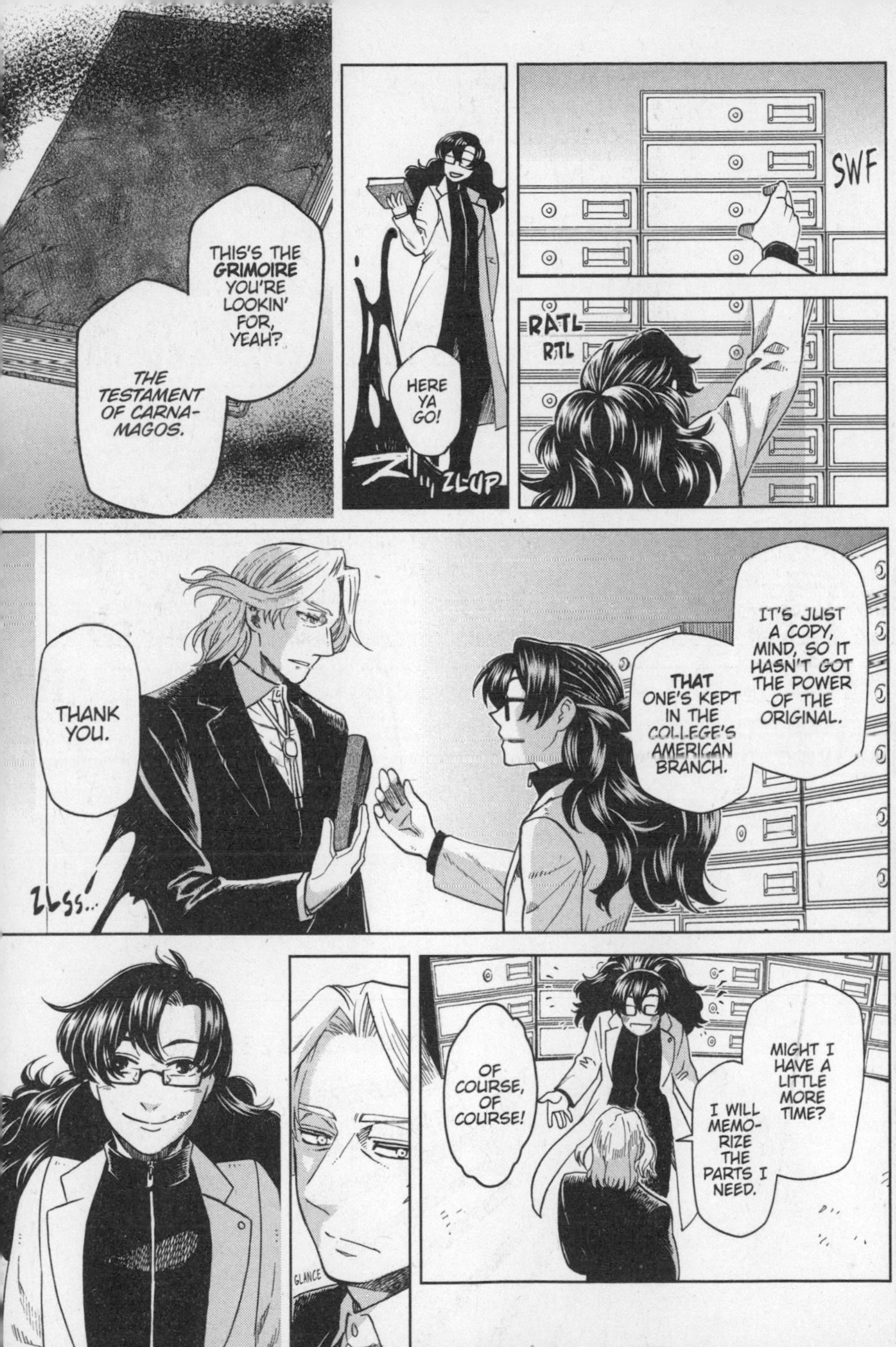
SWF
RATL
RTL
HERE YA GO!
ZLUP
THIS'S THE GRIMOIRE YOU'RE LOOKIN' FOR, YEAH?
THE TESTAMENT OF CARNA-MAGOS.
IT'S JUST A COPY, MIND, SO IT HASN'T GOT THE POWER OF THE ORIGINAL.
THAT ONE'S KEPT IN THE COLLEGE'S AMERICAN BRANCH.
THANK YOU.
ZLSS...
MIGHT I HAVE A LITTLE MORE TIME?
I WILL MEMO-RIZE THE PARTS I NEED.
OF COURSE, OF COURSE!
GLANCE

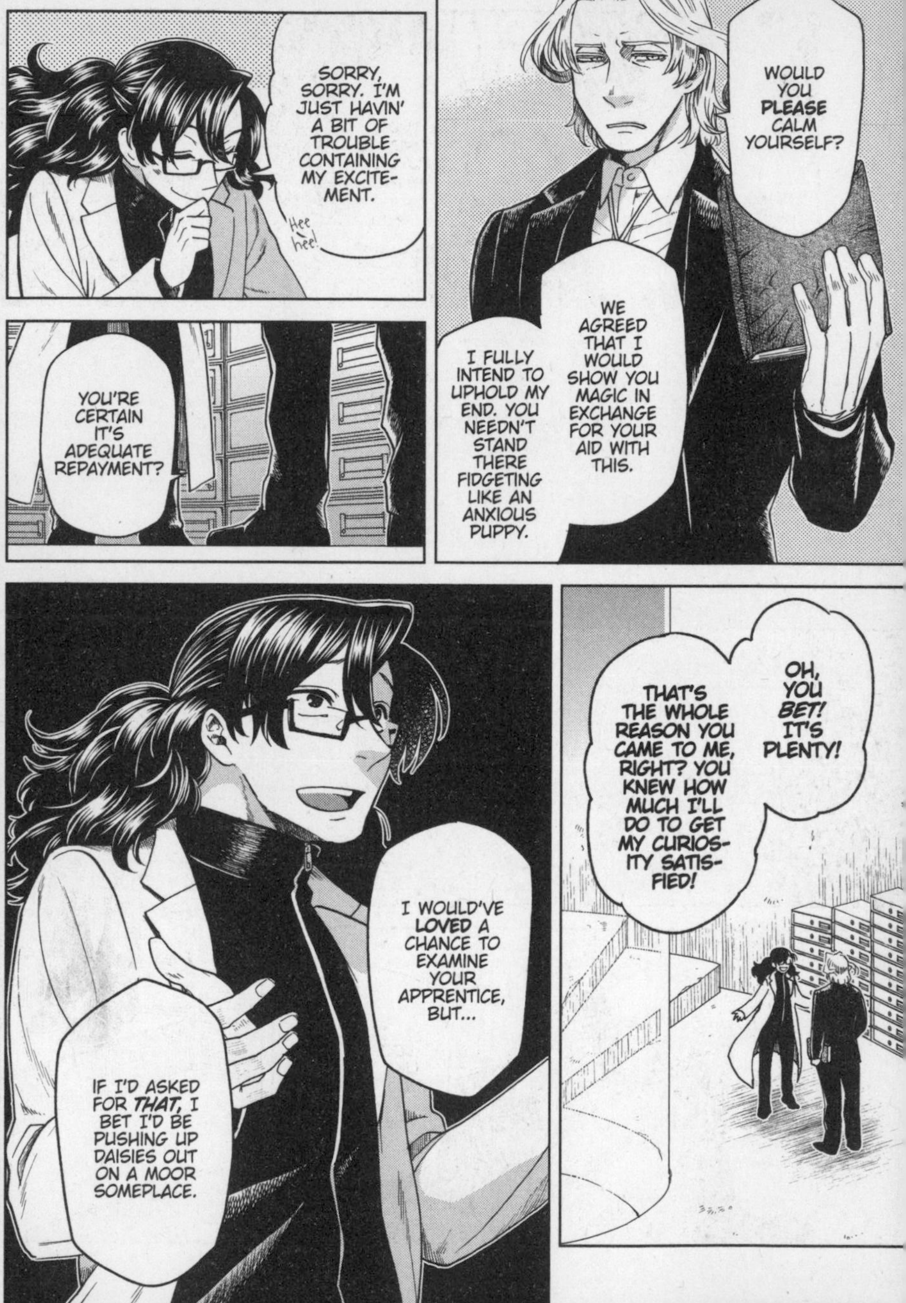
WOULD YOU PLEASE CALM YOURSELF?
WE AGREED THAT I WOULD SHOW YOU MAGIC IN EXCHANGE FOR YOUR AID WITH THIS.
I FULLY INTEND TO UPHOLD MY END. YOU NEEDN'T STAND THERE FIDGETING LIKE AN ANXIOUS PUPPY.
SORRY, SORRY. I'M JUST HAVIN' A BIT OF TROUBLE CONTAINING MY EXCITE-MENT.
Hee hee!
YOU'RE CERTAIN IT'S ADEQUATE REPAYMENT?
OH, YOU BET! IT'S PLENTY!
THAT'S THE WHOLE REASON YOU CAME TO ME, RIGHT? YOU KNEW HOW MUCH I'LL DO TO GET MY CURIOS-ITY SATIS-FIED!
I WOULD'VE LOVED A CHANCE TO EXAMINE YOUR APPRENTICE, BUT...
IF I'D ASKED FOR THAT, I BET I'D BE PUSHING UP DAISIES OUT ON A MOOR SOMEPLACE.

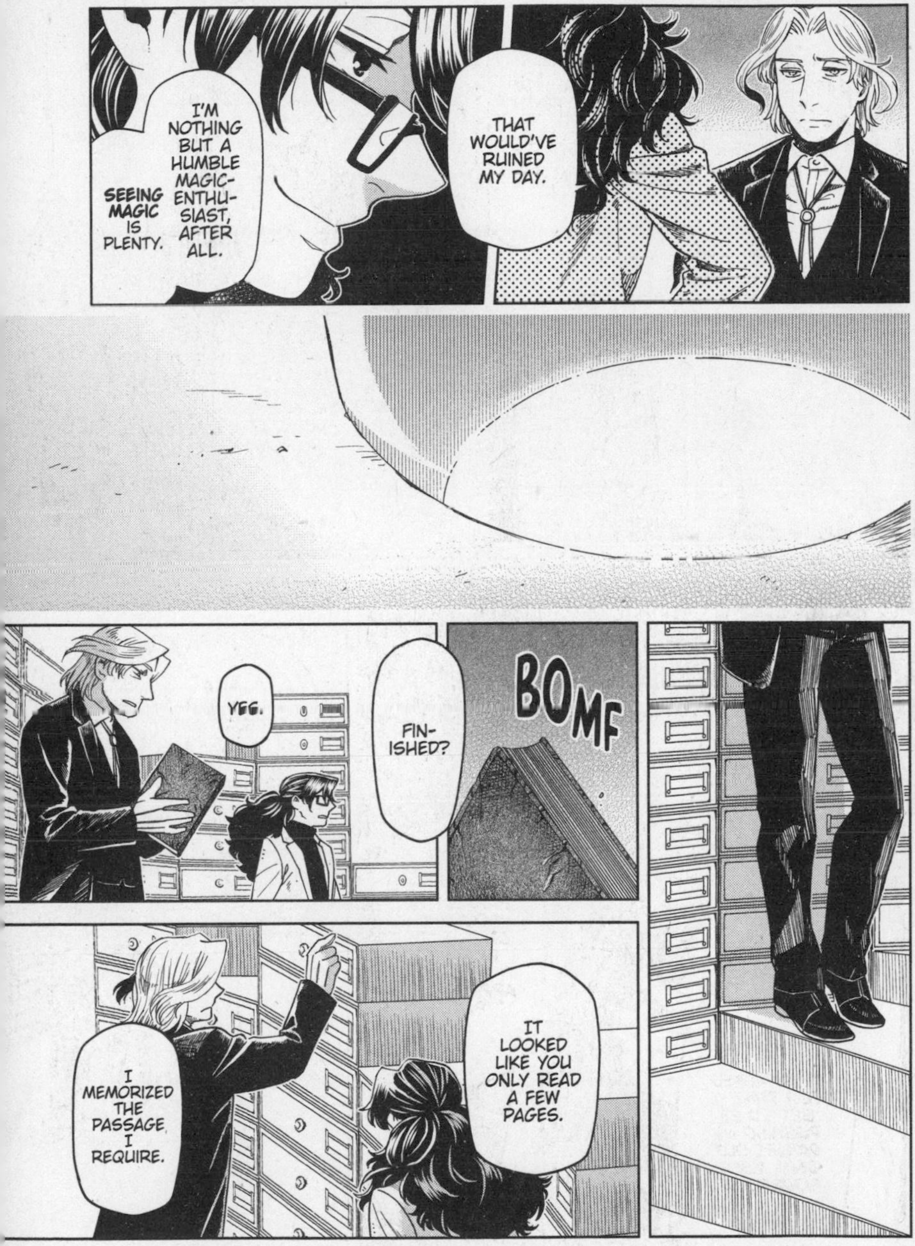
THAT WOULD'VE RUINED MY DAY.
I'M NOTHING BUT A HUMBLE MAGIC-ENTHUSIAST, AFTER ALL.
SEEING MAGIC IS PLENTY.
BOMF
FIN-ISHED?
YES.
IT LOOKED LIKE YOU ONLY READ A FEW PAGES.
I MEMORIZED THE PASSAGE I REQUIRE.

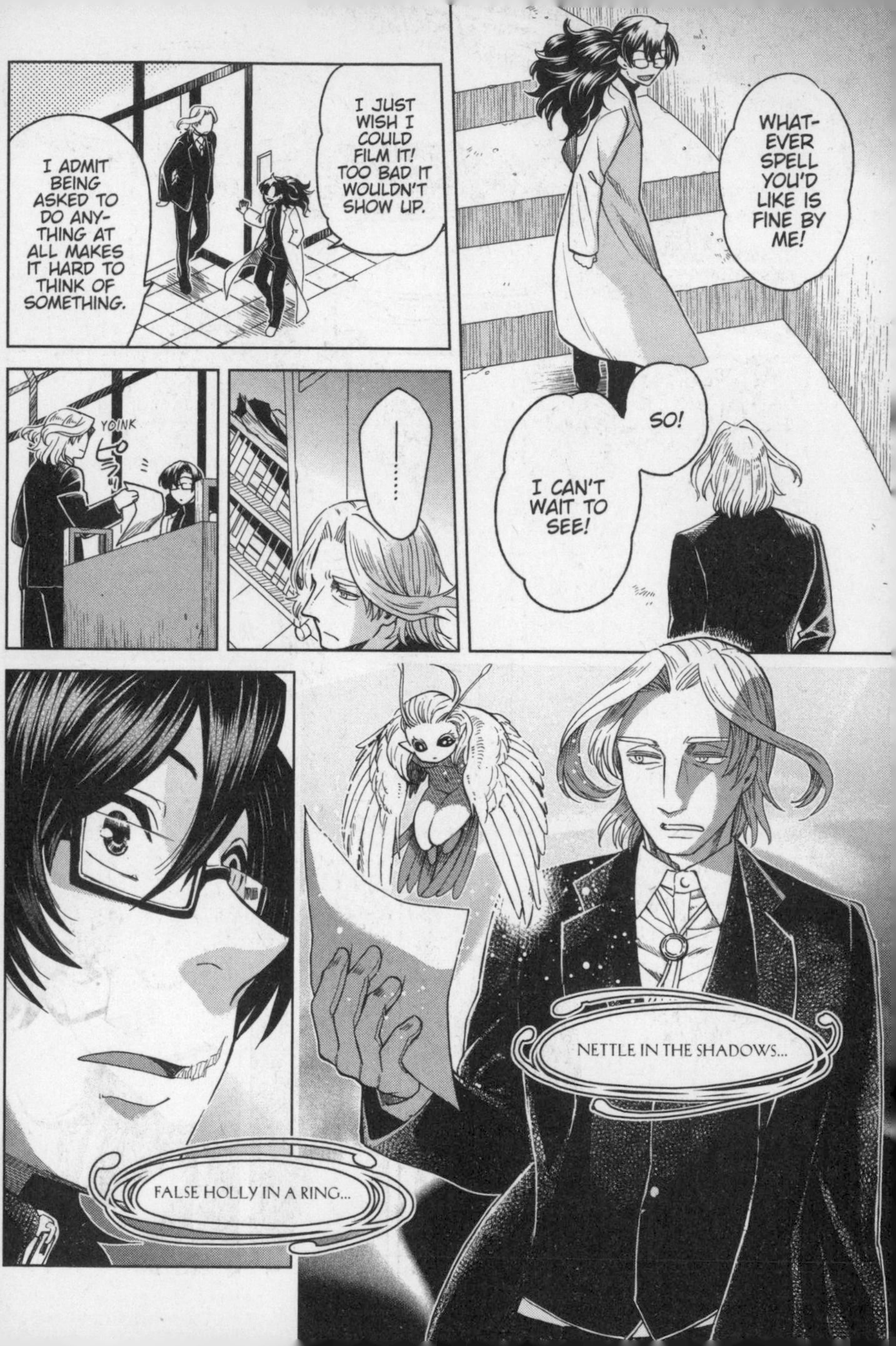
WHAT-EVER SPELL YOU'D LIKE IS FINE BY ME!
SO!
I CAN'T WAIT TO SEE!
I JUST WISH I COULD FILM IT! TOO BAD IT WOULDN'T SHOW UP.
I ADMIT BEING ASKED TO DO ANY-THING AT ALL MAKES IT HARD TO THINK OF SOMETHING.
!......
YOINK
NETTLE IN THE SHADOWS...
FALSE HOLLY IN A RING...

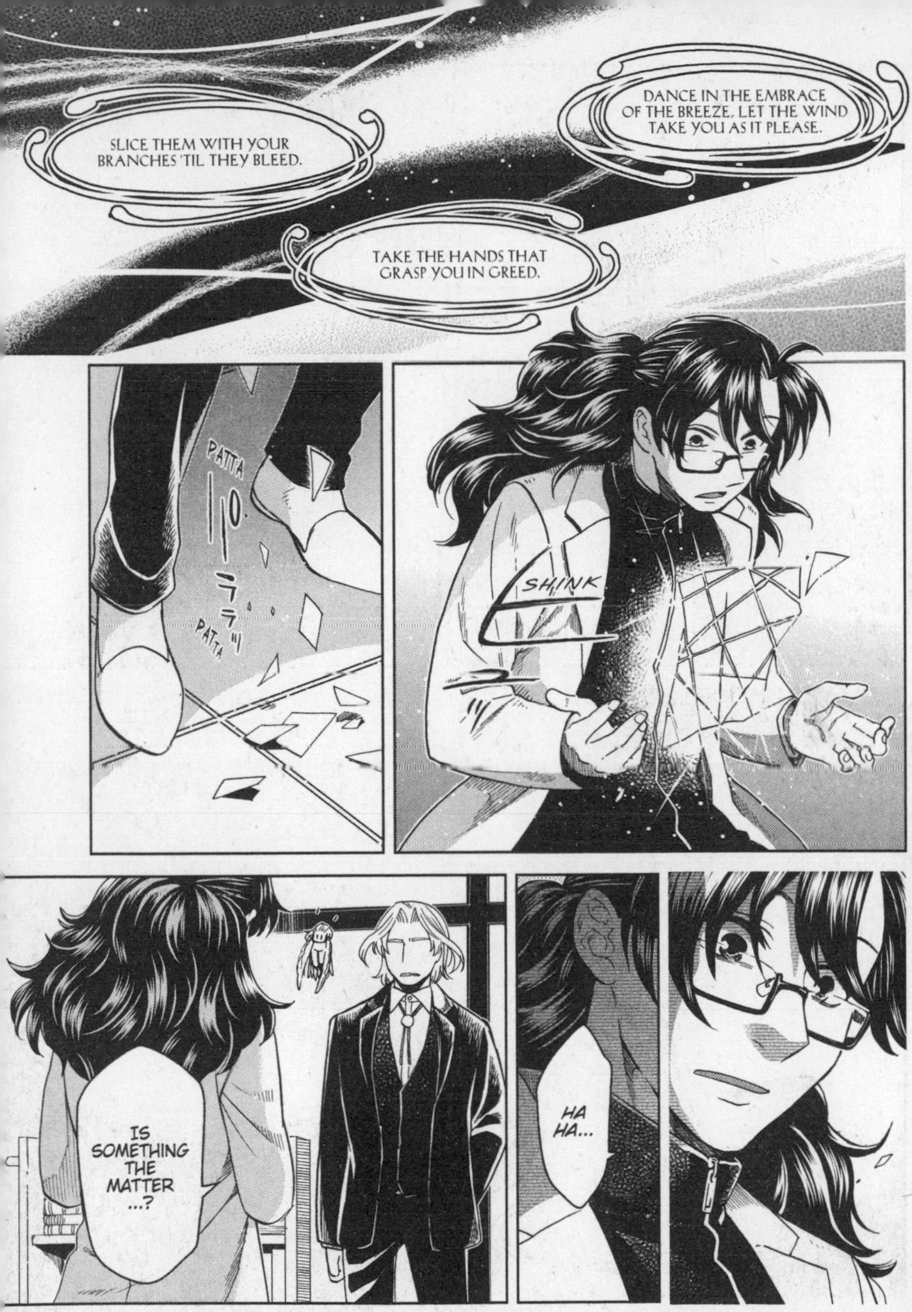
DANCE IN THE EMBRACE OF THE BREEZE, LET THE WIND TAKE YOU AS IT PLEASE.
SLICE THEM WITH YOUR BRANCHES 'TIL THEY BLEED.
TAKE THE HANDS THAT GRASP YOU IN GREED.
SHINK
PATTA
PATTA
HA HA...
IS SOMETHING THE MATTER ...?

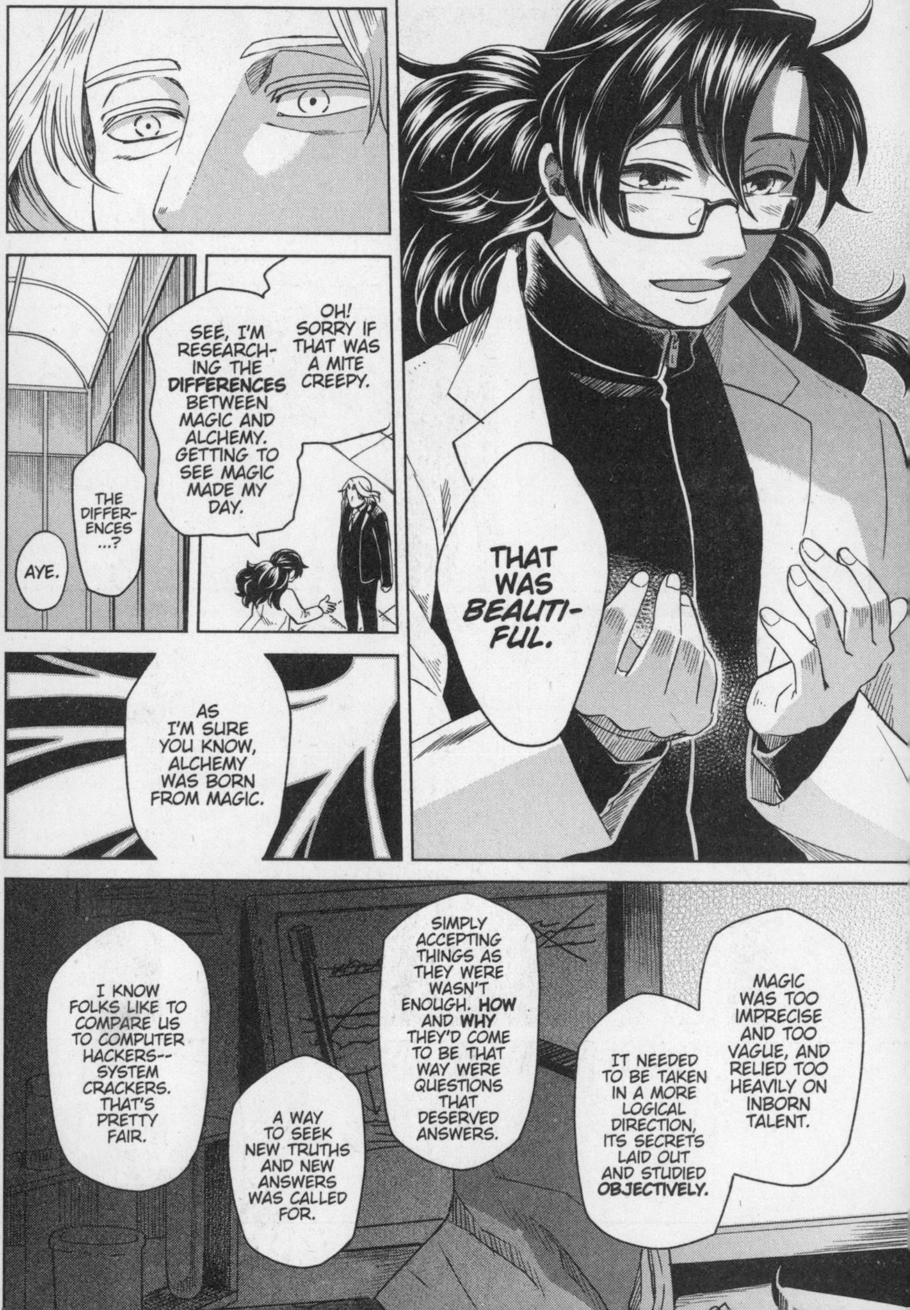
THAT WAS BEAUTIFUL.
OH! SORRY IF THAT WAS A MITE CREEPY.
SEE, I'M RESEARCHING THE DIFFERENCES BETWEEN MAGIC AND ALCHEMY. GETTING TO SEE MAGIC MADE MY DAY.
THE DIFFERENCES ...?
AYE.
AS I'M SURE YOU KNOW, ALCHEMY WAS BORN FROM MAGIC.
MAGIC WAS TOO IMPRECISE AND TOO VAGUE, AND RELIED TOO HEAVILY ON INBORN TALENT.
IT NEEDED TO BE TAKEN IN A MORE LOGICAL DIRECTION, ITS SECRETS LAID OUT AND STUDIED OBJECTIVELY.
SIMPLY ACCEPTING THINGS AS THEY WERE WASN'T ENOUGH. HOW AND WHY THEY'D COME TO BE THAT WAY WERE QUESTIONS THAT DESERVED ANSWERS.
A WAY TO SEEK NEW TRUTHS AND NEW ANSWERS WAS CALLED FOR.
I KNOW FOLKS LIKE TO COMPARE US TO COMPUTER HACKERS-- SYSTEM CRACKERS. THAT'S PRETTY FAIR.

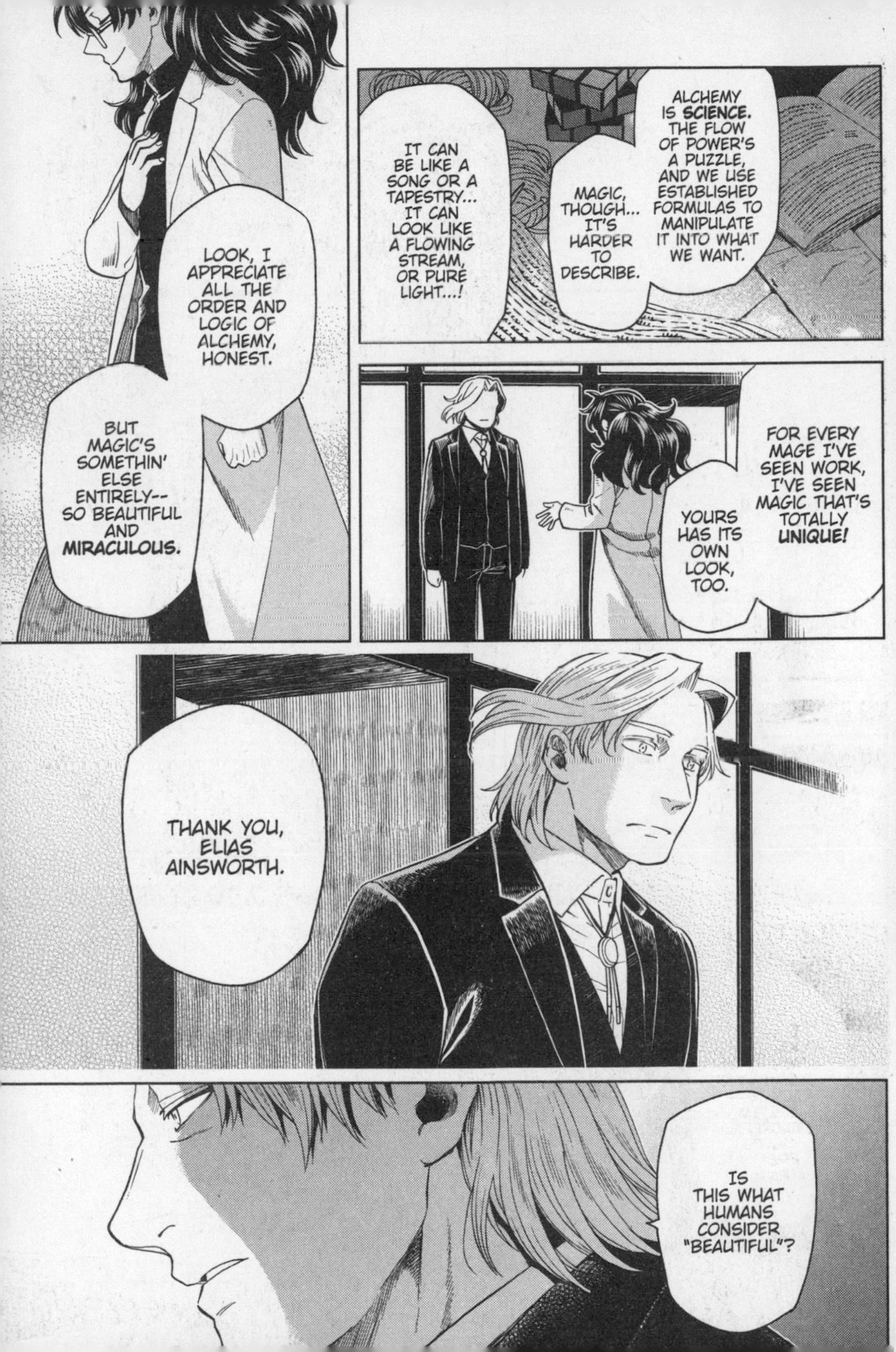
ALCHEMY IS SCIENCE. THE FLOW OF POWER'S A PUZZLE, AND WE USE ESTABLISHED FORMULAS TO MANIPULATE IT INTO WHAT WE WANT.
MAGIC, THOUGH... IT'S HARDER TO DESCRIBE.
IT CAN BE LIKE A SONG OR A TAPESTRY... IT CAN LOOK LIKE A FLOWING STREAM, OR PURE LIGHT...!
FOR EVERY MAGE I'VE SEEN WORK, I'VE SEEN MAGIC THAT'S TOTALLY UNIQUE!
YOURS HAS ITS OWN LOOK, TOO.
LOOK, I APPRECIATE ALL THE ORDER AND LOGIC OF ALCHEMY, HONEST.
BUT MAGIC'S SOMETHIN' ELSE ENTIRELY-- SO BEAUTIFUL AND MIRACULOUS.
THANK YOU, ELIAS AINSWORTH.
IS THIS WHAT HUMANS CONSIDER "BEAUTIFUL"?

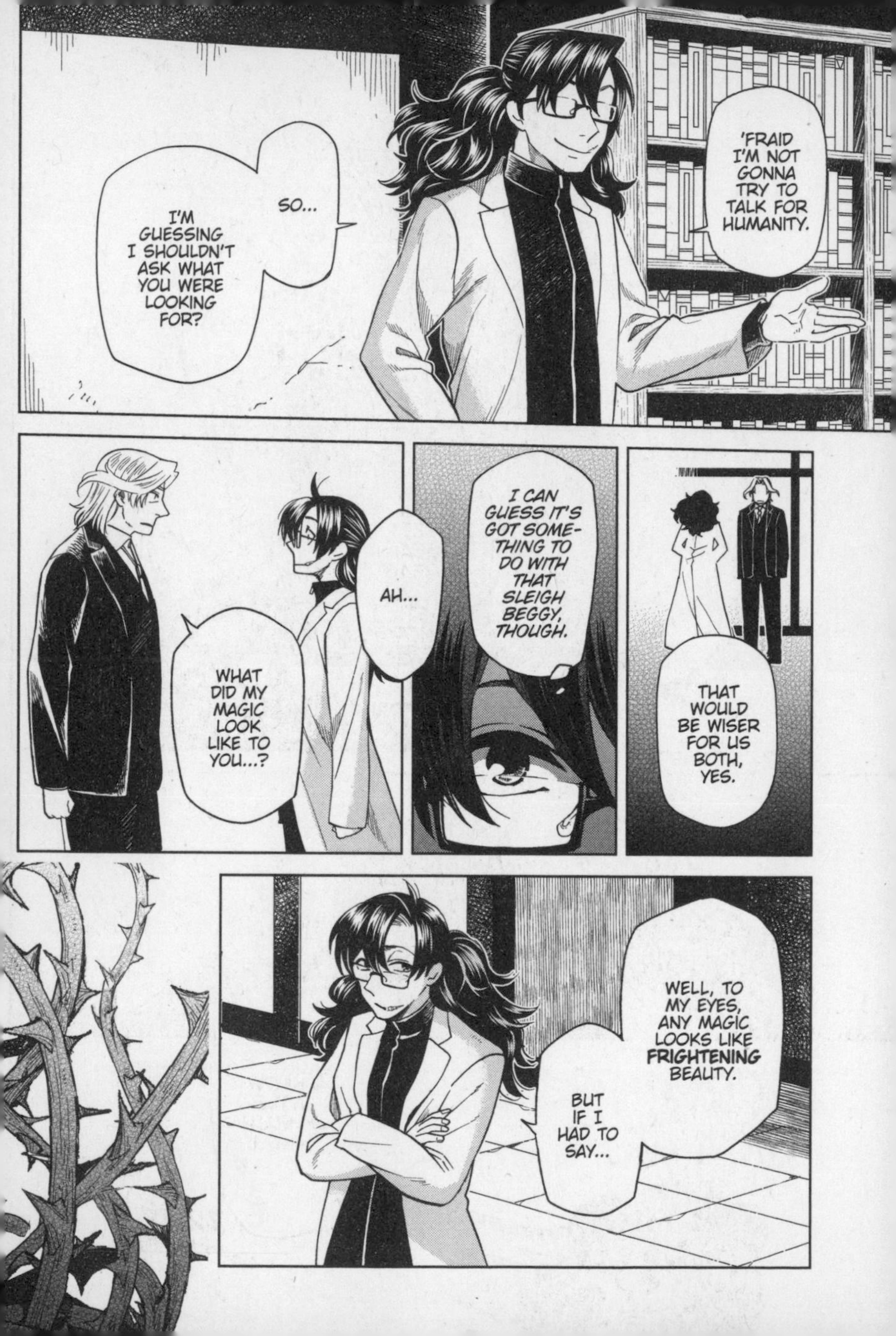
'FRAID I'M NOT GONNA TRY TO TALK FOR HUMANITY.
SO...
I'M GUESSING I SHOULDN'T ASK WHAT YOU WERE LOOKING FOR?
THAT WOULD BE WISER FOR US BOTH, YES.
I CAN GUESS IT'S GOT SOME-THING TO DO WITH THAT SLEIGH BEGGY, THOUGH.
AH...
WHAT DID MY MAGIC LOOK LIKE TO YOU...?
WELL, TO MY EYES, ANY MAGIC LOOKS LIKE FRIGHTENING BEAUTY.
BUT IF I HAD TO SAY...

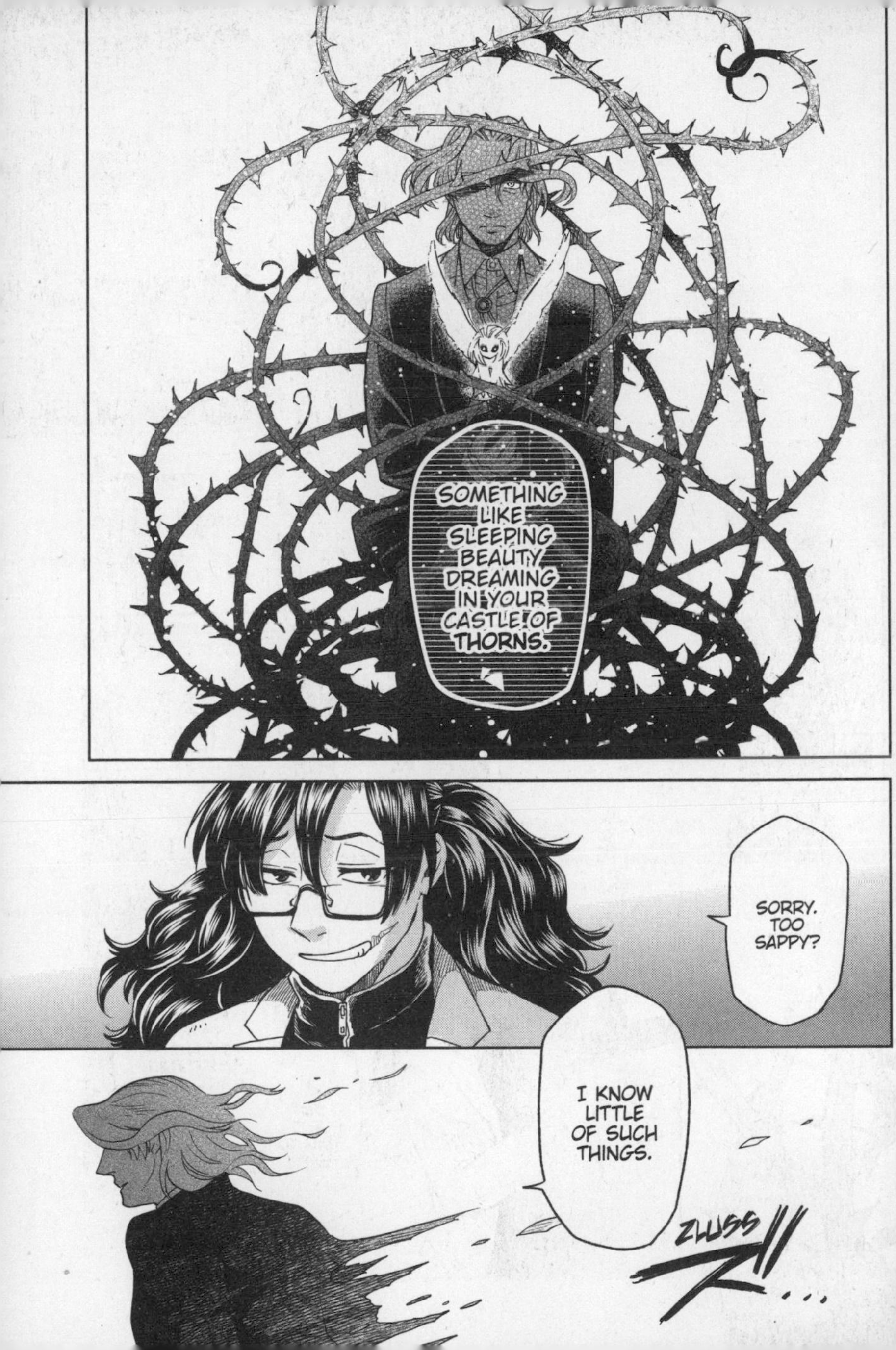
SOMETHING LIKE SLEEPING BEAUTY DREAMING IN YOUR CASTLE OF THORNS.
SORRY. TOO SAPPY?
I KNOW LITTLE OF SUCH THINGS.
ZLUSS
...

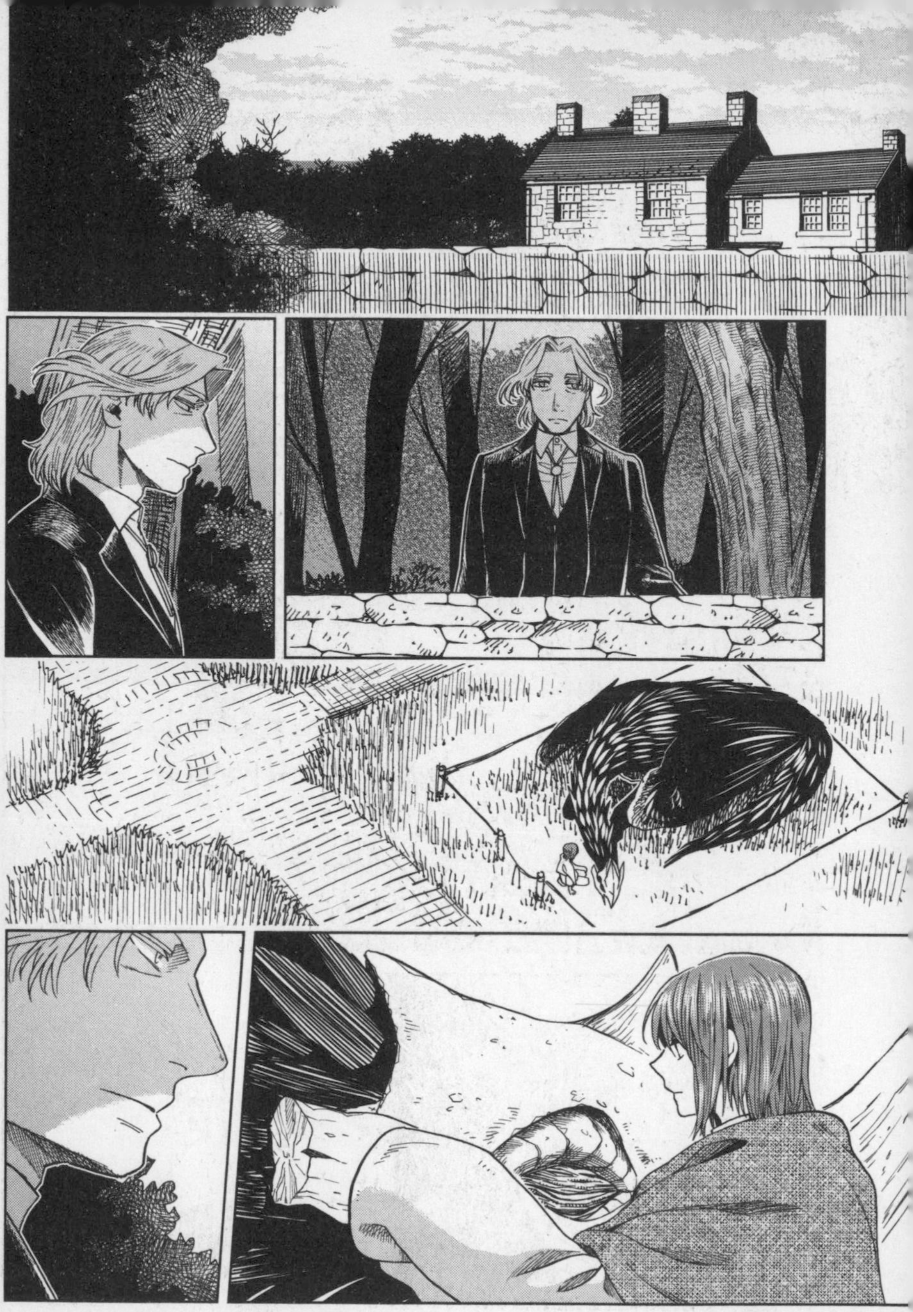

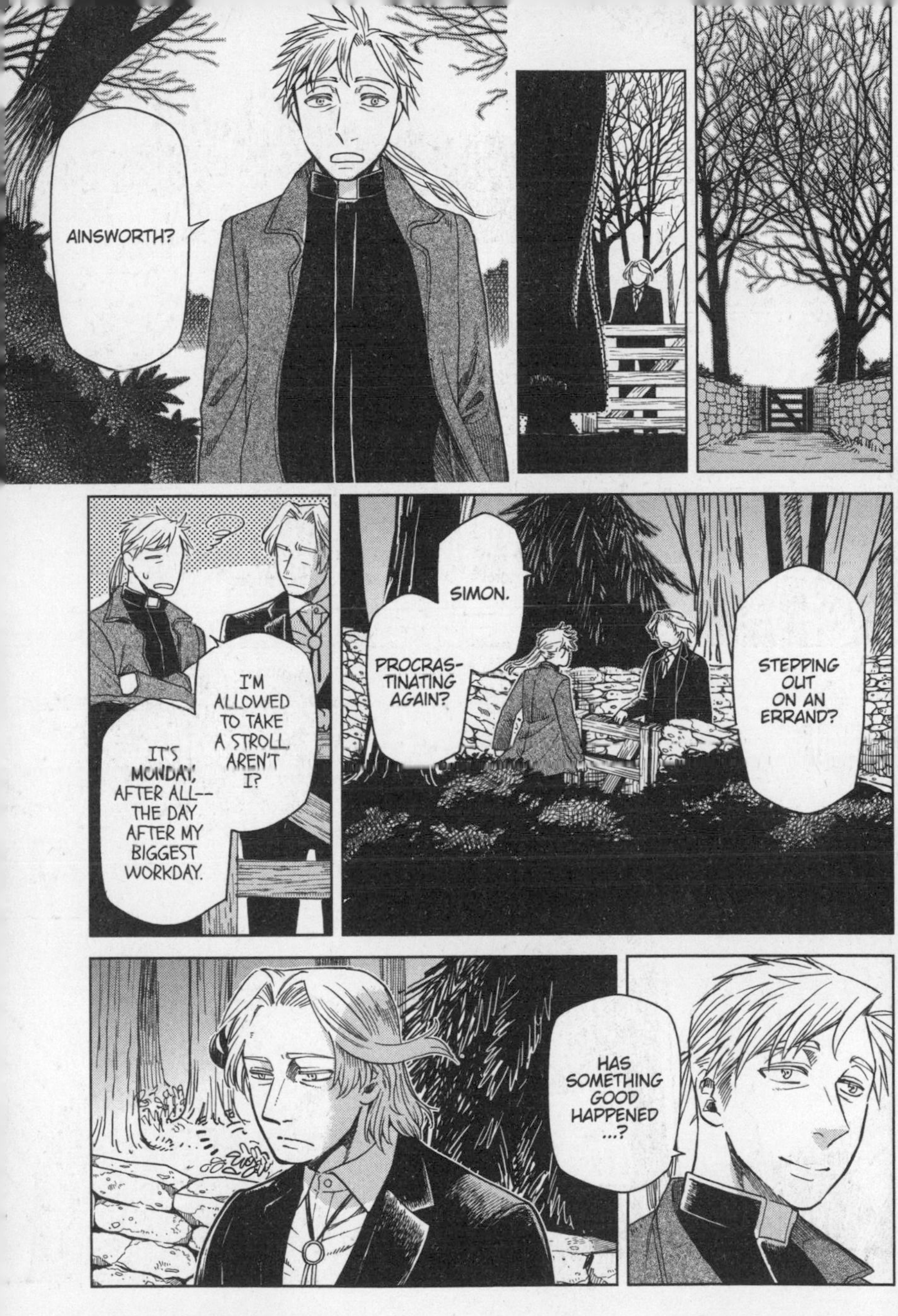
AINSWORTH?
STEPPING OUT ON AN ERRAND?
SIMON.
PROCRAS-TINATING AGAIN?
I'M ALLOWED TO TAKE A STROLL, AREN'T I?
IT'S MONDAY, AFTER ALL-- THE DAY AFTER MY BIGGEST WORKDAY.
HAS SOMETHING GOOD HAPPENED ...?

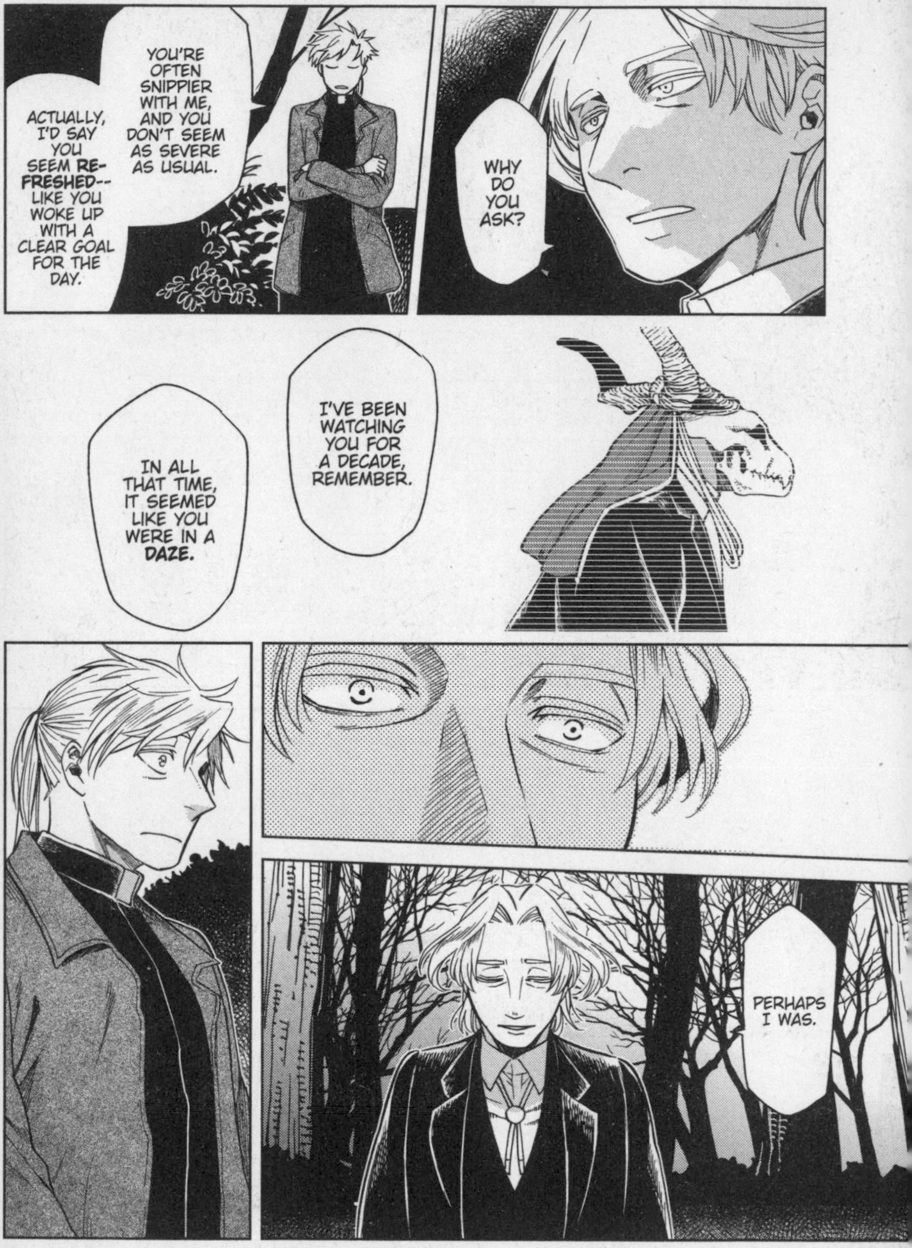
WHY DO YOU ASK?
YOU'RE OFTEN SNIPPIER WITH ME, AND YOU DON'T SEEM AS SEVERE AS USUAL.
ACTUALLY, I'D SAY YOU SEEM **REFRESHED**-- LIKE YOU WOKE UP WITH A CLEAR GOAL FOR THE DAY.
I'VE BEEN WATCHING YOU FOR A DECADE, REMEMBER.
IN ALL THAT TIME, IT SEEMED LIKE YOU WERE IN A **DAZE.**
PERHAPS I WAS.

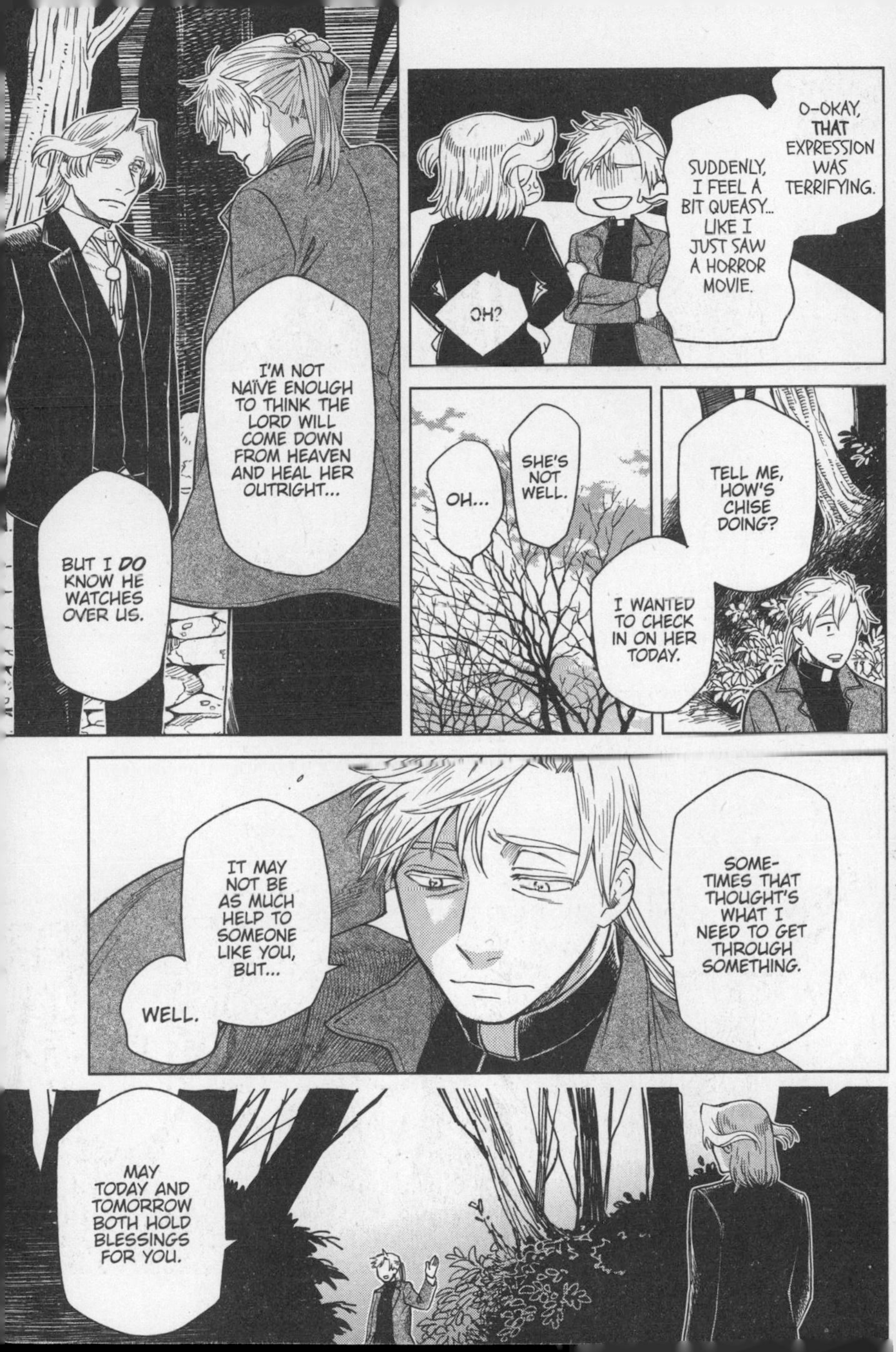
O-OKAY, THAT EXPRESSION WAS TERRIFYING.
SUDDENLY, I FEEL A BIT QUEASY... LIKE I JUST SAW A HORROR MOVIE.
OH?
TELL ME, HOW'S CHISE DOING?
I WANTED TO CHECK IN ON HER TODAY.
SHE'S NOT WELL.
OH...
I'M NOT NAÏVE ENOUGH TO THINK THE LORD WILL COME DOWN FROM HEAVEN AND HEAL HER OUTRIGHT...
BUT I DO KNOW HE WATCHES OVER US.
SOME-TIMES THAT THOUGHT'S WHAT I NEED TO GET THROUGH SOMETHING.
IT MAY NOT BE AS MUCH HELP TO SOMEONE LIKE YOU, BUT...
WELL.
MAY TODAY AND TOMORROW BOTH HOLD BLESSINGS FOR YOU.

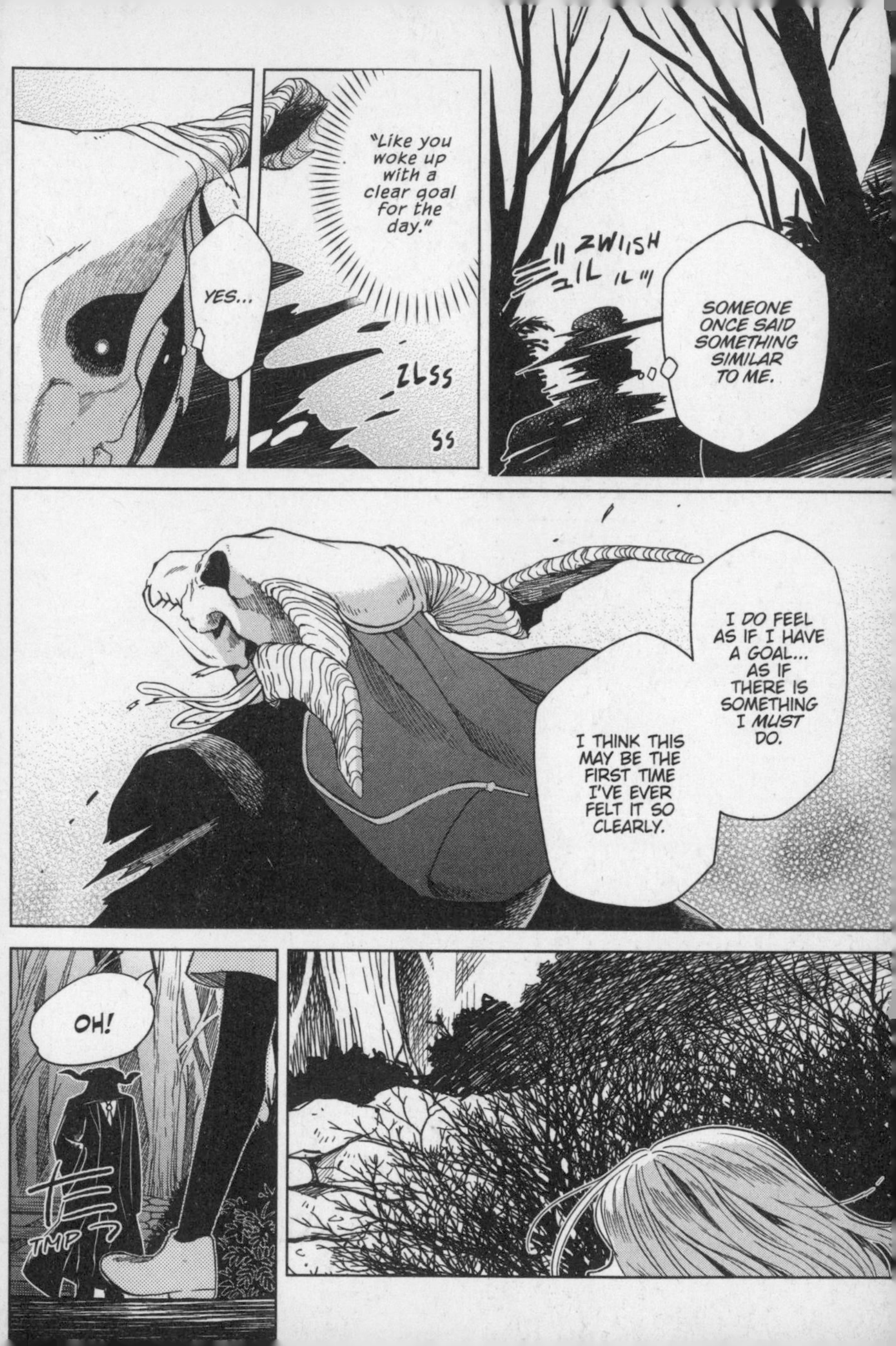
ZWISH
SOMEONE ONCE SAID SOMETHING SIMILAR TO ME.
"Like you woke up with a clear goal for the day."
ZLSS
SS
YES...
I DO FEEL AS IF I HAVE A GOAL... AS IF THERE IS SOMETHING I MUST DO.
I THINK THIS MAY BE THE FIRST TIME I'VE EVER FELT IT SO CLEARLY.
OH!
TMP

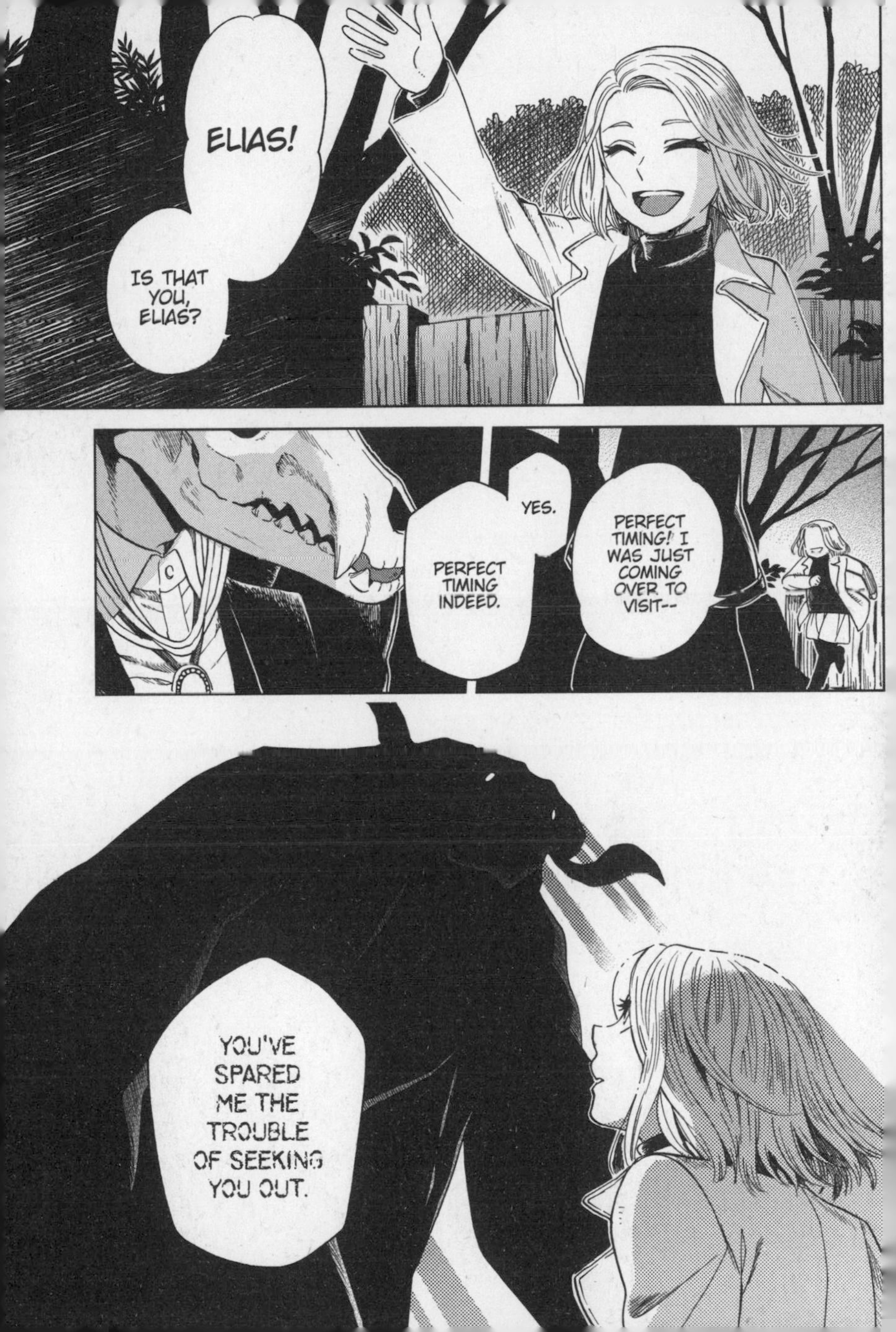
ELIAS!
IS THAT YOU, ELIAS?
PERFECT TIMING! I WAS JUST COMING OVER TO VISIT--
YES.
PERFECT TIMING INDEED.
YOU'VE SPARED ME THE TROUBLE OF SEEKING YOU OUT.

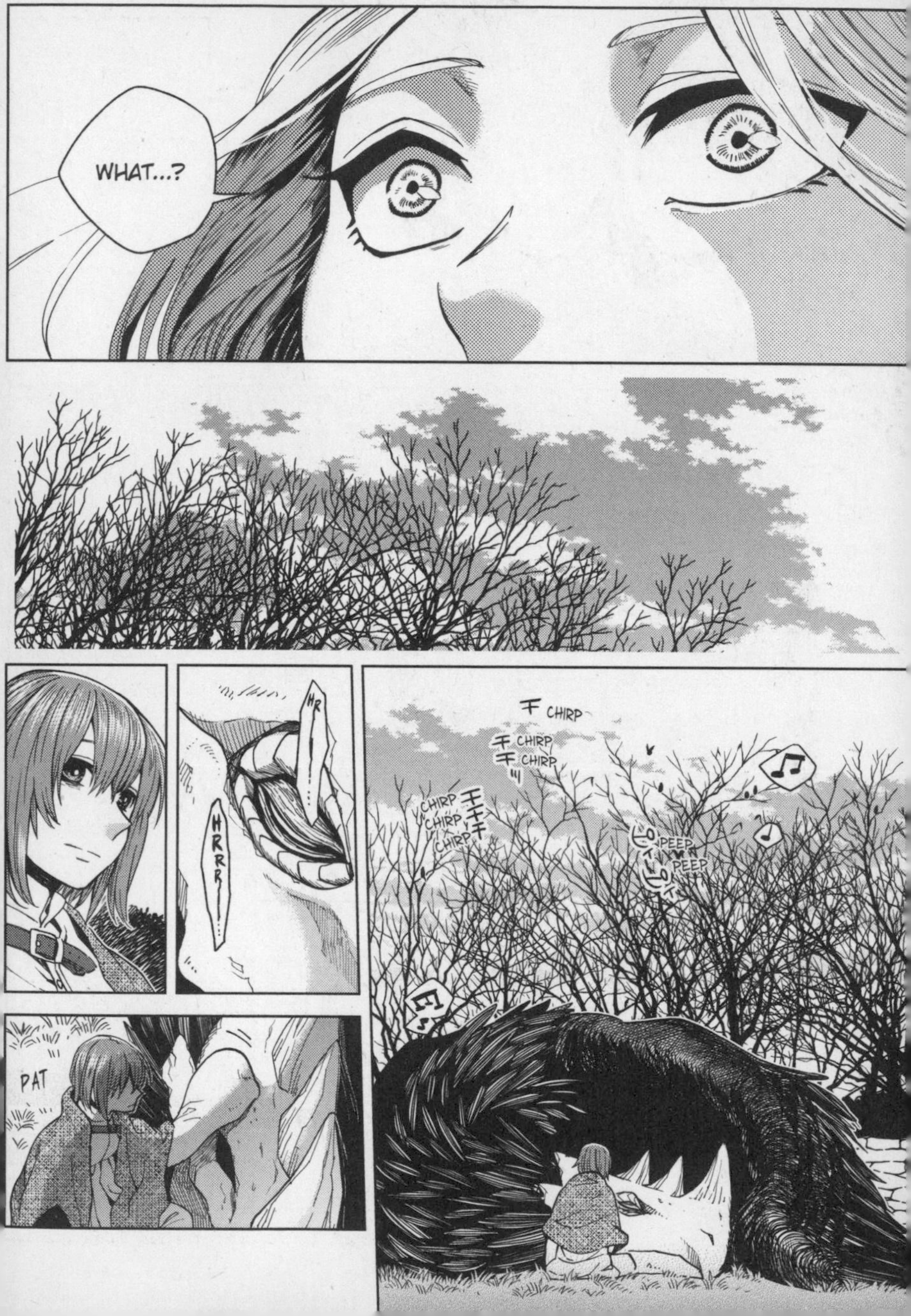
WHAT...?
CHIRP
CHIRP
CHIRP
CHIRP
CHIRP
CHIRP
PEEP
PEEP
HR...
HRRR...
PAT

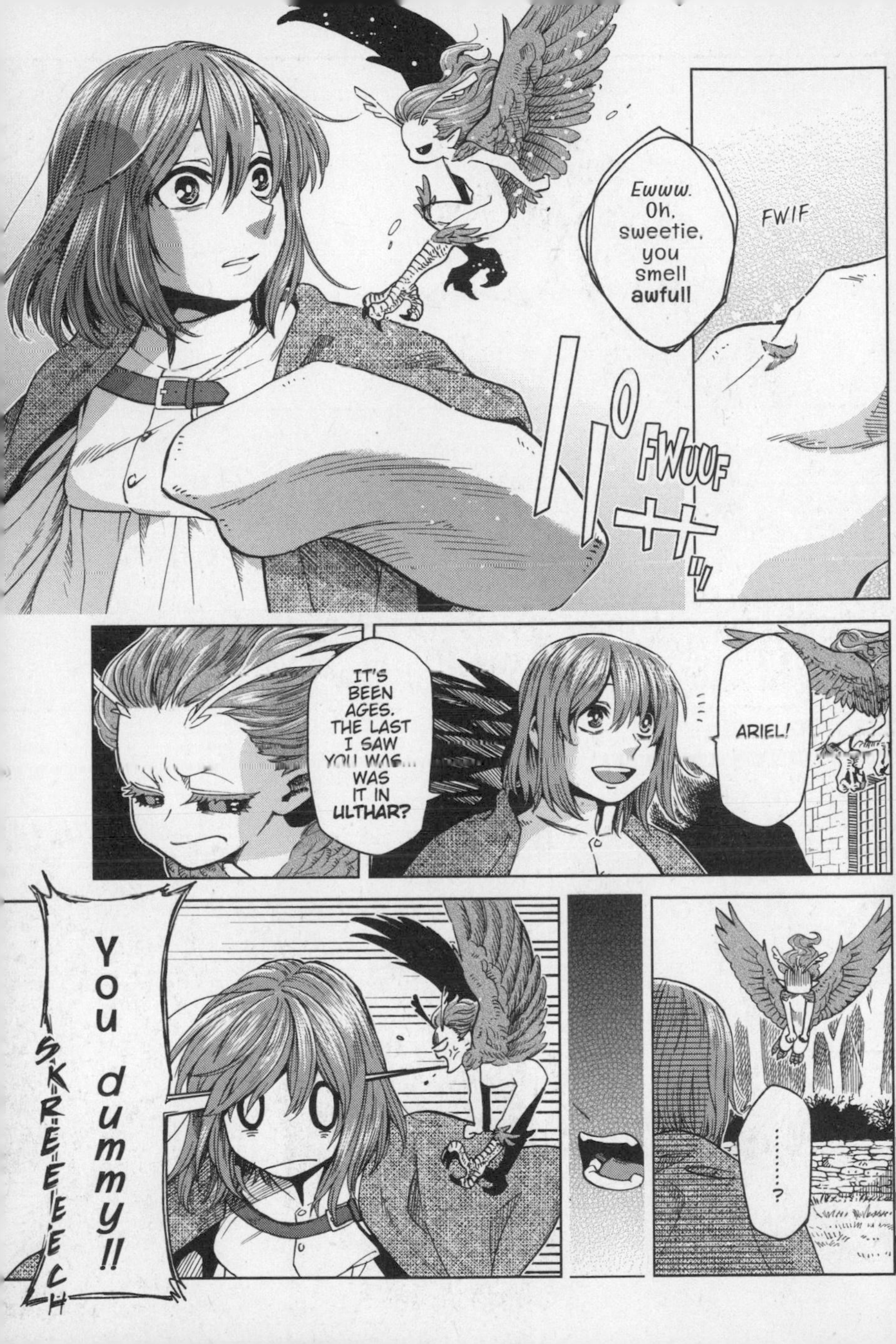
FWIF
Ewww. Oh, sweetie, you smell awful!
FWUUF
ARIEL!
IT'S BEEN AGES. THE LAST I SAW YOU WAS... WAS IT IN ULTHAR?
......?
You dummy!!
SKREEEECH

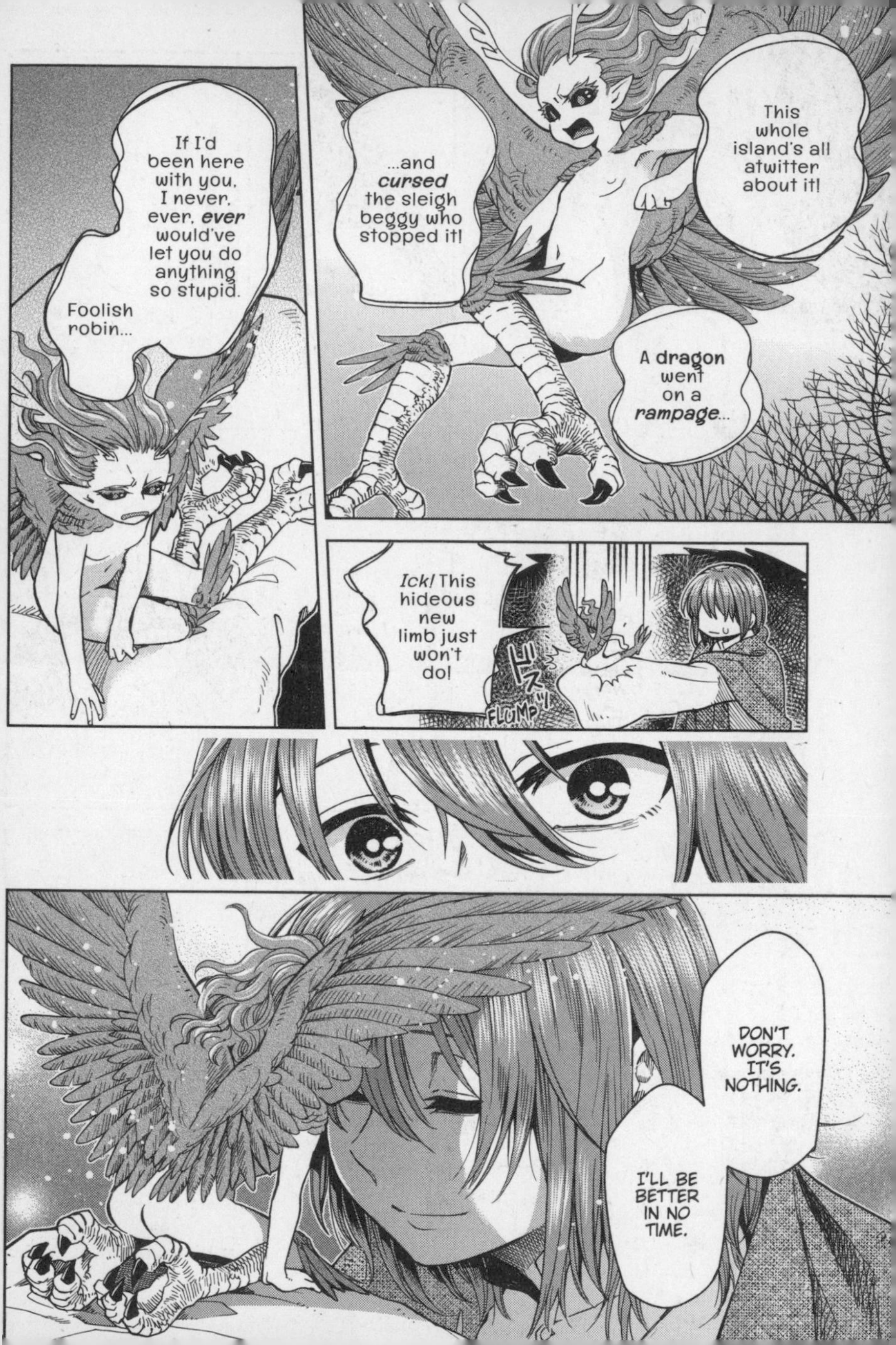
This whole island's all atwitter about it!
A dragon went on a rampage...
...and cursed the sleigh beggy who stopped it!
Ick! This hideous new limb just won't do!
FLUMP
If I'd been here with you, I never, ever, ever would've let you do anything so stupid.
Foolish robin...
DON'T WORRY. IT'S NOTHING.
I'LL BE BETTER IN NO TIME.

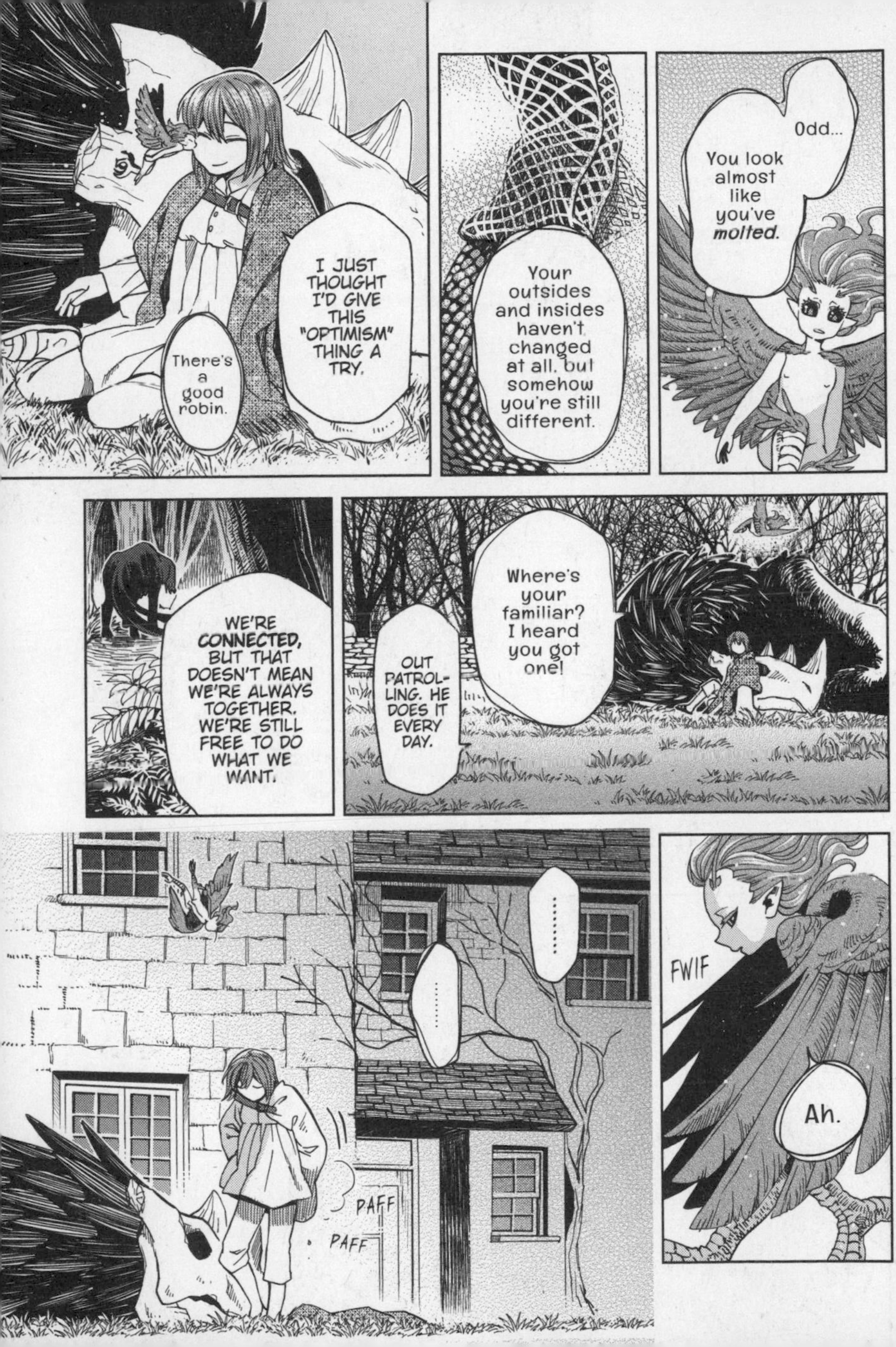
Odd...
You look almost like you've *molted*.
Your outsides and insides haven't changed at all, but somehow you're still different.
I JUST THOUGHT I'D GIVE THIS "OPTIMISM" THING A TRY.
There's a good robin.
Where's your familiar? I heard you got one!
OUT PATROLLING. HE DOES IT EVERY DAY.
WE'RE **CONNECTED**, BUT THAT DOESN'T MEAN WE'RE ALWAYS TOGETHER. WE'RE STILL FREE TO DO WHAT WE WANT.
FWIF
Ah.
......
......
PAFF
PAFF

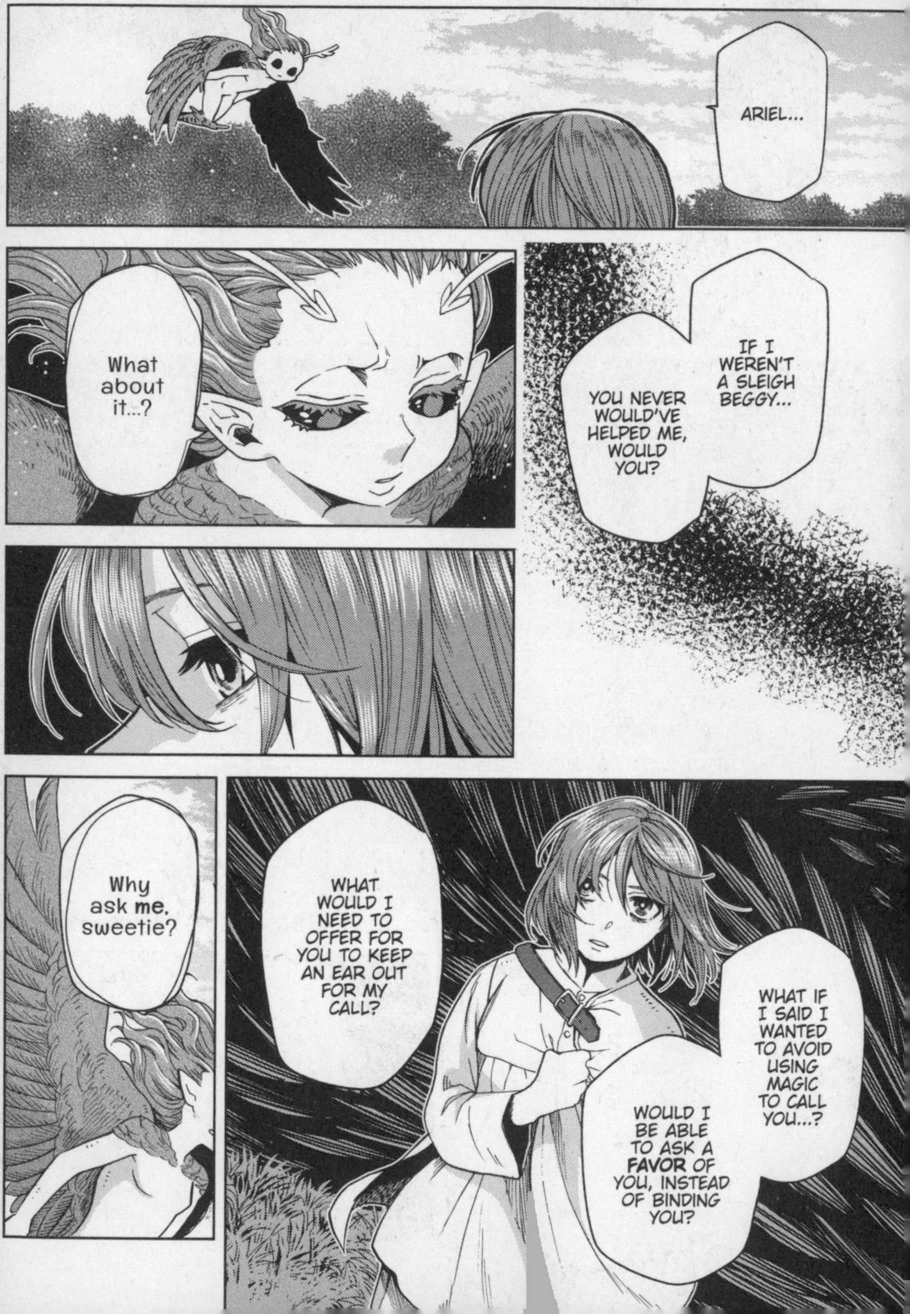

ARIEL...
IF I WEREN'T A SLEIGH BEGGY...
YOU NEVER WOULD'VE HELPED ME, WOULD YOU?
What about it...?
WHAT IF I SAID I WANTED TO AVOID USING MAGIC TO CALL YOU...?
WOULD I BE ABLE TO ASK A **FAVOR** OF YOU, INSTEAD OF BINDING YOU?
WHAT WOULD I NEED TO OFFER FOR YOU TO KEEP AN EAR OUT FOR MY CALL?
Why ask **me**, sweetie?

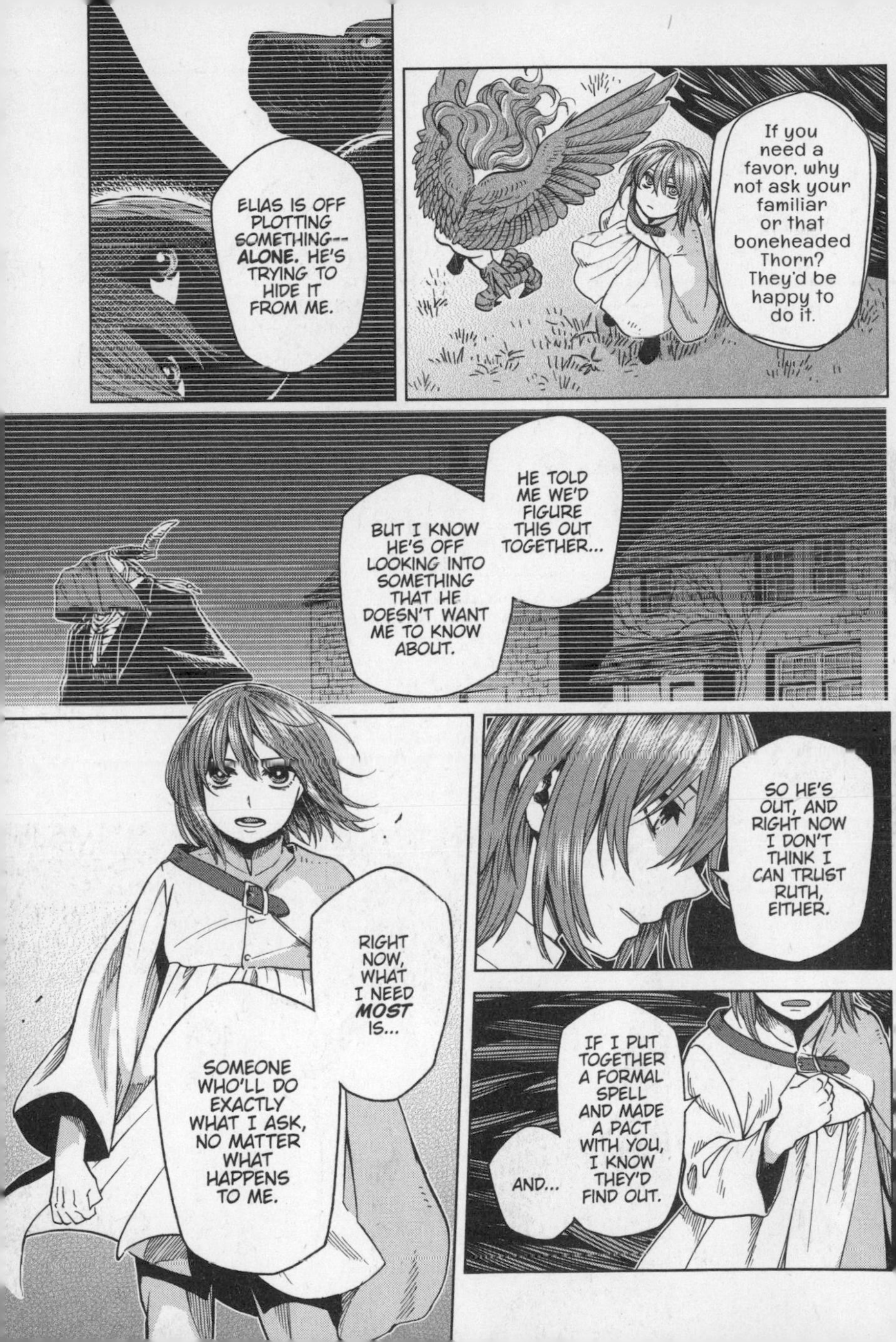
If you need a favor, why not ask your familiar or that boneheaded Thorn? They'd be happy to do it.
ELIAS IS OFF PLOTTING SOMETHING-- **ALONE.** HE'S TRYING TO HIDE IT FROM ME.
HE TOLD ME WE'D FIGURE THIS OUT TOGETHER...
BUT I KNOW HE'S OFF LOOKING INTO SOMETHING THAT HE DOESN'T WANT ME TO KNOW ABOUT.
SO HE'S OUT, AND RIGHT NOW I DON'T THINK I CAN TRUST RUTH, EITHER.
IF I PUT TOGETHER A FORMAL SPELL AND MADE A PACT WITH YOU, I KNOW THEY'D FIND OUT.
AND...
RIGHT NOW, WHAT I NEED ***MOST*** IS...
SOMEONE WHO'LL DO EXACTLY WHAT I ASK, NO MATTER WHAT HAPPENS TO ME.

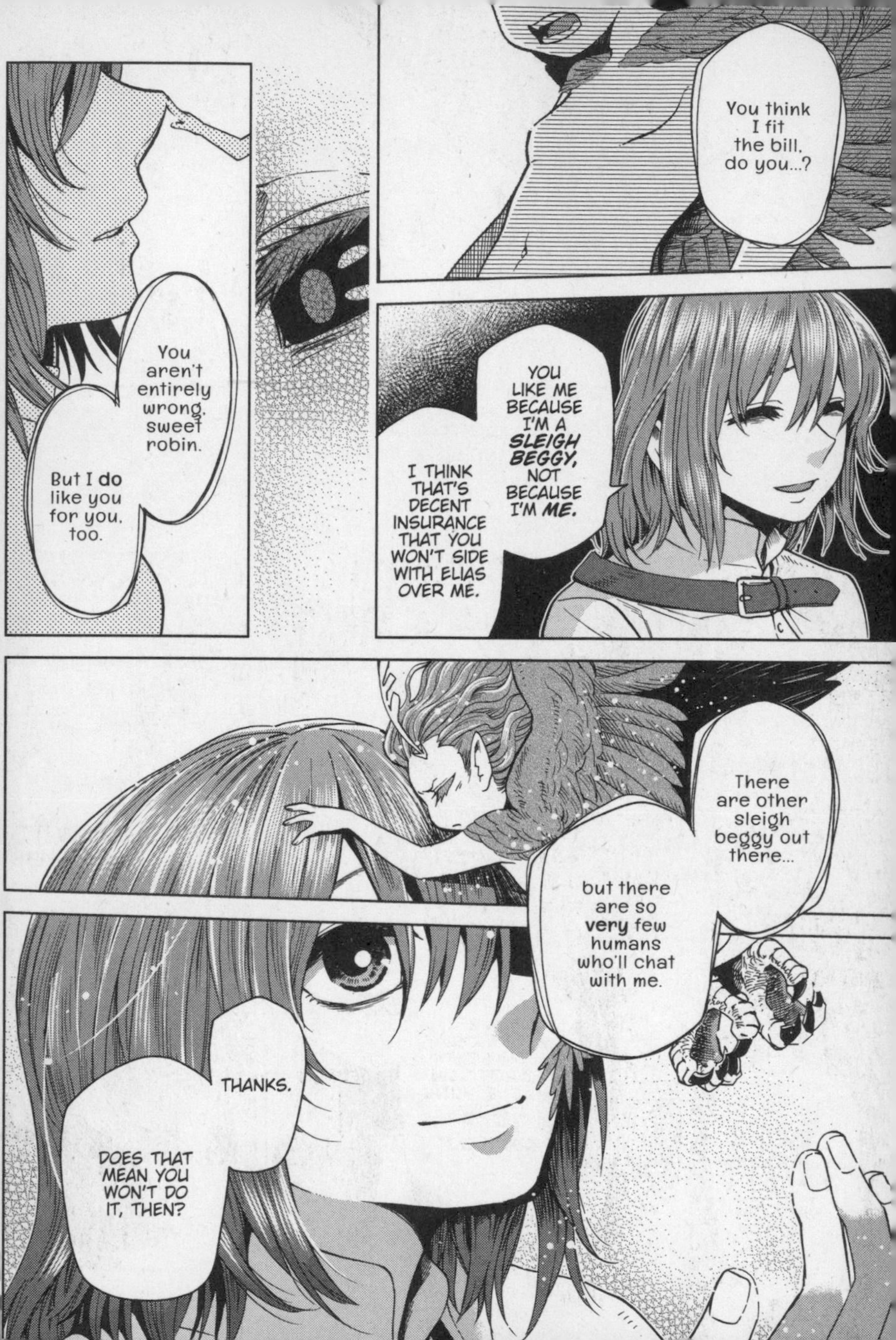
You think I fit the bill, do you...?
YOU LIKE ME BECAUSE I'M A SLEIGH BEGGY, NOT BECAUSE I'M ME.
I THINK THAT'S DECENT INSURANCE THAT YOU WON'T SIDE WITH ELIAS OVER ME.
You aren't entirely wrong, sweet robin.
But I do like you for you, too.
There are other sleigh beggy out there...
but there are so very few humans who'll chat with me.
THANKS.
DOES THAT MEAN YOU WON'T DO IT, THEN?

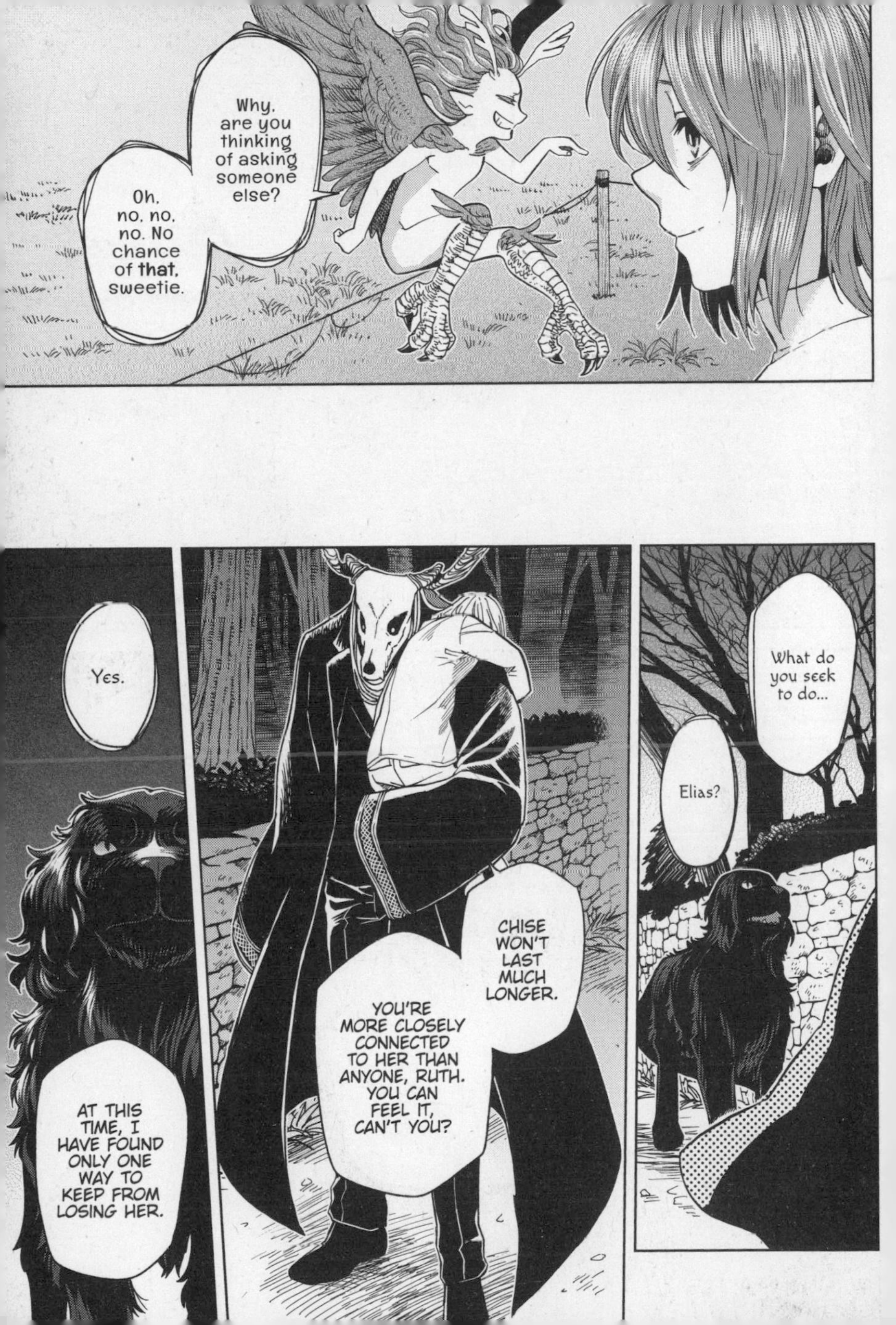
Why, are you thinking of asking someone else?
Oh, no, no, no. No chance of **that**, sweetie.
What do you seek to do...
Elias?
CHISE WON'T LAST MUCH LONGER.
YOU'RE MORE CLOSELY CONNECTED TO HER THAN ANYONE, RUTH. YOU CAN FEEL IT, CAN'T YOU?
Yes.
AT THIS TIME, I HAVE FOUND ONLY ONE WAY TO KEEP FROM LOSING HER.

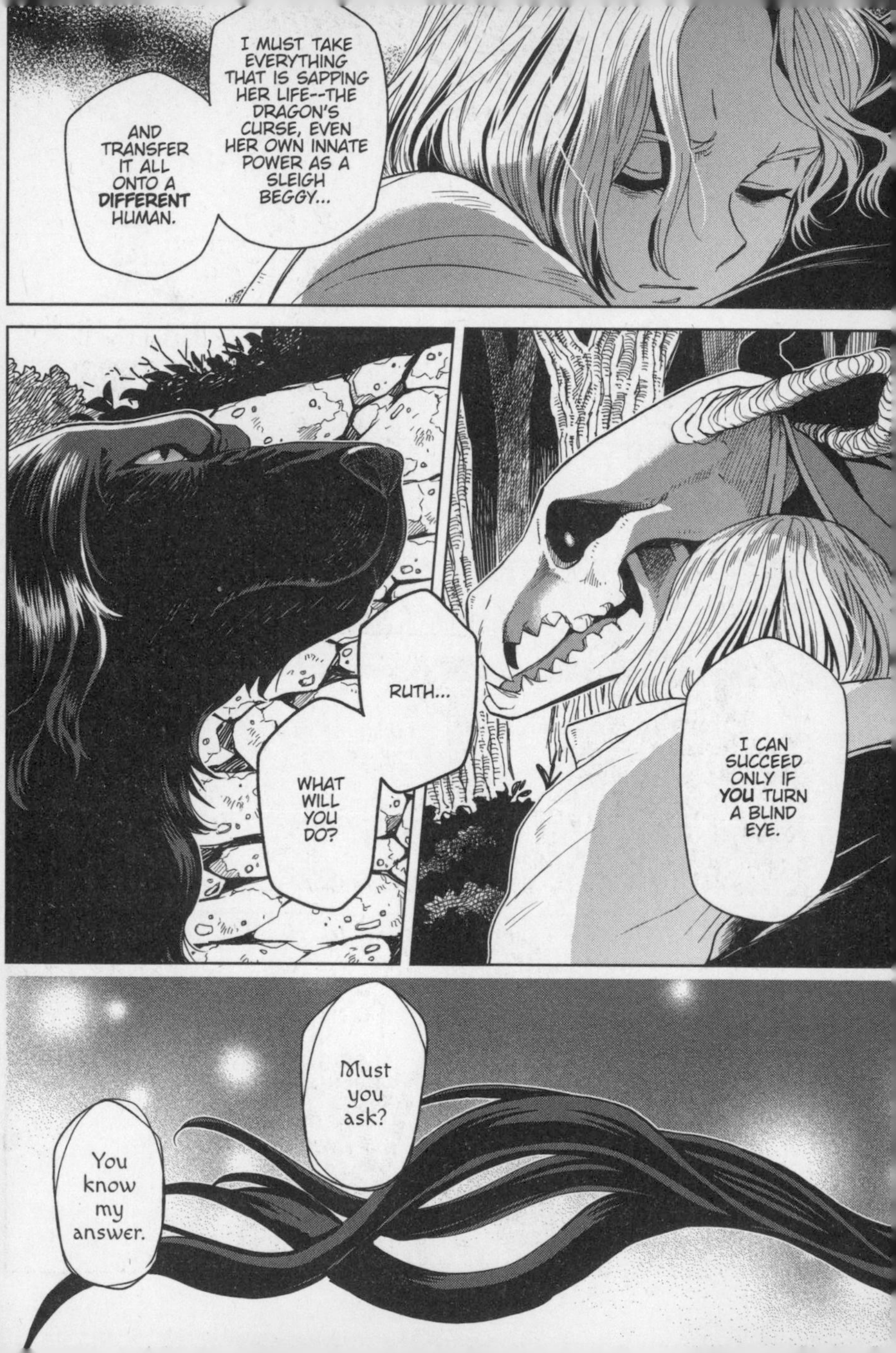
I MUST TAKE EVERYTHING THAT IS SAPPING HER LIFE--THE DRAGON'S CURSE, EVEN HER OWN INNATE POWER AS A SLEIGH BEGGY...
AND TRANSFER IT ALL ONTO A DIFFERENT HUMAN.
I CAN SUCCEED ONLY IF YOU TURN A BLIND EYE.
RUTH...
WHAT WILL YOU DO?
Must you ask?
You know my answer.

Chapter 40: What's bred in the bone will not come out of the flesh.

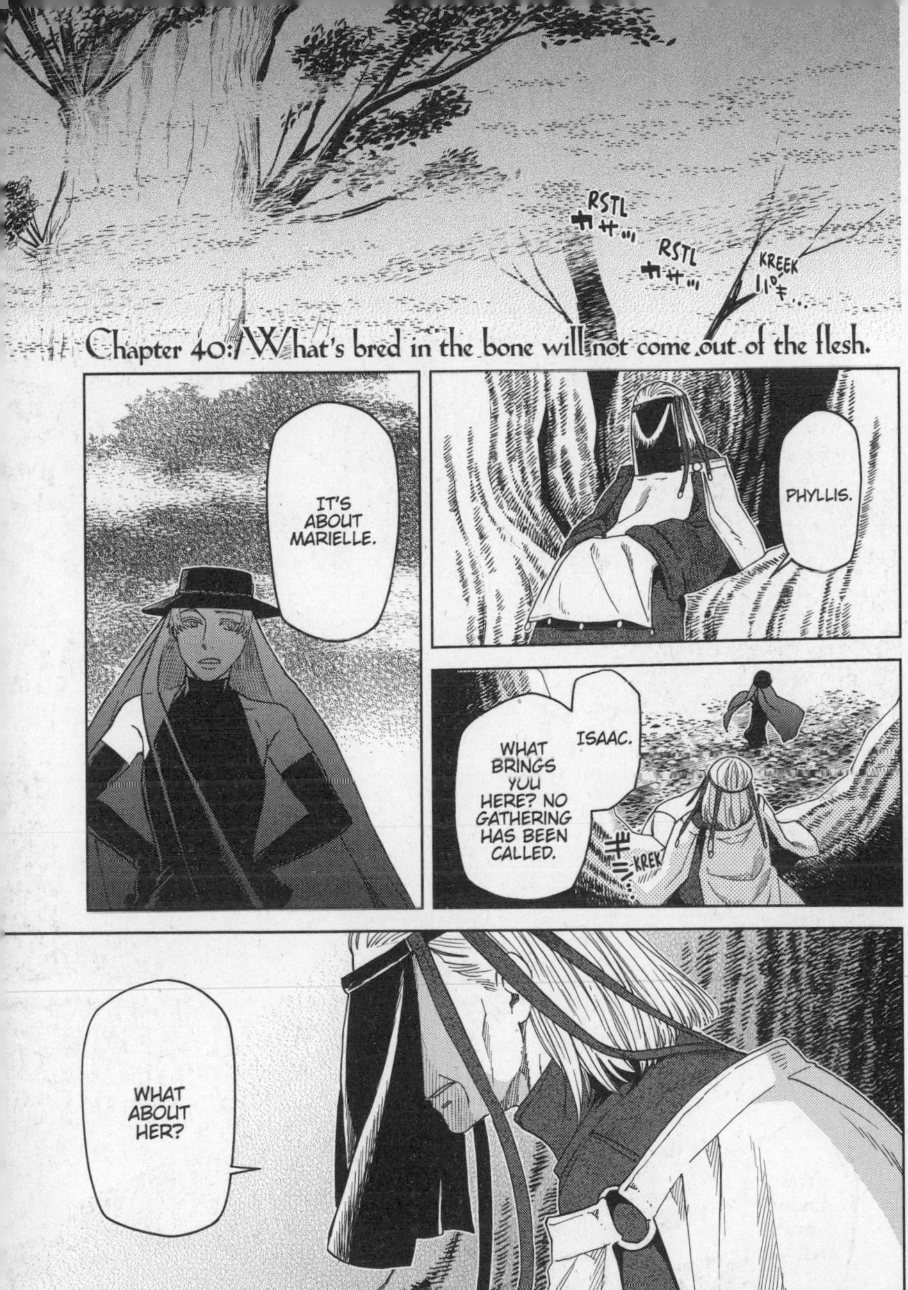
KREEK
RSTL
RSTL
PHYLLIS.
ISAAC.
WHAT BRINGS YOU HERE? NO GATHERING HAS BEEN CALLED.
KREK
IT'S ABOUT MARIELLE.
WHAT ABOUT HER?

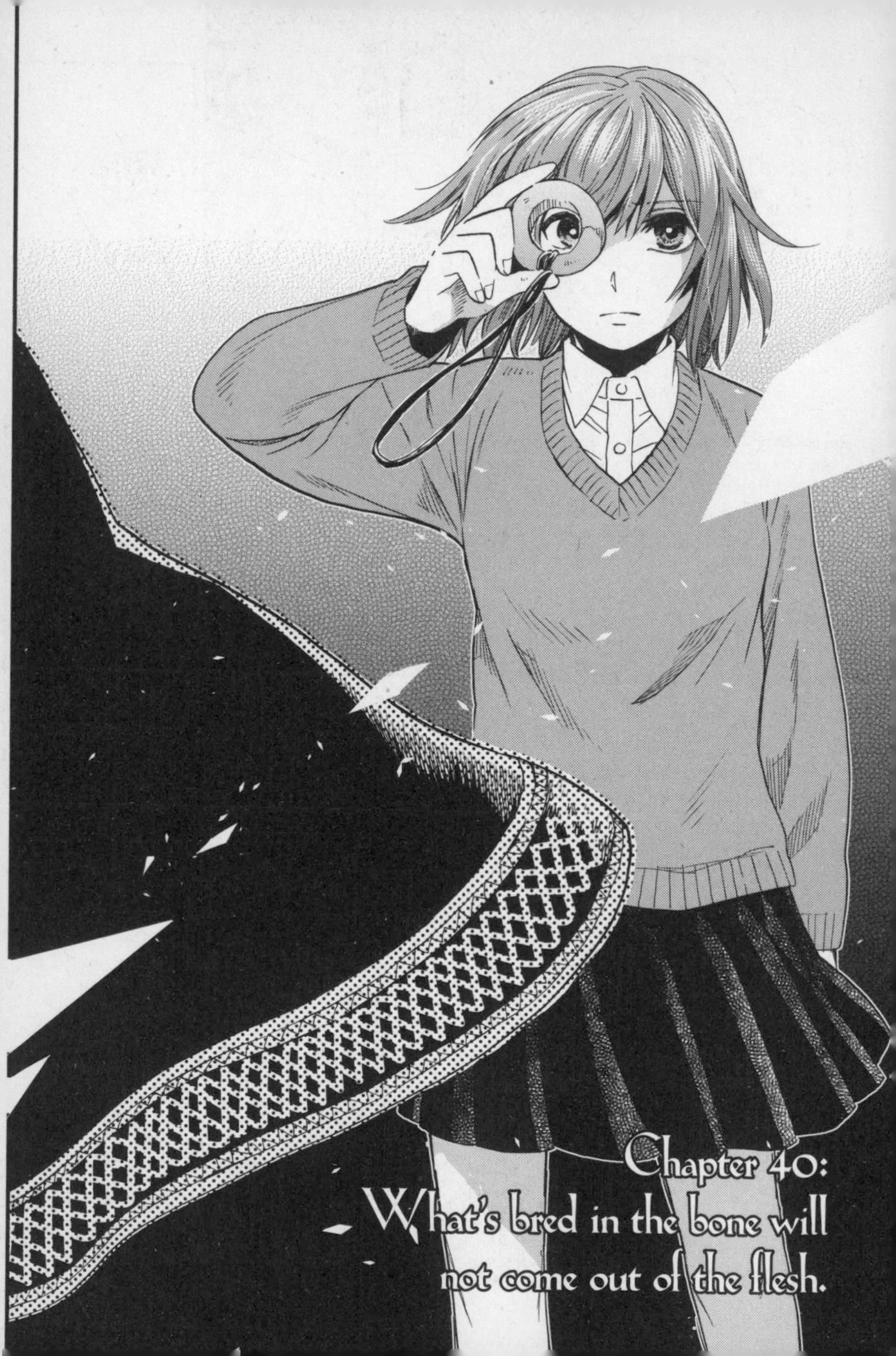
Chapter 40:
What's bred in the bone will not come out of the flesh.

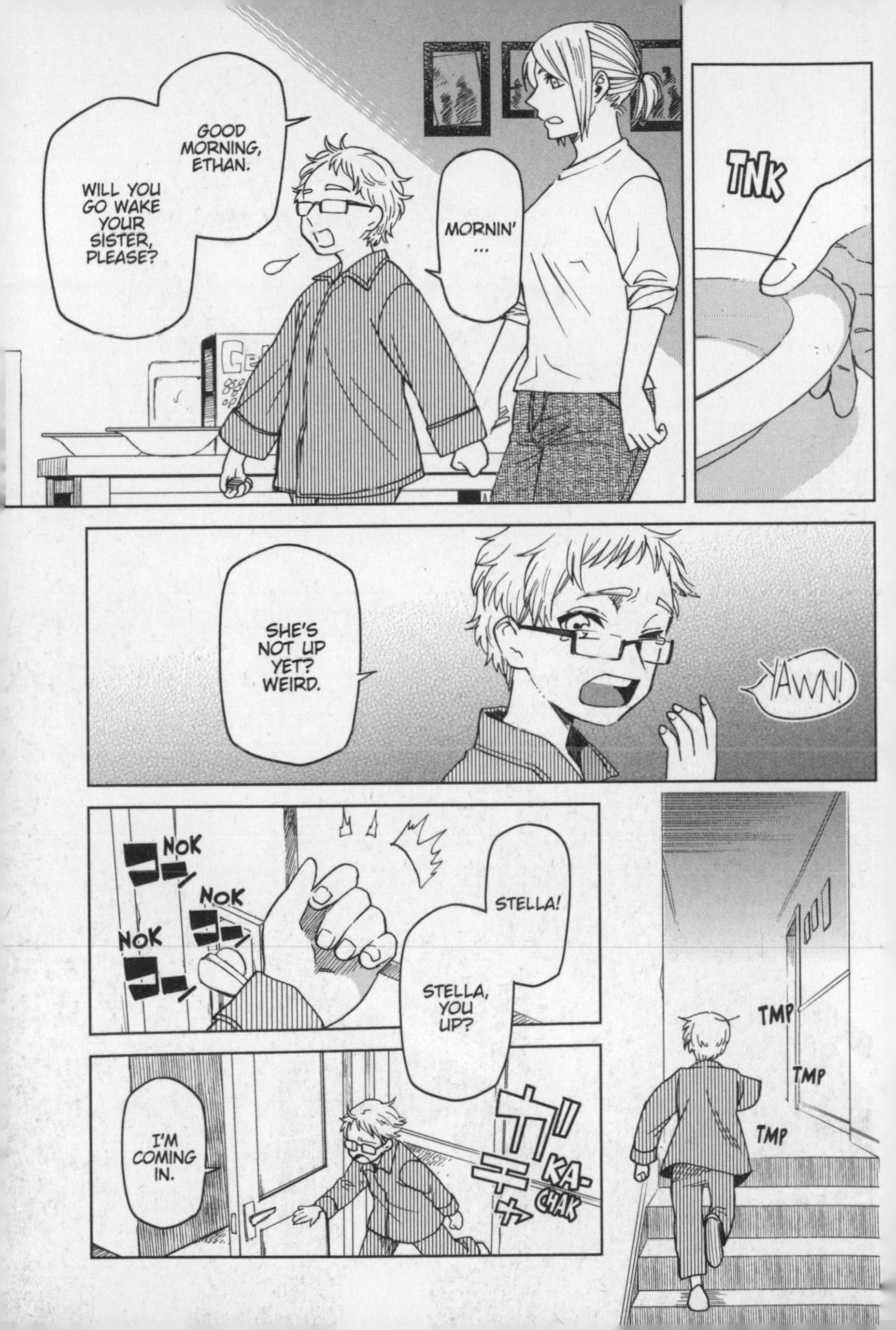
TNK
GOOD MORNING, ETHAN. WILL YOU GO WAKE YOUR SISTER, PLEASE?
MORNIN' ...
YAWN!
SHE'S NOT UP YET? WEIRD.
TMP
TMP
TMP
STELLA! STELLA, YOU UP?
NOK
NOK
NOK
KA-CHAK
I'M COMING IN.

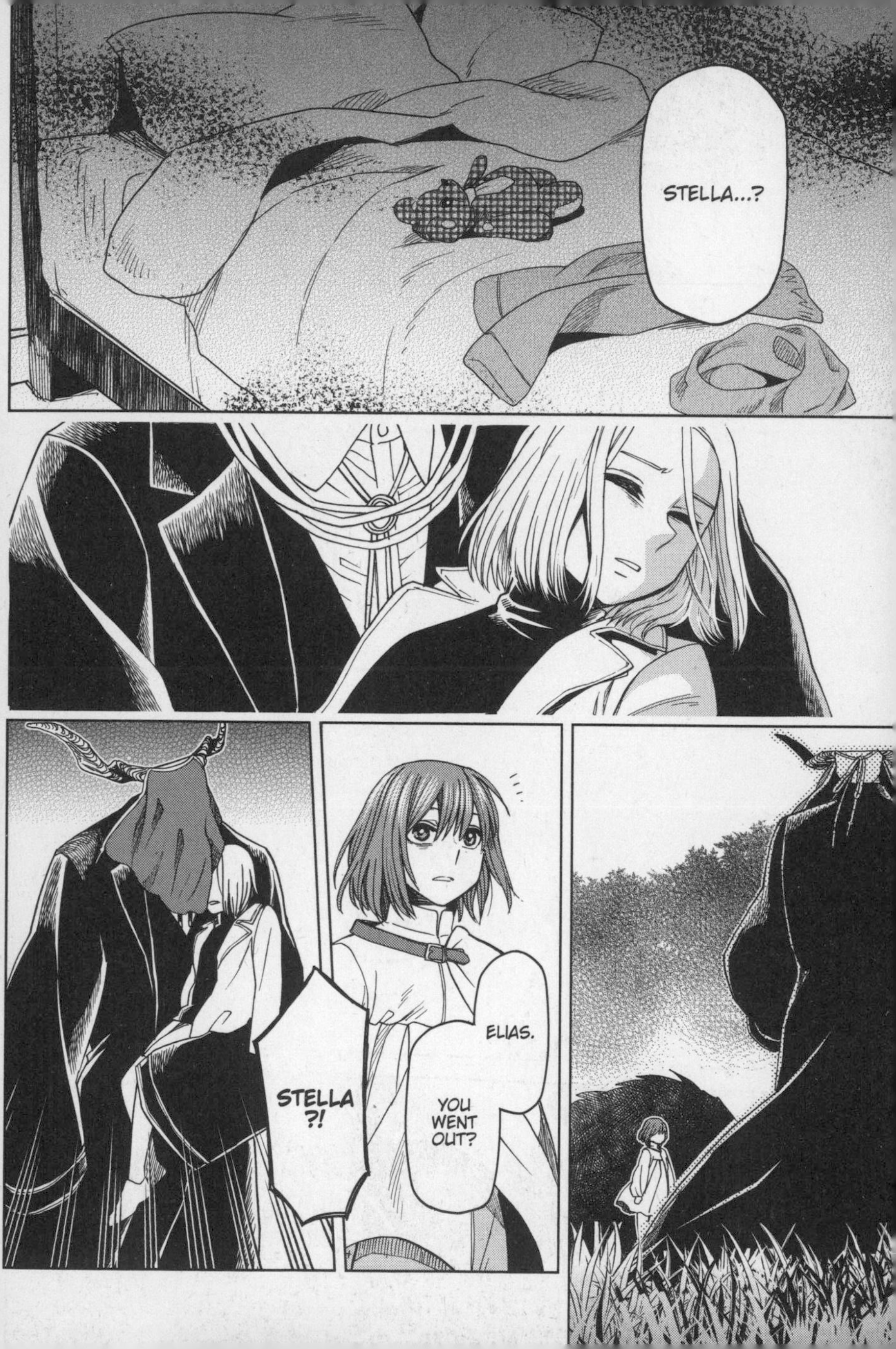
STELLA...?
ELIAS.
YOU WENT OUT?
STELLA ?!

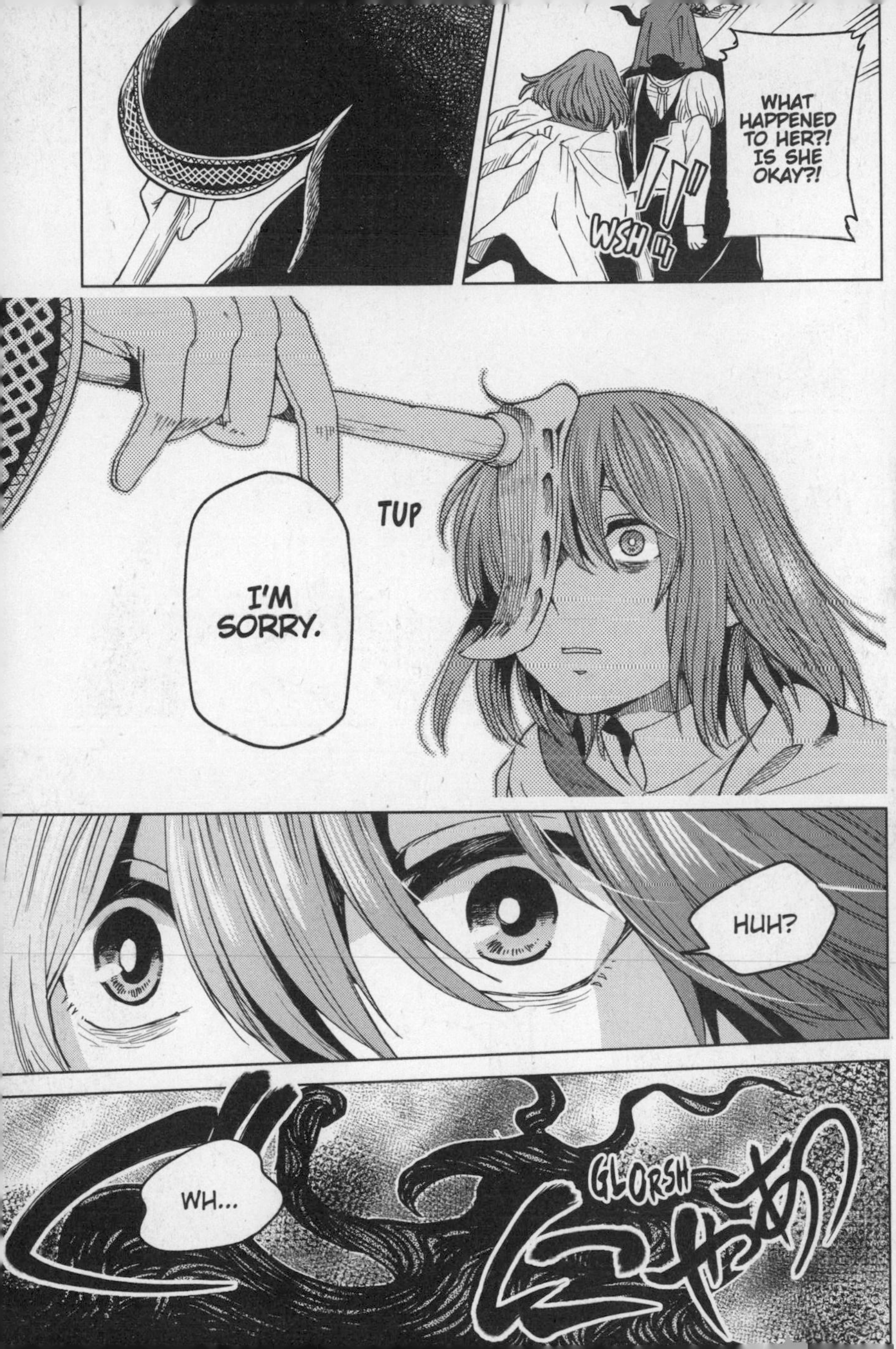
WHAT HAPPENED TO HER?! IS SHE OKAY?!
WSH
TUP
I'M SORRY.
HUH?
WH...
GLORSH

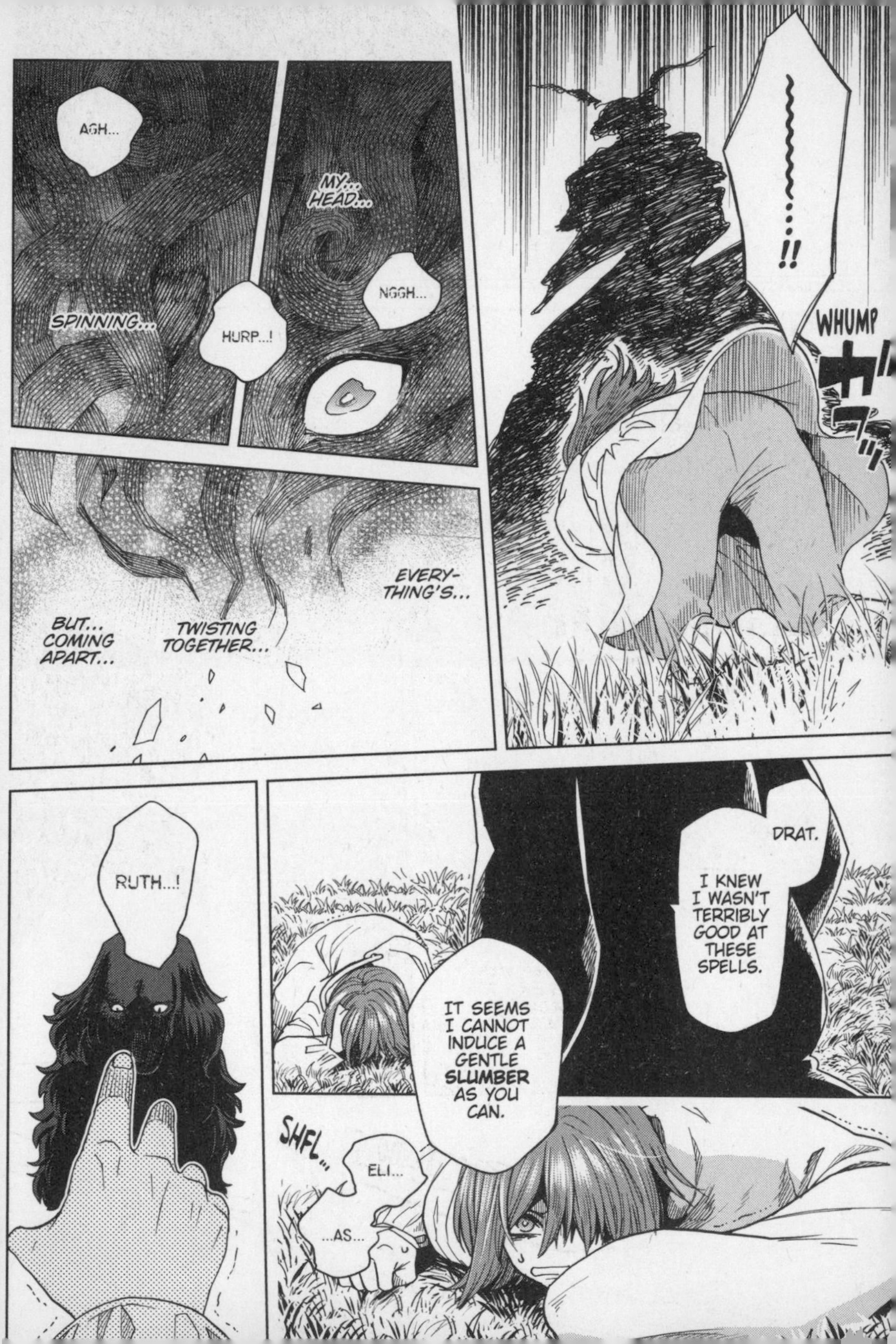
……!!
WHUMP
MY... HEAD...
NGGH...
HURP...!
AGH...
SPINNING...
EVERY-THING'S...
TWISTING TOGETHER...
BUT... COMING APART...
DRAT.
I KNEW I WASN'T TERRIBLY GOOD AT THESE SPELLS.
IT SEEMS I CANNOT INDUCE A GENTLE **SLUMBER** AS YOU CAN.
SHFL...
ELI...
...AS...
RUTH...!

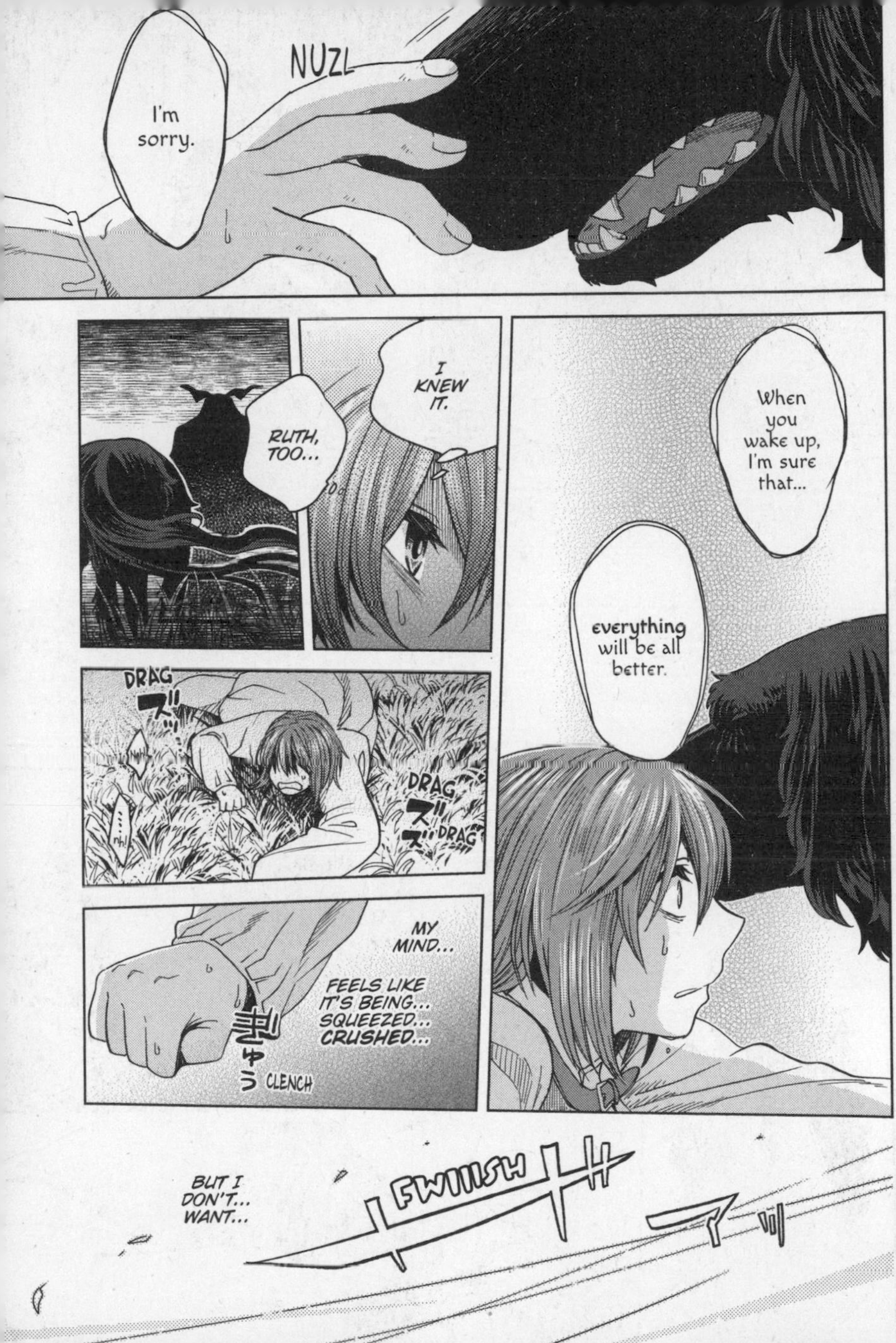
NUZL
I'm sorry.
When you wake up, I'm sure that...
everything will be all better.
I KNEW IT.
RUTH, TOO...
DRAG
ズッ
DRAG
ズズッ
DRAG
...nh!
MY MIND...
FEELS LIKE IT'S BEING... SQUEEZED... CRUSHED...
ぎゅう
CLENCH
FWIIISH
BUT I DON'T... WANT...

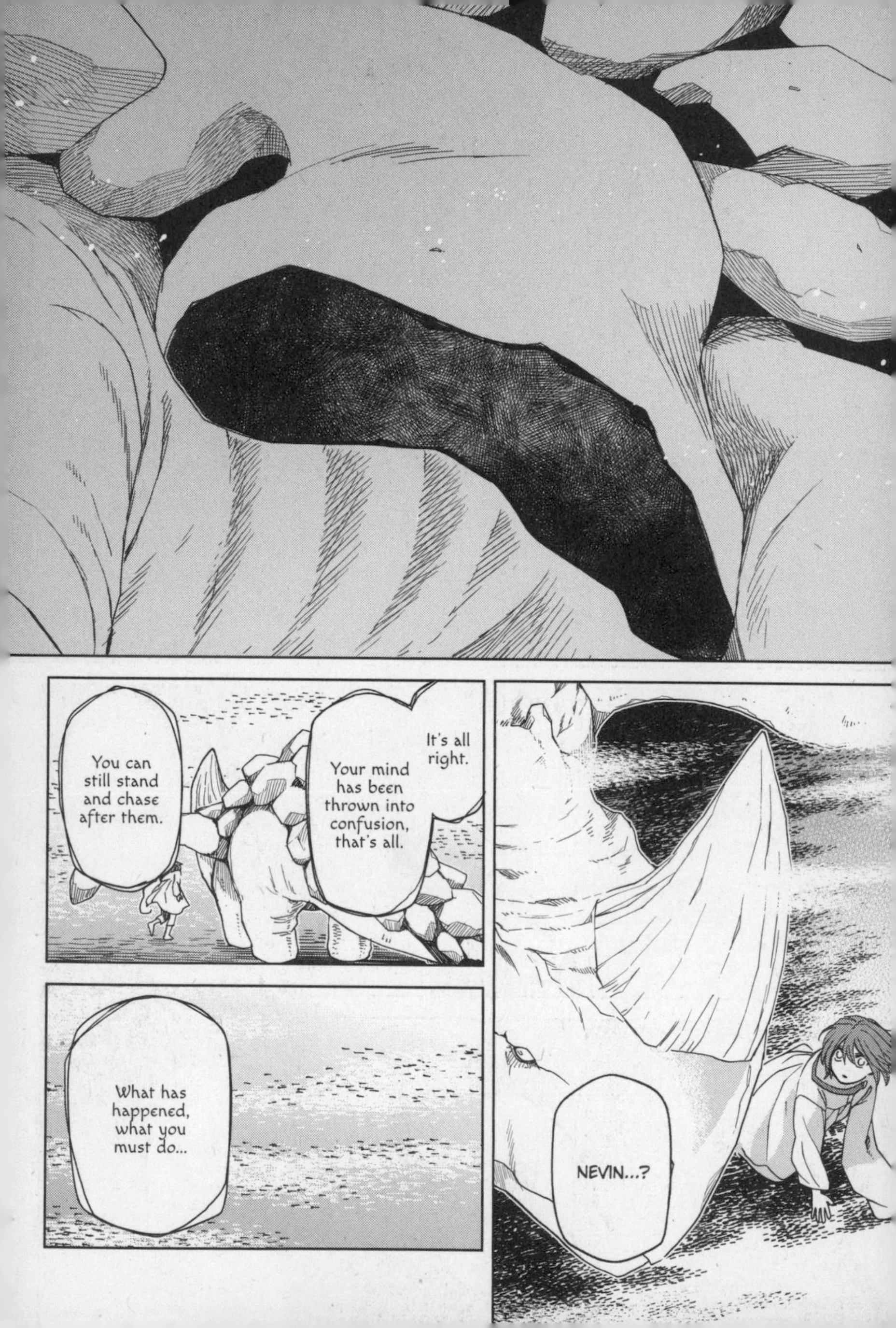
NEVIN...?
It's all right.
Your mind has been thrown into confusion, that's all.
You can still stand and chase after them.
What has happened, what you must do...

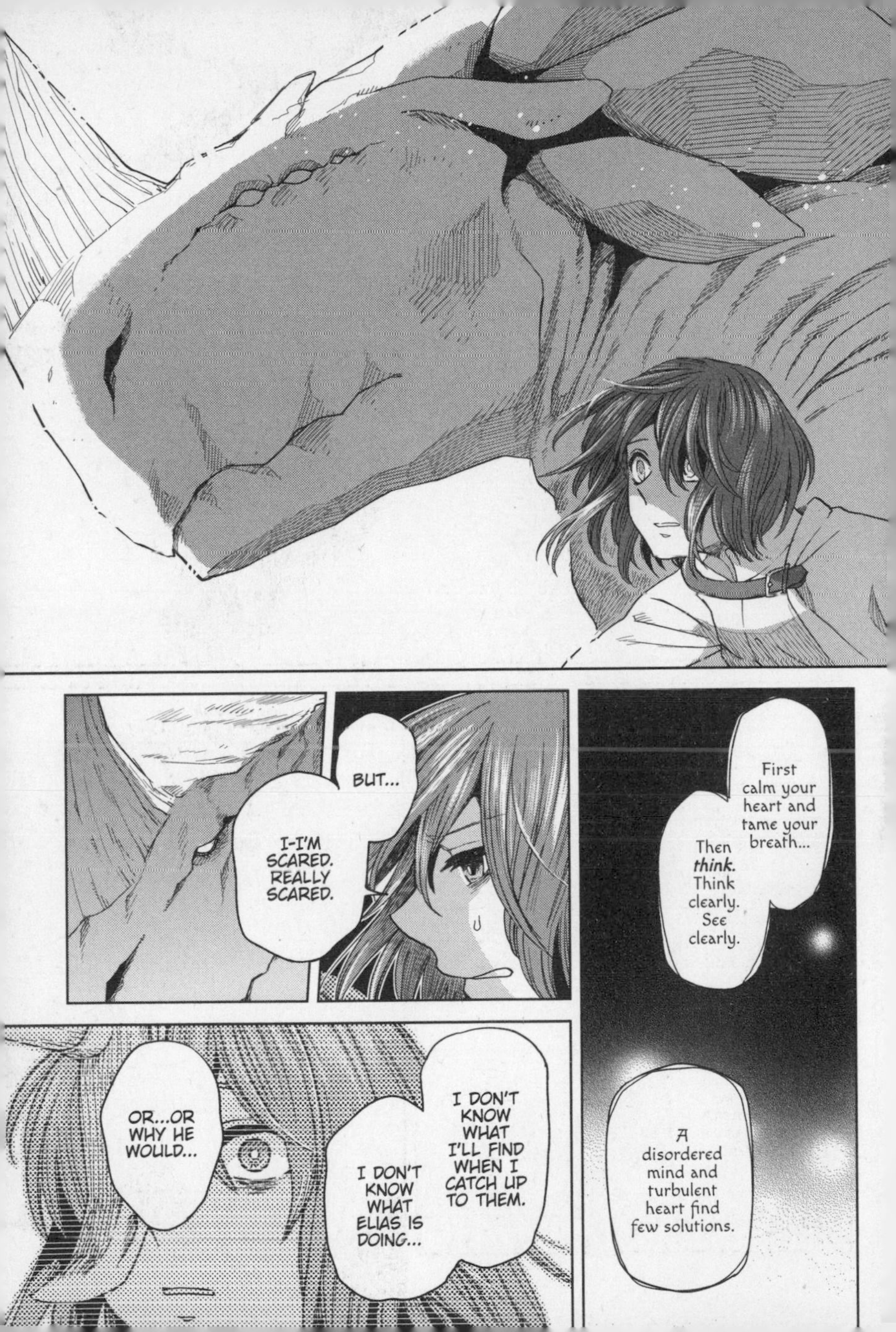
First calm your heart and tame your breath...
Then *think*. Think clearly. See clearly.
A disordered mind and turbulent heart find few solutions.
BUT...
I-I'M SCARED. REALLY SCARED.
I DON'T KNOW WHAT I'LL FIND WHEN I CATCH UP TO THEM.
I DON'T KNOW WHAT ELIAS IS DOING...
OR...OR WHY HE WOULD...

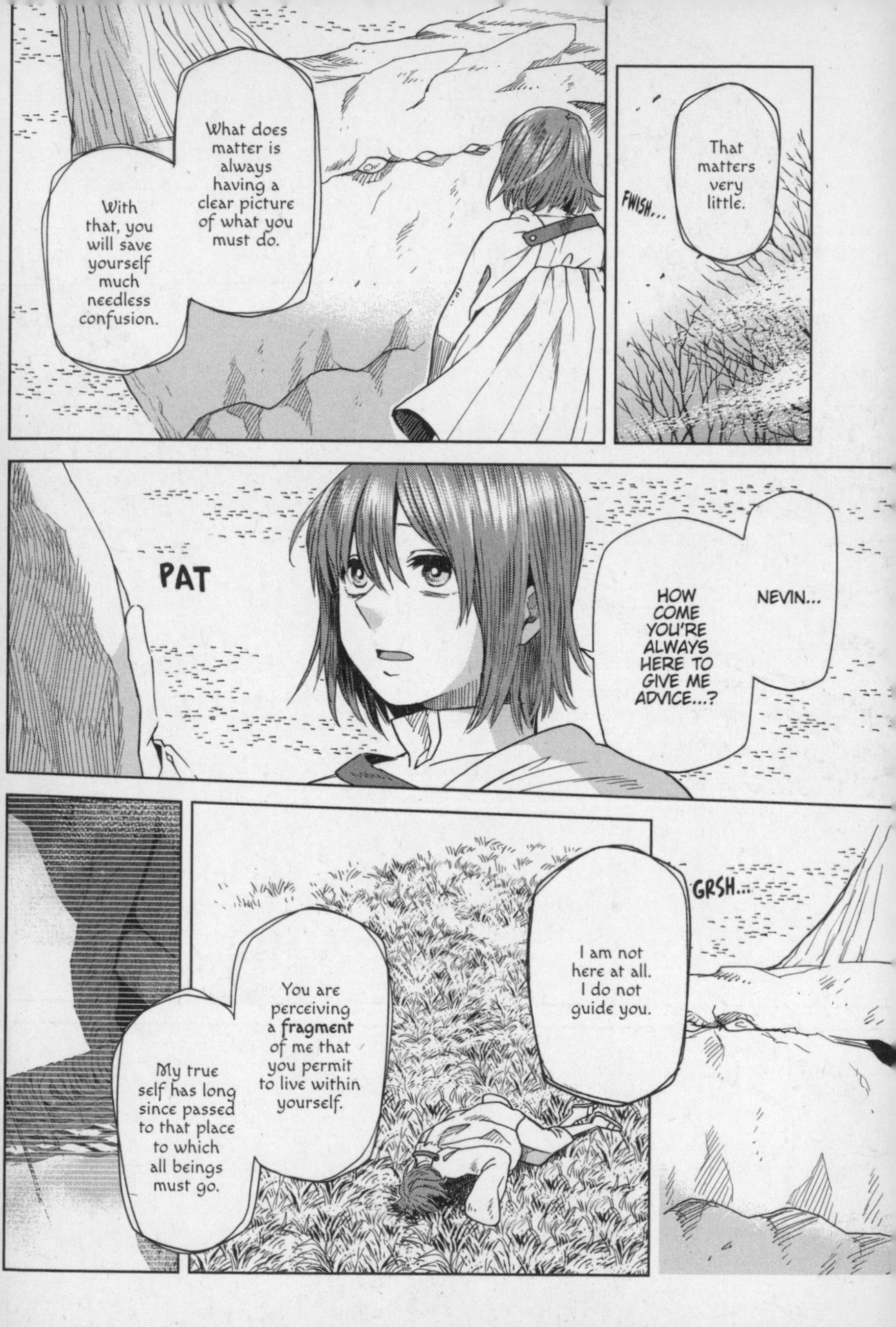
FWISH...
That matters very little.
What does matter is always having a clear picture of what you must do.
With that, you will save yourself much needless confusion.
NEVIN...
HOW COME YOU'RE ALWAYS HERE TO GIVE ME ADVICE...?
PAT
GRSH...
I am not here at all. I do not guide you.
You are perceiving a **fragment** of me that you permit to live within yourself.
My true self has long since passed to that place to which all beings must go.

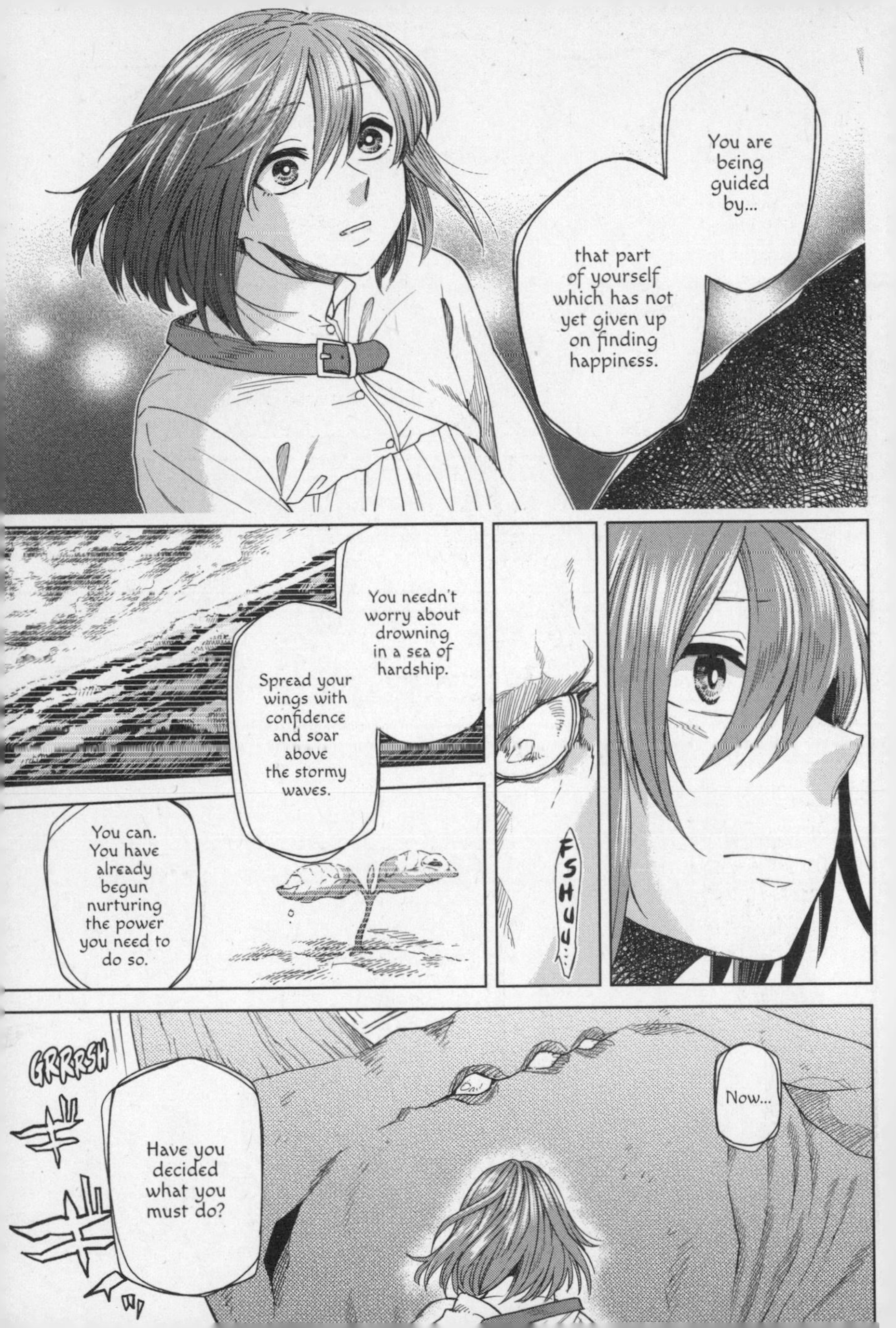
You are being guided by...
that part of yourself which has not yet given up on finding happiness.
FSHUU...
You needn't worry about drowning in a sea of hardship.
Spread your wings with confidence and soar above the stormy waves.
You can. You have already begun nurturing the power you need to do so.
Now...
Have you decided what you must do?
GRRRSH

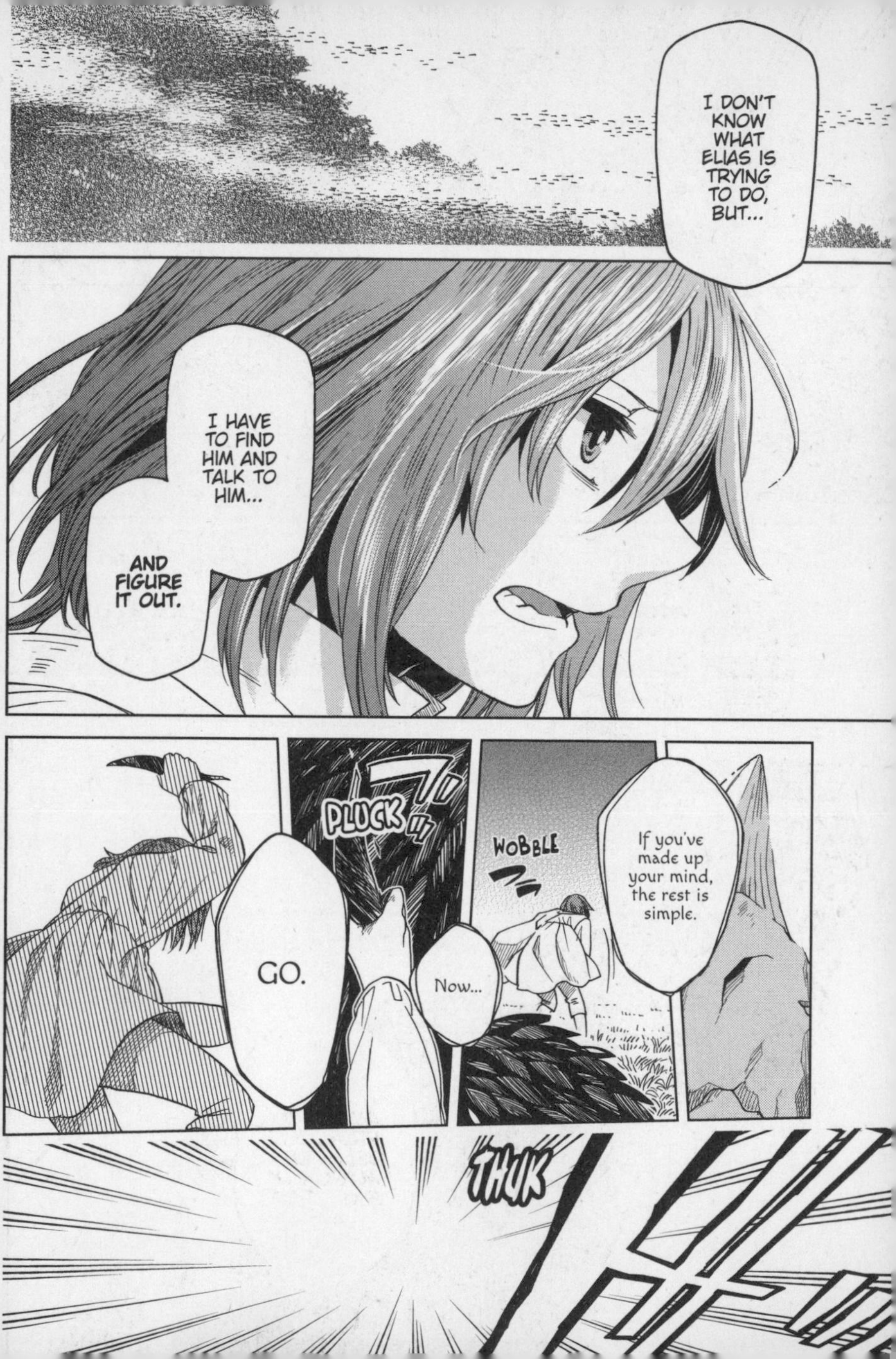
I DON'T KNOW WHAT ELIAS IS TRYING TO DO, BUT...
I HAVE TO FIND HIM AND TALK TO HIM...
AND FIGURE IT OUT.
If you've made up your mind, the rest is simple.
WOBBLE
Now...
PLUCK
GO.
THUK

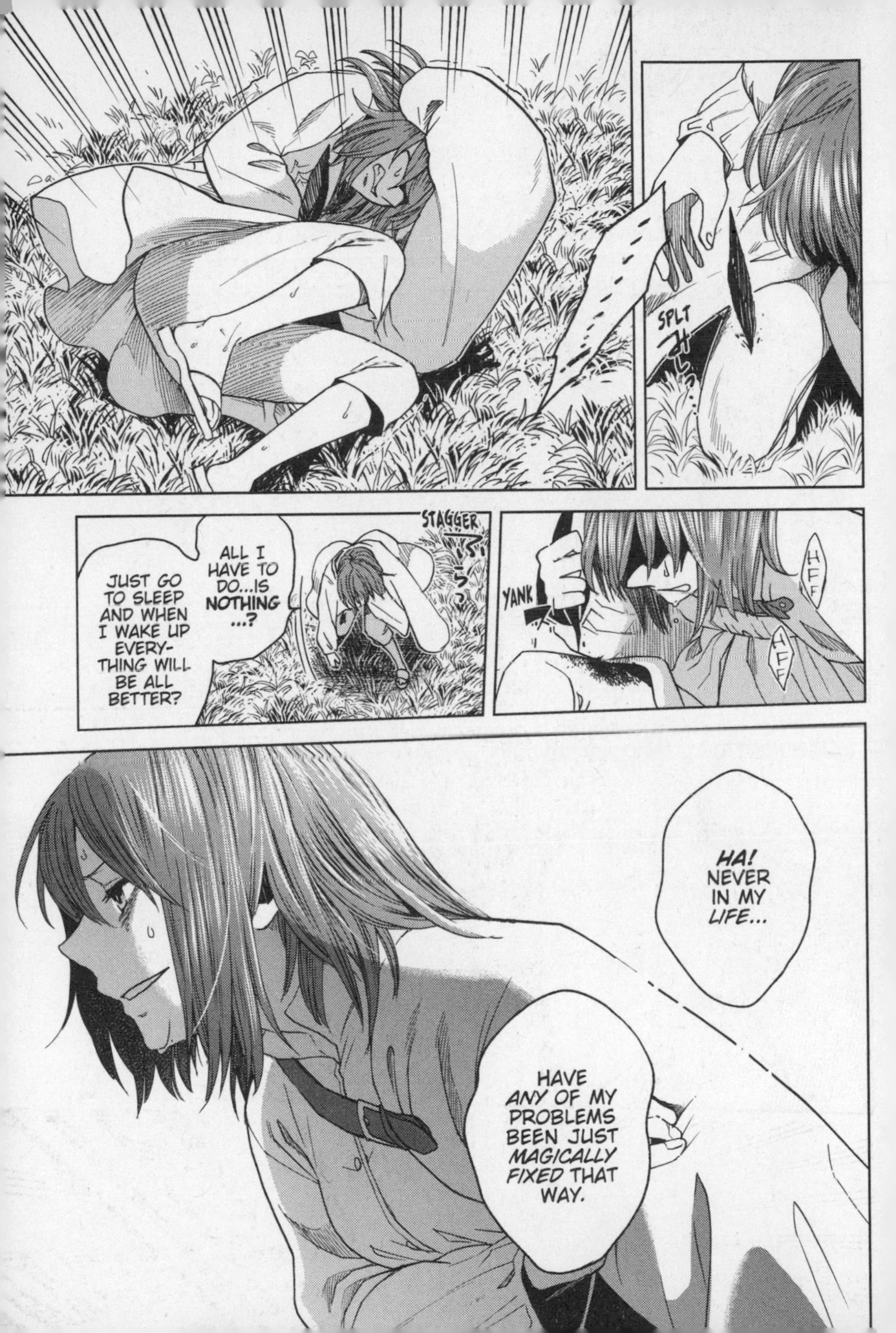
SPLT
YANK
HFF
HFF
STAGGER
ALL I HAVE TO DO...IS NOTHING ...?
JUST GO TO SLEEP AND WHEN I WAKE UP EVERY-THING WILL BE ALL BETTER?
HA! NEVER IN MY LIFE...
HAVE ANY OF MY PROBLEMS BEEN JUST MAGICALLY FIXED THAT WAY.

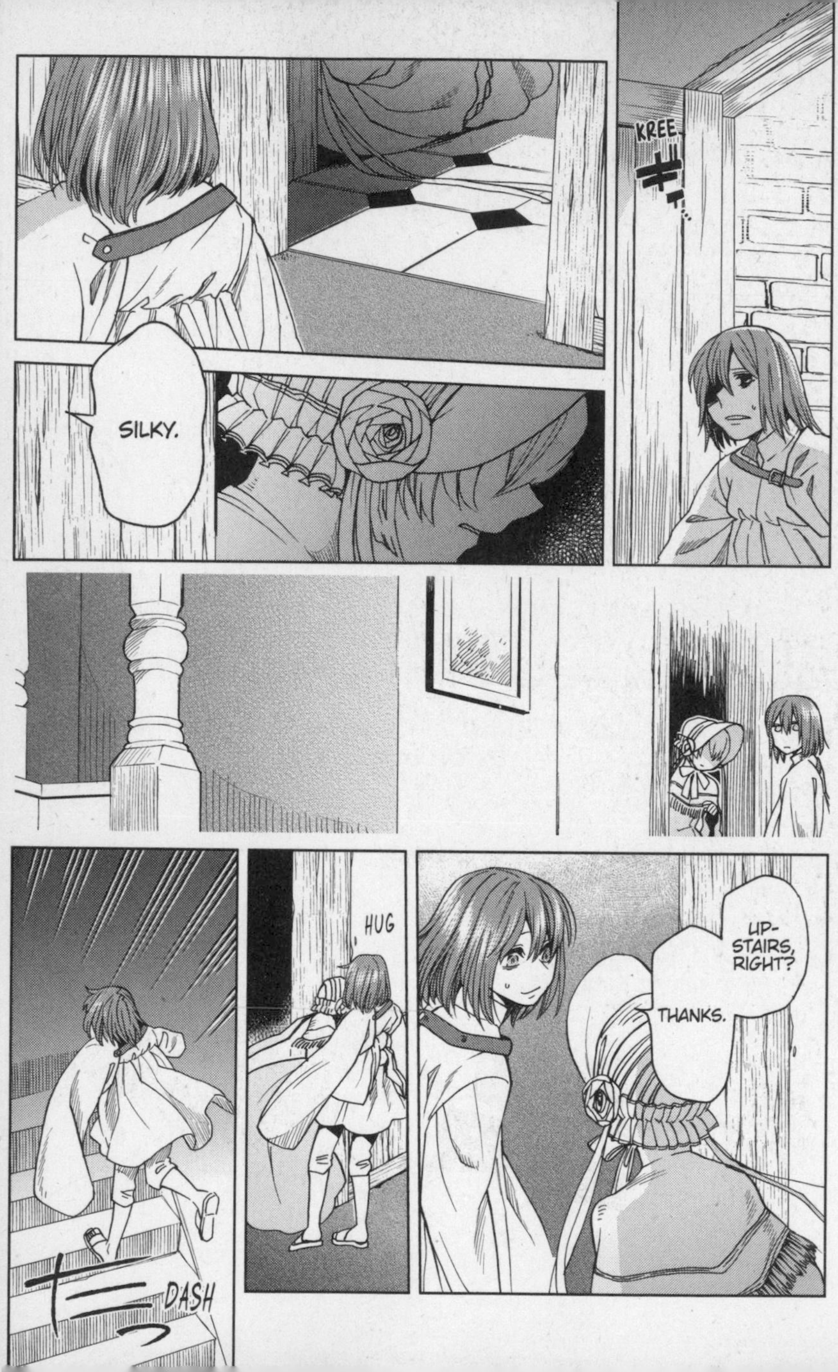
KREE
SILKY.
UP-STAIRS, RIGHT?
THANKS.
HUG
DASH

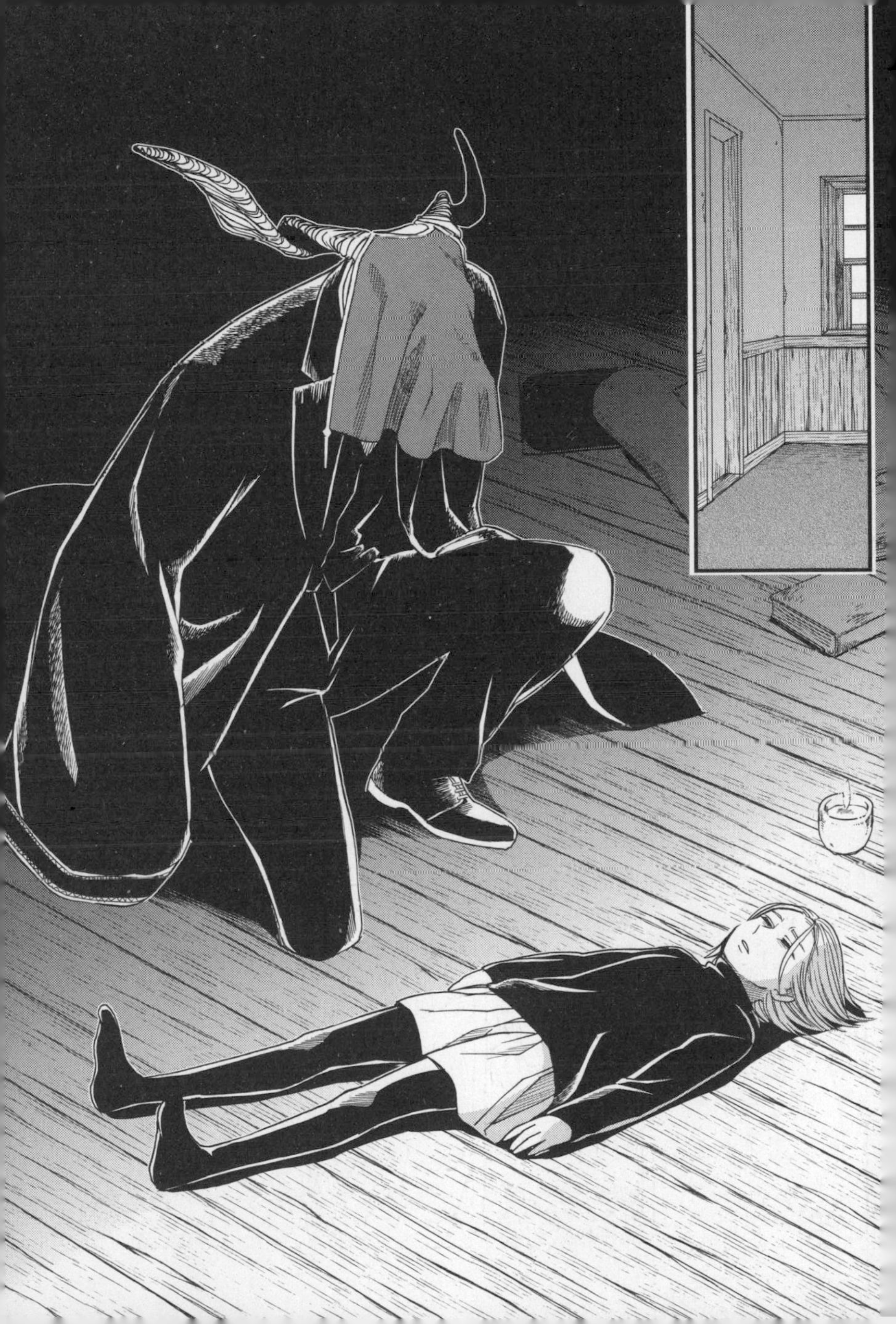

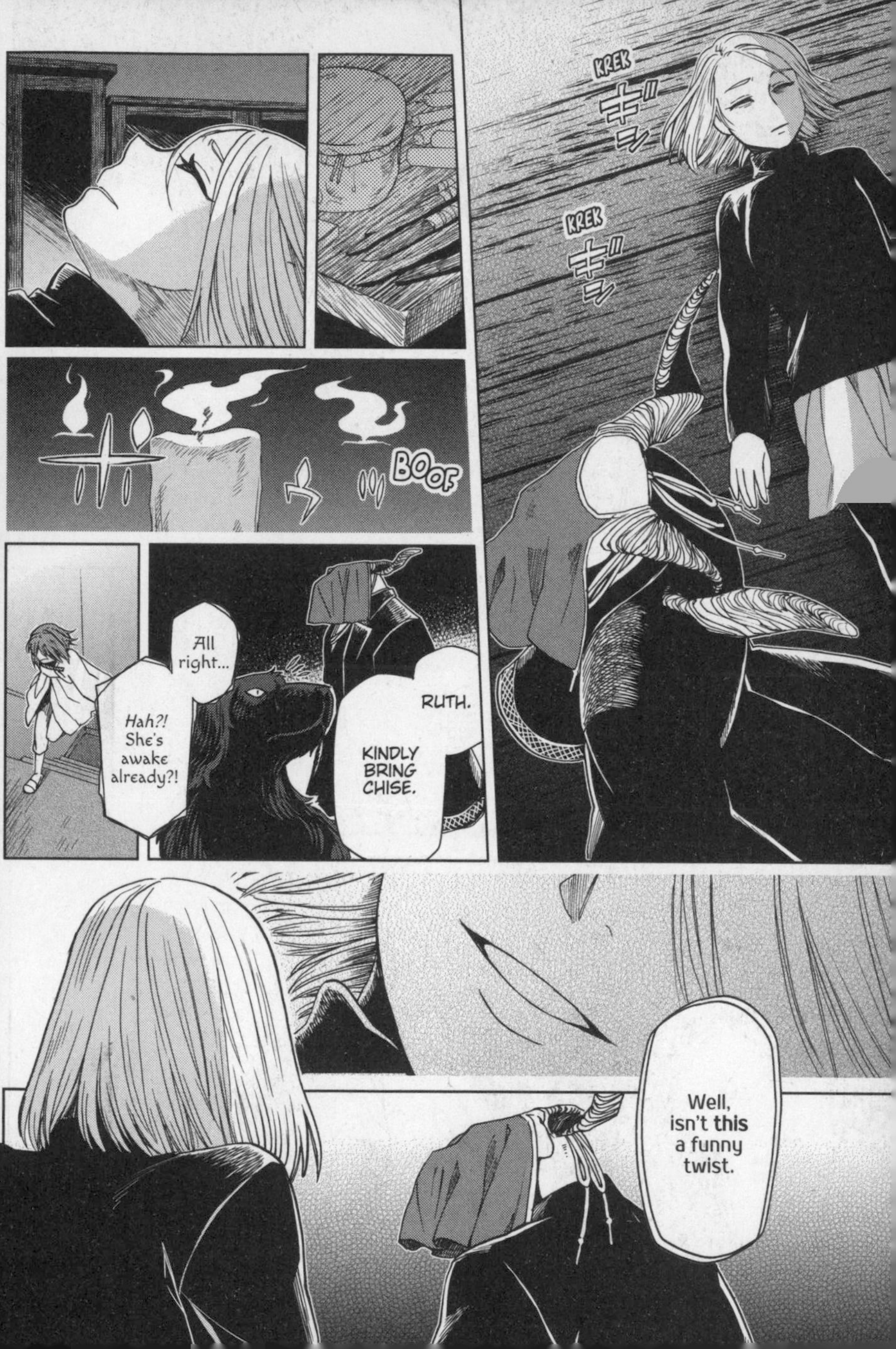
KREK
KREK
BOOF
RUTH.
KINDLY BRING CHISE.
All right...
Hah?! She's awake already?!
Well, isn't this a funny twist.

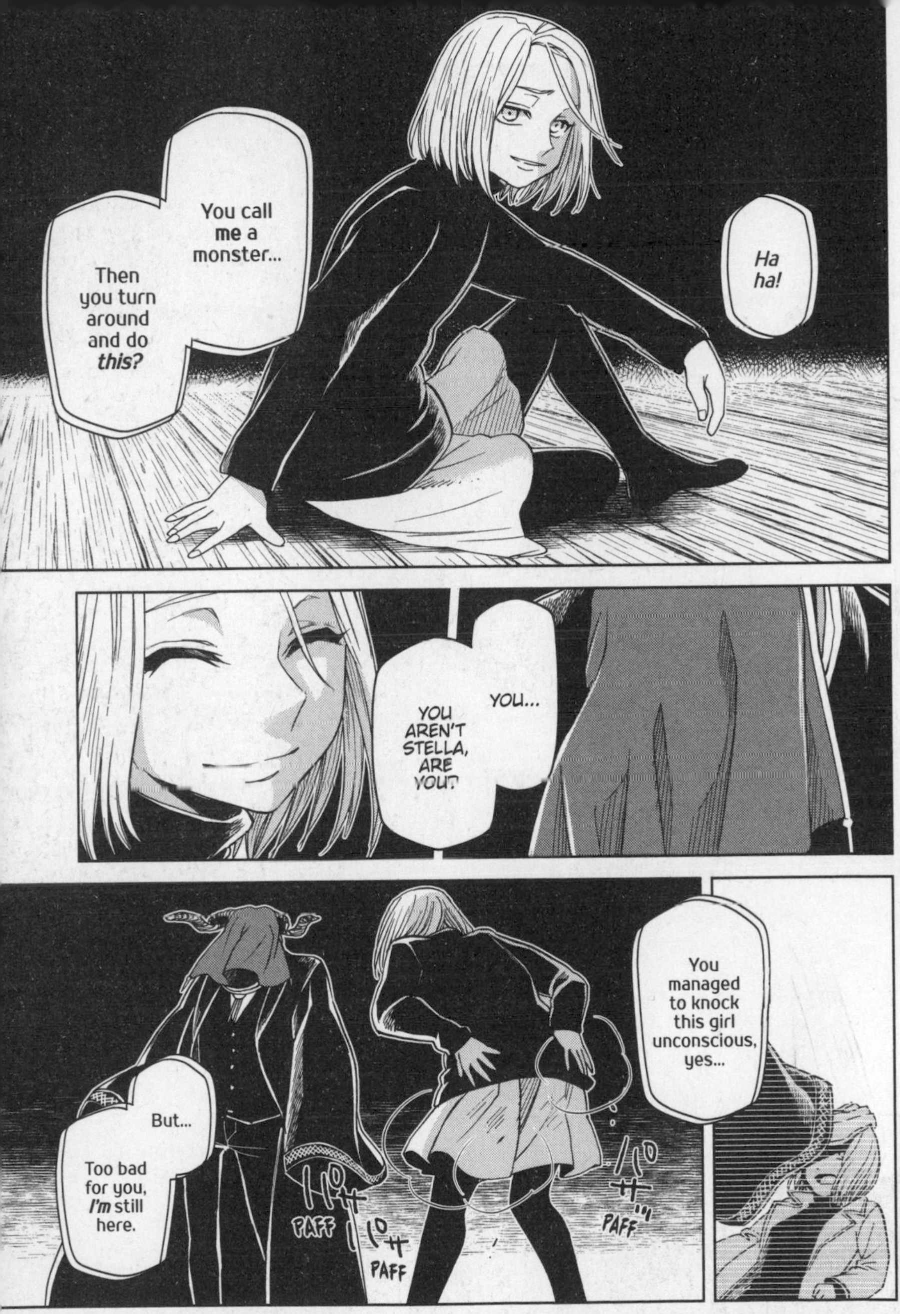
Ha ha!
You call me a monster...
Then you turn around and do *this*?
YOU...
YOU AREN'T STELLA, ARE YOU?
You managed to knock this girl unconscious, yes...
パッ PAFF
パッ PAFF
パッ PAFF
But...
Too bad for you, *I'm* still here.

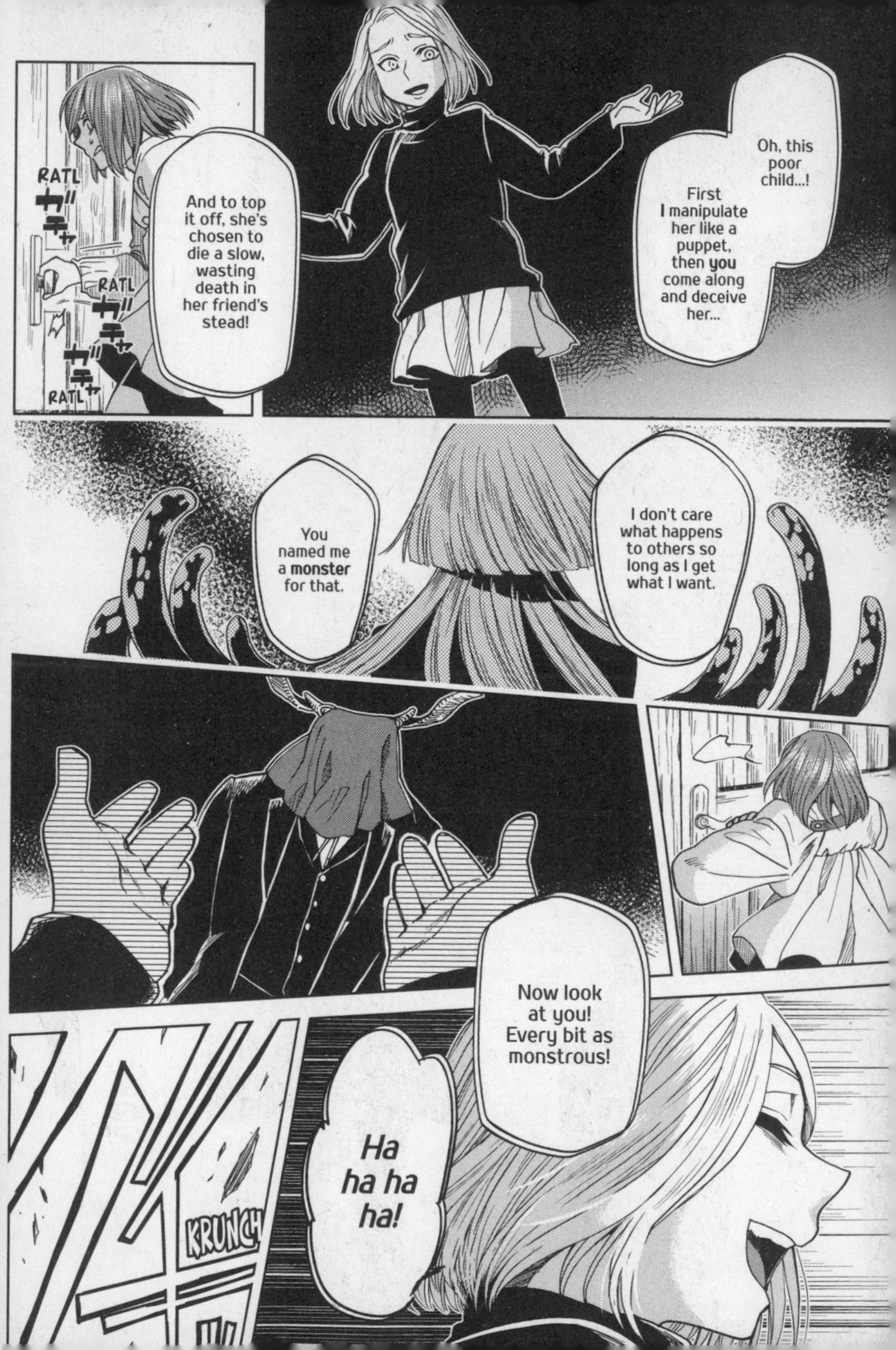

Oh, this poor child...!
First I manipulate her like a puppet, then **you** come along and deceive her...
And to top it off, she's chosen to die a slow, wasting death in her friend's stead!
RATL
RATL
RATL
I don't care what happens to others so long as I get what I want.
You named me a **monster** for that.
Now look at you! Every bit as monstrous!
Ha ha ha ha!
KRUNCH

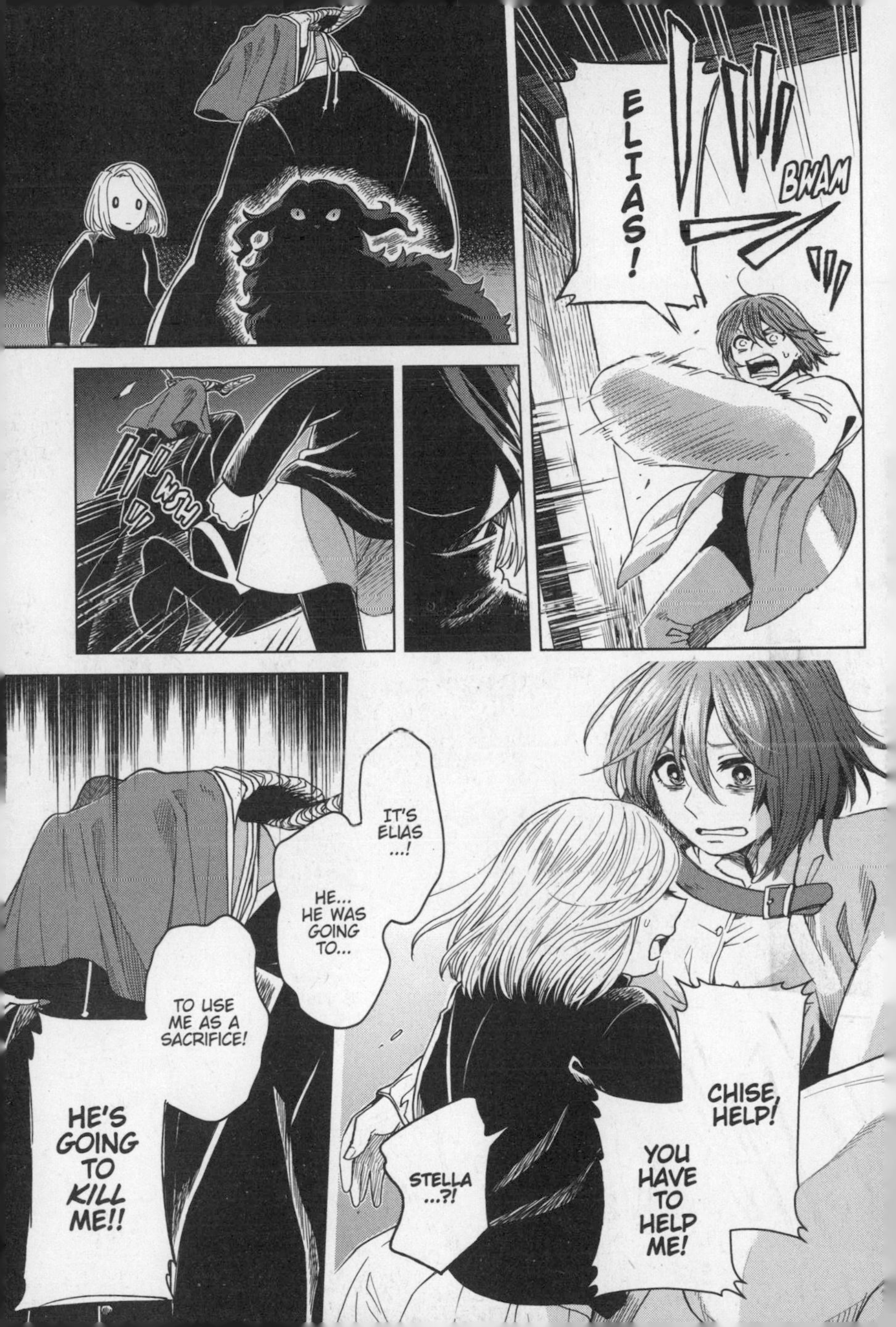
ELIAS!
BWAM
WSH
CHISE, HELP!
YOU HAVE TO HELP ME!
STELLA ...?!
IT'S ELIAS ...!
HE... HE WAS GOING TO...
TO USE ME AS A SACRIFICE!
HE'S GOING TO KILL ME!!

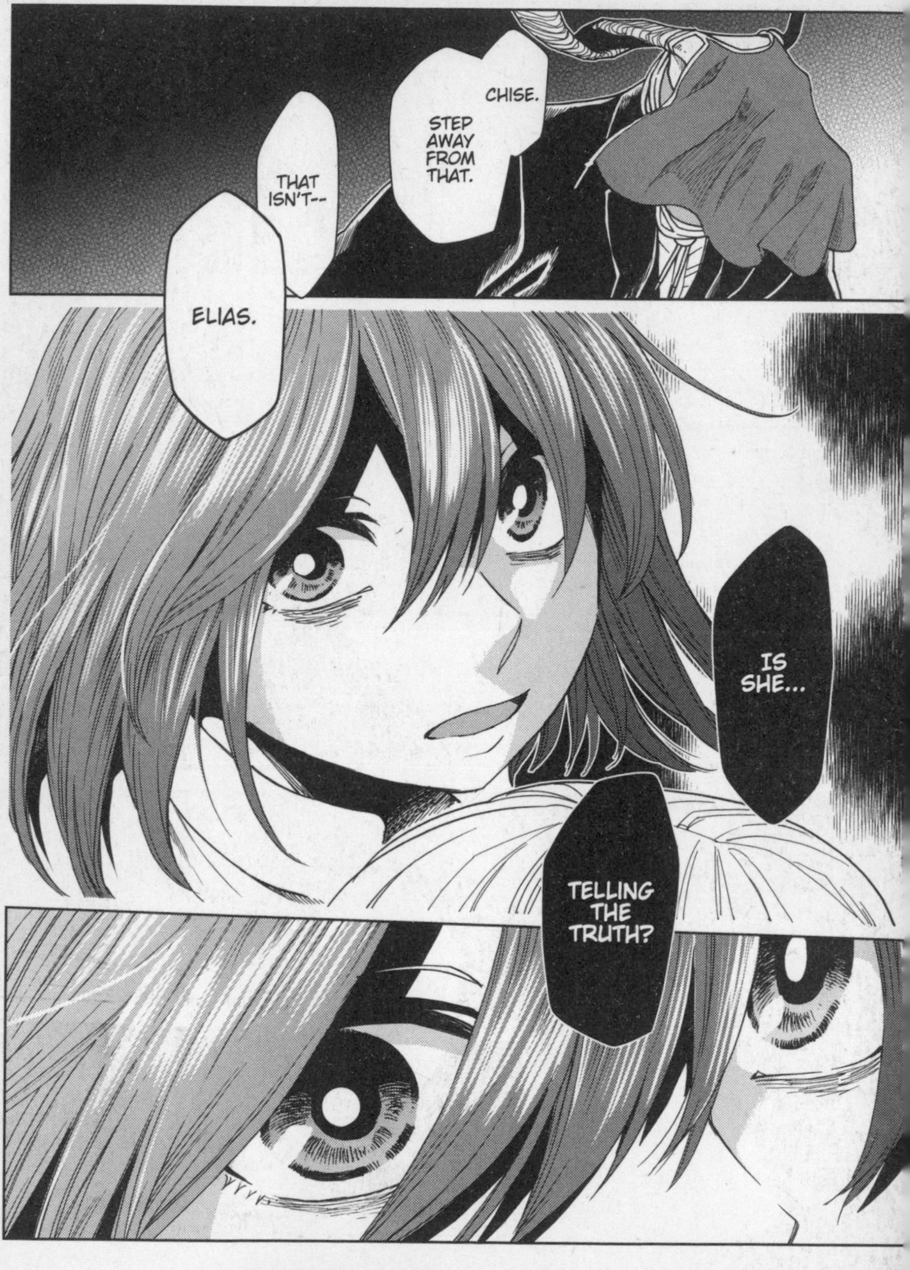
CHISE.
STEP AWAY FROM THAT.
THAT ISN'T--
ELIAS.
IS SHE...
TELLING THE TRUTH?

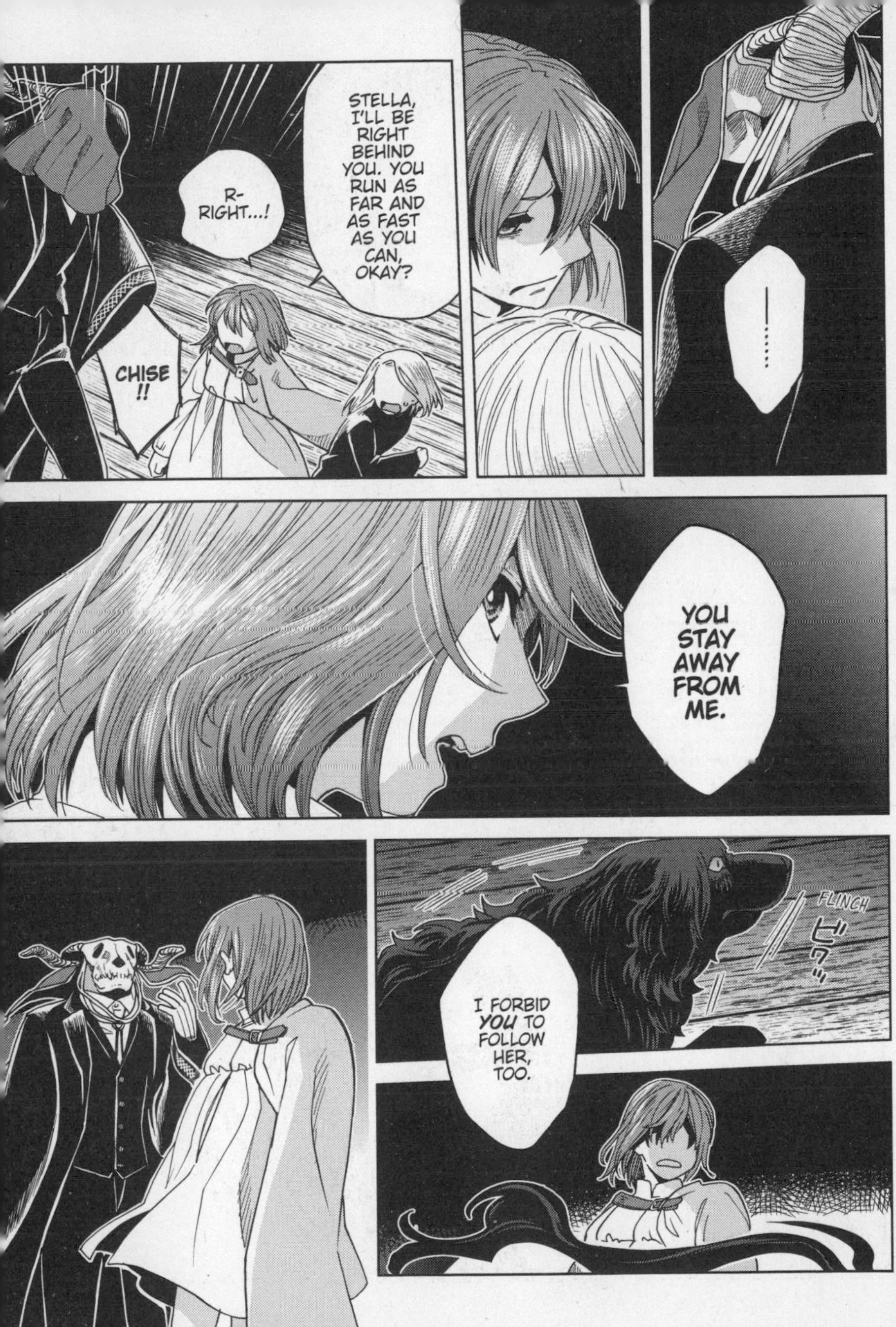
......
STELLA, I'LL BE RIGHT BEHIND YOU. YOU RUN AS FAR AND AS FAST AS YOU CAN, OKAY?
R-RIGHT...!
CHISE!!
YOU STAY AWAY FROM ME.
FLINCH
ビクッ
I FORBID *YOU* TO FOLLOW HER, TOO.

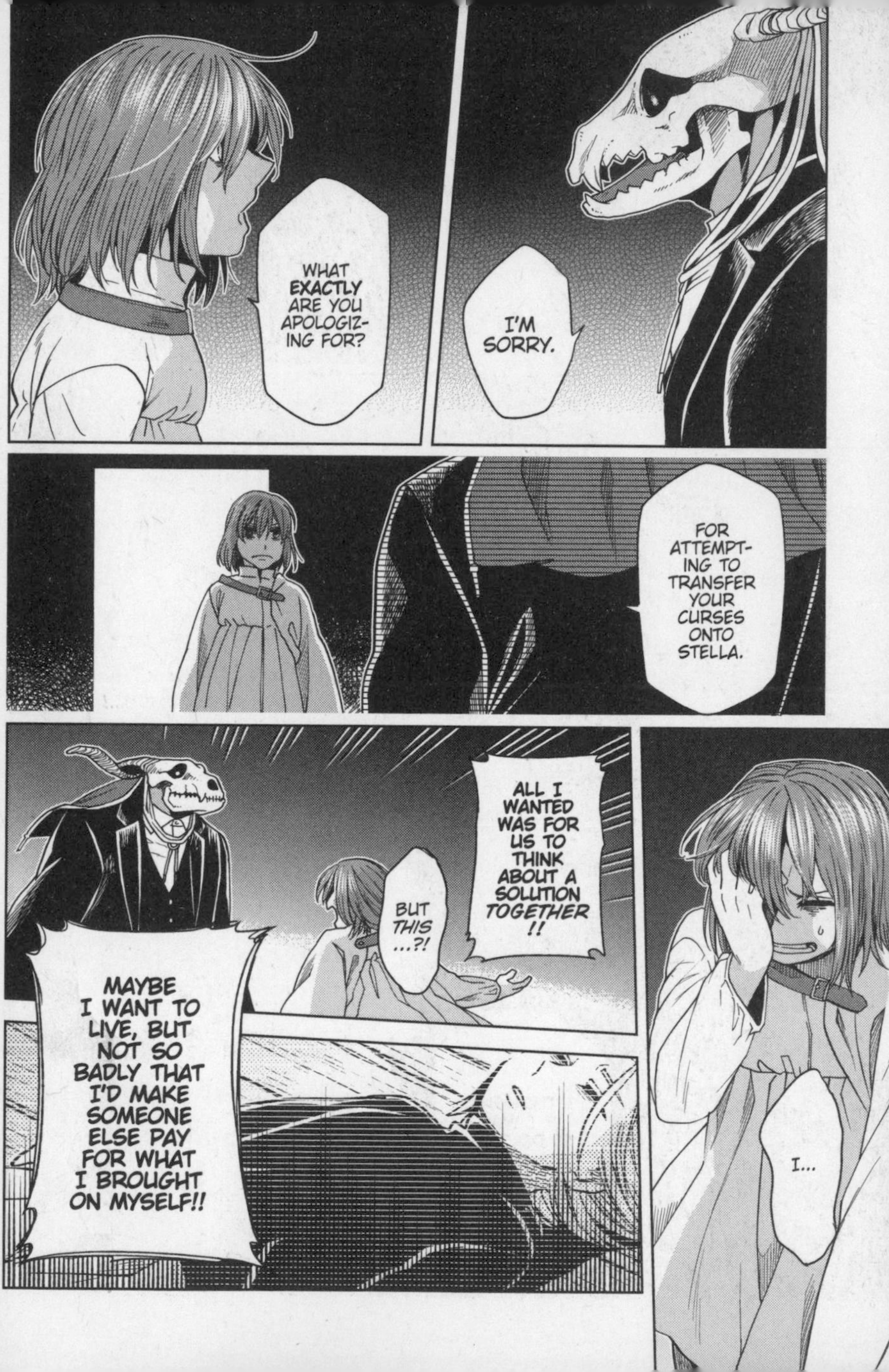
I'M SORRY.
WHAT EXACTLY ARE YOU APOLOGIZ-ING FOR?
FOR ATTEMPT-ING TO TRANSFER YOUR CURSES ONTO STELLA.
...
I...
ALL I WANTED WAS FOR US TO THINK ABOUT A SOLUTION TOGETHER!!
BUT THIS ...?!
MAYBE I WANT TO LIVE, BUT NOT SO BADLY THAT I'D MAKE SOMEONE ELSE PAY FOR WHAT I BROUGHT ON MYSELF!!

CHISE...

I'VE MADE NO PROMISES.

YOU SEEM SO CHILDLIKE SOMETIMES, BUT YOU'RE **NOT**...!

YOU'RE **CENTURIES** OLD...! YOU'VE LIVED SO MUCH LONGER THAN I HAVE!

BUT YOU...

......

Y...

YOU...!

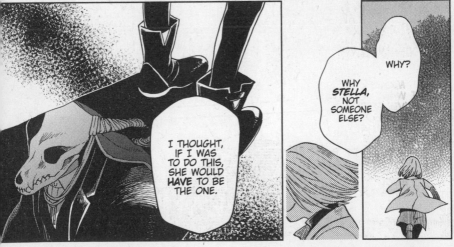

WHY?

WHY **STELLA**, NOT SOMEONE ELSE?

I THOUGHT, IF I WAS TO DO THIS, SHE WOULD **HAVE** TO BE THE ONE.

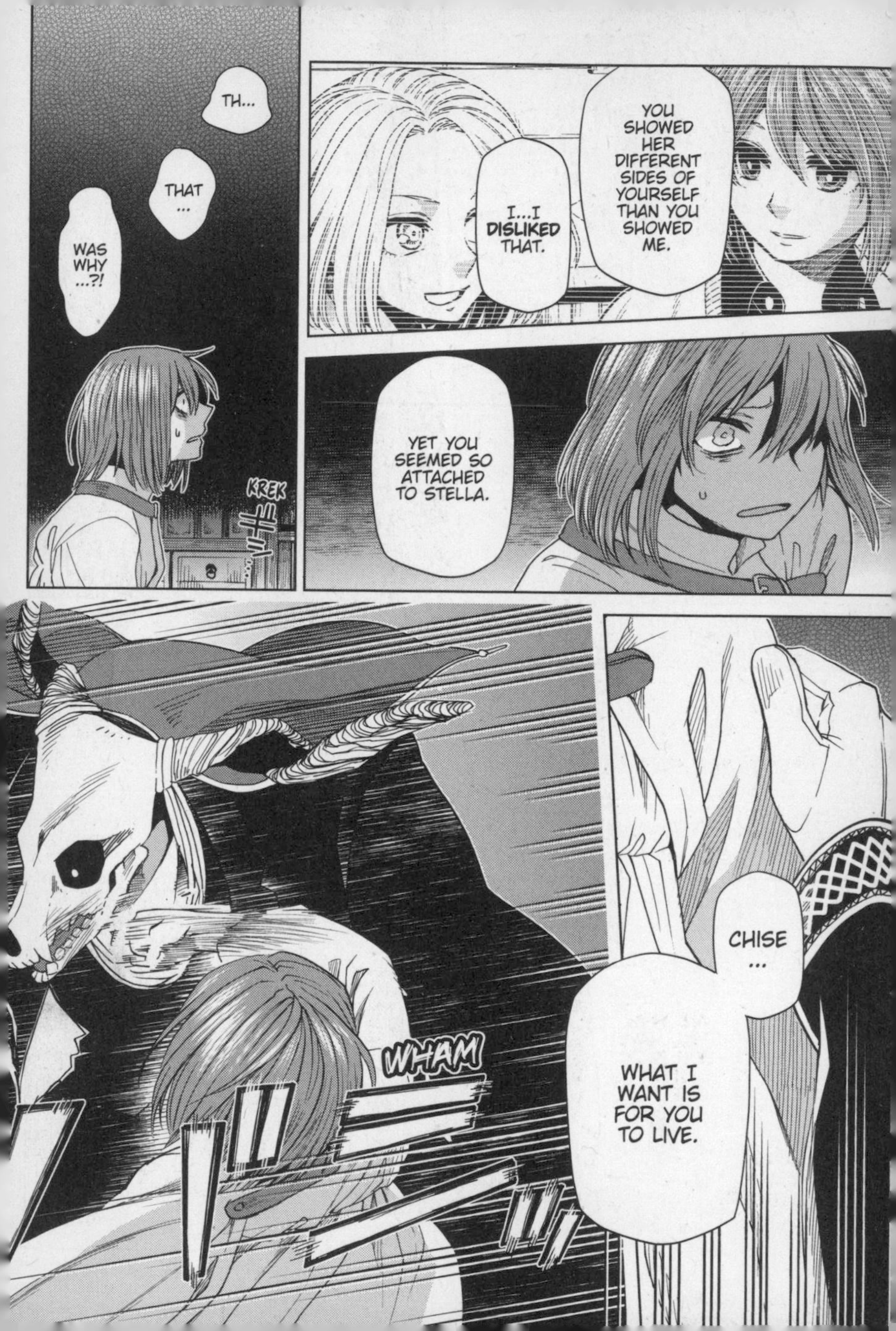
YOU SHOWED HER DIFFERENT SIDES OF YOURSELF THAN YOU SHOWED ME.
I...I **DISLIKED** THAT.
YET YOU SEEMED SO ATTACHED TO STELLA.
TH...
THAT ...
WAS WHY ...?!
KREK
CHISE ...
WHAT I WANT IS FOR YOU TO LIVE.
WHAM

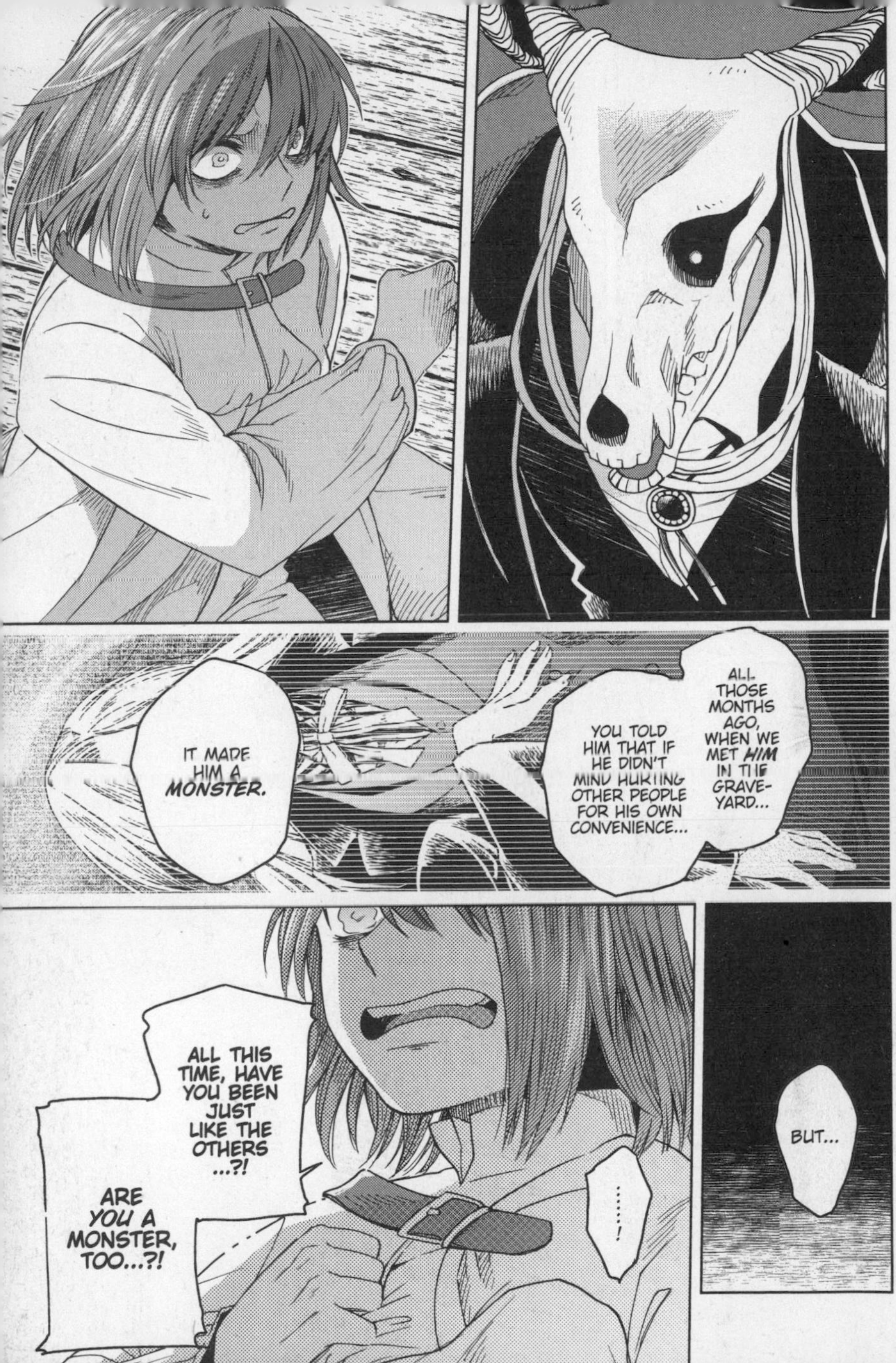
ALL THOSE MONTHS AGO, WHEN WE MET *HIM* IN THE GRAVE-YARD...
YOU TOLD HIM THAT IF HE DIDN'T MIND HURTING OTHER PEOPLE FOR HIS OWN CONVENIENCE...
IT MADE HIM A ***MONSTER.***
BUT...
......!
ALL THIS TIME, HAVE YOU BEEN JUST LIKE THE OTHERS ...?!
ARE *YOU* A MONSTER, TOO...?!

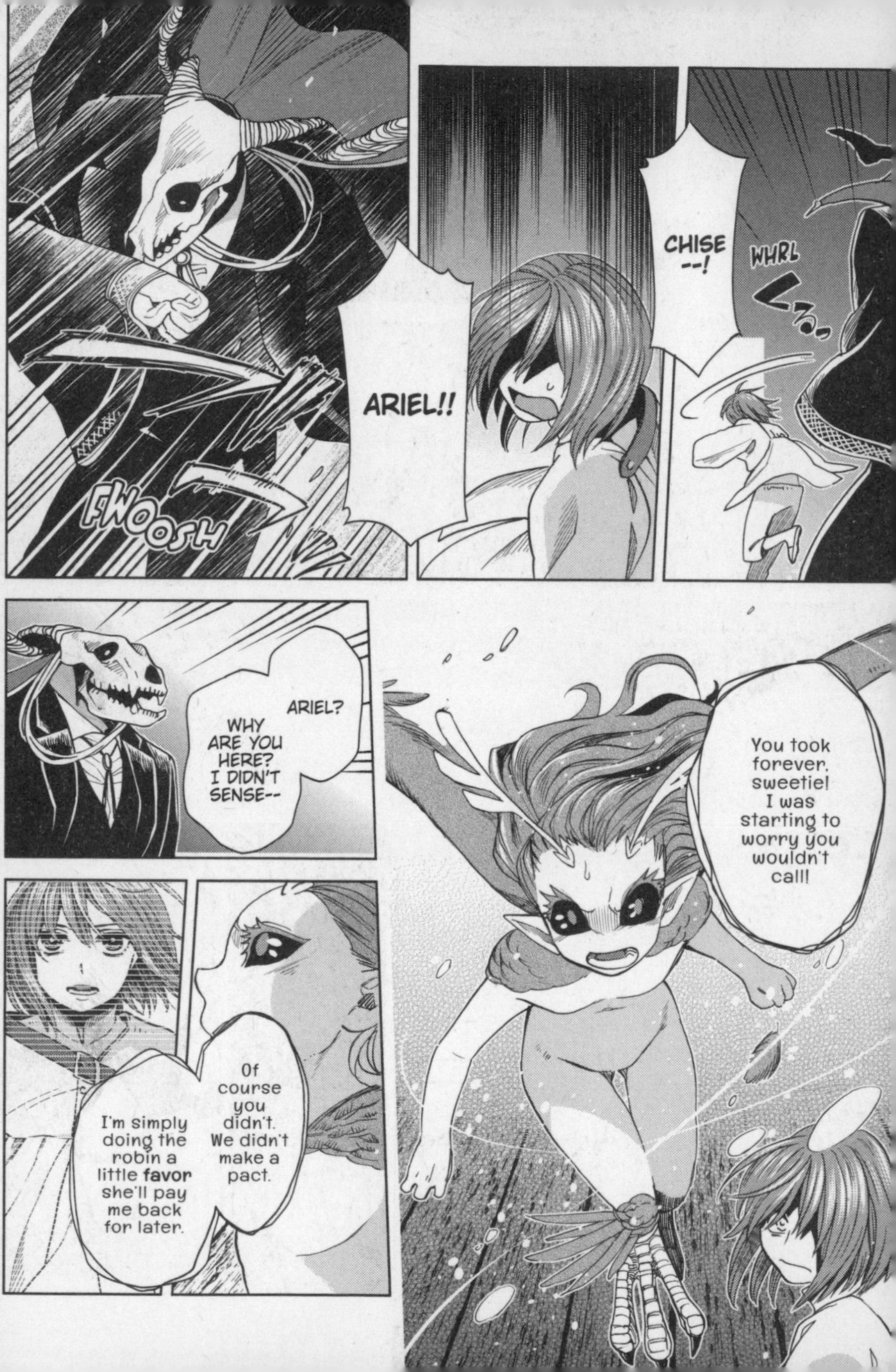
CHISE --!
WHRL
ARIEL!!
FWOOSH
You took forever, sweetie! I was starting to worry you wouldn't call!
ARIEL? WHY ARE YOU HERE? I DIDN'T SENSE--
Of course you didn't. We didn't make a pact.
I'm simply doing the robin a little **favor** she'll pay me back for later.

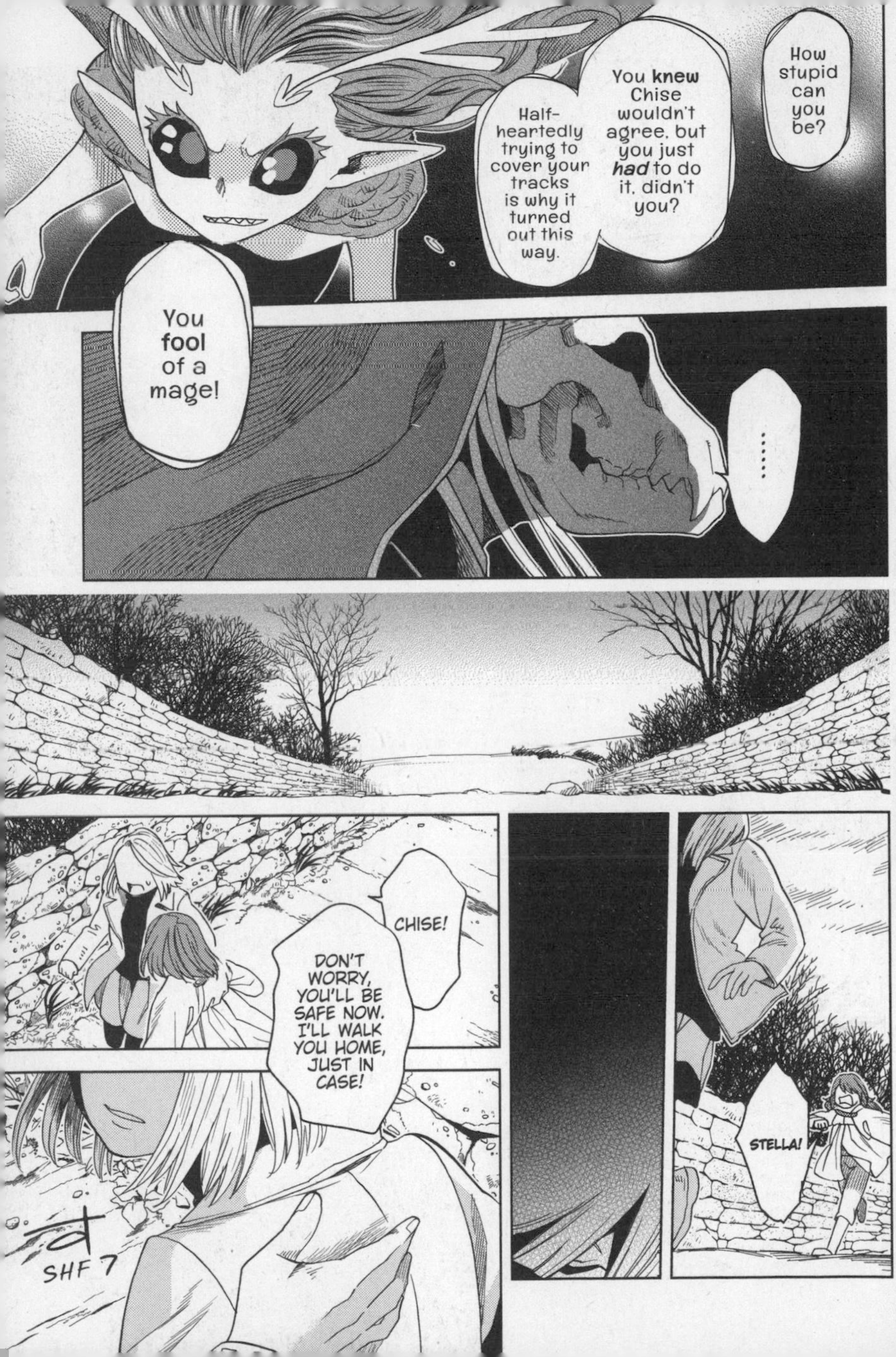
How stupid can you be?
You knew Chise wouldn't agree, but you just had to do it, didn't you?
Half-heartedly trying to cover your tracks is why it turned out this way.
You fool of a mage!
......
STELLA!
CHISE!
DON'T WORRY, YOU'LL BE SAFE NOW. I'LL WALK YOU HOME, JUST IN CASE!
SHF

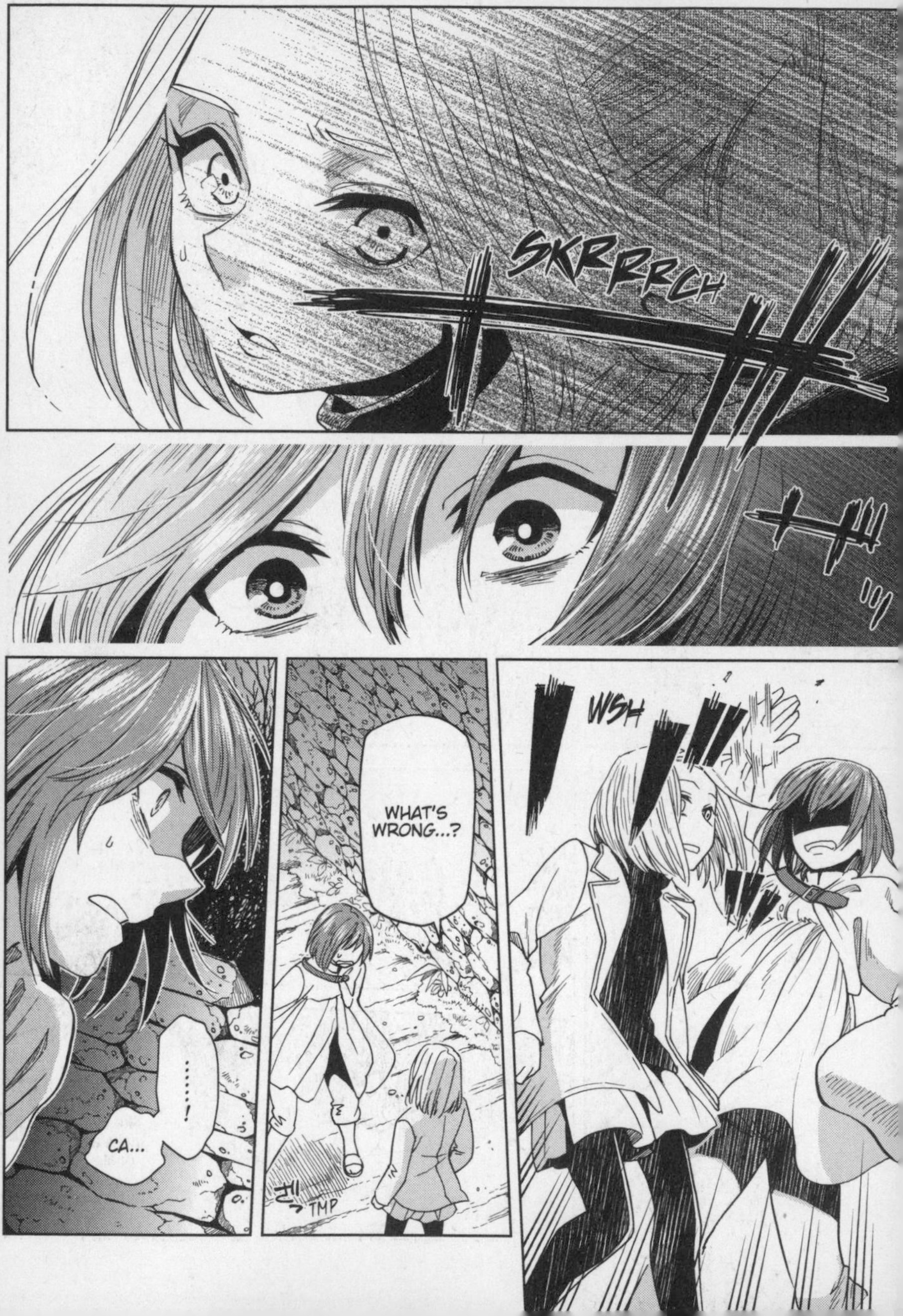
SKRRRCH
WSH
WHAT'S WRONG...?
TMP
......!
CA...

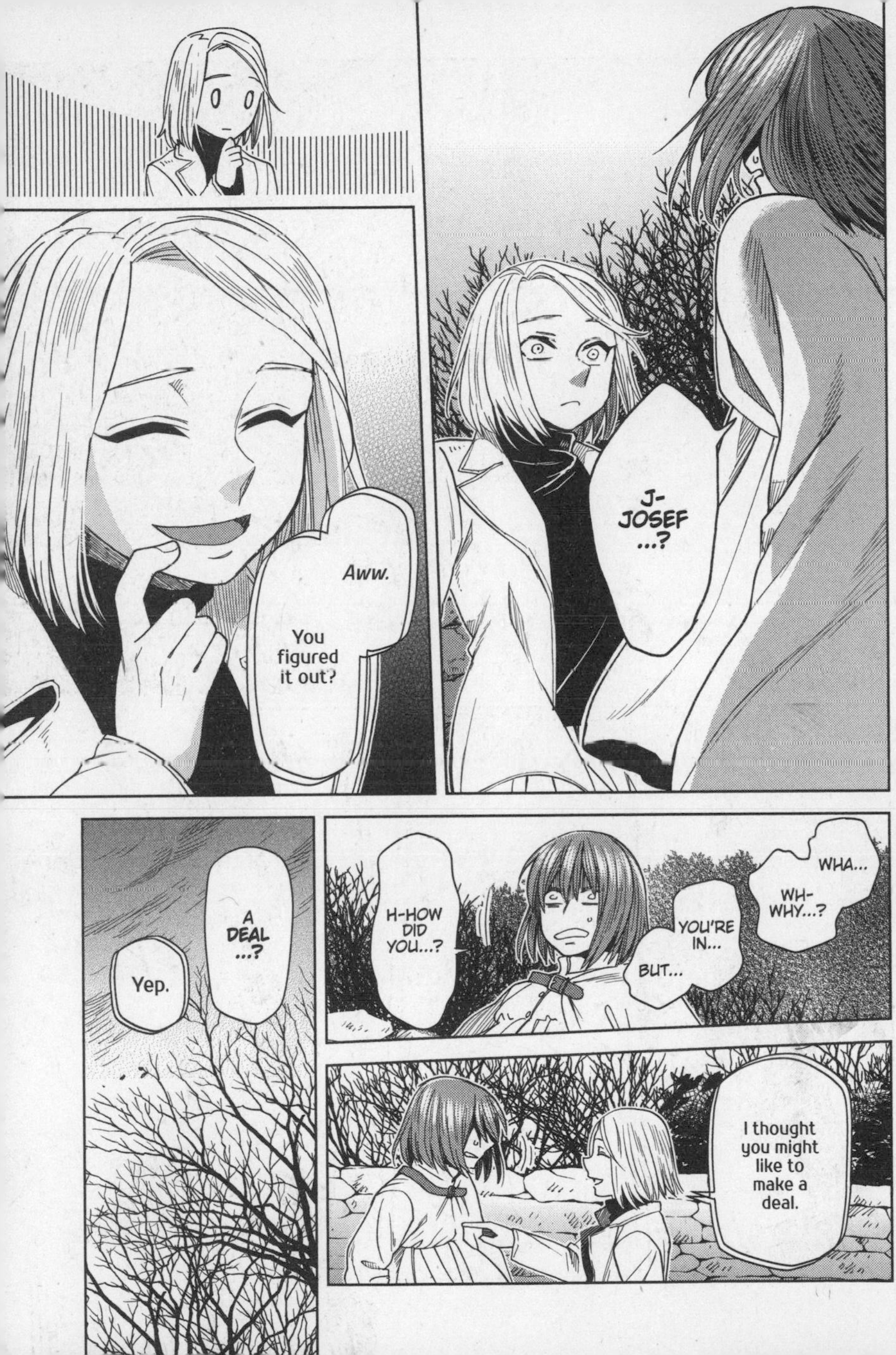
J-JOSEF ...?
Aww.
You figured it out?
WHA...
WH-WHY...?
YOU'RE IN...
BUT...
H-HOW DID YOU...?
I thought you might like to make a deal.
A DEAL ...?
Yep.

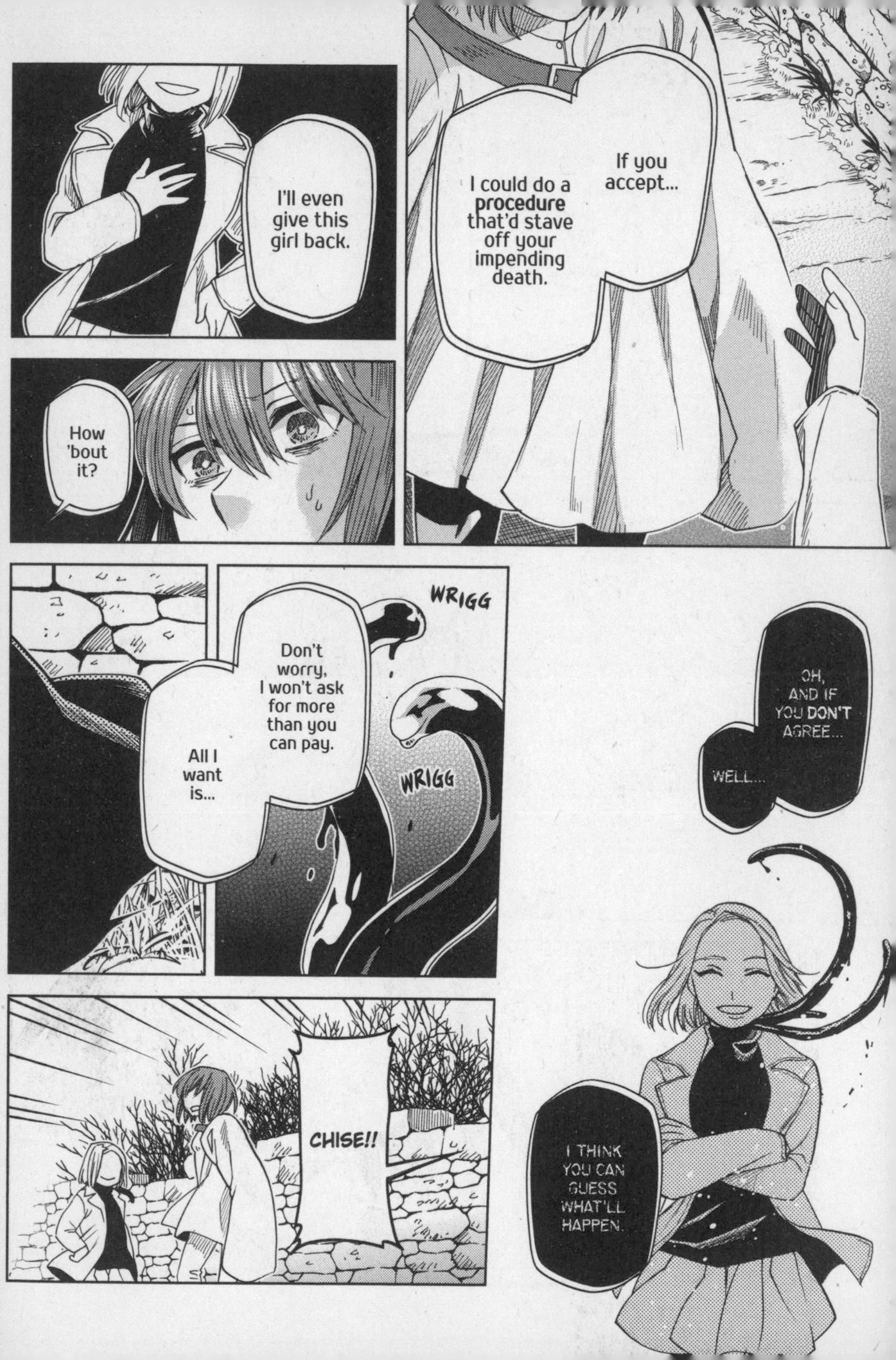
If you accept...
I could do a **procedure** that'd stave off your impending death.
I'll even give this girl back.
How 'bout it?
OH, AND IF YOU DON'T AGREE...
WELL...
I THINK YOU CAN GUESS WHAT'LL HAPPEN.
WRIGG
Don't worry, I won't ask for more than you can pay.
All I want is...
WRIGG
CHISE!!

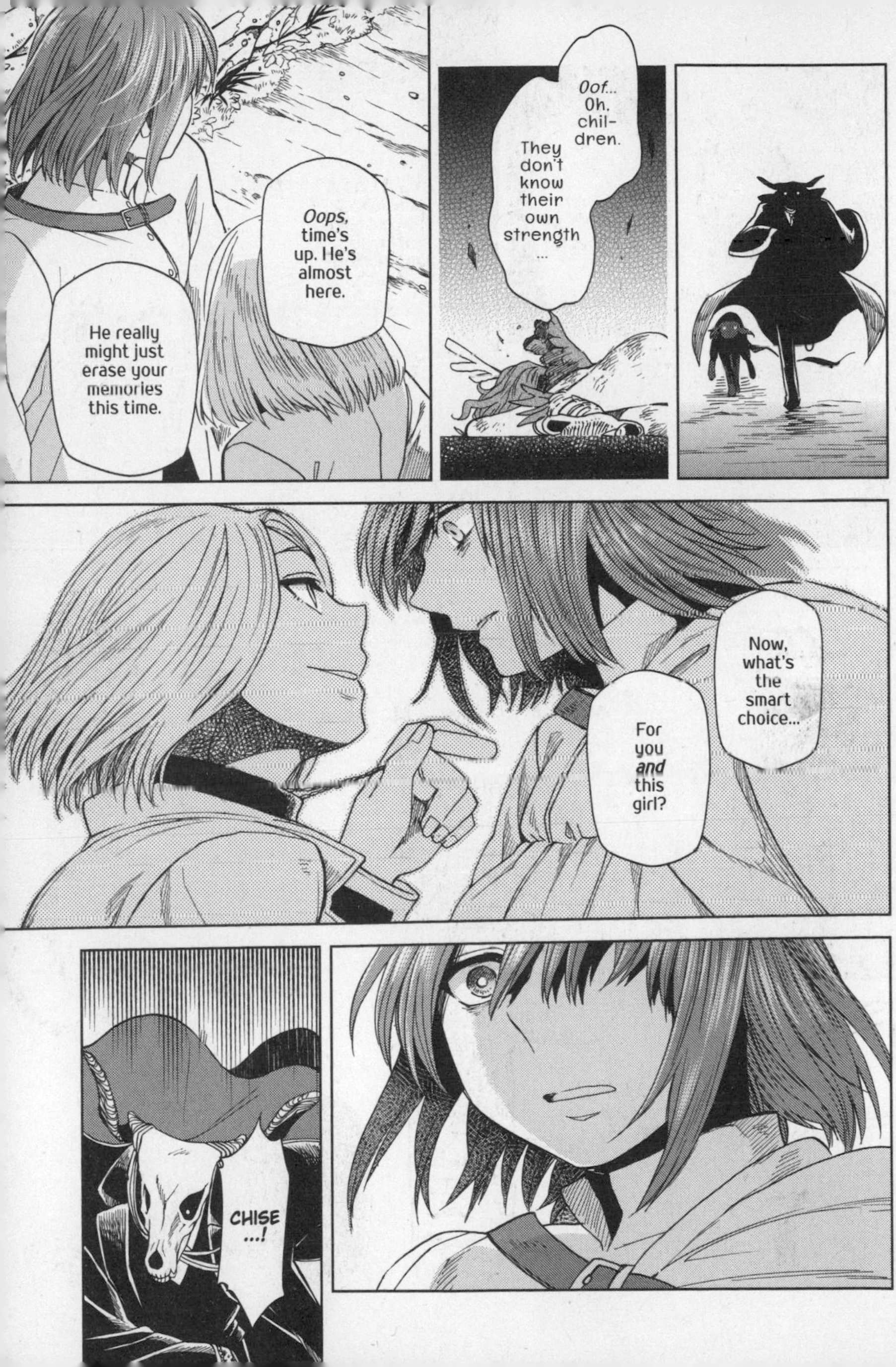
Oof... Oh, children.
They don't know their own strength...
Oops, time's up. He's almost here.
He really might just erase your memories this time.
Now, what's the smart choice...
For you ***and*** this girl?
CHISE ...!

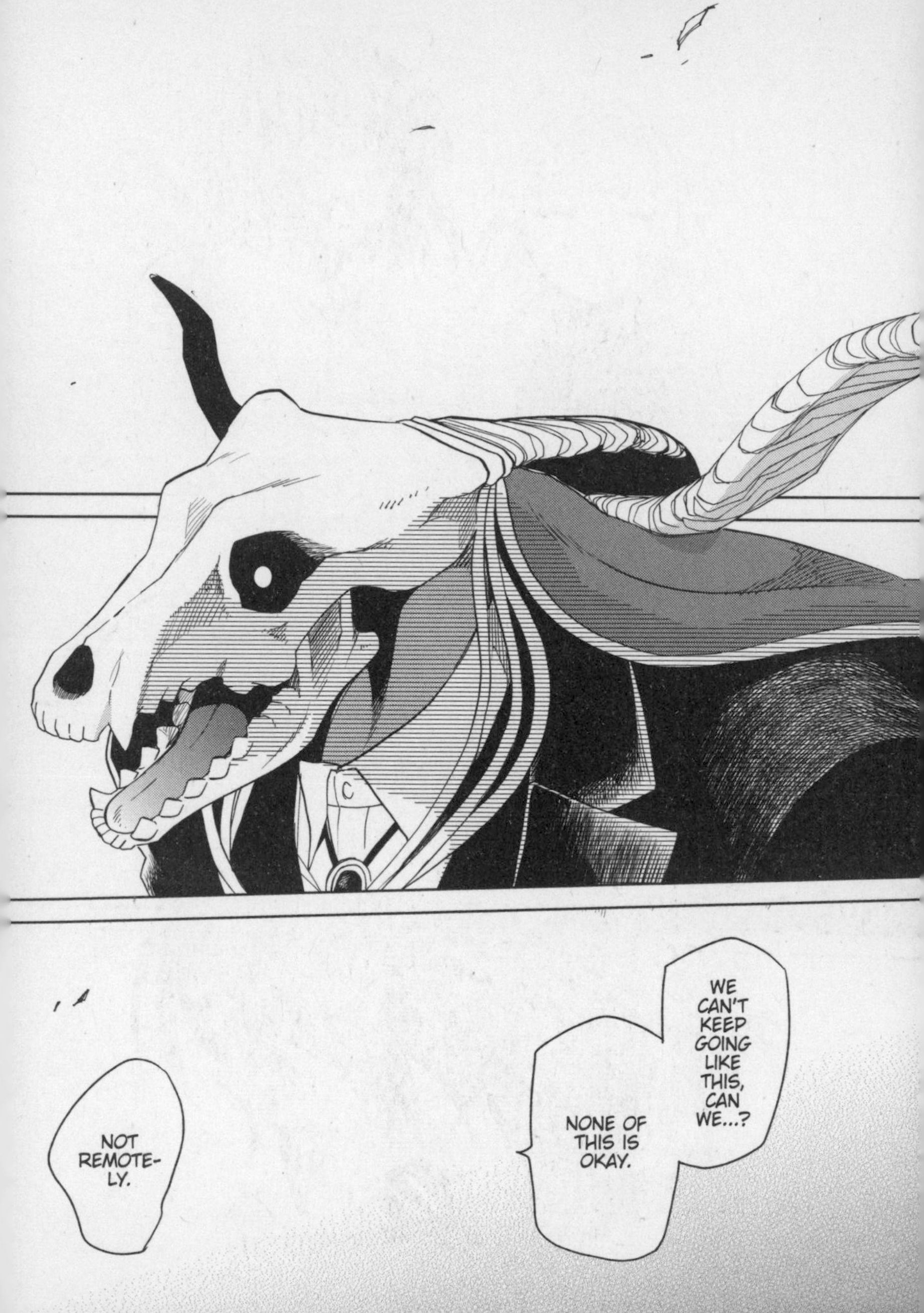
WE CAN'T KEEP GOING LIKE THIS, CAN WE...?
NONE OF THIS IS OKAY.
NOT REMOTE-LY.

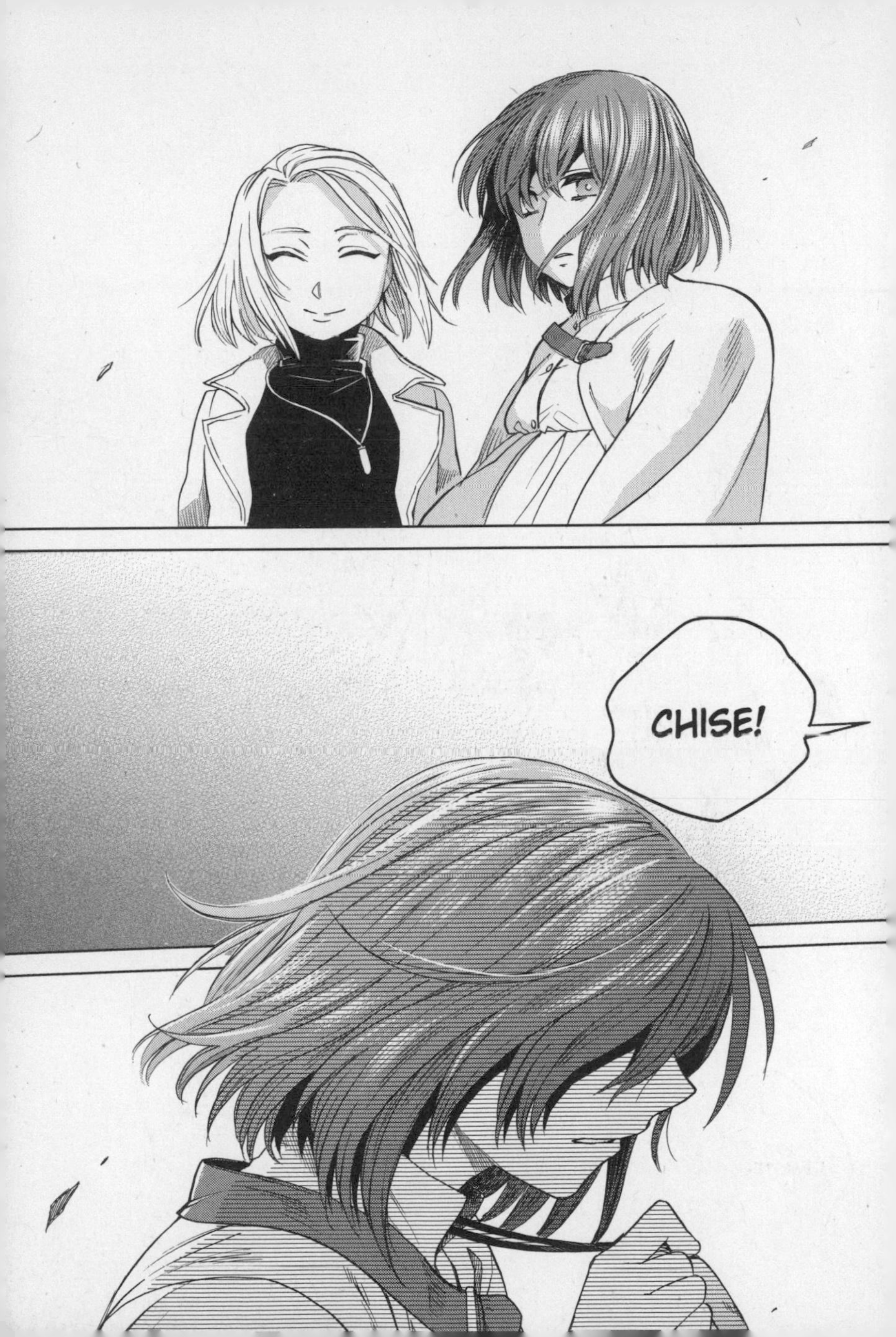
CHISE!

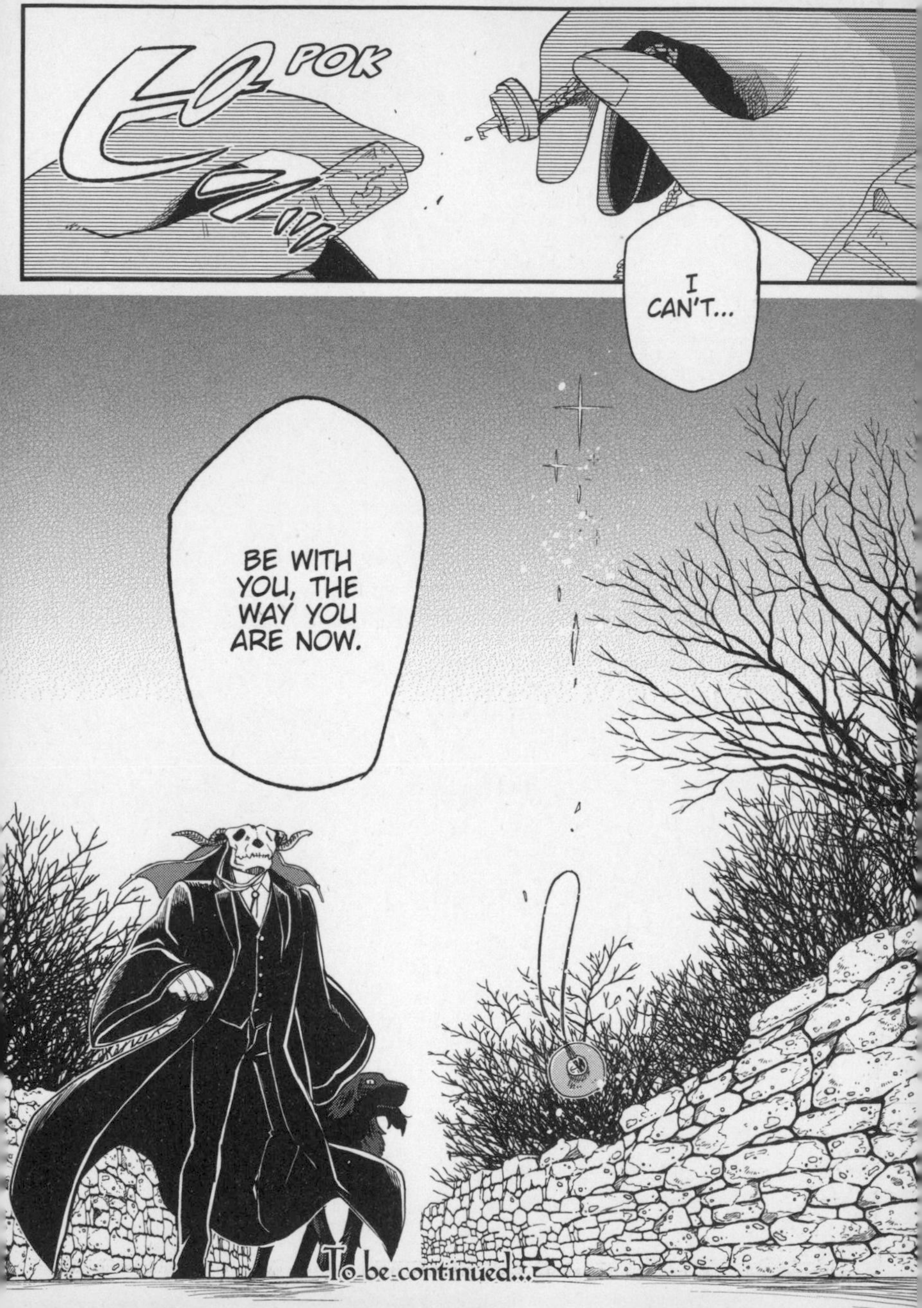
POK
I CAN'T...
BE WITH YOU, THE WAY YOU ARE NOW.
To be continued...

The Ancient Magus' Bride

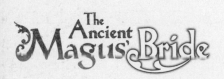

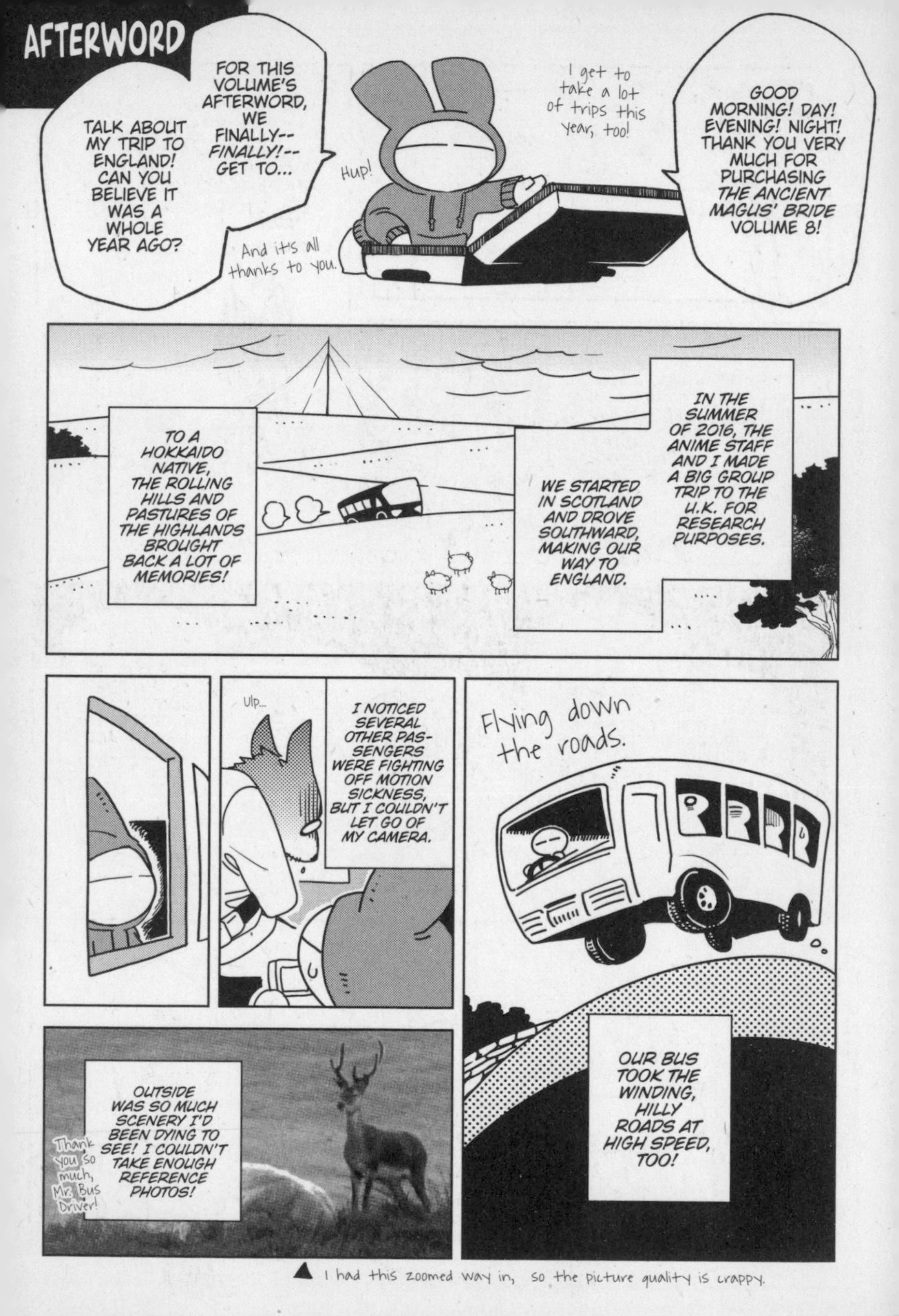
AFTERWORD
GOOD MORNING! DAY! EVENING! NIGHT! THANK YOU VERY MUCH FOR PURCHASING THE ANCIENT MAGUS' BRIDE VOLUME 8!
I get to take a lot of trips this year, too!
Hup!
FOR THIS VOLUME'S AFTERWORD, WE FINALLY-- FINALLY!-- GET TO...
TALK ABOUT MY TRIP TO ENGLAND! CAN YOU BELIEVE IT WAS A WHOLE YEAR AGO?
And it's all thanks to you.
IN THE SUMMER OF 2016, THE ANIME STAFF AND I MADE A BIG GROUP TRIP TO THE U.K. FOR RESEARCH PURPOSES.
WE STARTED IN SCOTLAND AND DROVE SOUTHWARD, MAKING OUR WAY TO ENGLAND.
TO A HOKKAIDO NATIVE, THE ROLLING HILLS AND PASTURES OF THE HIGHLANDS BROUGHT BACK A LOT OF MEMORIES!
Flying down the roads.
OUR BUS TOOK THE WINDING, HILLY ROADS AT HIGH SPEED, TOO!
Ulp...
I NOTICED SEVERAL OTHER PAS-SENGERS WERE FIGHTING OFF MOTION SICKNESS, BUT I COULDN'T LET GO OF MY CAMERA.
OUTSIDE WAS SO MUCH SCENERY I'D BEEN DYING TO SEE! I COULDN'T TAKE ENOUGH REFERENCE PHOTOS!
Thank you so much, Mr. Bus Driver!

▲ I had this zoomed way in, so the picture quality is crappy.

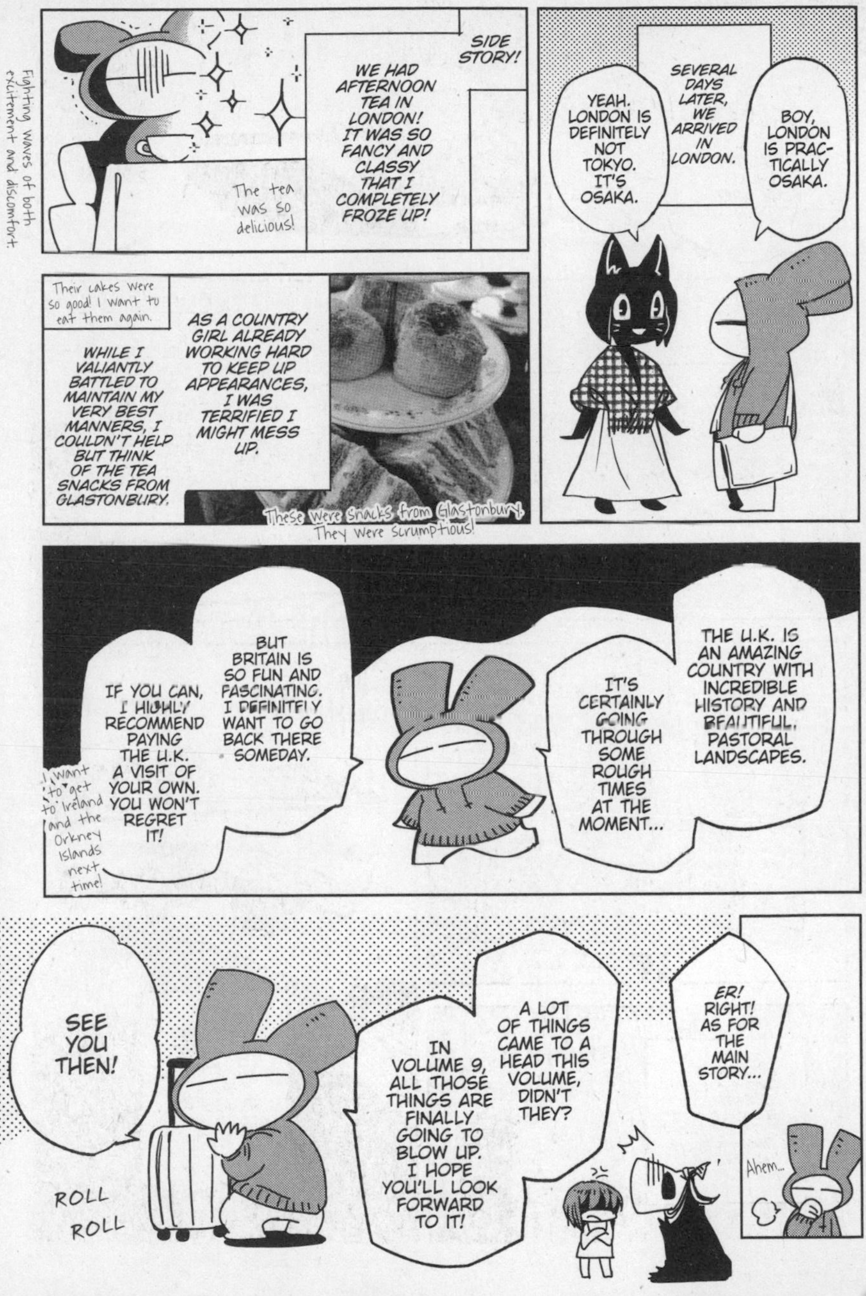
BOY, LONDON IS PRAC-TICALLY OSAKA.
SEVERAL DAYS LATER, WE ARRIVED IN LONDON.
YEAH. LONDON IS DEFINITELY NOT TOKYO. IT'S OSAKA.
SIDE STORY!
WE HAD AFTERNOON TEA IN LONDON! IT WAS SO FANCY AND CLASSY THAT I COMPLETELY FROZE UP!
The tea was so delicious!
Fighting waves of both excitement and discomfort.
Their cakes were so good! I want to eat them again.
AS A COUNTRY GIRL ALREADY WORKING HARD TO KEEP UP APPEARANCES, I WAS TERRIFIED I MIGHT MESS UP.
WHILE I VALIANTLY BATTLED TO MAINTAIN MY VERY BEST MANNERS, I COULDN'T HELP BUT THINK OF THE TEA SNACKS FROM GLASTONBURY.
These were snacks from Glastonbury. They were scrumptious!
THE U.K. IS AN AMAZING COUNTRY WITH INCREDIBLE HISTORY AND BEAUTIFUL, PASTORAL LANDSCAPES.
IT'S CERTAINLY GOING THROUGH SOME ROUGH TIMES AT THE MOMENT...
BUT BRITAIN IS SO FUN AND FASCINATING. I DEFINITELY WANT TO GO BACK THERE SOMEDAY.
IF YOU CAN, I HIGHLY RECOMMEND PAYING THE U.K. A VISIT OF YOUR OWN. YOU WON'T REGRET IT!
I want to get to Ireland and the Orkney Islands next time!
ER! RIGHT! AS FOR THE MAIN STORY...
Ahem...
A LOT OF THINGS CAME TO A HEAD THIS VOLUME, DIDN'T THEY?
IN VOLUME 9, ALL THOSE THINGS ARE FINALLY GOING TO BLOW UP. I HOPE YOU'LL LOOK FORWARD TO IT!
SEE YOU THEN!
ROLL
ROLL

SEVEN SEAS ENTERTAINMENT PRESENTS

The Ancient Magus' Bride

VOLUME 8

story and art by **KORE YAMAZAKI**

TRANSLATION
Adrienne Beck

ADAPTATION
Ysabet Reinhardt MacFarlane

LETTERING AND RETOUCH
Lys Blakeslee

COVER DESIGN
Nicky Lim

PROOFREADER
Shanti Whitesides
Erika Turner

ASSISTANT EDITOR
Jenn Grunigen

PRODUCTION ASSISTANT
CK Russell

PRODUCTION MANAGER
Lissa Pattillo

EDITOR-IN-CHIEF
Adam Arnold

PUBLISHER
Jason DeAngelis

THE ANCIENT MAGUS' BRIDE VOL. 8

Originally published in Japan in 2017 by MAG Garden Corporation, Tokyo.
English translation rights arranged through TOHAN CORPORATION, Tokyo.

ISBN: 978-1-626925-97-7

Printed in Canada

First Printing: February 2018

10 9 8 7 6 5 4 3 2 1

FOLLOW US ONLINE: ***www.sevenseasentertainment.com***

READING DIRECTIONS

This book reads from ***right to left***, Japanese style. If this is your first time reading manga, you start reading from the top right panel on each page and take it from there. If you get lost, just follow the numbered diagram here. It may seem backwards at first, but you'll get the hang of it! Have fun!!

1
2
3
4
5
6
7
8
9

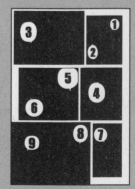